Risk Management in Public Administration

Konrad Raczkowski
Editor

Risk Management in Public Administration

palgrave
macmillan

Editor
Konrad Raczkowski
University of Social Sciences
Warsaw, Poland

ISBN 978-3-319-30876-0 ISBN 978-3-319-30877-7 (eBook)
DOI 10.1007/978-3-319-30877-7

Library of Congress Control Number: 2016946836

Printed on acid-free paper

This Palgrave Macmillan imprint is published by Springer Nature
The registered company is Springer International Publishing AG
The registered company address is: Gewerbestrasse 11, 6330 Cham, Switzerland

Contents

List of Figures

List of Tables

Introduction

Although risk is a feature that is deeply rooted in the practice of economic trading, there is still a wide knowledge gap as far as the determination of the theoretical rules underlying the creation and management of risk involved in individual economic actions is concerned. This is also, and perhaps particularly, true for the public sector, where individual management functions are burdened with constant strategic and operational risk that is political, economic, social, technological, legal, and environmental in character— and thus influenced by volatile cycles. There are two primary reasons behind this. The first is related to the fact that it is not possible to consider risk in fully logical terms, if the assumptions of neoclassical economics are not rejected or challenged, especially in regard to the rationality of human behaviour. The second is the existence of an intense causal relationship between taking risk and gaining an advantage, as well as incurring irrational losses in the case of excessive acceptance of risk under the circumstances of limited possibilities of risk dispersion. Additionally, we are faced with the phenomenon of incomplete information, as developed by the agency theory or transformed transaction costs theory within the framework of new institutional economics. It is also inconceivable to discuss risk management in the economy if we disregard individual management functions understood in classic terms, such as planning, organizing, managing, and controlling, which are applied in the theory of rationality of crime that is increasingly common in contemporary business relations. It is thus justified to claim that an economic entity strives for an increase in individual and/or collective utility in the contemporary economy, which is marked by certain behavioural and information asymmetry. Therefore, the objective of this book is to demonstrate the multifaceted nature of risk management in public administration in a form of an enrichment of finance theory, the theory of economics, and management theory, which might be pragmatically reflected in real economic trading and public administration. One could even claim that risk management in public administration should identify and constantly develop the capacity of an organization in order to achieve the result – measured with the efficiency of operation – of the capability of cooperation with the real economy – under the circumstances of continuous decrease in the number of court cases between the citizen and the state. At the same time, accounting standards for calculating budgetary expenses or proper integration of systems and processes, which may not stray from the global reality, should be sustained.

In the economic and financial context, the significance of the lack of an appropriate approach to economic risk management in public administration is greater than ever before. This is because public administration may be the creator of public policies which establish the organizational and economic order and simultaneously acts in the vital national interest, and takes care of business competition, social security, and the fair redistribution of incomes. Public administration is supposed to ensure that citizens have access to desired services and must, at the same time, strive for balance in decision-making situations where it is profitable to take extreme risks, if it may enable success. Such tasks may not be delegated to the free market exclusively in the hope that it will spontaneously redress social inequalities or take care of sustainable development.

Due to that fact, public administration must understand contemporary business models that are characterised by an increasing level of optimization in terms of limiting the tax base and/or attempting to introduce unfair competition on the market. It must understand that the power of international corporations is rising and active economic policies run by sovereign countries are becoming more and more limited, usually by means of indirect mechanisms of exerting influence and win-lose (or less often win-win) relationships. Such administrations must be aware that it is not the same thing for certain entities to accept compliance rules and to implement them in their practical business activity. Therefore, a question emerges whether if there is a lack of compliance of the accepted rules and principles with an actual activity, it is possible to limit or eliminate risk at all? The answer is clear—of course it is possible to limit or eliminate risk—but only provided that the administration adopts various perspectives of thinking and decision-making with respect to the same entities, situations, and events, which will reflect the particular course of action in the process of evaluation. Not everyone is a law-abiding citizen, nor are all economic entities, while the manner or thinking and acting of two even declaratively analogous entities may be radically different due to pursuance of secret objectives.

The following book fills the cognitive gap with respect to the possibilities of risk management in public administration and, due to its economic character enriched with a considerable number of case studies, it may indicate trends in risk development both from a micro- and macro-perspective. The book is comprised of fourteen chapters; each is preceded by a summary and followed by conclusions. Chapter 1 presents the theory underlying risk and risk management on micro- and macroeconomic levels. Chapter 2 contains an interesting description of the elimination of currency risk in the Transatlantic Trade and Investment Partnership by way of inserting a clause combining the Euro and the Dollar. Whereas an illustration of changes that credit ratings undergo due to the influence of credit spreads is provided in Chap. 3. Chapter 4 presents the elements of risk management, especially with reference to the public financial sector. The next chapter (Chap. 5) contains a description of the possibilities for management of public safety based on the concept of risk processes. Chapters 6, 7 and 8 elaborate on risk in economic activity in the light of the early warning system within the framework of the social economy and operations on the Internet. The next chapters (Chaps. 9, 10, 11 and 12) are concerned with the risk involved in intellectual capital, bank regulatory risk in the EU, the financial distress of public sector entities, and systemic risk in the insurance sector. The final two chapters (Chaps. 13 and 14) elaborate on extremely important issues in the contemporary economy, which are concentrated around the European tax gap in personal income taxes and VAT carousel fraud in selected European States.

As the scientific editor, I hope that the book presented to you will explain what risk management in the public administration and economy is, as there are still no widely acceptable standard constructions and scientific laws which would be, first and foremost, approved by the majority of researchers and simultaneously implemented in the practices of economic entities.

Konrad Raczkowski

1

What Does Risk Management in an Economy Really Mean?

Konrad Raczkowski and Piotr Tworek

1 Introduction

In economics, risk is regarded as a category that is quite hard to define in an explicit way. Neither in theory nor in practice is there a single universal definition which clearly identifies this category. The difficulty here lies in the very nature of risk, i.e. a phenomenon that is complex and multidimensional. As an interdisciplinary category, risk is addressed by a vast array of sciences, e.g. technical, social, natural and medical ones. Generally, there is no scientific discipline in which risk is not present in one way or another. This is also one of the reasons why risk is so difficult to interpret in science. In economics, too, risk has been a focus of research all over the world for many years, giving rise to various interpretations.

K. Raczkowski (✉)
University of Social Sciences, Warsaw, Poland

P. Tworek
University of Economics, Katowice, Poland

K. Raczkowski (ed.), *Risk Management in Public Administration*,
DOI 10.1007/978-3-319-30877-7_1

Risk may be analysed in macro-, meso- and micro-economic dimensions, and risk management is often regarded as constituting a separate scientific area, which is applicable and utilitarian in character. In business, risk is managed using a wide range of methods, techniques and tools, the applicability of such methods depending on the scale and type of operations carried out by a given entity.

Risk management in the commercial sector differs significantly from risk management in the public sector, in recognition of the differing objectives pursued by entities operating in private and public sectors. Attention should also be drawn to the threats which occur in activities conducted by so-called third sector entities, such as societies and associations carrying out social missions, which are increasingly eager to find out what risks they are exposed to in their operations. Today new kinds of threat are emerging in the public space, and have to be addressed by almost all entities, without exception. An obvious example is the risk of terrorism, which may affect individuals, commercial entities, public and social institutions. Thus there is a correlation between the two categories – public and commercial risk. A rise in global risk in the public space leads to specific consequences for commercial entities, including adverse financial effects. Equally, a rise in global risk in an economy results in a rise in individual risks these entities are exposed to. Therefore, there is a need to adopt an overall approach to dealing with risk and set out some universal risk management rules.

This chapter is intended as an introduction to the issues connected with risk management, perceived from global, general and system perspectives. In particular, we address the category of economic risk in relation to entities operating in the private and the public sectors. Effective risk management is translated into savings and these are sought after by all commercial enterprises, as well as public organisations and institutions. Such entities have to be able to identify risk, analyse it and then respond to it in the right way, in order to achieve their objectives. In the commercial sector this means maximising the value, while in the public sector it means increasing public value, including public trust in authorities. First we focus on the problems of risk management methodology, which is reviewed against the background of the general risk concept in economics.

2 Theory of Risk in the Economy

Risk, as an economic category, can be analysed in a variety of areas and across numerous dimensions. At the same time, it would be difficult to assign such analyses to individual sciences, such as management, economics or finance. Risk is, therefore, an interdisciplinary category. It is also a pervasive and dynamic phenomenon, which occurs in commercial activities, is inevitably associated with potential losses, demonstrates high intensity, and usually leads to a wide range of impacts and spans over time (Tworek 2010, 17). The situation in the public sector is slightly different, though. For public institutions the need to avoid potential losses does not necessarily have to be a top priority in their strategic management as they are publicly subsidized. When it comes to the private sector, however, risks have caused a number of entities operating in this sector to teeter on the brink of bankruptcy or collapse altogether. In particular, in times of economic crisis, global business risk grows, which can be seen in the world crisis of 2008–2015. The pervasiveness of risk means that it is present in any areas in which commercial or public entities operate. We can never be completely certain that no new risk factors are going to occur in an entity's business activities. Risk dynamics, in turn, refers to the intensity and volatility of this phenomenon over time, meaning that risks may occur in different guises and have different impacts on entities. It is not possible to find two entities that are completely identical and exposed to the same types of risk. Similarly, there are no two economies in the world, which are the same and thus vulnerable to the same risks. Also within one economy, some sections are more and some less risky. Almost every industry has its own specific risks which need to be addressed (Drucker 1964, 17–31).

Nevertheless, irrespective of the types of risk encountered by specific industries, risk is perceived in science as a strictly quantitative category. Since 1921, the notion of risk has been regarded as a measurable category, ruling out uncertainty (Knight 1921, 17). Since then the concept of risk has developed significantly, especially in the 1950s, when there was much progress in technology, including, significantly, the advent of computers. At that point risk started to be estimated using numerical methods. The approach to risk as a quantitative category, however, dates back to the Hindu-Arabic numeral systems (Bernstein 1997, 15). In particular, serious research into risk was conducted in the Renaissance (Bernstein 1997, 15). In a way this could be regarded as a significant development: the period in which *homo oeconomicus* was able to pursue goals as an economic and rational human being, focusing on maximising profits and making choices on an economic basis (Tworek 2013, 21–22). Such an attitude may readily be seen in modern commercial enterprises, in which every decision needs to be made having in mind the overriding goal of maximising profits (Tworek 2013, 22). Thus economic entities need to look for a variety of measures to minimize risks arising out of their decisions, because they carry out their day-to-day operations in an environment which is uncertain and volatile (Tworek 2013, 22). Risk is an inherent feature of any economic activity and, as such, should be dealt with using the right methodology. The methodical aspect of risk management in business is particularly important as the way in which risk should be handled is largely determined by the specific nature of an entity's operations: various entities control their risks in various ways. What also needs to be taken into account here is the behavioural dimension of risk management, i.e. propensity or aversion to risk (Hirschey and Nofsinger 2008, 89–260).

Modern scientists conducting research into business risk seem to believe that risk management and control are very high on the agenda in the world of business (Kendall 2000, 13), and risk, if ignored, will surely not disappear (Mulcahy 2003, 7). This outlook arises from the former concept of practical risk control (Arrow 1979, 7). Currently much attention is being paid to risk, in theory and in practice. The problem of risk has found full expression in modern theories of capital market investment, advocated by Nobel Prize winners in economics (Black and Scholes 1973, 637–659; Merton 1974, 449–470). All modern investment theories are fundamentally based on the risk diversification theory, commonly applied in science (Markowitz 1952, 77–91). A particularly valuable contribution to the science of risk management has been made by risk control studies carried out by economic entities in connection with decision-making (Kahneman and Tversky 1979, 313–327). Thus risk may be interpreted in a number of ways, but there are a few basic approaches to defining risk in science (Table 1.1).

A review of the concepts listed in Table 1.1 usefully demonstrates the complexity of defining risk and risk perception in the theory of economics. There are a variety of interrelations and interactions between the categories of risk and uncertainty. In addition, the progress made in the science of risk has led to the formulation of many follow-up theories. However, no matter how many theories and concepts are presented in scholarly literature, special attention should be focused on two essential trends in risk definition: the offensive and the defensive. For business practice, the defensive trend is of particular importance, with its understanding of risk as a purely negative phenomenon, meaning a loss in, a threat or damage to an enterprise or public organisation. This approach is adopted by insurers (Seog 2010, 18–92; Skipper and Kwon 2007, 3–26). In the theory of economics, the defensive trend is counteracted by the offensive trend (Arrow 1979; Drucker 1964), according to which risk may not only pose a threat but also provide an opportunity, and risk management should be looked upon as a way to improve the conditions in which a given entity operates. Effective and efficient risk management adds value to the entity and exemplifies a modern approach to corporate management (Dallas 2006, 52–86). Effective risk management in commercial enterprises or public organisations may provide numerous benefits and, in particular, substantial savings. In the theory of economics, there is also decision-making theory (Ackoff 1962, 24–52), which in practice means making decisions in the conditions of risk.

Whatever the perception and interpretation of risk in science, from the practical point of view it is important for business to be well-informed about risk. Based on the available data about potential future threats, risk may be described using the distribution of probability, i.e. the probability of a given risk occurring in the future is calculated. If the risk does not occur, no risk consequences will be experienced. This is the mathematical approach to the concept of risk in economics, and can be expressed using the following formula:

$$R = p \cdot c$$

Table 1.1 Scientific trends in defining risk: overview of concepts

I. Classical foundations of risk definition
1. Risk results from operating in unrecognized conditions, uncertainty about the areas of operations, signals about the nature of random events
2. Risk is difficult, often unpredictable, potential changeability of consequences of an event
3. When defining risk it is advisable to relate an objective element, i.e. strictly understood risk, to a subjective element, i.e. the state of mind, such as uncertainty, where risk is an objective correlate of the subjective uncertainty
II. The defensive trend in risk definition
1. Risk is a negative phenomenon: the threat of a negative deviation from the target, the possibility of making a wrong decision, the threat of achieving a negative result
2. Uncertainty is a subjective category, while risk is an objective one
3. This approach provides the basis for the theory of insurance, with the presence of such notions as: a random event, a random accident, accidental damage, danger and hazards of physical, moral and spiritual nature
III. The offensive trend in risk definition: risk characteristics
1. Risk is an inherent feature of any business activity and a potential source of losses or gains. Risk as a negative term in the economic sense, and its positive counterpart is an opportunity
2. Risk is a function of uncertainty, which always accompanies it. Uncertainty is a statistical phenomenon, while risk is a dynamic one. Risk is a dynamic category, closely connected with acts or omissions
3. When defining risk, subjective and objective elements may be distinguished. Subjective elements are: firstly, an economic entity's awareness of hazards connected with an undertaking it opts to participate in or the business it conducts; secondly, uncertainty whether these hazards are going to occur in a specific case, and if they do, what losses they are going to cause; thirdly, a decision to bear responsibility for the events which may take place. The objective elements include: firstly, the undertaking or the business which are exposed to risk; secondly, the events which cause risk, their probability and time of occurrence; and thirdly, the size of losses which may result
IV. Decision-making theory
1. Decision-making in the conditions of uncertainty and risk is based on game theory, in which, unlike probability theory, there is a possibility to choose one of many possible courses of actions
2. Risk accompanies decision-making problems, but only these ones in which there is no certainty as for the results of the decision (i.e. these are not determined). Risk may appear in such decisions independently (in probabilistic situations) or in connection with uncertainty (in strategic situations)

Table 1.1 (continued)

3. The analysis of decision-making tasks must be combined with an analysis of the environment in which these decisions are to be made, namely: uncertainty, dynamics and complexity
V. Neoclassical framework for risk definition
1. Risk related to business activities requires a point of reference, such as the category of profit, the value of which, in the conditions of uncertainty, is variable
2. Risk is not tantamount to uncertainty. Risk is measurable uncertainty
3. Propensity to risk is determined by the value of expected profits

Source: Own elaboration based on Karmańska et al. 2008, 59–60

where R means risk, p is the probability of risk (threat) occurrence, and c are consequences of the risky event (threat). That is how scholarly papers tend to quantify risk (Mitchell 2003, 178–188; Kallman 2005, 57–58; Pickett 2006, 40–55; Murphy 2008, 39; Brown 2008, 184–185). As there is an abundance of factors which cause global risk in the economy, many types of risk need to be taken into account at the same time. This idea is reflected in the following formula:

$$R = \sum_{i=1}^{n} p_i \cdot c_i$$

where p_i means the probability of i-risk occurrence and c_i means its consequences. The presented formula, when looking at its origin, is just an extension of the previous formula and shows the total of expected consequences caused by a given risk, i.e. if the risk does not occur, no risk consequences have to be dealt with and vice versa. In business these negative risk consequences are most often expressed as financial effects (losses). This entails that a risk carried by an entity comes with a cost. At the same time, risk consequences are an integral part of a commonly known and thoroughly researched notion of risk mechanism (Flanagan and Norman 1993, 48), according to which every risk has its source, i.e. the cause of risk, and brings about certain effects (consequences) (Smith and Merritt 2002, 8). For example, inflation is a risk factor in an economy, as it leads to a rise in banking interest rates and thereby increases the cost of capital.

As a result, borrowers have to pay higher interest to their banks. Inflation is a macroeconomic risk factor, which is just one of many risk sources in the economy. Microeconomic factors constitute another source of risk, and are more important from the point of view of a specific entity's operations., Global risks to the economy may similarly be grouped as endogenous or exogenous, macroeconomic or microeconomic in kind. The literature presents this subject in a very broad way (Kendall 2000; Holliwell 2001, 2–29).

3 Uncertainty Versus Risk

In the classical approach to risk definition, uncertainty is regarded as an unmeasurable category (Knight 1921, 17). However, in the neoclassical framework for an analysis of risk attributes, risk is not in the same category as uncertainty, but is limited to measurable uncertainty (Karmańska et al. 2008, 59–60). According to the offensive trend, however, risk is a function of uncertainty (Table 1.1). Following this approach, uncertainty in business is always accompanied by risk. It may be assumed that risk results from uncertainty, so risk is a much more narrow term than uncertainty. Furthermore, risk can even be considered an effect of uncertainty and, as such, risk changes along with uncertainty (Willett 1951, 6). Risk may also be treated as the total of uncertainties and losses a given entity is exposed to (Jannadi and Almishari 2003, 493), where a loss means a direct effect of risk (according to the risk mechanism), namely:

$$\text{Risk} = \text{Uncertainty} + \text{Loss}$$

This equation largely results from the practical aspects of risk management, where risk in commercial activities means an unexpected increase in costs of the entity's operations. (Uff and Odams 1995, 28). This appears to be a substantively correct interpretation of risk in economics, where risk is directly reflected in the accounting approach to risk management. No matter how uncertainty and risk are understood, however, and how these two categories interact, both uncertainty and risk have a common denominator, i.e. the future which cannot be fully predicted. Therefore, every decision about the future bears lower or higher risk, which refers primarily to the category of investment decisions (Aggarwal 1993, 9–30; Hartman 2007, 417–468; Pike and Neale 2003, 275–303). Thus in the theory of economics a division is made between decisions made in conditions of certainty and those made in uncertainty. There is also one more type of condition in which decisions may be made – the condition of surety, which basically means the absence of any doubts (Williams et al. 2002, 28). There are mutual interactions and dependencies between these three types of condition. This division is connected with the amount of information about the future that a decision-maker possesses, which can mean: a total lack of information, complete information that a given event is bound to occur, and incomplete information about probability of risk occurrence. This issue is illustrated in Fig. 1.1.

Since the future implies uncertainty, and there is a risk which occurs as an inherent feature of any investment project carried out over time (Gitman et al. 2011, 126–138; Pike and Neale 2003, 79–99; Royer 2002,

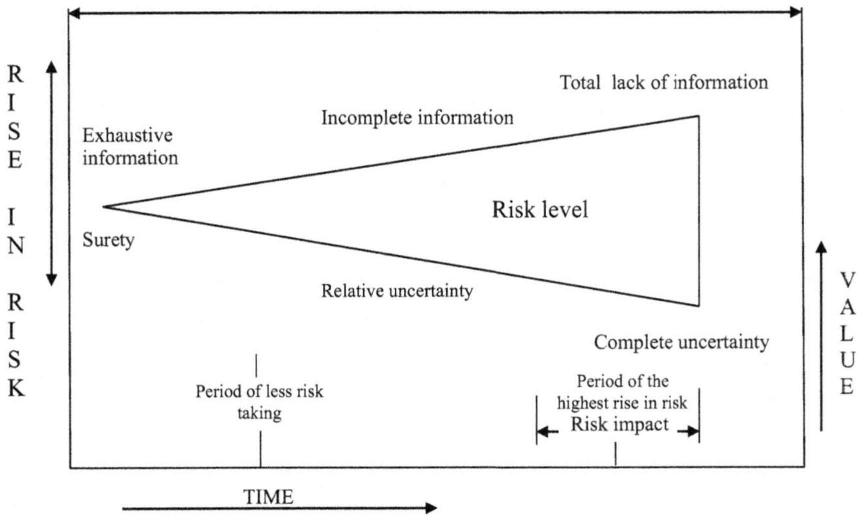

Fig. 1.1 Dependencies between risk, information and uncertainty, against the background of time (*Source*: Own elaboration based onHeerkens 2003, 133; Wideman 1992, II-5)

3–61; Kendrick 2003, 56–98; Chapman and Ward 2002, 86–115) a risk condition always appears when a given project or a decision may lead to a set of specified results, and the decision-maker is aware of all possible results and able to estimate the likelihood of every one (Nowak 2010, 12). Surety (Fig. 1.1) occurs when the future results of the project under consideration are known at the moment the entity undertakes to perform it, while uncertainty occurs when investment projects undertaken by the enterprise may lead to one or more possible results (Nowak 2010, 12). Therefore, uncertainty results from a lack of complete information about the future (Young and Tippins 2001, 7–8), so it should be identified with the complete inability to predict and define the risks (Cleden 2009, 4–5), which is simultaneously connected with a threat and the inability to achieve specific results (Kolluru et al. 1996, 8.53). Summing up, the higher uncertainty, the higher risk and vice versa (Fig. 1.1). That is why more risky investments are expected to bring a higher rate of return, to compensate for the risk to be borne, in form of a premium. In this context, risk is perceived as an effect of unmistaken anticipation of the future by the business person and the profit is a compensation for the uncertainty the business person has to face (Knight 1921, 20–21).

Just like risk, uncertainty may also be divided into endogenous and exogenous. At the same time, sources of uncertainty, in a commercial enterprise, may be identified and divided into external and internal. Internal uncertainty of the enterprise as a system includes, first of all, the objective uncertainty due to the limited predictability and ambiguity of behaviours demonstrated by the people in the enterprise's surroundings —in its regulatory sub-system (unreliability of informative and decision-making objects) and the real sub-system (the process of transformation of material and energy supplies); secondly, the subjective uncertainty related to unreliability of real processes; and thirdly, the structural uncertainty resulting from mutual relations between the elements of the enterprise system (Jędralska 1992, 16–17). The same way of thinking may apply to the macroscale, where uncertainty in an economic system may also be divided into endogenous uncertainty and exogenous uncertainty, with the sources of uncertainty broken down into internal and external ones.

In conclusion, just like risk, the category of uncertainty cannot be explicitly identified by forming a single all-purpose definition, which could be commonly applicable. This issue is broadly presented in economic literature and makes a popular topic of scientific debates (Smith 2003, 57–87). In particular, the answers are being sought to the following questions – How can we define uncertainty in a conclusive way? Can it be measured? If so, what measurements and methods should be used? (Tworek 2013, 26). In science uncertainty management and risk management may even work as two separate notions (Petit 2012, 540). Irrespective of the definitions of uncertainty and risk, as well as the interdependencies between these economic categories, the key difference lies in the fact that uncertainty cannot be quantified, while risk can be estimated using appropriate measurements and quantitative methods, including risk simulation (Haimes 2004, 56–112; Grey 1995, 15–38; Molak et al. 1997, 25–78; Perry 2007, 43–58; Raftery 1994, 35–89; Schuyler 2001, 67–156).

4 Risk in Private and Public Economy

4.1 Risk in the Commercial Sector

As emphasized in the introduction, risk in the commercial sector may be analysed in a very broad way, on macro-, meso- and microeconomic scales. This applies to risk factors, as well as risks as such. Scholarly literature devotes a lot of attention to the problem, as the phenomenon of risk in economics evolves in time. In commercial activities, new risk sources have emerged due to the developments in financial markets. There are also increasingly complex and risky financial instruments. The origin of the current economic crisis of 2008–2015 can be traced back to the financial markets, that is why it is so severe and painful in its consequences. Generally speaking, the risk factors in the commercial sector may be divided into the factors which contribute to global risk in the economy, such as a fall in GDP, a decrease in exports and industrial output, a growing deficit in foreign trade, a rise in state expenditure on social needs and related welfare schemes, an unstable economic situation (strikes, social unrest, etc.), higher rates of inflation and unemployment in the economy, volatile and weak currency and an increased tax burden (Tarczyński and Mojsiewicz 2001, 142). The major factors which reduce global risk in the economy, in turn, include: a rise in GDP, an increase in exports and industrial output, higher demand for manufacturers' products, a drop in the inflation rate, a drop in energy prices, lower taxes and the development of investment incentive schemes (Tarczyński and Mojsiewicz 2001, 142). To elaborate, the sources of risks in economic activities may be divided into the following groups of factors (Kosiński 2000, 11–12):

(a) '... factors related to the type of company (ownership, management structure, concentration of the decision-making power, sources of funding);
(b) factors related to the operational strategy (reasons why a strategy is to be implemented, accepted strategy assumptions, strategy selection);
(c) factors related to the current financial standing of the enterprise (liabilities, debts, seizures and pledges, receivables, disputed claims, possible creation of working capital, petty cash, financial liquidity);
(d) factors related to a country's general economic situation (budgetary debt towards society, budgetary debt towards external sources of funding for the deficit, the size of the budget deficit, structure of budget income allocation, structure of budget revenue allocation, administrative limits on salary rises in the economy, the impact of the budget structure and its imbalance on inflation, possibilities to export domestic goods – the existence of limitations or preferences, possibilities to import goods – the existence of limitations or preferences, the structure of domestic exports, the structure of domestic imports, the exchange rate policy, the possibility for investors to purchase foreign currencies, limitations to participation of domestic or foreign partners (the use of protectionism, the need to purchase concessions, the use of title assignment, licences and other types and forms of limiting third party participation in any given type of activity);
(e) factors related to competition (the existence of domestic and foreign rivals in a given field of production, manufacture of equivalent

or similar products by other entities which are not industry-related, the possibility for competition to use dumping, possible smuggling, how organized the competition is – official competition and the so-called grey zone, possible monopoly-like connections among competitors);

(f) factors related to economic and political risks in foreign markets (a possible direct entry into a given market – the need to use intermediaries/promotors, the knowledge of trading habits in a given market, the knowledge of living standards in the market (minimum, average and maximum), the knowledge of policies carried out by the state and regional authorities and their consistency in the past – possible forecasts, possible establishment/cancellation of agreements between the authorities in the given market and one's own authorities – possible fluctuations and long-lasting changes in trading relations (e.g. the most favoured nation clause);

(g) factors related to foreign exchange risk (the ability to estimate the rate of inflation/deflation in a given market or in a given country, the ability to forecast currency devaluation/revaluation in a given market or a country, how mutual relations between these factors are determined, how the impact of attractiveness of goods on currency rate fluctuations—or a reverse phenomenon—is evaluated);

(h) factors related to the political situation in a given country (the size of political parties in the country, how disperse political interests of specific parties are, the number of political parties in parliament—their possible regionalisation, differences in programs of specific parliamentary parties—the possibility to form a coalition or strong opposition groups, mutual relations between the government and parliament, the role of the president, the influence of non-parliamentary groups (banks, state and governmental administration, the church, non-parliamentary parties, other) on passing of acts and regulations with country-wide, regional or local impact, the role and influence of trade unions on actions of the government, parliament, behaviour of non-parliamentary groups).'(Kosiński 2000, 11–12).

Summing up, the reasons why risks appear in commercial activities include, first of all, a lack of reliable information about the future and the current macro- and microeconomic conditions; secondly, the insufficient number of methods which can be employed to explain cause and effect relationships between economic values from the past and the forecast economic phenomena; thirdly, the use of simple planning methods which fail to take into account the nature of the phenomena which occur in reality; fourthly, high dynamics and complexity of economic activities; fifthly, changes in the environment and, in particular, legal regulations (Bizon-Górecka 1998, 98). No matter which criterion is used to divide risk factors in the commercial sector, the phenomenon which is referred to in economics as the vicious circle should always be kept in mind, in the systemic approach to risk management and at the strategic level. This means that some risk factors may result from other risk factors and this, consequently, may lead to a further series of unfavourable events. Therefore, risks, when analysed from the point of view of how the state operates and is governed, may be divided into competition, country, criminal, economic, environmental, financial, informational, legal, market, operational, personal, political, product and industry, reputation, resources, technological, war and terrorism risks (Holliwell 2001, 2). When looking at risks in the commercial sector from the microeconomic perspective, i.e. through the operation of economic entities in general, the following types may be distinguished (Tarczyński and Mojsiewicz 2001, 20–22) :

(a) credit risk (a risk of a financial loss in a situation when an enterprise the financial institution cooperates with stops paying their liabilities);
(b) market risk (a risk that a loss may be incurred as a result of change in assets, owned by the enterprise, which are to be sold);
(c) operational risk (one of the broadest risk categories, which tends to be defined as the risk of a loss as a result of unreliable systems, insufficient control, human error or mismanagement);
(d) business risk (related to economic activities conducted by the enterprise and resulting from specific investment decisions aimed at implementation of its development strategy);
(e) legal risk (related to possible losses as a result of activities carried out by the enterprise and falling beyond some legal framework or regulations, including the inability to enforce contractual terms).

The key categories of risks faced by commercial enterprises are presented in Fig. 1.2.

Figure 1.2 presents the whole range of risks, providing a general outline of global risks faced by a commercial enterprise. Depending on the industry, risk factors as well as risks themselves appear with varying intensity. Therefore, risks will be managed differently e.g. in a commercial bank and in an industrial enterprise. From among the risk factors listed above, special importance should be attached to the financial risk, which may take different forms and be interpreted in different ways in business practice. This is most often connected with cash flow problems and growing debts of the enterprise (Brealey et al. 2007, 456–477; Saunders and Cornett 2011, 496–518; Nersesian 2004, 177–263; Murphy 2008, 137–172; Watson and Head 2007, 152–174; Gitman 2006, 419–490).

4.2 Risk in the Public Sector

Risk in the public sector has its own unique profile. Both in theory and in practice one can come across different interpretations of public risk. However, so far the attempts to come up with an unequivocal definition of this category have not been successful. The difficulty in defining risk in the public sector results from the fact that there is a wide range of public entities and institutions, of differing types and profiles. In addition, the public space also comprises commercial entities, and that is why the statistic division between the public and the commercial entities—in the public and the private sector—starts to blur. All over the world, many economic initiatives are carried out by private-public partnerships, one of the reasons being risk diversification (Akintoye et al. 2003, 31–91; Yescombe 2007, 42–244). The best example of the public risk category might be the risk which occurs in public healthcare. According to The American Society for Healthcare Risk Management, risk in the healthcare sector is referred to as a patient safety risk (Carroll 2009, 2). Another type of risk in the public arena is a risk connected with terrorist attacks, as mentioned in the introduction to this chapter. Since the attack on the World Trade Center on September 11, 2001 and the terrorist attacks in London in 2005, this

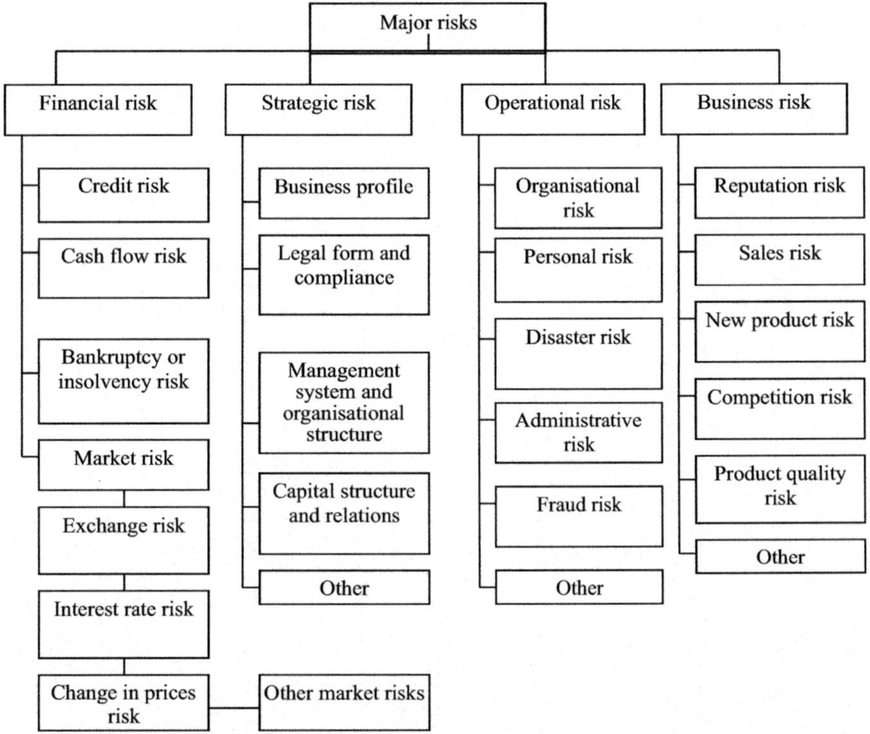

Fig. 1.2 Types of risks in economic activities of private sector entities (*Source*: Own elaboration based on: (Tarczyński and Mojsiewicz 2001, 23; Kuziak 2011, 23))

category has been particularly broadly researched and a lot of efforts have been made to counteract this risk (Fischbacher-Smith and Fischbacher-Smith 2013, 330). The knowledge of risk management in the public sector is promoted by such organisations and associations as The Public Risk Management Association (PRAM) and the Public Utilities Risk Management Association (PURMA) in the USA, or The Public Risk Management Organisation, the European counterpart of PRAM. In the American public sector, there is an independent managerial function—a public risk manager, who performs the same role as a risk manager employed in a corporation. Public risk managers deal with risk management, especially in big public and governmental institutions, but also support the entire process of governance in public entities. They are also responsible for achievement of an organisation's results, which may be defined in a different way, both in theory and in practice (Pestieau and Tulkens 2006, 346–347). Therefore, difficulties may arise in the interpretations of the values which should provide the basis for risk estimation in public organisations. This problem is now being widely debated in scholarly papers (Brown and Osborne 2013, 187–190; Osborne and Brown 2013, 157–160; Carmen and Dobrea 2006, 126; Spinki 2012, 101–118). It also involves the impact of risk on performance measurement in public organisations, which is directly connected with the difficulty in defining risk, often perceived by public organisations as the possible occurrence of deviations from expected results (Fone and Young 2007, 12). Such a risk definition is compliant with the mathematical interpretation of risk. But no matter how risk is defined in activities carried out by public organisations, the risk mechanism invariably remains the same, i.e. every risk has its cause and leads to specific effects (risk consequences) (Tworek 2014, 313–325). In healthcare services, for example, it may be assumed that risk can be caused by the failure to provide sterile conditions and comply with medical procedures in public hospitals, which may lead to hospital infections (a risk of a patient's loss of health) and, consequently, even to a patient's death as the most tragic effect of the risk (Tworek 2014, 313–325). The hospital may be exposed to the threat of litigation and, as a consequence, a claim for compensation, meaning that risk in its final manifestation may take the form of additional unpredictable expenses for a healthcare entity (the economic dimension of risk) (Tworek 2014, 313–325). In addition to the financial implications, there are many reasons why risk in the public sector should be managed, e.g. damage to the organisation's reputation in the eyes of the general public (Barrett 2014, 459), disruptions due to new technologies and IT systems (Brookfield and Fischbacher-Smith 2014, 5),communication problems and disruptions in information flow inside public organisations (Smith and McCloskey 1998, 41), difficulties related to logistics and public transport, poor quality of public services (Osborne and Brown 2013, 157), disruptions in internal communication (Bennet et al. 2010, 4), corruption and fraud (Jackson 2013, 330), as well as the harmful effects of natural forces. Irrespective of the types of risks a public organisation is exposed to, or their source, the most important thing from the practical point of view is the correct identification of these risks, which is often regarded as the key part of the risk management process (Chapman 2001, 151). This results, first of all, from the belief that any mistakes made at this stage of a risk management process may lead to incorrect risk assessment and, consequently, the failure to come up with the right risk responses (Tworek 2015, 196–210). In particular, there are three basic phases of risk management process, namely:

(a) risk identification, which means the recognition of risk sources and the determination of basic risk subcategories;
(b) risk analysis and assessment, which involves risk estimation and determination of its impact on the public organisation;
(c) risk response, which means the selection of the right methods and ways of preventing the risks which have previously been identified and quantified (Tworek 2012, 126).

The graphic illustration of these phases is given in Fig. 1.3, which gives an idea diagram of the risk management process in a public sector organisation or institution. The four-phase structure of the risk management process, as shown in Fig. 1.3, results from the need to complete the flow chart with step four monitoring and control of public risk. Public organisations mostly focus on determining the effects of risk management and indicating possible drawbacks and irregularities in this respect. Therefore, monitoring and control are necessary to establish whether any additional

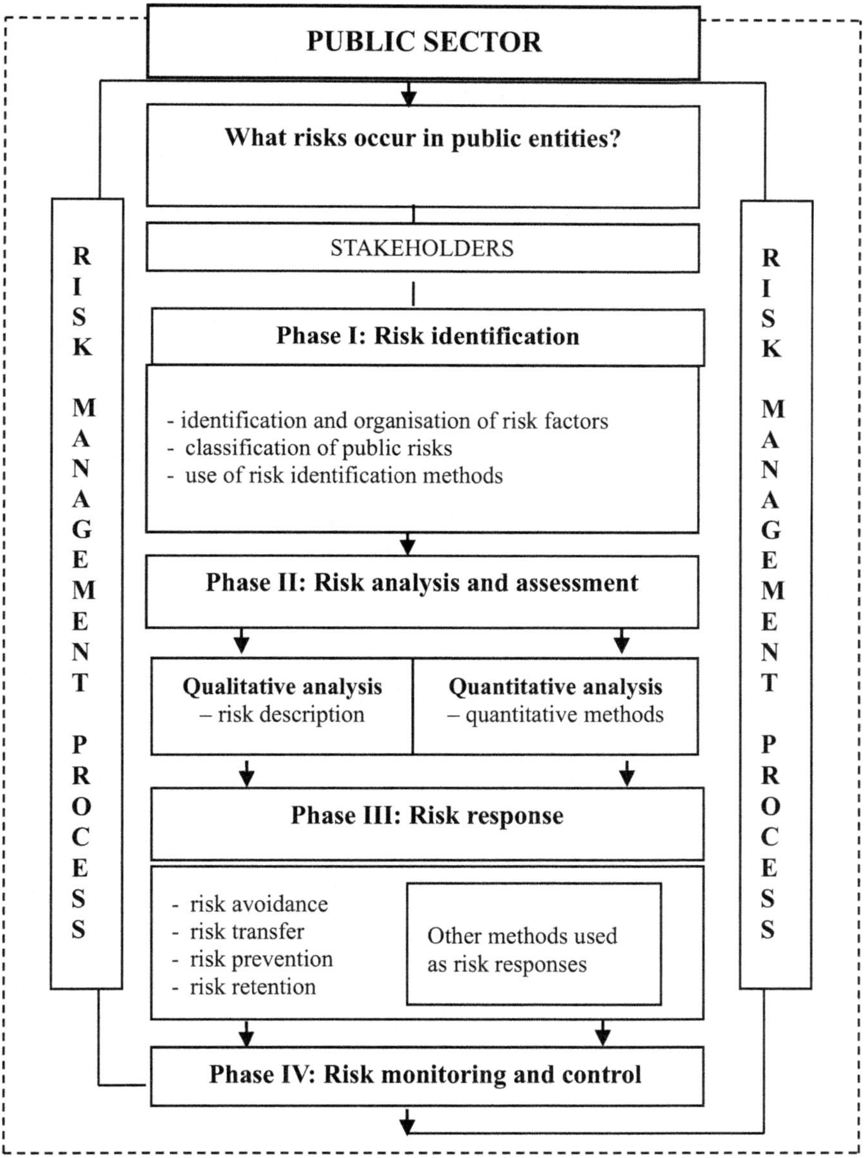

Fig. 1.3 Risk management process in public institutions (*Source*: Own elaboration based on: (Tworek 2012, 129–133))

measure or method should be used in order to make the risk management activities more effective (Tworek 2013, 158). What risks occur in a public organisation? To find an answer to that question a thorough analysis of stakeholders has to be conducted (Fig. 1.3), as many risk factors in the public sector come from its environment. In phase 1, i.e. the risk identification process, public risk managers have to decide which methods should best be used to identify the risks properly. A checklist is a highly effective method, which is widely employed all over the world. In the United States pilots flying passenger planes read and verify checklists before every take-off to ensure that risks related to their flights are eliminated. Not all risks, however, can be predicted and prevented, and this applies, in particular, to so-called Acts of God. Examples of these risks include natural disasters, such as Hurricane Katrina in the USA in 2005, which almost completely destroyed and crippled the public space in New Orleans, Louisiana (Tworek 2015, 196–210). The majority of public institutions in the affected area stopped working at that time, and the authorities went as far as to announce a state of emergency, summoning the National Guard and the military forces, as part of the crisis management efforts (Tworek 2015, 196–210). In the risk identification process, in addition to the classic checklist, risk managers in public organisations may also take advantage of other techniques, e.g. brainstorm, desktop research, internal audit and controls, hazard and operability study (HAZOP) or business analyses, which address specific areas of an organisation's operation by describing internal processes as well as exogenous factors that may affect these processes (FERMA 2002, 15). Having been identified, risks are analysed and assessed (phase 2), using appropriate methods. Due to the difficulties experienced during risk quantification in the public sector, it is most advisable to follow the complementary approach to risk analysis, combining qualitative and quantitative methods. Here the rules of probability calculus are applied to determine the likelihood of a given risk, based on historical data. Risk matrixes are created and specific scales are assigned for potential risks which may occur, broken down into very low, low, moderate, high and very high. In practice, there is an array of quantitative methods which might be used, e.g. a decision tree analysis or a sensitivity analysis, derived from the field of corporate finance. In public organisations which have their risks estimated, appropriate risk responses may be identified (phase 3), and these reactions may be of different kinds (Fig. 1.3).

The best way to secure risks in a public institution is to take out insurance (risk transfer), which may involve a combination of two or more risk responses at the same time (Edwards and Bowen 2005, 136). Risk can also be avoided altogether or, to the contrary, it may equally well be accepted (risk absorption) (Bennet et al. 2010, 12–22). Risks can also be mitigated, to a certain extent, e.g. by putting in place evacuation procedures in case of fire (Tworek 2015, 196–210). All such activities and measures are subject to monitoring and control (phase 4), and a person responsible for this process in a public organisation is a risk manager. In various organisations, risk management may be carried out in various ways, i.e. some of the phases shown in the figure may be parallel, and other may come earlier or be omitted. It is important, however, to ensure that the methods applied in risk identification, risk quantification and risk responses are used complementarily. This will make risk management highly effective. One should not forget, however, about the attitudes of individuals who draw conclusions in this respect, as this is connected with their perception of risk (Smallman and Fischbacher-Smith 2003, 8). Another thing that needs to be borne in mind is the political aspect of public institutions, which involves the identification of political risk. It may, therefore, be concluded that risk management protects the public entity, adding to its value, as it contributes to the fulfilment of the entity's goals by:

(a) providing the systemic framework, to make the entity's further operation coherent and controlled;
(b) enhancing the decision-making process, planning and identifying priorities, using the wide-ranging knowledge about the entity's operations, the degree of uncertainty, opportunities and threats;
(c) enabling more effective allocation of capital and resources available to the entity;
(d) reducing uncertainty in non-core operations;
(e) protecting and building up the entity's assets and image;
(f) supporting the development of the entity's human potential and knowledge base;
(g) improving the efficiency of the public organization (FERMA 2002, 4).

5 Modern Approaches to Risk Management in Theory and Practice: Methodical Aspects

There is no single and universal risk management formula which could be fully applicable and appropriate for every entity, without exception. There is also no risk management methodology which could be widely and uniformly adopted, i.e. there are no methods which could work in every case and in every entity. There are, however, some universal rules—devised by appropriate institutions and organisations that promote risk management knowledge worldwide—which could be followed by entities in their risk management processes. The following UK organisations should be listed here – The National Forum for Risk Management in the Public Sector (ALARM), The Association of Insurance and Risk Managers (AIRMIC) and The Institute of Risk Management, which have jointly developed the risk management standard of FERMA (Federation of European Risk Management Associations). This standard recommends certain methods and procedures for managing risks but its main advantage is the fact that it is not only applicable to commercial enterprises but also to other entities, including public organisations, i.e. so-called third sector. In the context of public risk, PRAM and PURMA should also be mentioned here, as they advocate and promote the application of ISO 31000:2009 *Risk Management: Principles and Guidelines*, which is basically an extension of the previously existing Australia and New Zealand standard of AS/NZS 4360:2004, largely based on the solutions established by FERMA, focusing on the alignment of risk management terminology and the process-based approach to risk management (Tworek 2014, 318). The standard of COSO II: *Enterprise Risk Management: Integrated Framework*—developed in 2004 by COSO (The Committee of Sponsoring Organisations of the Treadway Commission) in the USA, is equally important from the point of view of business practice. Both COSO II and ISO 31000:2009 refer to commercial activities, and the risk management methodology proposed there is mainly applicable to big corporations. There are many similar standards available internationally, such as Austrian ONR 49000:2004 *Risikomanagement für Organisationen und Systeme: Begriffe und Grundlagen* or Japanese JIS Q 2001:2001 *Guidelines for Development and Implementation of a Risk Management System.* A huge contribution to risk management knowledge has been made by the International Risk Management Institute (IRMI), an American organisation which holds an annual conference in the USA devoted to the issues of risk management in the commercial sector. The IRMI has developed 101 risk management rules, which make an excellent practical guidebook for managers of any industry or profession (Construction Risk Management... 2010, I.B.1). Adherence to these rules may contribute to an effective reduction in the global risk every organisation in any country and economic system is exposed to (Tworek 2010, 63). The 101 risk management rules provide a set of guidelines which help to streamline the corporate management process, taking into account technical, organisational, administrative and cultural aspects. (Construction Risk Management... 2010, I.B.1). These rules are versatile in their character and may be applied by numerous entities, including the public sector (Tworek 2010, 63). All these standards, as well as the institutions promoting them, recommend an organised approach to risk management. Looking at practical aspects of risk management, the key standards, of those mentioned above, include AS/NZS, COSO II and FERMA (see Table 1.2).

Table 1.2 presents 12 key characteristics of the standards listed there, with AS/NZS 4360:2004 being the most important standard and providing the basis for ISO 31000:2009, including the supporting documents of ISO Guide 73:2009 – Vocabulary and ISO/IEC 31010:2009 Risk Assessment Techniques. Today this standard provides the foundation, worldwide, for risk management, and its implementation brings a number of tangible benefits for corporations. First of all, it focuses on the goal of risk management in an enterprise, i.e. value creation; secondly, risk management principles are largely aligned with Enterprise Risk Management solutions, which is particularly evident when analysing the key components of the risk management process; thirdly, the contents of the standard comprise the three stages that need to be completed and the actions that need to be taken in order to implement the standard successfully in practical operations (Tworek 2013, 203). This standard indicates specific methods which may be employed to identify risks e.g. brainstorming, expert panel, and estimate risks, e.g. risk simulation

Table 1.2 Risk management standards: 12 key characteristics

AS/NZS 4360:2004

1. A possibility of something happening that impacts on a company's objectives. It is the chance to either make a gain or a loss and is measured in terms of likelihood and consequence. It addresses negative and positive aspects of risk
2. Culture, processes and structures directly focused on making gains and controlling threats at the same time
3. The standard may be applied in any organization
4. A general description in the standard plus a brief expansion in a handbook
5. Identifying entities involved in risk management and formal documents to support the risk management system
6. Objective setting is embedded in the risk management process
7. The standard does not pay much attention to risk identification. It emphasizes the need of regularity, no matter whether risk is controlled by an organization or not. The standard provides some guidance about the information needed to identify risk, a method of identification and documentation which closes this stage of the process
8. In the guidelines part, estimation criteria and risk appetite concept are described. No references to historic events when determining assessment criteria
9. Reporting and communication issues are presented in the first part of the standard
10. The standard provides separate descriptions of risk activities, bringing positive and negative effects. The main part of the standard outlines an analysis of costs and benefits of every risk response, but more details about it (qualitative and quantitative analyses) can be found in the guidelines part
11. Continuous monitoring combined with drawing conclusions are vital in risk management process. The guidance part provides, e.g. a detailed description of monitoring and measuring effectiveness of risk management process
12. The standard refers to this issue in a very general way and discusses the following: assessment of practices used so far: provision of support from top level management, establishing responsibilities, ensuring appropriate resources

Enterprise Risk Management – COSO II

1. A possibility that an event will occur and have a negative impact on the achievement of objectives. It addresses negative and positive (opportunities) aspects of risks
2. Conducted by an entity's board of directors, management or any other personnel. This process is applied in strategy setting and across the company, designed to identify potential events that may affect the entity, manage risk which is within its risk appetite and provide reasonable assurance regarding the achievement of entity objectives

Table 1.2 (continued)

3. Universal standard designed mainly for American listed companies
4. A very detailed description of stages within the risk management process
5. Objective setting is a stage of the risk management process. It emphasizes that risk management should be correlated with the achievement of strategic objectives. Four types of objectives are distinguished: strategic, operations, reporting and compliance
6. Within risk identification, the standard refers to the analysis of a company's internal and external environment, which may be a source of events that have a positive or negative impact on the strategy implementation (suggests a catalogue of internal and external factors). COSO II provides detailed information about risk identification techniques (with examples)
7. No separate section about estimation. Some references to risk estimation may be found in the section on risk assessment and risk response
8. COSO II anticipates that reporting and communication should follow risk response and control activities
9. COSO II distinguishes four possible risk responses: avoiding, reducing, sharing or accepting risk. It provides a brief analysis of costs and benefits. More details can be found in the volume on Application Techniques
10. COSO II distinguishes two kinds of monitoring – ongoing (in progress) and ad hoc. The standard provides a detailed description of the observation process, including the subjective and objective scope of reporting
11. The standard outlines the roles and responsibilities of: board of directors, managers, CRO, financial officers, internal auditors and external parties. The supplementary part includes detailed examples of job descriptions for CRO, CEO, audit committee and risk committee
12. Even the best risk management system does not necessarily ensure that the objectives are met. COSO indicates the following limitations: management process, human error, circumvention of controls, costs of risk responses
FERMA Standard
1. The combination of the probability of an event and its consequences. The standard draws attention to both positive and negative aspects of risks but focuses primarily on the former ones
2. The process whereby organizations methodically address the risks
3. The standard may be applied in any type of organization, including those in the public sector
4. A very general description of the risk management process and its stages
5. Entities participating in the process are identified and it is recommended that general internal regulations should be established
6. No special section dealing with goal setting. The impact of risk management on achievement of strategic goals is emphasized

(*continued*)

Table 1.2 (continued)

7. Risk identification is treated as part of risk analysis, which comprises risk description and risk estimation. Few directives are given in this area. It is recommended that risk identification should be conducted in a methodical way to ensure that all activities are defined. An appendix to the standard includes a short list of risk identification techniques
8. As soon as the risk evaluation stage is completed, risks need to be referred to pre-agreed criteria and a decision about further actions should be taken
9. Reporting and communication (internal and external) are discussed before the risk response section
10. FERMA does not pay much attention to this issue. It is underlined that risk control and mitigation are part of risk responses, just like risk avoidance, transfer and financing
11. Monitoring should bring information about risk identification and appropriate control actions to be taken
12. The standard specifies the roles and scope of responsibility of: the Board of Directors, Business Units, the Risk Management Function and Internal Audit. In addition, it deals with a risk management policy and resources needed to implement the risk management process

Source: Own elaboration based on Kasiewicz 2011, 93–96, The Association of Insurance

(Tworek 2013, 203). It also presents concrete solutions regarding risk responses, such as. risk avoidance or risk retention, depending on the size of risk (Fig. 1.3). The standard is an attempt to formally structure the risk management process, as well as laying foundations for the holistic approach to risk management, in which all the risk identification and quantification methods, as well as risk responses used within the process, are to be employed in a complementary and complete way. The vital thing, however, is the fact that it forms the basis for an integrated risk management concept, which is currently the most modern way of looking at risk in the theory of economics. The integrated risk management concept in a modern organisation should mean, in particular, that:

(a) risk is managed in all areas of the organization's operation;
(b) the organization clearly identifies who manages risk and bears responsibility for that—a risk manager;
(c) a complete range of risk management methods are employed in a complementary way;

(d) risk management is carried out on the macro-, meso- and microeconomic scale and it concerns, primarily, competition, including rivalry in the international market;
(e) risk management supports the overall governance of the organization and is regarded as a separate management support function in an entity;
(f) risk management is an ongoing and reliable process, and it also analysed as a process;
(g) effective risk management reduces the global risk for an organization (Tworek 2013, 205).

6 Risk Management in Macro-Organisations: A Systemic Approach

Can risk be managed with reference to a specific macro-organisation, such as a nation state, by public space representatives who have been appointed to do so? Of course, it can – through a network of formal and non-formal institutions which provide the framework but are analysed in terms of capacities, owing to which the system, as a whole, can operate (Raczkowski 2015, 9–10). This means that an improvement introduced in one institution—no matter how desirable— may not only fail to contribute to the state's operations, but may even cause a threat, if no corresponding improvements are introduced in other institutions. To put it simply, people resist any changes if these changes are likely to affect them. On the other hand, however, in the democratic system individuals are not subject to the direct mechanisms of command or control. As a result, the task faced by every authority (not just the executive one) is to make effective use of political tools, within the framework of public policies, which will lead to co-operation and network management (Kickert et al. 1997), encourage or even force the individual members of the society to behave in a desirable way (Salamon 2002, 600–610). This network character of the macro-organisation is also utilized in the matrix form, where the same single activity falls simultaneously under a number of structures. This means that managers of one structure not only have to be able to manage within different structures, but also need to be flexible and willing to be managed by other structures (Sy and Cote 2004, 437–455).

The state's intervention in the market, connected with the need to disperse the risk, is usually successful in the short or medium run, while the long-term consequences of such intervention do not necessarily prove satisfactory and may lead to a delay in the introduction of the desirable reforms, if the currently applied solution is not regarded as problematic (Frame et al. 2015, 25–52). In the democratic system a political party or parties which, at the given time, form the government tend to focus more on short-term political benefits, instead of encouraging a debate about vital issues and paying more attention to actual social and economic needs, and that leads to a systemic risk of a non-moderated structure (Baker 2015, 266). The risk in macro-organisations should, therefore, be analysed looking at the global environment and, in particular, at the biggest and most influential economies such as the USA or China. In the public private partnerships of the fastest growing world economy (China), the key risks include, in order of importance (Ke et al. 2011): government's intervention, poor political decision-making, financial risk, government's reliability, market demand change, corruption, subjective evaluation, interest rate change, immature juristic system and inflation. At the same time, China may already have generated some risk in the real estate market, which is an essential part of the Chinese economy, and too many leveraged buyouts (Wu et al. 2015, 3–35), risks insolvency or even may cause another global crisis, especially if accompanied by a rise in interest rates and a fall in demand. According to the Global Risk Management Survey (Global Risk Management… 2015, 8) the key risks for enterprises include, in order of importance:

(a) damage of reputation or brand (usually due to unfair competition);
(b) economic slowdown or slow recovery (putting the profitability of operations at risk);
(c) regulatory/legislative changes (leading to a risk when making investment decisions);
(d) increasing competition (as a natural free market process, which however creates asymmetry between the way entities are treated and the way they behave);

(e) failure to attract or retain top talent (noticing that real true leaders add value but not everyone is capable of becoming one);
(f) failure to innovate/meet customer needs (which would result in the need to restructure);
(g) business interruption (as far as it concerns any forms of disruptions in operations—both on the part of individuals/private entities, as well as public entities);
(h) third party liability (e.g.: a risk that no adequate insurance may be arranged, due to increased risk exposure related to an entity's business profile);
(i) computer crime/hacking (as technological and actual disruptions to—or discontinuation of—operations and/or data theft);
(j) property damage (a serious risk if the property is not insured, the insurance sum is not estimated or the assets cannot be reproduced in due time).

This clearly shows that different actors are exposed to different risks, which result from their specific geographies, industries, economic and social features.

Nevertheless, according to Ameyaw and Chan (2015, 447–448), governments, just like investors, have to be aware that risk is a dynamic category, have to be able to properly analyse risk factors and prioritize them, as required in any risk management process. Therefore, if we assume that a macro-organisation, e.g. a state, is obliged by constitution to ensure specific public goods for citizens, then the state's efficiency or inefficiency is reflected in the way its institutions co-ordinate their activities, even if affected by recurring economic crises or natural disasters (Hanson 2006, 480–494). The risks which occur in this sphere of the macro-organisation's intervention are of at least six types (political, financial, economic, social, environmental and technological), and affect, to a greater or lesser degree, all its structures—from the general and systemic one (the state) to key subsystems (enterprises, households); see Table 1.3.

An extremely useful tool in risk management during humanitarian crises and natural disasters, as well as for systemic risk management, is

Table 1.3 Threats to institutional risk management: the systemic approach

No.	Risk type	Early warning system	State risk	Enterprise risk	Household risk
1	Political	Government actions; opinion polls; parliamentary elections	Incompetent institutional staff; particularity of interests	Increased risk in business operations	Worse functioning of selected households
2	Financial	Trends and events; poor risk management	Transfer of global financial risks	More difficult access to capital; higher operating costs	Lower possibility to fulfil the needs; utility-based classification of goods and services
3	Economic	Trends and events; poor risk management	Mismatch between an economic strategy and a public policy	Uncontrolled market game; asymmetry in competitiveness of economic entities	Absorption of risk, mainly financial, social, psycho- logical
4	Social	Government actions; opinion polls; parliamentary elections	Higher demand for financial resources; increasing rigid budget expenditure	Low productivity; accidental and chronic vocational illnesses; high costs of employment	Social exclusion; high costs of social security; inability to make one's own living

5	Environmental	The condition of ecosystems; current state of people's heath	Unsuitable environmental strategies; distorted communication of environmental risk	Risk investments; new production technologies in agriculture and industry	Higher illness rate (including cancer); worse quality of life
6	Technological	The number of cyberattacks; R&D expenditure; innovativeness	Insufficient protection against cyberattacks; low percentage of public digital services; low expenditure on innovations	Low reliability of ICT systems; ineffective protection of technology copyrights; high commercialisation costs of new technologies	Digital and technological exclusion; living in the virtual world only (an epidemic of loneliness)

Source: Own elaboration

INFORM, which was developed co-operatively by the Inter-Agency Standing Committee Task Team for Preparedness and Resilience and the European Commission, with fourteen other global organisations: the OECD (Organisation for Economic Co-operation and Development), UNICEF (United Nations International Children's Emergency Fund), UNDP (The United Nations Development Programme), GFDRR (Global Facility for Disaster Reduction and Recovery), ACAPS (The Assessment Capacities Project), WHO (World Health Organisation), OCHA (Office for the Co-ordination of Humanitarian Affairs), UNHCR (United Nations High Commissioner for Refugees). INFORM helps to gain the understanding of— and illustrates the threats posed by— humanitarian crises, which may occur in 191 world countries surveyed. It offers a simple way to optimize the decision-making process in all kinds of crisis situations. It addresses three aspects of risk, namely (Index for Risk Management… 2015, 2–19):

(a) lack of coping capacity (a lack of necessary institutions and infrastructure);
(b) vulnerability (socio-economic, vulnerable groups);
(c) hazard and exposure (natural, human).

INFORM was used to illustrate risk management values for 12 selected countries (Fig. 1.4, Table 1.4), ranging from the highest level in the world (Singapore) to the lowest one (Somalia).

A valuable feature of the index is the fact that it reflects changes in risk over time and across geographic locations. In terms of trade, business development, decisions about tourist destinations and decisions made by governments this information is highly appreciated. When making decisions about the actual allocation of available resources, in order to stay ready and react to any crisis or disaster which may occur, it may determine the distribution of funds and attention. Another important issue in risk management carried out by a macro-organisation is resilience, defined as 'the ability of people, households, communities, countries and systems to mitigate, adapt to, and recover from shocks and stresses in a manner that reduces chronic vulnerability and facilitates inclusive growth' (USAID

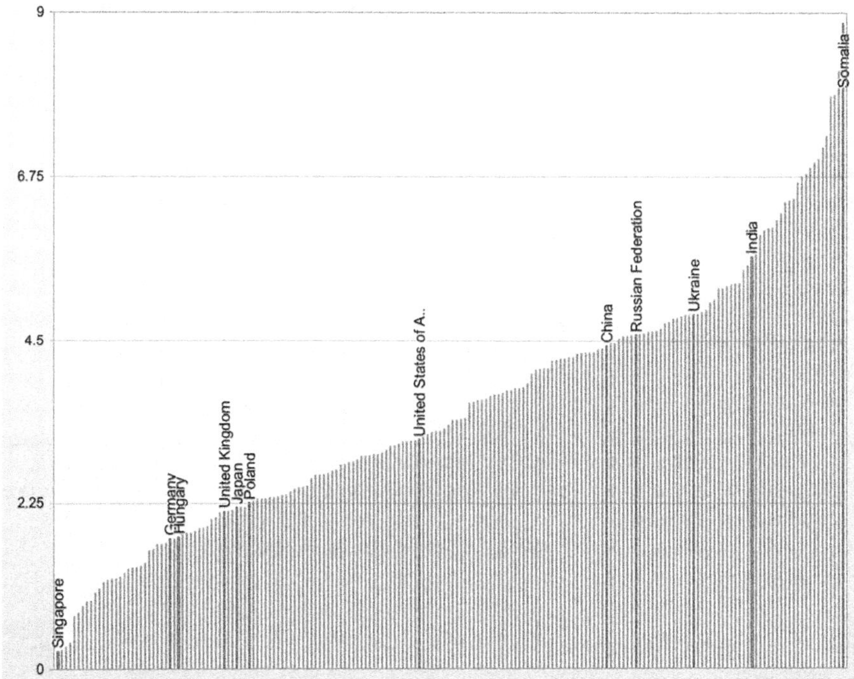

Fig. 1.4 Distribution of risk management values based on INFORM in selected world countries (*Source*: Own elaboration based on: Index for Risk Management. Results 2015, INFORM, Brussels: Inter-Agency Standing Committee (http://www.inform-index.org/Results/Global))

2012). Every micro-organisation belonging to a macro-organisation demonstrates different resilience and, consequently, perceives and handles risk in a different way. Managers of such organisations, who focus their efforts on risk dispersion, have to employ control techniques and methods, within the management process, which may fail to ensure effectiveness and efficiency (Hashagen et al. 2009, 92–103). What needs to be highlighted here, however, is the fact that such control has to follow a practical approach, make practical recommendations and suggest actual improvements to be introduced to the management system, which is key for establishing the process, instead of simply reporting the results of risk (Rooney and Cuganesan 2015, 132–159).

Table 1.4 Distribution of detailed risk management indices, based on INFORM in the selected world countries

Country	Risk management index	LCCI	VI	H&EI
Singapore	0.24	1.2	0.56	0.02
Germany	1.8	1.8	2.0	1.6
Hungary	1.8	2.0	1.5	1.9
United Kingdom	2.1	1.8	2.0	2.8
Japan	2.2	2.1	0.89	5.6
Poland	2.3	3.3	2.0	1.8
United States	3.1	2.6	2.1	5.6
China	4.4	4.1	2.9	7.4
Russian Federation	4.6	4.9	3.3	6.0
Ukraine	4.9	5.6	3.0	7.0
India	5.7	5.3	4.4	7.6
Somalia	8.9	9.6	8.4	8.6

Source: Own elaboration based on: (Index for Risk Management. Results 2015, INFORM, Brussels: Inter-Agency Standing Committee (http://www.inform-index.org/Results/Global))

LCCI lack of coping capacity index, *VI* vulnerability index, *H&EI* hazard & exposure index

7 Conclusion

Risk management requires a systemic approach. The theory of economics is full of modern concepts and theories about this. No matter how risk management is viewed, however, it is a practical dimension of knowledge: an applied science. In particular, at the times of economic downturn, the notion of global risk gains significance, and its impact can clearly be seen in the commercial and public sectors alike. The existence of risk in the public space, for example, means that risk concerns, to a greater or lesser degree, all entities, irrespective of their size, business model, status, and so on. Every entity is affected, in one way or another, by negative consequences of risks, which are ultimately expressed in financial terms. Due to this economic aspect, risk needs to be managed in a comprehensive and formalised way, at macro, meso and micro level. To this end, a variety of methods, techniques and tools should be used and the person responsible for a risk management process should be a risk manager. Risk, however, needs to be handled differently in the public and private sectors. First of all, the specific nature of activities carried out by an entity which manages risk has to be taken into account. Irrespective of the entity's profile and the risk management area, the thorough implementation of the right procedure should lead to tangible benefits for the entity, such as significant savings. The bottom line is that risk management means savings and today this is a prerequisite for any modern management process. At the same time, risk management is an integral part of strategic management and supports organisational governance. It is not possible to list all the scientists who have researched this field, and this chapter has merely attempted to outline the key concepts. In particular, the interdisciplinary character of risk in business makes it a challenge to come up with one explicit definition of this conceptual category. Moreover, risk as an economic category has to be perceived and analysed globally. Risk is pervasive in the public space and often results from the nature of the economic system. It is inseparably linked to political risk as a country's economic policy cannot effectively be separated from political decisions. This is the source of the difficulties encountered when trying to interpret risk in economics.

Bibliography

Ackoff, L. R. (1962). *Scientific method: Optimizing applied research decisions*. New York/London: Wiley.

Aggarwal, R. (1993). *Capital budgeting under uncertainty*. Englewood Cliffs: Prentice-Hall.

Akintoye, A., Beck, M., & Hardcastle, C. (2003). *Public-private partnership. Managing risks and opportunities*. Oxford: Blackwell Publishing Ltd.

Ameyaw, E. E., & Chan, A. P. C. (2015). Risk ranking and analysis in PPP water supply infrastructure projects. An international survey of industry experts. *Facilities, 33*(7/8), 428–453.

Arrow, J. K. (1979). *Eseje z teorii ryzyka (Essays it the theory of risk bearing)*. Warsaw: PWN.

Baker, K. (2015). Multi-level governance: The missing linkages. *Critical Perspectives on International Public Sector Management, 4*, 321–342.

Barrett, P. (2014). New development: Risk management – How to regain trust and confidence in government. *Public Money & Management, 34*(6), 459–464.

Bennet, P., Calman, K., Curtis, S., & Fischbacher-Smith, D. (2010). *Risk communication and public health*. Oxford: Oxford University Press.
Bernstein, P. (1997). *Przeciw bogom. Niezwykłe dzieje ryzyka, [Against the gods: The remarkable story of risk]*. Warsaw: WIG-Press.
Bizon-Górecka, J. (1998). *Metodyka zarządzania ryzykiem w produkcji budowlanej [Risk management methodology in construction production]*. Bydgoszcz: Akademia Techniczno-Rolnicza.
Black, F., & Scholes, M. (1973). The pricing of options and corporate liabilities. *Journal of Political Economy, 81*, 637–654.
Brealey, A. R., Myers, C. S., & Marcus, J. A. (2007). *Fundamentals of corporate finance*. New York: McGraw-Hill.
Brookfield, D., & Fischbacher-Smith, D. (2014). Conceptualising and responding to risk in IT projects. *Risk Management, 16*(3), 195–230.
Brown, T. J. (2008). *The handbook of program management. How to facilitate project success with optimal program management*. New York: McGraw-Hill.
Brown, L., & Osborne, P. S. (2013). Risk and Innovation: Towards a framework for risk governance in public services. *Public Management Review, 15*(2), 186–208.
Carmen, N., & Dobrea, R.C. (2006). Adapting risk management principles to the public sector reforms. *Administrație și Management Public, 6*, 126–130.
Carroll, R. (2009). *Risk management handbook for health care organizations*. Hoboken: Wiley.
Chapman, J. R. (2001). The controlling influences on effective risk identification and assessment for construction design management. *International Journal of Project Management, 19*(3), 147–160.
Chapman, C., & Ward, S. (2002). *Managing project risk and uncertainty. A constructively simple approach to decision making*. Chichester: Wiley.
Cleden, D. (2009). *Managing project uncertainty*. Farnham: Gower Publishing.
Construction Risk Management, Volume I. (2010). Dallas: International Risk Management Institute, Inc.
Dallas, F. M. (2006). *Value & risk management*. Oxford: Blackwell Publishing.
Drucker, P. (1964). *Managing for results: Economic tasks and risk-taking decisions*. London: Heinemann.
Edwards, J. P., & Bowen, A. P. (2005). *Risk management in project organizations*. Oxford: Elsevier.
FERMA. (2002). *A risk management standard*. London: FERMA.
Fischbacher-Smith, D., & Fischbacher-Smith, M. (2013). The vulnerability of public spaces: Challenges for UK hospitals under the 'new' terrorist threat. *Public Management Review, 15*(3), 330–343.

Flanagan, R., & Norman, G. (1993). *Risk management in construction*. Oxford: Blackwell Publishing.

Fone, M., & Young, C. P. (2007). *Managing risks in public organizations*. New York: Palgrave Macmillan.

Frame, W. S., Fuster, A., Tracy, J., & Vickery, J. (2015). The Rescue of Fannie Mae and Freddie Mac. *Journal of Economic Perspectives, 29*(2), 25–52.

Gitman, J. L. (2006). *Principles of managerial finance*. Boston: Pearson Education.

Gitman, J. L., Joehnk, D. M., & Smart, B. S. (2011). *Fundamentals of investing*. Boston: Pearson Education Limited.

Global Risk Management Survey. (2015). London: AON Empower Results.

Grey, S. (1995). *Practical risk assessment for project management*. Chichester: Wiley.

Haimes, Y. Y. (2004). *Risk modeling assessment and management*. Chichester: Wiley.

Hanson, A. (2006). Organizational responses and adaptations after 9-11. *Management Research News, 29*(8), 480–494.

Hartman, C. J. (2007). *Engineering economy and the decision-making process*. New York: Pearson Education.

Hashagen, J., Harman, N., Conover, M., & Sharma, J. (2009). Risk management in banking: Beyond the credit crisis. *Journal of Structured Finance, 15*(1), 92–103.

Heerkens, R. G. (2003). *Jak zarządzać projektami? [How to manage the projects?]*. RM: Warsaw.

Hirschey, M., & Nofsinger, J. (2008). *Investments: Analysis and behaviors fundamentals of corporate finance*. New York: McGraw-Hill Companies.

Holliwell, J. (2001). *Ryzyko finansowe. Metody identyfikacji i zarządzania ryzykiem finansowym [The financial risk manual. A systematic guide to identifying and managing financial risk]*. Warsaw: K.E. Liber.

Index for Risk Management. Results 2015. Inform. Brussels: Inter-Agency Standing Committee. http://www.inform-index.org/Results/Global

Jackson, P. (2013). Debate: Fraud risk management in the public sector. *Public Money & Management, 33*(1), 6–8.

Jannadi, A. O., & Almishari, A. (2003). Risk assessment in construction. *Journal of Construction Engineering and Management, 129*(5), 492–500.

Jędralska, K. (1992). *Zachowania przedsiębiorstw w sytuacjach niepewnych i ryzykowanych [How enterprises behave in uncertain and risky situations]*. Katowice: Wydawnictwo Akademii Ekonomicznej.

Kahneman, D., & Tversky, A. (1979). Prospect theory: An analysis of decision under risk. *Econometrica, 47*, 263–292.

Kallman, J. (2005). What is risk? *Risk Management, 52*(10), 57.

Karmańska, A. (2008). *Ryzyko w rachunkowości [Risk in accounting]*. Warsaw: Difin.

Kasiewicz, S. (2011). *Zarządzanie zintegrowanym ryzykiem w przedsiębiorstwie w Polsce [Integrated risk management in a Polish enterprise]*. Warsaw: Oficyna Wydawnicza Wolters Kluwer Business.

Ke, Y., Wang, S., Chan, A. P., & Cheung, E. (2011). Understanding the risks in China's PPP projects: Ranking of their probability and consequence. *Engineering, Construction and Architectural Management, 18*(5), 481–496.

Kendall, R. (2000). *Zarządzanie ryzykiem dla menedżerów. Praktyczne podejście do kontrolowania ryzyka [Risk management for executives]*. Warsaw: K.E. Liber.

Kendrick, T. (2003). *Identifying and managing project risk. Essential tools for failure-proofing your project*. New York: American Management Association.

Kickert, W. J. M., Klijn, E. H., & Koppenjan, J. F. M. (Eds.) (1997). *Managing complex networks: Strategies for the public sector*. London: Sage.

Knight, H. F. (1921). *Risk, uncertainty, and profit*. Boston: Hart, Schaffner & Marx.

Kolluru, V. R., Bartell, M. S., Pitblado, M. R., & Stricoff, S. R. (1996). *Risk assessment and management handbook for environmental, health and safety professionals*. New York: McGraw-Hill.

Kosiński, J. (2000). Ryzyko i niepewność w działalności gospodarczej [Risk and uncertainty in economic activities]. *Ekonomika i Organizacja Przedsiębiorstwa, 2*, 10–12.

Kuziak, K. (2011). *Pomiar ryzyka przedsiębiorstwa. Modele pomiaru i ich ryzyko [Enterprise risk measurement. Measurement models and related risk]*. Wrocław: Wydawnictwo Uniwersytetu Ekonomicznego.

Markowitz, H. M. (1952). Portfolio selection. *Journal of Finance, 7*(1), 77–91.

Merton, R. (1974). On the pricing of corporate debt: The risk structure of interest rates. *Journal of Finance, 29*, 449–470.

Mitchell, W. V. (2003). Consumer perceived risk: Conceptualisations and models. *European Journal of Marketing, 33*(1/2), 163–195.

Molak, V. (1997). *Fundamentals of risk analysis and risk management*. Boca Raton: CRC Press LLC.

Mulcahy, R. (2003). *Risk management. Tricks of the trade® for project managers*. Minneapolis: RMC Publications.

Murphy, D. (2008). *Understanding risk. The theory and practice of financial risk management*. London: Chapman & Hall/CRC.

Nersesian, L. R. (2004). *Corporate financial risk management. A computer-based guide for nonspecialists.* Westport: Praeger Publishers.
Nowak, E. (2010). *Rachunkowość w zarządzaniu ryzykiem w przedsiębiorstwie [Accounting in corporate risk management].* Warsaw: Polskie Wydawnictwo Ekonomiczne.
Osborne, P. S., & Brown, L. (2013). *Handbook of innovation in public services.* Cheltenham: Edward Elgar Publishing Limited.
Perry, P. (2007). *Risk assessment. Questions and answers: A practical approach.* London: Thomas Telford.
Pestieau, P., & Tulkens, H. (2006). Assessing and explaining the performance of public enterprises: Some recent evidence from the productive efficiency viewpoint. In P. Chander, J. Drèze, C. K. Lovell, & J. Mintz (Eds.), *Public goods, environmental externalities and fiscal competition, selected papers on competition, efficiency and cooperation in public economics by H. Tulkens.* New York: Springer Science+Business Media, LLC.
Petit, Y. (2012). Project portfolios in dynamic environments: Organizing for uncertainty. *International Journal of Project Management, 5*(30), 539–553.
Pickett, S. H. K. (2006). *Enterprise risk management. A manager's lourney.* Hoboken: Wiley.
Pike, R., & Neale, B. (2003). *Corporate finance and investments.* Harlow: Pearson Education Limited.
Raczkowski, K. (2015). *Zarządzanie publiczne, Teoria i praktyka [Public management. Theory and practice].* Warsaw: PWN.
Raftery, J. (1994). *Risk analysis in project management.* London: E & FN SPON.
Rooney, J., & Cuganesan, S. (2015). Leadership, governance and the mitigation of risk: A case study. *Managerial Auditing Journal, 30*(2), 132–159.
Royer, S. P. (2002). *Project risk management. A proactive approach.* Vienna: Management Concepts.
Salamon, L. M. (2002). The tools approach and the new governance. In S. L.M. (Ed.), *The tools of government.* New York: Oxford University Press.
Saunders, A., & Cornett, M. M. (2011). *Financial institutions management. A risk management approach.* New York: McGraw-Hill.
Schuyler, J. (2001). *Risk and decision analysis in projects.* Newtown Square: Project Management Institute.
Seog, H. S. (2010). *The economics of risk and insurance.* Chichester: Wiley.
Skipper, H., & Kwon, W. (2007). *Risk management and insurance. Perspectives in a global economy.* Oxford: Blackwell Publishing.

Smallman, C., & Fischbacher-Smith, M. (2003). Patterns of managerial risk perception: Exploring the dimensions of manager' accepted risks. *Risk Management, 5*, 7–32.

Smith, N. J. (2003). *Appraisal, risk and uncertainty*. London: Thomas Telford.

Smith, D., & McCloskey, J. (1998). Risk and crisis management in the public sector: Risk communication and the social amplification of public sector risk. *Public Money & Management, 18*(4), 41–45.

Smith, G. P., & Merritt, M. G. (2002). Managing consulting project risk. *Consulting to Management, 13*(3), 8.

Spinki, C.I. (2012). Decision theory and risk management in public organizations: A literature review. *Revista de Gestión Pública, 1*(1), 89–126.

Sy, T., & Cote, S. (2004). Emotional intelligence: A key ability to succeed in the matrix organization. *Journal of Management Development, 23*(5), 437–455.

Tarczyński, W., & Mojsiewicz, M. (2001). *Zarządzanie ryzykiem [Risk management]*. Warsaw: Polskie Wydawnictwo Ekonomiczne.

Tworek, P. (2010). *Ryzyko wykonawców przedsięwzięć inwestycyjnych [Contractors' risk]*. Katowice: University of Economics.

Tworek, P. (2012). Integrated risk management in construction enterprises – Methodical approach. *Journal of Economics & Management, 8*, 125–135.

Tworek, P. (2013). *Reakcja na ryzyko w działalności przedsiębiorstwa budowlano-montażowego [Risk responses in the operations of a construction and assembly enterprise]*. Warsaw: Difin.

Tworek, P. (2014). In J. Gołuchowski & A. Frączkiewicz-Wronka (Eds.), *System zarządzania ryzykiem jako źródło wiedzy o zagrożeniach w organizacjach publicznych w Polsce [Risk management system as a source of knowledge about threats faced by public organisations in Poland], Technologie wiedzy w zarządzaniu publicznym 2013*. Katowice: Wydawnictwo Uniwersytetu Ekonomicznego.

Tworek, P. (2015). In K. Z. Kapuścińska, S. Lachiewicz, & M. Matejun (Eds.), *Wykorzystanie listy kontrolnej w zarządzaniu ryzykiem w organizacjach publicznych [The use of a checklist in risk management carried out by public organisations], Współczesne organizacje wobec wyzwań zarządzania ryzykiem – aspekty poznawcze*. Łódź: Wydawnictwo Politechniki Łódzkiej.

Uff, J., & Odams, M. A. (1995). *Risk, management and procurement in construction*. London: King's College London.

USAID, (2012). Building resilience to recurrent crisis. Available at: www.usaid.gov/sites/default/files/documents/1870/USAIDResiliencePolicyGuidanceDocument.pdf. Accessed 14 July 2015.

Watson, D., & Head, A. (2007). *Corporate finance. Principles & practice*. Harlow: Pearson Education Limited.

Wideman, M. R. (1992). *Project & risk management. A guide to managing project risks & opportunities*. Newtown Square: Project Management Institute.
Willett, H. A. (1951). *The economic theory of risk and insurance*. Philadelphia: University of Pennsylvania.
Williams, A. C., Smith, L. M., & Young, C. P. (2002). *Zarządzanie ryzykiem a ubezpieczenia [Risk management and insurance]*. Warsaw: Wydawnictwo Naukowe PWN.
Wu, J., Gyourko, J., & Deng, Y. (2015, July). *Evaluating the risk of Chinese housing markets: What we know and what we need to know* (NBER working paper series). Cambridge.
Yescombe, R. E. (2007). *Public-private partnership. Principles of policy and finance*. Oxford: Elsevier Ltd.
Young, C. P., & Tippins, C. S. (2001). *Managing business risk. An organization-wide approach to risk management*. New York: American Management Association.

2

Elimination of Exchange Rate Risk in TTIP by Inclusion of a Clause Linking Dollar and Euro

Katarzyna Żukrowska

1 Introduction

There are various reasons why the two main world currencies should be linked and this could be achieved by making it a condition in the Transatlantic Trade and Investment Partnership (TTIP) which is currently being negotiated. However, such a solution could be seen as a further obstruction to concluding the negotiations, which have been on-going since 2013. Their conclusion was planned for the end of 2015. This chapter indicates why such a linkage is needed and why the TTIP is seen as a political, not a purely economic, issue, as free trade agreements are usually considered to be. Following an introduction, five merit points and conclusions are given to explain. why the exchange rate should be included in the TTIP. Then the state of the on-going negotiations is discussed, which is followed by a consideration of the advantages of the TTIP and some criticisms of the proposed agreement. Finally there is an

K. Żukrowska (✉)
Warsaw School of Economics, Warsaw, Poland

K. Raczkowski (ed.), *Risk Management in Public Administration*,
DOI 10.1007/978-3-319-30877-7_2

argument as to why this already complex agreement should be further complicated by a seemingly problematic solution.

2 Exchange Rate in an Investment and Trade Partnership

Negotiations over the TTIP started in July 2013, which means that they have already lasted over two years. This seems a relatively short period in comparison to the 14 year-long WTO (World Trade Organization) negotiations started in Doha (Qatar) in 2001. The TTIP is not the first attempt to institutionalize mutual economic relations between the EU and the USA. Closer co-operation between the two trading areas was proposed in the mid- 1980s (Transatlantic Declaration… 1990). Yet, despite several statements on the need for liberalization and barrier reduction, negotiations of an agreement bringing this about never commenced. In 2008, in response to the global financial crisis, G-20, a group of major world economies, was established, to make decisions on the co-ordination of economic, financial, and exchange rate policies. G-20 consists of the G-7 (Canada, France, Germany, Italy, Japan, the UK, the USA), BRIC countries (Brazil, Russia, China, India), Saudi Arabia, and representatives of the EU, ECB, WTO and IMF. The presidency rotates among the heads of states or governments of the countries forming the G-20.

Establishing the G-20 meant that a bigger group of states than the G-7 took responsibility for global guidance. The formation of G-20 could also be seen as a stimulus for closer co-operation between the EU and the USA. as could the increased role of the Asian states in the world economy and the prolonging of the Doha Round negotiations within the WTO. The TTIP is seen as an open agreement, which means that other countries will be able to join. It is also intended to be an agreement that will adjust to the needs of its members and expand in scope, if required. TTIP has been negotiated in parallel with TPP (Trans-Pacific Partnership). negotiations for which started in 2011. The states in the TTP are: Australia, Brunei, Canada, Chile, Japan, Malaysia, Mexico, New Zealand, Peru, Singapore, US, and Vietnam. The Republic of South Korea is also interested in joining, and potential joiners include: Taiwan, Philippines, Laos, Cambodia, Thailand, Indonesia, Cambodia, Bangladesh and India. The most economically powerful and dynamic economy of China is not a member. Negotiations started as the Trans-Pacific Strategic Economic Partnership Agreement (TPSEP or P4) in 2005 and their conclusion was anticipated in 2012. However, a growing number of problems and then an increase in the number of participating states prolonged the negotiations. Finally, the formula of the agreement was also changed and it was relabelled as the TPP. One might ask why TPP is mentioned here. The answer is simple: the parallel negotiations of TPP and TTIP create pressure on the participants, concerning the first agreement rent, deriving from its application in practice which is seen as profit for the participants (Congleton and Hillman 2015, 307–330).

A number of economists state that the twenty-first century is an age in which global institutional ties are being replaced by regional ones. The EU and USA can be seen in this process as hubs which stimulate liberalization. Enough to mention that in the past both the EU and the USA have signed agreements on free trade with Mexico and South Korea. The EU recently negotiated an agreement with Japan, India and concluded negotiations with Canada. Canada, the USA and Mexico form NAFTA (North American Free Trade Agreement), negotiated in 1990 and extant since 1994. The USA is negotiating the TPP. The Asian dimension of trade liberalization is given a fast track status in the USA (Pacific and... 2015), which means that the US government supports the trade policy and welcomes liberalization. The summit in Bali set the elimination of border bureaucracy within the WTO as a priority.

The arguments used in support of TTIP are of a different character. They are based on the following premises: (1) change in the nature, conditions and direction of trade flows; (2) role of the EU and the USA in world trade and their mutual turnover share in world totals; (3) new growth impulse anticipated for both markets and the world economy from more intensive mutual relations between the EU and the USA; (4) the significance of negotiated conditions for global solutions; (5) new nature of production within EU and US markets, dominated by Small and Medium (S&M) companies, for which non-tariff barriers (NTB) seem to be a problem in increased expansion of trade; (6) the growing role of China and other emerging economies in world trade, which diminishes (relatively) the share of the EU and the USA in some markets.

The information given in Table 2.1 below shows that, prior to the launch of the negotiations on TTIP, a number of solutions had been

Table 2.1 Stages of development of mutual relations between the EU and USA

1995	1998	2007	2011	2013
New transatlantic agenda	Transatlantic economic partnership	Transatlantic economic council	EU and US high level working group on employment and growth	Recommendations of group concerning Transatlantic trade and investmrnt partnership (TTIP).
Co-operation in area of creating political and economic partnership. Promotion of peace, stability in the world. Deepening of institutional and economic ties.	Elimination of barriers in industrial goods trade and services. Activities undertaken to accept mutually compatible technical norms and standards as well as professional qualifications. Opening of the market for public tenders, solutions concerning intellectual property and protection of the environment. Co-operation in favour of liberalizing world trade within the WTO.	Liberalization of mutual trade. Promotion of investment. Co-ordination of protection of the financial markets. Protection of intellectual property. Participation of business representatives in bilateral summits.	Employment and economic growth are considered as two main topics calling for quick solutions and support by common policies.	Recommendations of working group to establish TTIP and start of negotiations July 2013. May 2014 – beginning of 5th negotiations round.

Source: Author's compilation, based on information about bilateral relations between the EU and the USA

suggested and laws that were introduced after 1995 were co-ordinated and took into account the prospect of future co-operation in production and trade. This co-ordination represents 15 years of closer co-operation in preparing laws and adjusting institutions and 13 years of closer co-operation before the TTIP negotiations started, and reflects the direction of structural change in the economies of the EU and the USA, with changes in the trade of industrial goods followed shortly by growth in FDI (foreign direct investment), services and intellectual property rights.

Why is the exchange rate linking important today? A number of economists will say that it will additionally complicate the negotiations, which are complex enough, and that the proposed clause would provoke different types of anti-TTIP protest. The TTIP concentrates principally on NTB (non-tariff barrier) reduction. Tariff barriers are relatively low in trade between the EU and the USA, the average level being approximately 2 %. This protection varies in different fields and is not the same in case of the Common European Tariff used in the European Trade Policy and the US tariff. Nevertheless reducing these tariff barriers would also be a stimulus to mutual trade in the future. Reducing non-tariff barriers is expected to result in greater profits. Those barriers are time-consuming measures of protection which transnational corporations (TNCs) can cope with but are a real challenge for small and medium companies (S&MC). Currently TNCs dominate the foreign trade of the EU and USA and hold the view that SMCs will not gain anything from a reduction of NTBs. This is a misconception, as reducing NTBs could result in a dramatic increase in foreign trade for S&MCs by removing their current problems in overcoming the high costs of acquiring the required technological, veterinary and phitosanitary certificates. Obtaining these certificates necessitates employing people who can arrange all the documentation and prove that the firm's product is safe to use in both markets by meeting the safety requirements of one of them.

The exchange rate, more precisely the level of the exchange rate, is one of the most often used NTBs. Appreciation of the exchange rate is a tool for 'opening a market', by using the currency to make imports cheaper and exports more costly. Of course, the relationship between two exchange rates is quite complex, as both can change their values in different directions. Nevertheless, post-2008 experience has shown that it is a workable measure since most states have used the value of their exchange rates to protect their markets. This is not a significant new development in trade policy as a way to deal with conditions in which the selling of goods abroad has become more difficult. Devaluation of the exchange rate has thus been used post-2008 to improve the competitiveness of exports and thus increase their volume in a difficult climate A lower value of exchange rate simultaneously protects one's own market, while an appreciation in the rate 'opens up' the market for imports, stimulating structural change by making imports more and exports less price competitive. This measure worked in the European Monetary Union upon the introduction of the euro, making production costs more comparable to the time when states were using their national currencies. This stimulated quicker development of the peripheral markets of the EU (Irish, Greek, Spanish and Portuguese) and slowed the development of the central markets (French, German, British, Dutch).

This was the situation in 2002 when euro banknotes came into circulation. In 2004, the European Union went through the biggest enlargement in its history, accepting 10 new members, of which 8 were at a much lower level of development than the EU average. The introduction of the euro and the enlargement of the market have resulted in acceleration of the EU economies as a whole. Approval on lifting trade barriers is easier to get, naturally, when the economy is flourishing and the opposite is equally true: support for reducing barriers drops when the economy slows down. This is a simple fact. It remains true despite most politicians and people of the European and North American markets believing that trade increases prosperity and the lifting of barriers stimulates mutual trade. There is less awareness that moving to more sophisticated types of production gives more added value to goods with the same engagement of production factors, which in turn makes a society richer faster. The policies applied in developed, or more precisely post-industrial, economies are designed to maintain existing jobs and not to move the production factors from one engagement to another. Protection of jobs is a costly activity for all states. It is mitigated by different tools introduced internationally but in practice only partially effective. These tools incorporate convergence criteria (limiting state expenditure), control of presence of the state in the economy (in EU competition policy, in WTO control of state engagement). After the 2008 financial crisis, the EU supported its policy in this area by additional solutions: a European Semester, six-pack and two-pack (all aimed at curbing an increase in state expenditure).

It is difficult to say what would have happened if a different solution had been chosen, as the economy is comprised of processes and once the time to act has passed, we can only talk about the solutions which were in fact introduced and put into practice. Nevertheless, we can guess that without the euro as a currency of currently 19 states (with 9 member states outside the European Monetary Union) we would be witnessing much higher tensions in Europe than we have now, as states with national currencies would devalue their currencies to protect their markets. Such a tactic was much used before the EMU, and was effectively used in most of the peripheral economies, as they were then called, of Ireland, Spain, Portugal and Greece. Italy, an initial and funding member state of the European Economic Community (EEC), also applied a policy of devaluation of the Italian lira, until the currency was linked with Deutsche Mark within the exchange rate mechanism (ERM).

Looking back to the initial stages of creation of the EEC, we can see that the elimination of trade barriers within the European Community and establishing a common European Trade Policy resulted in a policy of continued devaluation of exchange rates of the member states. This procedure was curbed in 1970 by measures in the Werner Plan, which was supposed to introduce a common European currency within ten years. The plan was not fulfilled, due to objective difficulties: namely the financial shocks to capital markets caused in 1971 by the departure of the US dollar from the gold standard (15 August 1971) and in 1973 by the energy crisis (1973). One proposal from the Werner Plan was introduced, however, regulate mutual proportions of the national currencies of the EC member states. This was known under the popular name of the 'snake in the tunnel' (One currency… 2015).

The transformation of Poland in 1989 suspended the use of tariffs on foreign trade after introducing convertibility of the Polish zloty, which started a deep devaluation and set the Polish currency at its real value. Suspension of tariffs was backed by arguments that devaluation and tariffs applied in parallel would cause increased protection, not liberalization, of external contacts of the market, and liberalization was one of the conditions of the shock-therapy. Tariffs were reduced according to the agreed schedule set forth in the Europe Agreement or free trade agreement with EFTA (European Free Trade Agreement) and CEFTA (Central European Free Trade Agreement) but were not applied in practice to trade as they were suspended and the role of protecting tool was overtaken by exchange rate which was devalued and protective by losing value (Żukrowska 2010).

In the post-2008 financial crisis, the exchange rate was one of the frequently used mechanisms for protection. States did not appreciate their exchange rates to the level of the real value of the currency, gaining competitiveness and protection of their national markets. In other states, where possible, the exchange rate value was lowered. In these states, different solutions were used to achieve this loss of exchange rate value (Washington 2012; Voda 2012, 136). Devaluation was the protection tool most frequently used in Asian states during the last 2008+ crisis.

In sum, the EU and the USA need to include an exchange rate clause in the TTIP as they try to move the world economy towards a new order in which the two partners will play an important role, an order which has been referred to as *Pax Transatlantica* (Dunin-Wąsowicz 2015, 135–150). The two markets – European and American – already play an important role internationally and they can still use their high share in world GDP, imports and exports of world trade in goods and services, followed by FDI imports and exports. Together they form the world's biggest markets in real terms – measured by potential consumer and investment markets, and constitute complementary economies, so it is in their interests to eliminate the barriers which currently limit their mutual trade. By co-operating more closely, both economies can become more competitive and achieve higher rates of growth in the both markets, influencing remaining markets at the same time. According to F. E. Kydland and E. C. Prescott (Lectures by… 2015), the performance of national economy in each state is strongly conditioned by state policy.

After the 2008 crisis, a number of economists took it for granted that pumping money into national economies would mean a return to active financial intervention in the old style. It was not recognised that the most effective financial stimulus was lending (not giving) money, and this only once, not repeatedly. When financial support was repeated, as happened in some cases, economic recovery was poor (Żukrowska 2013).

3 Where Are We in the TTIP Negotiations?

The EU and the USA approved the start of negotiations on free trade between their markets during the 39th summit of G-8 (Prime Minister... 2013), which took place in Lough Erne Resort, County Fermanagh, in Northern Ireland, Great Britain 17–18 June 2013.[1] The first round of negotiations took place in Washington in 2013. The EU negotiators are representatives of individual DGs of the EC, together with a group of specialists. Ignacio Garcia Beiero is the EU chief negotiator, while Damien Levie is his deputy. Mr Fernando Perreau de Pinnick is the merit co-ordinator of negotiations on the side of the EU.[2] The USA is represented by the Secretary of State, who is responsible for foreign economic relations. Dan Mullaney was appointed the chief negotiator on the US side. David Weiner acts as his deputy. Kate Kalutkiewicz is the assistant to negotiator, while Isabella Detwiler acts in capacities of a coordinator.[3] In case of approving important political decisions, they are always undertaken by Karel De Gucht, chancellor of Trade Directorate in the EC and Mike Froman, secretary of state responsible for trade in the USA.

The negotiations are conducted in rounds and take place alternately in the USA and in Belgium. The scope of negotiations, as well as their character and the goals set for reaching agreement, make the process extremely demanding for the negotiators. The ground for TTIP negotiations was prepared in advance, in 2011–2012. In 2011, a common EU-American High Level Working Group on Jobs and Growth (HLWG) was established. In 2012, from March to June, social consultations were conducted within the framework of the HLWG on behalf of the EC. In 2011, between May and July, a primary version of the report prepared by the HLWG was produced. In February 2013, the corrected, completed

[1] The summit was the sixth G-8 summit G-8 to be organized in UK. Earlier the summits were organized in London (1977, 1984, 1991), Birmingham (1998) and Gleneagles (2005).

[2] List of Lead Negotiators for the Transatlantic Trade and Investment Partnership (TTIP).

[3] List of Lead Negotiators for the Transatlantic Trade and Investment Partnership (TTIP). The Office of the United States Trade Representative (USTR).

and final version of the HLWG report was submitted. A month later, in March 2013, the EC prepared guidelines and directions concerning the negotiations. This was done in parallel with a presentation of the expected impact of TTIP on the economies of the EU states. The US Trade Representation to the EU notified the European Parliament of the start of the negotiations. Between April and June, social consultations were carried out in the territories covered by the future agreement. In June 2013, the TTIP negotiations officially started. In the months of January and February 2014, the American Trade Representation to the EU prepared a report in which barriers for small and medium (S&M) US companies exporting to the EU market were enumerated.

The EU has experience in forming trade regulations, which resulted from Articles 207 and 218 of the Tratato de Funcionamiento de la Union Europea (TFUE). This means that the representative of the EC acts in name of the EU and the Member States. Since the Lisbon Treaty, the EU foreign trade contracts also cover flows of FDI (foreign direct investment) (Treaty of… 2007).

The conditions negotiated by the EC have to be presented to the Board of Ministers for approval before signing. Also, the European Parliament has to be informed of the conditions and submit an opinion on them. These procedures are required before the documents can be formally accepted and closed.

The negotiation mandate (directives for negotiation) for representatives of the Commission in the EU–US talks on TTIP were approved by the European Board of Ministers of Trade. Information on this mandate is not made public. Some elements of the instruction are publicly accessible, however. They cover such information as: (1) scope of the mandate; (2) more detailed information on the goals of the negotiations and their main direction. Neither the EU nor the USA has published closed chapters, due to the negotiations of the accession mandates of states from East-Central Europe (enlargement 2004/2007+).

The TTIP treaty will consist of three parts consisting of 24 chapters, divided into conditions on the following areas:

(a) market access
(b) regulatory issues and non-tariff barriers (NTB)

(c) regulations relating to common global challenges within the trading area

Up to now there have been nine rounds of negotiations:

(a) First Round: 7–12 July 2013, Washington DC
(b) Second Round: 11–15 November 2013, Brussels
(c) Third Round: 16–21 December 2013, Washington DC
(d) Fourth Round: 10–14 March 2014, Brussels
(e) Fifth Round: 19–23 May 2014, Arlington, USA
(f) Sixth Round: 13–18 July 2014, Brussels
(g) Seventh Round: 29 September-3 October 2014, Chevy Chase, USA
(h) Eight Round: 2–6 February 2015, Brussels
(i) Ninth Round: 20–24 April 2015, New York

The part of the agreement dealing with market access has been approved, the level of tariffs and remaining forms of market protection are being considered as problems, still to be negotiated. The aim of the negotiators is to agree the lowest level of barriers limiting the access to the two markets for industrial and agricultural goods. The average level of tariffs is estimated at 2 % but there are variations in customs tariffs. For example, a 10 % customs tariff is applied to cars imported from the USA, while cars imported from the EU to the USA are only subject to a 2.5 % tariff. The reverse situation is seen in case of railway carriages: here, the USA applies a 14 % customs tariff to imports from the EU, while the EU applies a much lower tariff of 1.7 % on such imports from the US. The goal of the negotiations is to totally eliminate tariffs on mutual trade, which can have an impact on mutual turnover and improve competitiveness globally through increased institutional competition, combined with economies of scale and lower components costs. The negotiations will also address the issue of the origin of food products, to which both partners apply different regulations. The European Union aims to start a regular dialogue with the USA on anti-dumping practices and use of subsidies.

Together with commodity trade, both economies enjoy a big share in the world service market. In this area, the goal of the negotiations is to improve access in both markets, harmonizing regulations on access, mobility, licensing, and so on, changes which in the USA require approval not only federally but also by individual states. The service market is a broad area which includes telecommunication, ports, port-services, mobility (the approval of qualifications and access to the market); licensing (audit, legal advising, management consultancy), and new for industries important for the European economy as a whole, as well as for the member states (telecommunication, e-trade, social services, water). In the field of culture, the TTIP aims to introduce flexible measures, taking into consideration the rules applied in individual states. This involves agreement on regulations for the media and film industry with their various models and conditions.

In the case of personal data, TTIP would not introduce changes to current conditions. As such, this problem is not negotiated within the TTIP framework, and conditions concerning this issue will guarantee protection of personal data in the EU states, following the law regulations which were introduced in this area by EU regulations.

As far as investment is concerned, TTIP intends to liberalize investment at federal and sub-federal levels, while ensuring investment protection. New solutions in this field need to be approved by all member states. It should be added here that both the EU and US investors follow similar evaluations of the ranking agencies like Standard and Poor, Moody's or Fitch. Those rankings were established earlier in the US market. All currencies of the future TTIP market enjoy IMF supervision of currency convertibility and macrostabilization measures. In the case of investor-to-state dispute settlements (ISDS), TTIP will offer better conditions in comparison to the individual agreements previously signed with the USA. Finally, all states are members of OECD, which monitors capital transfers in the short, medium and long term. A particular problem is the access to state tenders at central and local level, where new measures could increase competition and provide the state with better deals. Alongside customs protection and barriers, which work in similar ways, it is also proposed to lift non-tariff barriers (NTB). and to solve the problem commonly known as non-border trade barriers, i.e. requirements for security or diversified environmental, health, food, sanitary, veterinary, hygienic, and agricultural standards. This involves harmonization on such matters as certificates, permits, identity confirmation, information given on the origin of imports, or contents and so on. All such requirements place a burden on exporting or importing companies, less so for transnational corporations (TNC) more so for S&M companies, which predominate in both markets (Table 2.2).

Generally, the NTB average protection for both services and industrial goods is higher for EU exports to the US market than vice versa. This means that TTIP would be more advantageous for the EU states than for American companies. At the same time, USA production is on average more competitive than European: people are more entrepreneurial and markets more flexible, a situation reflected in the USA's faster recovery after the 2008+ crisis. GDP growth in the USA is 3.5 %, while in EMU states it is 1.0 % (*The Economist...* June 2015, 78). Closer co-operation in such conditions, especially when interest rates reach a similar level, could stimulate growth strongly in both markets.

As far as co-operation in the area of regulatory and legal solutions is concerned, the TTIP is not limited to trade, but also incorporates the transfer of services, including in due course financial services. Since achieving convergence in such areas is time-consuming, it is necessary to let the TTIP have a 'living' character which would allow future adjustments to regulations to meet new conditions. Such elasticity of approach has a specific meaning and can be seen as one of the important requirements of defining the goals of fixed and intransgressible timing.

Concerning global trade challenges, it is necessary to take into account the specific issues and differences between the EU and USA, such as the protection of products and brands, which are geographically specific (e.g. Dijon mustard, Polish "oscypek" cheese, champagne). In this field, there is a need for measures which target 'trade and sustainable development'. The EU and USA will need to agree on job markets and environmental protection in the context of internationally approved standards, but these agreed measures must also stimulate mutual trade, and enable transfer of energy sources and energy, as well as addressing the problems of S&M and state-owned enterprises.

A report, which was ordered by the European Commission from the CEPR (Consortium for Economic Policy and Advice) in 2013 predicted that 80 % of the advantages of TTIP will result from elim-

Table 2.2 NTB index by branches (from 0 to 100)

Sector	EU export to USA	USA export to EU
Services		
Travels	35.6	17.6
Transport	39.9	26.3
Financial services	29.7	21.3
ICT	20.0	19.3
Insurance	29.5	39.3
Communication	44.6	27.0
Construction	45.0	37.3
Other business services	42.2	80.0
Personal, cultural, recreation services	35.8	35.4
Average range of NTB protection in services	**35.8**	**33.7**
Branches of goods		
Chemical	45.8	53.2
Pharmaceutical	23.8	44.7
Cosmetic	48.3	52.2
Biotechnological	46.1	50.2
Machines	50.9	36.5
Electronic	30.8	20.0
Office equipment, communication and information equipment	37.9	32.3
Medical, measurement and testing equipment	49.3	44.5
Automobile	34.8	31.6
Airplanes and space	56.0	55.1
Food and beverages	45.5	33.6
Iron, steel and metal products	35.5	24.0
Textiles, clothes and footwear	35.6	48.9
Wood, paper and paper products	30.0	47.1
Average protection level NTB in industrial products	**40.7**	**37.4**

Source: Ecorys (2009), quoted after CEPR Report 2013

inating and reducing of NTBs. because mutual tariff barriers, as mentioned earlier, are relatively low while the value of mutual trade is high (Table 2.3).

Market protection, with use of NTB measures, can take different forms, such as import quotas, direct limitations of market access, voluntary export restraints, different types of regulations and norms, which cause costly differences in products (e.g. difference voltage tension or adjustments in car systems). Some of the NTBs are easy to remove. Such a move only requires political will. Others seem to be more dif-

Table 2.3 Economic relations between the EU and US markets in 2011, 2012 and 2013 (trade in industrial foods, services and capital transfers in mln euro)

Contents	2011	2012	2013
Trade EU–USA in industrial goods			
EU import	192	206.5	196
EU export	264.1	292.8	288.2
Balance	72.1	86.3	92.2
Trade EU–USA in services			
EU import	134.7	138.0	3.3
EU export	141.1	148.1	6.9
Balance	148.9	163.0	14.1
FDI transfer EU–USA			
EU import	–	–	1655
EU export	–	–	1536.4
Balance	–	–	118.6

Source: The European Commission

ficult to eliminate, especially when such measures enable the achievement of political goals outlined in a state's policy. The former EU Trade Commissar, Lord Mandelson, suggested three possible ways to solve this sort of problem: (1) common approval of widely understood comparable standards, at their lowest level; (2) harmonization of approved standards and norms applied in different law systems; (3) long-term convergence of regulation in respect of new measures or their regulation on an international level. Such solutions could be applied in case of the EU and USA. For example, in EU and American markets there are different technical requirements for motor vehicle security. In both cases, the measures are safe. The simplest solution in this case is to accept that requirements in both cases guarantee security, making common rules unnecessary and that both regulations can function in parallel. This is an example of 'harmonization' of established laws and standards (*brownfield*), while in case of the new laws and standards, the solutions would be common (*greenfield*).

There are calculated advantages deriving from lifting the NTB barriers in the future. The TTIP agreement has to take into account the number of such barriers which limit the access to certain market for goods and services exported from markets of individual states today. A CEPR Report in 2013 estimates which NTBs can be realistically reduced and what kind of impact this can have on advantages from the increased mutual turnover (Table 2.4).

The EU is the second largest market for the USA, while the USA is the biggest market for the EU. Analysing the mutual turnover of the two markets and calculating their share in world trade shows the current weight of the two markets, and gives the possible scale of influence of future bilateral trade and FDI liberalization on other economies. This is especially true when creation and reallocation effects are taken into account, which will be followed by changed institutional competitiveness. At the second stage, mutual liberalization should stimulate increased rates of growth as a reaction to higher intensification of competition (enforcing reduction of costs following the increased scale of production and shrinking unit costs) (Table 2.5).

The immediate effects of such liberalization are projected through different scenarios: (1) limited to tariffs reduction; (2) reduction of barriers only for services; (3) reduction limited to market of public tenders, as shown in Table 2.6. The figures give a clear picture. On the one hand, we expect positive effects in both EU and US economies. On the other hand, we can see shrinking rates of growth in other markets, which might act

Table 2.4 Five main trade partners of the EU and the USA: export, import and balance in 2013 (ml € and mld $)

Five main EU trading partners in ml euro			
	Export	Import	Balance
USA	288.2	196	92.2
Switzerland	169.6	95.3	74.3
China[a]	148.3	280.1	−131.8
Russia	119.8	206.5	−86.7
Turkey	77.8	50.4	27.4
Five main trading partners of the USA in ml US$			
Canada	301.6	332.6	−31.0
European Union	262.2	387.6	−125.4
Mexico	226.1	280.5	−54.4
China	121.7	440.4	−318.7
Japan	65.2	138.6	−73.4

[a]Without Hong Kong

Source: EUROSTAT, US Census Bureau, World Bank, own calculations

as a push-factor for others to join TTIP, or it might stimulate the Doha negotiations, or possibly both (Table 2.6).

TTIP is not intended to disadvantage any markets. It has to be seen as an arrangement which can help to overcome the deadlock of low rates of growth, which entails falling rates of growth in other countries.

Table 2.5 Ten biggest world economies

Market	GNP in ml US$	GNP per capita in 1000 US$	
EU	17,958.1	29.6	5
USA	16768.1	53	2
China	9240.3	6.8	9
Japan	4919.6	38.6	4
Brazil	2245.7	11.2	8
Russia	2096.8	14.6	7
India	1878.8	1.5	10
Canada	1826.8	51.9	3
Australia	1560.4	67.5	1
Rep Of South Korea	1304.6	26	6
World	**75593**	**10.6**	

Source: Own compilation, based on EUROSTAT data

Table 2.6 Changes of GNP (in mln euro) in 2027 assuming limited liberalization and a 20 % external impulse

Contents	Tariffs reduction only	Reduction of barriers only for services	Reduction limited to market of public tenders
EU	23.753	5.298	6.367
USA	8.447	7.356	1.875
Other	−7.903	−117	−1.595
Remaining OECD	−5.065	726	−668
Changes in incomes			
Central Europe	−292	26	4
Mediterranean states	580	60	−8
PRC	2289	−1.713	−856
India	−489	137	79
ASEAN	−832	337	−263
MERCOSUR	−363	182	−5
Low income states	−228	39	47
Rest of World	−2.344	90	75

Source: CEPR Report 2013

What we have witnessed recently is a slowing of growth in BRICS, a group which was previously seen as a driver of growth in the world economy during the post-2008 crisis. Since the last evaluation of financial stability risks by the IMF in April 2015. such risks have increased (GFSR… 2015). The EU and USA are acting together to return to their previous role as locomotives of the world economy (Mann 2015). As previously mentioned, the main focus of TTIP liberalization is on NTBs, not tariffs, which differ but in general are relatively low. Elimination, or at least reduction, of NTBs can change the conditions of mutual trade, which has special significance for S&M companies, which are predominant in creating GDP and jobs. The lifting NTBs through FTA agreements signed with Canada, Mexico and Korea show that the share of S&M companies in trade also is increasing. This can also happen in mutual relations between the EU and US markets when barriers are eliminated. The TNCs can afford costs of NTBs much easier than the S&M companies. This means that elimination of NTBs is advantageous for S&M companies (Table 2.7).

The potential of both partners in mutual trade is significant and the TTIP can have an important direct impact on competitiveness, as well as an indirect one whereby this competition stimulates growth.

Table 2.7 Turnover EU with the USA, basic indicators

Indicator	Unit	Period	Import	Export	General value of turnover	Balance
Last year	Mln euro	2013	196.098	288.263	484.361	92.166
Position as a partner		2013	3	1	1	
Share in the EU trade	%	2013	11.7	16.6	14.2	
Dynamic of growth in year terms	%	2012–2013	−5.0	−1.7		
Average dynamic of growth in year terms	%	2009–2013	6.0	9.1		

Source: European Union Trade in goods with USA, Directorate General for Trade, European Commission 27.08.2014

4 Advantages and Criticism of TTIP

Most of the advantages of the TTIP have already been mentioned. In this section, we can divide them into groups, using different criteria. They can have direct and indirect impact on rates of growth in the EU and USA. They can also stimulate mutual turnover and enable participation in trade of S&M companies, which until now have been taking part in trade on a limited scale, mainly due to NTBs. Acting together, the EU and the USA can re-establish sustained world economy growth, which is needed as BRICS are running out of steam in this capacity. The TTIP is shaped in such way that it is open for states who would like to join this initiative. Moreover, this open formula means that the agreement can be extended to other economies. For those economies joining the agreement, it will accelerate the introduction of practices characteristic of advanced market economies, for the rest it will speed up introduction of practices which enable them to build a stable base for market democracies. In sum, the TTIP, if concluded can have important internal and external implications.

Without the TTIP we might expect to see the slowing-down of the world economy, limited improvement of competitiveness, and possibly the weakening of the euro as a result of the Euro crisis or Greek financial crisis. Integrated EU and USA markets could shoulder such crises more easily.

As far as criticism of the TTIP is concerned, it is argued that countries covered by the agreement have individual interests and traditions. This is true of US states, as well as of member states of the EU. There are also specific interest groups which are openly against the agreement and criticize the limited release of information on the substance of negotiations. Finally, there are interest groups who accept that while the terms of the TTIP would improve access to the latest scientific and technological findings at the same time this could result in unfair competition in certain fields such as chemical fertilizers, which in the USA are produced with low-priced shale gas. The list of problems is generally limited as the negotiators knew from the start which issues were likely to be controversial and they have removed these from the negotiations, saying that all such controversial matters will be dealt with one by one after the agreement has been signed. Such problematic areas include MGO, personal data protection, and state support in some areas (e.g. agricultural subsidies in the EU).

The TTIP could conflict with WTO proposals. The Doha negotiations, according to experts, are firmly deadlocked. When signed, the TTIP could accelerate the conclusion of a global agreement on liberalizing trade and services. Or, conversely, it could undercut the current round of negotiations, preventing the fulfilment of six decades of GATT/WTO trade liberalization agreed in 8 consecutive rounds, the Doha round being the ninth, if we take all GATT and WTO rounds together. If concluded, the TTIP would mean that the world is ready for open regionalism, which has already been proven by such agreements as the TPP (Trans Pacific Partnership between the USA and 11 Pacific states, and also by the USA–Korean FTA and the EU–Korean FTA, NAFTA and the EU–Mexico, EU–Canada FTA, EU–ASEAN FTA (in negotiations) (International Market… 2015).

The geographic direction of the signed agreements can be seen as following a dynamic or a static dimension. Overlapping trade agreements cause a situation in which streams of capital from the EU and USA markets compete with one another and producers sell their goods on European and American markets (Free Trade… 2015). The specific feature of the signed agreements is that they exclude China.

Rejection or postponement in concluding the TTIP gives the advantage to TPP (Trans Pacific Partnership) between the USA and eleven Pacific states. This agreement, if concluded and activated, would cover approximately 40 % of world GDP and approximately 30 % of world trade. The parallel negotiations of TTIP and TPP resemble the situation of the 12 countries that negotiated membership of the EU in the 1990s, divided into two groups: Copenhagen and Luxembourg (the names deriving from the towns where negotiations started). The first group of applicants was annoyed by the number of closed chapters by the time of the second one, which was used to speed-up the negotiations. In the case of EU membership treaties, states were scared that despite the fact that they have started negotiations earlier, they would end them later and this would result in later EU membership. This fear was leveraged by EU officials, who tried to 'manage the queue to the EU'. Finally, all states joined the EU on 1 May 2004, with exception of Bulgaria and Romania, who joined the EU three years later, in 2007.

In the case of the TTIP and TTP, it is not a matter of membership but of institutional competition. The group of states who are able to establish and conclude an agreement on trade and capital liberalization will gain months or years of advantage over those who are not able to finalize negotiations. It is significant that China, at this stage of negotiations, is excluded from the deals. Rough estimates indicate that this exclusion on its own could stimulate the rate of growth in Europe and the USA by 1 % annually. Even better results are expected in case of the Pacific states, a fact that gives a strong motive for speedy conclusion of the agreement.

As it was mentioned earlier, the criticisms of TTIP stem from different sources. Interest groups are concerned about social issues, fearing that some of the standards approved in Europe will be lost or lowered. There is also concern over health, security and technical standards. This is the case, despite the fact that both the EU and US standards are often guarantees as far as both markets are concerned, which leads negotiators to assume that if a product is guaranteed as safe and is approved in the home market, this would also be the case for the other's market, without a need for further adjustments. That would apply in the many cases where standards are already in place, while in the case of new rules, new common solutions could be imposed through the agreement.

Criticism of the TTIP in Europe also extends to the fact that signing up to such an agreement would distance the EU from the dynamic markets of Asia and cause the European market to be driven by more static American protocols. At the same time, a USA–Asian agreement is seen as an indirect influence for change, which could be replaced by stronger and more dynamic ties established within a direct agreement with the Asian states. Given this situation, it would be a good idea to negotiate a EU–Asia Pacific Free Trade agreement in parallel. Such a move would pose a challenge to the role of the WTO, which has for six decades has enabled the reduction of trade barriers. Regional and inter-regional arrangements could be temporary drivers, which would lead towards more global and complex solutions, to give an effective stimulus to the regions which they cover.

The TTIP might be regarded as a starting point through which spill-over effects will stimulate changes in remaining economies, not included into the deal.

5 Why Do We Need to Make the Negotiations More Complicated Adding the Exchange Rate to the Deal?

Returning to the issue of the monetary clause in the TTIP, we need to say that there are strong arguments in favour of such a solution as evidenced by current economic, financial or political events, such as the Greece crisis or the Russia–Ukraine war. This war is conducted by states bordering the EU. Moreover, President V. Putin talks about regaining former Soviet power, which suggests that he wants to draw in independent states like Ukraine, Uzbekistan, Belarus, Kazakhstan, Georgia, Moldova, Tajikistan, Azerbaijan, and later possibly also three Baltic states which are members of NATO and the EU: Estonia, Lithuania and Latvia. This might be followed by an attempt to rebuild former spheres of influence in the former Warsaw Pact states and COMECON. This possibility, since the annexation of Crimea in April 2014, has affected the outlook of NATO and EU states.

The EU followed the USA's decision to impose embargoes on a list of politicians and business people who co-operate closely with Kremlin (Ćwiek-Karpowicz and Secrieru 2015). Sanctions on Russia by the EU were expanded and the period of their application was prolonged in April 2015 (EU-Ukraine Relations… 2015). In response, Russia has imposed an embargo on food and agricultural imports from EU states, with a consequent scarcity of goods in the Russian market and an increase in prices. A situation of accelerating inflation, followed by slow-down in the Russian economy does not bode well for liberalization or co-operation with the outside world.

These factors can have a strong impact on the values of the euro and the dollar, adjustments to which usually influence exchange rates of the remaining currencies. This means that the positive gains from eliminating tariff and non-tariff barriers can be diminished or cancelled out by changes in the exchange rates of main currencies. In such a case, expected positive stimuli on growth would be replaced by some negative effects that, in turn, would result in the fall of rates of growth. The prospect of such a scenario would dampen support for liberalization of trade, in addition to slowing growth rates and increasing tensions between states. This is a real as well as an undesirable possibility, especially in conditions in which European economies are not able to accelerate their rates of growth by even 2 % annually, while the USA economy grows by 3.2 %. The BRIC and then all other economies also slow down.

None of the prognoses (OECD, IMF, regional and national forecasts) are optimistic. They show that the world economy needs a strong kick. Such a kick could be achieved when TTIP and TTP are concluded. Nevertheless, the effect of those agreements might be much smaller than foreseen by the papers previously quoted in this chapter, if a clause on currency linkage is not part of the deal. Exclusion of that solution would not improve the economic results on a macro-level, namely the rates of growth, but might even lower them in comparison to the initially expected and predicted level.

The depreciation of the euro against the dollar would result in reduced global turnover. European imports would fall as a result, followed by a decline in trade between non-EMU and EMU states within the EU. This can produce a further slow-down of peripheral economies in the EU, affecting all macroeconomic indicators such as convergence criteria. With the measures that have been introduced in areas to tighten control of fiscal policies, the end result could be the enforcement of very tough measures, which would be be difficult to maintain, especially since many states are already suffering the effects of excessive budget deficit.

An acceleration of the world economy is also needed because further liberalization will only gain support in favourable economic conditions. Acceleration could result in the return to WTO negotiations, followed by a number of economies joining the regional agreements that offer open terms. On the other hand, a lack of acceleration could produce increased tensions between states, regions, nationalities with new conflicts added to current ones. Nevertheless, there is still a lack of action in the specific areas that could hasten the rates of growth of the main economic centres and of the world economy as a whole, viz. liberalization and the linkage of the two main exchange rates: dollar and euro. This could even be a broader measure in which all reserve currencies are linked. The linkage of the dollar and the euro should be seen as basic anchor for the world financial system, resulting in common strategies like the co-ordination of policies or intervention when tensions occur. Such tensions may have different sources and results. To take the case of Greece: Greece is obliged to pay consecutive financial commitments to the IMF, holders of the state treasury bonds and the ECB. Difficulties in this show that growth in taxation can bring a short-term improvement of the proportions between the revenues to budget and the expenditures, but in the longer run it results in lowered revenues, as investors move their business to less highly taxed economies. Greece not only badly needs a solution that will reduce its external obligations, postponing the payments until such a time when the country can pay, but it also need a new credit injection, which has to be followed, not by an increase of taxes, but by improvement in collecting them. It should be said that collecting taxes efficiently is not a problem unique to Greece (Table 2.8).

Greece, despite the engagement of IMF, ECB and EC, was not able to change its economy by reforming it or accelerating the rate of growth enough to decrease unemployment. Rather, there was increased public debt, caused by the budget deficit. Greece's financial obligations include loans from European Financial Stability Facility (EFSF), established in

Table 2.8 Greece macro indicators (public debt, unemployment and rates of growth) 2007–2015

Contents	2007	2008	2009	2010	2011	2012	2013	2014	2015[a]
Public debt as % of GDP	106.1	105.4	112.9	129.7	146.0	171.3	156.9	175.0	177.1
Budget deficit as % of GDP	−5.7	−6.5	−9.8	−15.7	−11.1	−10.2	−8.7	−12.3	−3.7
Dynamics of growth in %	3.5	−0.4	−4.4	−5.4	−8.9	−6.6	−3.9	0.8	0.5
Unemployment	8.4	7.8	9.6	12.7	17.9	24.5	27.5	26.5	25.6

Source: tradingeconomics.com.eurostat
[a]*Prognoses*

2010 to support the European economies hit by the crisis. Greece owes €145 bln and is the biggest debtor. In sum, external debts of the state are estimated at $240 bln. The second biggest creditor is the IMF. The table below illustrates Greece's financial obligations. It was unable to pay its obligations of 1.6 bln to IMF in June 2015. The obligations indicate total amounts which the state should pay in coming months till the end of 2015 (Table 2.9).

Data in Tables 2.8 and 2.9 show that Greece's external debt needs to be restructured, which means the reduction and postponement of payments. Yet this, accompanied by an additional stabilization loan, will not solve the problem and financial tension will return. The impact on the value of exchange rate of euro seems to be obvious.

Moreover, Greece needs to diversify its economy, which now heavily relies on two industries: agriculture and tourism. The latter gives incomes for eight of the year only.

Recurring tensions result in consecutive phases when Greece is due to pay her interests and installments and have to be solved by bringing the system to certain equilibrium. This seems to be difficult given that Greece voted in a referendum against the EU–ECB–IMF conditions for further loans, demonstrating that the country prefers to stay in EMU. Prime Minister Aleksis Cipras is strongly backed by his nation, but politicians and institutions in Europe do not trust Greece, or the promises given by the state and its government. Smaller amounts of credit, pumped into Ireland, Portugal, Spain or Italy brought about better results than those offered to Greece. Greece external debt amounted to 240 bln euro and in June 2015 the country was offered a further 79 bln euro.

Solidarity of the EU states and a positive solution to the Greek problem can play an important role internationally, especially in regions which follow a path of integration similar to the European model. Such a solution will also stabilize the euro and eliminate financial tensions

Table 2.9 Financial obligations of Greece July–December 2015 (in bln euro)

Contents	July	August	September	October	November	December
Amounts due (in sum)	3.4	4.4	5.1	2.7	–	1.2

Source: Financial Times (http://www.ft.com/intl/fastft/354841/efsf-wont-demand-immediate-repayment-from-greece)

caused by the decreasing value of the EU currency. All this shows that the solution to the Greek problem is badly needed, but it cannot be quick or temporary, as this might lead to another crisis in Europe.

6 Conclusion: Is TTIP Realistic and Do We Really Need a Currency Clause in It?

The article argues that there is a need both to conclude the negotiations over the TTIP and to include a clause to keep the exchange rates of the euro and dollar in relatively stable proportions one to another. Otherwise, there is a danger that the liberalization brought about by the elimination of tariffs, even when it is followed by significant reduction of NTBs, could result in an increase of protection through the expedient of exchange rate depreciation. This possibility is illustrated in the Greek crisis, which has had a strong impact on the value of euro and remaining currencies, causing the euro to lose and other currencies to gain value. This problem has occurred several times recently. A second factor that urges the lining of the two main currencies is the Russian–Ukraine war, which engages states that have borders with the EU and thus strongly increases the risk of change in value of the dollar and euro exchange rates. The third argument made in this article is that regulations introduced in bilateral, regional and global arrangements all reduce the prospects of protecting national markets by raising tariffs, – as was done in the crisis of the 1930s. Also, protection in NTB areas is strongly controlled, although NTBs are seen still as an effective measure that controls access to certain markets. Nevertheless, they are the subject of negotiations in interregional agreements such as TTP or TTIP. In such complicated circumstances, the exchange rate and some additional arrangements are seen as tools of protection. This was the case historically in the EEC, when customs borders between states were eliminated. Such a practice was stopped by the introduction of 'snake in the tunnel', as part of the Weber Plan, which was supposed to lead the EEC towards a common currency in ten years 1970–1980. Exchange rates were also used as protection tool in Poland in the early stages of its transformation after 1989, when convertibility was introduced. Finally, the exchange rate, namely devaluation or slower depreciation of currency in comparison to the real exchange rate value, was used as a protectionist tool in the crisis 2008+. In view of these examples, it is necessary to include a clause to link the values of the two main world currencies, the euro and the dollar, in the TTIP agreement. Otherwise, demolishing tariff and non-tariff barriers to trade will not effectively integrate the American and the internal European markets.

Bibliography

Traditionally Printed Sources

Congleton, R. D., & Hillman, A. H. (Eds.) (2015). *Companion to the political economy of rent seeking*. Northampton/Cheltenham: Edward Elgar Pub.

Currency War. (2013, March 11). Canada has to devalue or get hurt. *Canadian Business*. http://www.canadianbusiness.com/economy/currency-war.

Ćwiek-Karpowicz, J., & Secrieru, S. (Eds.) (2015). *Sanctions and Russia*. Warsaw: PISM.

Dunin-Wąsowicz, M., & Jarczewska, A. (Eds.). (2015). *TTIP – Transatlantyckie Parnerstwo w dziedzinie handlu I inwestycji. Nowy etap instytucjonalizacji współpracy UE – USA*. Warszawa: Wydawnictwo Naukowe Scholar.

European Union. Trade in goods with USA, Directorate General for Trade, European Commission (2014, August 27).

EUROSTAT. (n.d.). US Census Bureau, World Bank, own calculations.

EU-Ukraine Relations. (2015, April 24). Facts Sheets, EC. Brussels. 1504424/05.

Lectures by Professor Finn E. Kydland and Professor Edward C. Prescott, Nobel Prize Winners in Economics in 2004. The poor economic performances in the EU and the US: Problems are political, not economic, 24.06.2015, Warsaw.

List of Lead negotiators for the Transatlantic Trade and Investment Partnership (TTIP). (n.d.). The Office of the United States Trade Representative (USTR).

Minister. (2013, December 19). Written Ministerial statement. UK 2013 Presidency of G-8.

One Currency for One Europe. The Road to the Euro (2015). Economic and financial affairs. European Commission. http://ec.europa.eu/economy_finance/publications/general/pdf/the_road_ to_euro_en.pdf

Pacific and European Trade Deals May be Back on Track as US Senate Votes Again, The Guardia, 13.05.2015. http://www.theguardian.com/us-news/2015/may/13/senate-obama-trade-tpp-ttip-fast-track-bill

Reducing Transatlantic Barriers to Trade and Investment. An economic assessment final project report, 2013, March. Prepared under implementing framework Contract Trade 10/A21/A16. J. Francois (leader). CEPR, London 2013.

Treaty of Lisbon Amending the Treaty on European Union and the Treaty Establishing the European (Community, 2007/C 306/01). http://eur-lex.europa.eu/legal-content/EN/TXT/PDF/? uri=CELEX:12007L/TXT&from=EN

Voda, D. (2012). *Inflation-proof your portfolio: How to protect your money from the coming government hyperinflation*. Hoboken: Wiley.

Washington, R. A. (2012). Devaluation. What happens after the fall. July 10th. http://www.economist.com/blogs/freeexchange/2012/07/devaluation

Żukrowska, K. (Ed.). (2010). *Transformacjasystemowa w Polsce*. Warszawa: SGH.

Żukrowska K. (Ed.). (2013). Kryzys gospodarczy 2008+ test dla stosowanej polityki. Metody przeciwdziałania i ich skuteczność. Oficyna Wydawnicza SGH: Warszawa.

Internet Sources

Free trade agreement. (2015). https://ustr.gov/trade-agreements/free-trade-agreements. Accessed 23 June 2015.

GFSR. Market Update (2015). http://www.imf.org/external/pubs/ft/fmu/eng/index.asp. Accessed 06 June 2015.

International Market., Industry, Entrepreneurship and SME's (2015). http://ec.europa.eu/enterprise/policies/international/facilitating-trade/free-trade/index_en.htm#h2-1. Accessed 21 June 2015.

Mann, C. L. (2015). *Economic outlook and interim global economic assessment, 2–4 June*. Paris: OECD.

Negotiations rounds – press material. (2015). http://ec.europa.eu/trade/policy/in-focus/ttip/documents-and-events/#negotiation-rounds. Accessed 12 June 2015.

One Currency for One Europe. The Road to the Euro. 2015 Economic and Financial Affairs. European Commission. http://ec.europa.eu/economy_finance/publications/general/pdf/the_road_to_euro_en.pdf.

Pacific and European Trade Deals May be Back on Track as US Senate Votes Again, The Guardia, 13.05.2015. http://www.theguardian.com/us-news/2015/may/13/senate-obama-trade-tpp-ttip-fast-track-bill. Accessed 15 May 2015.

tradingeconomics.com.eurostat (n.d.).

Transatlantic Declaration. (1990). Declaration on US-EC relations. http://useu.usmission.gov/1990transatlantic_ declaration.html. Accessed 22 May 2015.

3

The Effect of Countries' Credit Ratings on Credit Default Swap Spreads

Patrycja Chodnicka-Jaworska

1 Introduction

Credit rating agencies play an important role in the financial system of an economy. At the moment there are three important agencies: Standard & Poor's (S&P), Fitch, and Moody. They specialize in analysing the creditworthiness of corporate and sovereign issuers of debt securities (Elkhoury 2008). Their basic goal is to help to avoid information asymmetry between investors and capital borrowers regarding creditworthiness. Millon and Thakor (1985, 1403–1422) propose a role for 'information-gathering agencies', such as credit rating agencies, based on information asymmetries. They argue that credit rating agencies are formed to act as 'screening agencies', certifying the values of the companies they analyse. In their opinion, credit rating agencies can reduce a company's capital costs, by certifying their market value. Boot et al. (2006) argue that rating

P. Chodnicka-Jaworska (✉)
Univeristy of Warsaw, Warsaw, Poland

K. Raczkowski (ed.), *Risk Management in Public Administration*,
DOI 10.1007/978-3-319-30877-7_3

agencies could be seen as information-processing agencies that speed up the dissemination of information to financial markets.

Government officials generally co-operate with credit rating agencies. Credit ratings are especially used when estimating foreign countries' credit rating risk. Countries strive to receive high credit ratings so as to improve their position in the international debt market. According to previous research (Jaramillo and Tejada 2011; Ferri et al. 1999, 335–255), the higher the risk presented by credit ratings, the higher the interest rates that borrowers have to pay for their capital.

Sometimes the credit rating estimate is different from that expected. Accordingly, the basic goal of this article is to analyse how countries' credit ratings influence the cost of capital. The analysis is prepared based on the long- and short-term country credit ratings granted by S&P's and Moody's Investor Services for 35 countries between 2005 and 2013. For a better understanding of the problem, linear regression, static and dynamic panel data models have been deployed. This chapter analyses how fast the cost of the capital measured by the CDS premium responds to a shift in countries' credit ratings. It also investigates whether change in risk classification (variation in the speculative or investment group of credit ratings) influences the cost of the capital.

I begin with a brief overview of the background literature. Next the data description and the methodology of the analysis is presented, followed by the empirical analysis and some concluding remarks.

2 Literature Review

The importance of credit rating agencies and their rules is underlined by the European Commission (2013), according to which credit rating agencies have a major impact on financial markets, with ratings being closely followed by and impacting upon financial agencies, governments and market players (i.e. investors, borrowers, issuers). Sovereign ratings play a crucial role for rated countries, since their downgrading has the effect of making borrowing more expensive.

A case in point is the CDS market and credit ratings, with several recent papers documenting the frequent utility of CDS at-market spreads in giving an early prediction of credit ratings (Hull et al. 2004, 2789–2811; Flannery et al. 2010, 10–31; Chava et al. 2012; Lee et al. 2014).

Credit ratings are taken into consideration when making investment decisions. Graham and Harvey (2001, 187–243) discovered that credit ratings are the second highest determinant for chief financial officer's (CFO's) decisions on the capital structure. Nearly 52 % of respondents said that credit ratings were important or very important in how they choose the appropriate amount of debt for their company.

Changes in credit rating statements have a negative effect on the cost of capital, first by exerting a strong influence on the coupon of bonds, then by complicating the competition between investments. Companies expecting a rating change issue less net debt relative to net equity than companies not expecting a change.

Patel, Evans and Burnett (1998, 408–418) found that liquidity affects whether speculative-grade bonds experience abnormal positive or negative returns. If companies incur higher interest rates in less liquid markets, in accordance with a credit rating, they may try to avoid these rating levels. Also, in difficult economic times certain credit rating levels may make it impossible for a company to raise debt capital (Stiglitz and Weiss 1981, 393–410).

Money market funds, which make up a significant portion of commercial paper investment, invest almost exclusively in A1-rated paper, and A1- rated commercial paper also has more favourable company liquidity requirements than lower rated paper (Hahn 1993, 45–67).

The CDS premium is exploited as the measure of the cost of the capital. As noted by Callen et al. (2009, 1363–1394), although CDS premiums are related to credit ratings issued by rating agencies, it can be observed that there is quite a wide variation in CDS spreads for companies having a given rating. The relationship can be observed in the market by looking at a CDS premium associated with a given rating. Daniels and Jensen (2005) studied the relationship between CDS spreads, credit spreads of corporate bonds and credit rating changes using principal component analysis, regression as well as event study methodology. Both corporate credit and CDS spreads react to rating changes, CDS spreads exhibit greater sensitivity than corporate bonds. Micu, Remolona and Wooldridge (2006) suggest that both corporate bond and CDS spreads should change by about the same magnitude; negative rating announcements that result from changes in a company's leverage should lead to a greater CDS price impact and two credit rating changes should be more informative than one. Negative reviews are found to have the greatest impact on BBB- rated companies, in contrast to the expectation that the trading of 'restricted investors' should only have a temporary price impact. Positive rating announcements are found to result in less tightening of CDS spreads, most noticeably for BB rated companies just below the investment grade threshold. Larger companies by market capitalization are found to be affected less by a positive rating announcement as compared to a negative one, but the impact of positive announcements tends to be stronger for split-rated companies. Carr and Wu (2009) studied the similarities between equity option implied volatility and CDS spreads. Villouta (2006) investigated how empirical tests of liquidity in the corporate bonds and CDS markets has an effect on the arbitrage relationship that links these markets, through analysing the effect of liquidity proxies on the CDS basis, as well as on trading strategies that seek to profit from arbitrage due to misalignment between the markets. Das and Hanouna (2009, 1837–1857) identified and extracted the implied forward curve of recovery and default rates on an issue using the CDS spread curve. Schneider, Sogner and Veza (2010, 1517–1547) examined the relationship between the loss given default (LGD) and probability of default (PD) by looking at the former across ratings as a crude proxy for credit quality. This mostly affects broad ranges in the CDS maturity spectrum, where changes in CDS spreads at the discontinuity is mostly positive, and the one-year CDS spread exhibits time-series variation that higher maturity spreads do not share. Ashcraft and Santos (2007) investigated the possible effect of the CDS market in reducing the cost of debt for corporate borrowers, including both corporate bonds and bank loans.

Previous research suggests that credit ratings influence a company's cost of capital (Kliger and Sarig 2000, 2879–2902; Jorion et al. 2005, 309–330; Kisgen and Strahan 2010, 4324–4347; Chen et al. 2005). Restrepo (2013) shows that the sovereign ceiling represents a meaningful institutional friction and in this channel credit ratings have an important effect on borrowing costs in the private sector. There is an estimated differential effect of contractions and relaxations in the sovereign ceiling on the bond spreads of companies that are exactly at the sovereign bounds, relative to companies that are near but not at the bound. The spreads of bound companies increase significantly relative to those of non- bound firms. Companies that are bound tend to be rated more unfavourably, and their default rates tend to be lower relative to non- bound firms.

The important information is the length of time it takes for the financial market to react to countries' credit rating changes. Lee, Naranjo and Sirmans (2014) analysed this for US companies. According to their findings, the at-market spreads of 5-year CDS contracts react at least 90 days prior to S&P's credit rating changes, with a further impact when the credit rating changes occur.

The analysis of countries' credit ratings was undertaken by Alasakka and Gwilym (2010, 79–97). They took into consideration lead–lag relationships in sovereign credit ratings across five agencies. According to their researches, the upgrade of credit ratings is much higher (the downgrade lower) for the sovereign issuer having a recent upgrade (downgrade) by other agencies. They find that lagged credit ratings are a particular agency influence on recent credit ratings on others. They also researched how particular credit ratings change. S&P's is more sensitive than other agencies, and Moody's is the first mover in upgrades.

These credit rating changes were verified by Ismailescu and Kazemi (2010, 2861–2873). They studied the impact of countries' credit rating changes on the CDS spreads for emerging economies. According to their research, a two-day lag in credit rating exerts positive changes on the cost of capital. They only observed increases in credit rating for the period covered by their research, but negative changes, which are very important for the prediction of the cost of the capital, were not observed. Consequently, the present author adopts monthly frequency of observation.

Daily data are also incorporated into the analysis by Bergman et al. (2013). They studied CDS for GIIPS countries (Greece, Italy, Ireland, Portugal and Spain). Lucas et al. (2013) observed the signals of credit rating agencies and the spill-over effects to other countries' exchange rates in the region. The outlook and watch signals, according to their studies, have a stronger impact on the cost of the capital than credit rating changes. They also found that negative information from S&P's,

Moody's and especially Fitch had an impact, only positive predictions from Moody's caused a change in the market.

The impact of the countries' credit ratings on the CDS spreads are verified by Aizenman, Binici and Hutchison (2013). They analysed the influence of credit rating changes on the sovereign spreads in the European Union, and investigated the macro and financial factors that account for the varying time periods for credit rating change. They use monthly data for 2005–2012 across 26 countries. They found that changes of ratings are informative, economically important and highly statistically significant in panel models even after allowing for a host of fundamental domestic and global factors and investigating various functional forms, time and country groupings and dynamic structures. To estimate the influence of the credit ratings on the CDS spreads, they used dynamic panel data models. The credit rating upgrade decreases CDS spreads by about 45 basis points on average for EU countries. However, the association between credit rating changes and spreads shifted markedly between the pre-crisis and crisis periods. European countries had quite similar CDS responses to credit rating changes during the pre-crisis period, but large differences emerged during the crisis period between the now highly-sensitive GIIPS group and other European country groupings (EU and Euro Area excluding GIIPS, and the non-EU area). They also found a complicated non-linear pattern dependent on the level of the credit rating. They found high sensitivity, implying a large change in spreads for a given change in ratings, at the very low end of credit ratings. Their ratings curve is U-shaped with high sensitivity at the very low end of credit ratings, fairly low sensitivity at the moderately low end and very high end. Middle ratings are quite sensitive to credit rating changes. The results are robust when including the credit 'outlook' or 'watch' signals by credit rating agencies. Contagion from rating downgrades in GIIPS to other euro countries is not evident once own-country credit rating changes are taken into account. The analysis proposed by Aizenman, Binici and Hutchison (2013) is based on S&P's and Fitch credit ratings. In their analysis they do not test the impact of investment and speculative degrees on the CDS spreads.

The above-mentioned research took into account the impact of the credit rating standing on the cost of the capital for the private sector. I would like to analyse how countries' credit ratings influence the cost of the capital measured by CDS premium.

3 Methodology

My research addresses the question of how a country's credit rating affects the cost of capital. For the purposes of the estimation process as an independent variable, credit rating data published by S&P and Moody's were used. Moody's long-term Issuer Rating, S&P long-term Issuer Rating and S&P short-term Issuer Rating were collected from the Thomson Reuters database. Credit ratings for particular countries over 2005–2013 were taken into consideration. The decision about the time frame is due to the limited availability of macroeconomic determinants for all countries and small changes in the credit rating assessment. As a result, credit rating evaluations for 35 countries[1] are studied.

Due to the nature of the data, it was decided to use static and dynamic panel models. The final version of static panel data model is presented in the form of Eq. (3.1), a dynamic panel data model is presented in the Eq. (3.2).

$$y_{i,t} = \sum_{k=0}^{n} \beta_k x_{j,t-k} + \theta_t T_t + \mu_j + \varepsilon_{j,t}, \quad n = 0 \tag{3.1}$$

$$y_{i,t} = y_{i,t-1} + \sum_{k=0}^{n} \beta_k x_{j,t-k} + \theta_t T_t + \mu_j + \varepsilon_{j,t}, \quad n = 0 \tag{3.2}$$

where: $y_{i,t}$ dependent variable means the CDS premium in basic points;
$x_{j,t}$ is a vector of explanatory variables, i.e.:

$$x_{i,j} = \left[\text{moodys}_{j,t}, \text{splong}_{j,t}, \text{spshort}_{i,j}\right],$$

where: $\text{moodys}_{i,j}$ is the Moody's long-term issuer credit rating for European countries, $\text{splong}_{i,j}$ is S&P's long-term issuer credit rating for

[1] Austria, Belgium, Croatia, Cyprus, Czech Republic, Denmark, Estonia, Finland, France, Germany, Greece, Hungary, Iceland, Ireland, Italy, Malta, Netherlands, Norway, Poland, Portugal, Slovak Republic, Slovenia, Spain, Sweden, Switzerland, United Kingdom, Ukraine, Belarus, Bulgaria, Latvia, Lithuania, Macedonia, Romania, Russian Federation, Turkey.

European countries, $spshort_{i,j}$ is S&P's short-term issuer credit rating for European countries.

To examine the link between the influence of the country's credit standing on the cost of capital, static panel data models were employed. Static models were included with models with fixed and random effects estimator. To decide between fixed and random effects, the Hausman test was used, where the null hypothesis is that the preferred model is random effect model (Greene 2008). This basically tests whether the unique errors are correlated with the regressors, and the null hypothesis is that they are not. Moreover, the Breusch–Pagan Lagrange Multiplier test was harnessed so as to help to decide between the random effects regression and a simple OLS regression. The null hypothesis is that variance across entities is zero. There is no significant difference across the units.

In order to test the applicability of the model panel GMM estimator based on first differences Arellano and Bond (FDGMM), the Sargan test was deployed to examine the reliability over identifying conditions that are not used in the estimation process. The second test is the autocorrelation Arellano–Bond test. The null hypothesis assumes no autocorrelation of the random component. The accuracy of the data which the study used was tested by the Wald test.

In the context of the decomposition of credit ratings on numeric variables, the linear method was used. It assumes a linear variation of the relation between ratings.

The research analysed the impact of a country's credit rating on the CDS premium in a sample of investment and speculative notes by using linear regression (Eq. 3.3), static panel data models (Eq. 3.4) and dynamic panel data models (Eq. 3.5) (Table 3.1).

$$y_{i,t} = \alpha_k + \beta_k x_{i,t} + \varepsilon_{i,t}, \tag{3.3}$$

$$y_{i,t} = \sum_{k=0}^{n} \beta_k x_{j,t-k} + \theta_t T_t + \mu_j + \varepsilon_{j,t}, \qquad n = 0 \tag{3.4}$$

$$y_{i,t} = y_{i,t-1} + \sum_{k=0}^{n} \beta_k x_{j,t-k} + \theta_t T_t + \mu_j + \varepsilon_{j,t}, \qquad n = 0 \tag{3.5}$$

Table 3.1 The codification system of the credit rating assessment

Moody's long-term Issuer Rating (foreign)		S&P's long-term Issuer Rating (foreign)		S&P's short-term issuer credit rating (foreign)	
Rating	Code	Rating	Code	Rating	Code
Aaa	100	AAA	100	A-1+	100
Aa1	95	AA+	95	A-1	83,33333
Aa2	90	AA	90	A-2	66,66667
Aa3	85	AA–	85	A-3	50
A1	80	A+	80	B	33,33333
A2	75	A	75	C	16,66667
A3	70	A–	70	NR	0
Baa1	65	BBB+	65	SD	–5
Baa2	60	BBB	60		
Baa3	55	BBB–	55		
Ba1	50	BB+	50		
Ba2	45	BB	45		
Ba3	40	BB–	40		
B1	35	B+	35		
B2	30	B	30		
B3	25	B–	25		
Caa1	20	CCC+	20		
Caa2	15	CCC	15		
Caa3	10	CCC–	10		
Caa	5	CC	5		
C	0	NR	0		
WR	–5	SD	–5		

Source: Own elaboration

4 Findings

Previous research suggests that credit rating exerts an influence on the cost of capital, but it strictly depends on the definition of the cost of capital. Table 3.2 illustrates the Spearman correlation coefficients of the variables analysed. Then, the relationship between the individual variables is highlighted.

The analysis of the Spearman correlation coefficients between the independent variables suggests a strong correlation between credit ratings. The phenomenon is a communication effect. As a result, we can observe the sensitivity of the credit rating changes by particular credit rating agencies to decisions on credit rating assessment proposed by other

Table 3.2 The Spearman correlation coefficients

	Splong	Spshort	Moody's	CDS
Splong	1.0000			
Spshort	0.9651	1.0000		
Moody's	0.9682	0.9391	1.0000	
CDS	−0.8138	−0.7823	−0.8061	1.0000

Source: Own elaboration

competitive agencies. In addition, the strong negative relationship may be noted between countries' credit ratings and CDS premium.

One of the basic goals of this paper is to analyse how the CDS premium responds to the countries' credit ratings changes. First, the paper analyses the impact of countries' credit rating on the CDS premium for a full sample, both for the speculative and investment notes. Static and dynamic panel data models are proposed. The decision on the use of the method outlined is strictly connected with the cross-section analysis, where we can observe the influence of the time-series and political division on the phenomenon investigated. The results obtained from the analysis are set out in Table 3.3.

The analysis of the received static panel data models suggests the existence of the strong negative correlation between the level of credit rating notes and the cost of capital. The increase in the credit rating results in the decrease of the CDS premium by nearly 32 basis points for long-term issuer credit ratings given by S&P's Investor Service, and 25 basis points for short-term issuer credit ratings. The weaker dependence is observed for the evaluations presented to Moody's. Correction of interest follows the end of the month, except that it is stronger for the long-term issuer credit ratings offered by S & P's.

The subgroup analysis, taking into account the level of speculative and investment notes, is presented in Table 3.4. As expected with the increase of credit ratings, as for the whole group of observations, similarly for the individual sub-samples, the levels of the CDS premium increase. While keeping the other factors ceteris paribus, in the case of raising the countries' credit ratings proposed by S&P's in the group of investment notes, the CDS premium level drops by 6 basis points. A much stronger decline in CDS premiums is observed for the sub-sample speculative notes, as

Table 3.3 Impact of European countries' credit ratings on the CDS premium

	S&P's long				S&P's short				Moody's			
Independent	FE		Arellano–Bond		FE		Arellano–Bond		FE		Arellano–Bond	
variables	Coef.	p	Coef.	P	Coef.	P	Coef.	p	Coef.	P	Coef.	p
CDS												
L1.			1.48	0.00			1.49	0.00			.90	0.00
Credit rating												
–.	–32.24	0.00	–25.06	0.00	–25.15	0.00	–1.10	0.76	–20.48	0.00	–5.71	0.00
L1.			28.63	0.00			5.41	0.13			5.53	0.00
_cons	2626.01	0.00	–371.77	0.00	2046.04	0.00	–415.53	0.00	1793.24	0.00	36.80	0.21
Sargan			0.9967				0.9998				vce(robust)	
AB (1)											0.1197	
AB (2)											0.2678	
Wald			0.0000				0.0000				0.0000	
Hausman	0.0000				0.0000				0.0000			
BP	0.0000				0.0000				0.0000			
F	0.0000				0.0000				0.0000			

Source: Own elaboration

much as 92 basis points. It can therefore be concluded that there is a high sensitivity to changes in financial market ratings for countries that have low credibility ratings.

Similar results can be observed in the case of ratings assigned by Moody's. However, the relationship examined has a slightly weaker nature, because with the increase in ratings in the group of investment ratings, CDS premium drops to only about 5 basis points. In contrast, higher-rated speculative results in a decrease in premiums by 51 points.

Thus the observed relationship confirmed the higher sensitivity of the financial market to changes in countries' speculative credit ratings that received the investment note. The next step of the analysis is to examine the influence of political divisions and risk classification. Static panel data models are used and the calculations received are summarized in Table 3.4. The analysis relates only to long-term countries' credit ratings proposed by S&P's and Moody's. There is a stronger negative impact of speculative credit ratings on the CDS premium by political division.. Countries that received the investment degree have lower CDS premiums by nearly 300 basis points. The risk classification is unimportant for Moody's long-term issuer credit ratings for countries. The impact of the countries' credit ratings is weaker for notes proposed by Moody's than those by S&P's.

In comparing these test results, it is observed that the negative impact of the investment notes on the CDS premium proves to be stronger for the static panel data models than for linear regression methods. The same applies to the ordinary last squares method where the relationship received is stronger for notes given by S&P's (Table 3.5).

The next task is to investigate how fast the financial market responds to the credit rating changes. For testing this, monthly credit ratings and CDS premiums data are used. First, the implications of countries' credit rating notes given by S&P's are analysed, indicating that the changes in credit ratings have an impact on the CDS premium in the same month. As with the previous tests, the effect of the risk classification is noticeable. The impact of countries' previous credit ratings is neutralized by current notes.

Earlier credit ratings do not have the significant impact on the CDS premium. The financial market reacts immediately to the credit rating assessment.

Table 3.4 The impact of credit rating on the CDS premium, taking into account the level of speculative and investment notes

	Investment S&P's long		Speculative S&P's long		Investment Moody's		Speculative Moody's	
CDS	Coef.	P	Coef.	P	Coef.	P	Coef.	P
Credit rating	−6.062013	0.000	−92.47821	0.000	−5.615212	0.000	−51.26132	0.000
_cons	662.2716	0.000	4471.901	0.000	626.6554	0.000	2709.589	0.000
No obs.	1529		450		1567		300	
F(1, 1527)	898.45		124.08		885.60		23.03	
Prob> F	0.0000		0.0000		0.0000		0.0000	
R-squared	0.3704		0.2169		0.3614		0.0717	
Adj R-squ.	0.3700		0.2151		0.3610		0.0686	
Root MSE	137.54		1950.1		130.66		2095	

Source: Own elaboration

Table 3.5 The impact of credit rating on the CDS premium while taking into account the level of speculative and investment notes by using static panel data models

	S&P's long-term issuer credit rating				Moody's long-term issuer credit rating			
CDS	Coef.	P>t	Coef.	P>t	Coef.	P>t	Coef.	P>t
Credit rating	–49.90895	0.0000	–35.39844	0.000	–23.22962	0.000	–14.60517	0.000
lnws	312.6712	0.014	214.851	0.074	181.1693	0.137	–34.16117	0.742
_cons	3654.636	0.000	2683.556	0.000	1846.578	0.000	1380.067	0.000
Number of obs	1979		1979		1867		1867	
Number of groups	33		33		32		32	
F	0.0000		0.0000		0.0000		0.0000	
Hausman	0.0000		0.0000		0.0000		0.0000	
Xttest	0.0000		0.0000		0.0000		0.0000	
Method	FE		RE		FE		RE	

Source: Own calculations

Table 3.6 provides the results for Moody's. Countries' credit ratings from previous months are unimportant, as with S&P's. The basic difference between these samples is that the impact of the current month's credit rating is weaker than in previous samples.

The influence of S&P's long-term issuer credit rating is more important than degrees given by Moody's. This result differs from that presented by previous research. According to the findings of Lucas et al. (2013), Moody's role is the more important. By that reckoning, the impact of the Moody's degrees should be stronger than S&P's. In all estimations, using different models, for the European financial market, the more significant impact on the CDS premium is influenced by S&P's notes (Table 3.7).

The use of dynamic panel data models produces different results. A strong relationship between the groups of ratings is observed. The cross-country analysis suggests that the investment rating given by S&P's reduces the cost of capital measured by CDS premium. The changes in credit rating have an impact in the same month, showing that the capital market responds immediately to such changes. The system dynamic panel data models estimation proposed by Arellano, Bover and Blundell, and Bond suggests a stronger negative impact of the higher credit rating on the CDS premium.

Table 3.6 The impact of S&P's long-term issuer credit ratings on the CDS premium, using dynamic panel data models

	Arellano–Bond		Arellano–Bover/Blundell–Bond	
CDS	Coef.	P>z	Coef.	P>z
CDS				
L1.	1.479698	0.000	1.456637	0.000
S&P's long				
–.	–26.63839	0.000	–42.47574	0.000
L1.	28.36332	0.000	37.59795	0.000
inws	123.4231	0.066	223.0178	0.000
_cons	–333.4441	0.002		
Number of obs	1898		1937	
Number of groups	33		33	
Wald	0.000		0.000	
Sargan	vce(robust)		1.000	
AB1	0.0002		0.2882	
AB2	0.6741		0.2836	
Method	One-step		Two-step	

Source: Own calculations

Table 3.7 The impact of Moody's long-term issuer credit ratings on the CDS premium by using dynamic panel data models

	Arellano–Bond		Arellano–Bover/Blundell–Bond	
CDS	Coef.	P>z	Coef.	P>z
CDS				
L1.	.9036427	0.000	.9116131	0.000
Moodys				
–.	−5.666651	0.007	−5.947088	0.000
L1.	5.589696	0.005	6.90096	0.000
inwm	−10.05186	0.608	−34.45057	0.004
_cons	37.56814	0.194		
Number of obs	1787		1825	
Number of groups	32		32	
Wald	0.000		0.000	
Sargan	vce(robust)		1.0000	
AB1	0.1199		0.1281	
AB2	0.2673		0.2790	
Method	One-step		Two-step	

Source: Own calculations

The next step of the analysis is to establish the impact of countries' credit ratings on the cost of capital. Observations relate only to the moment of the change of notes by the credit rating agency. The results confirm the previous findings. The analysis strongly underlines the importance of changes in the ratings. As in the previous sample, the impact of the track record of credit ratings is insignificant for the changes in the cost of the capital in current period (Table 3.8).

The analysis using the static and dynamic panel data models only for the moment of change in credit ratings corroborates the negative correlation between the investment credit rating degrees and CDS premium. The relationship is weaker for the reduced sample. The increase by one note in countries' credit rating decreases the CDS premium by nearly 200 basis points, using the methods employed by Arellano–Bond. The systemic panel data models exert a weaker impact on the CDS premium. According to foregoing analysis, countries' credit rating affects the cost of the capital and this is observed during the same month. Therefore, it is not necessary to use the dynamic panel data models for the estimation process. The results received by taking into consideration static panel data models gives quite similar results (the increase in country's credit rating by one note reduces the CDS premium by 20 basis points). The grouping of data also emphasizes the quite rare change in countries' credit ratings (only 18 observations divided by 6 groups of data). Thus a strong impact of the constant on the cost of capital is observed. Given the division of the risk groups of countries' credit ratings, the impact of the reclassification between speculative and investment degree is weaker for the reduced sample (Table 3.9).

Table 3.8 The impact of S&P's long-term issuer credit ratings on the CDS premium, using dynamic panel data models for the moment of countries' credit ratings change

	Arellano–Bond		Arellano–Bover/Blundell–Bond	
CDS	Coef.	P>z	Coef.	P>z
CDS				
L1.	−.0046118	0.989	.7819252	0.000
Splong				
–.	−33.87298	0.029	−20.81807	0.100
L1.	9.002106	0.289	22.88353	0.021
Inws	100.1457	0.475	16.08528	0.812
Number of obs	18		24	
Number of groups	6		6	
Wald	0.0000		0.0000	
Sargan	0.0658		vce(robust)	
AB1	0.8956		0.1415	
AB2	0.7430		0.4555	
Method	One-step		One-step	

Source: Own calculations

Table 3.9 The impact of S&P's long-term issuer credit ratings on the CDS premium, using static panel data models for the moment of countries' credit ratings change

CDS	Coef.	P>z	Coef.	P>z
Splong	−19.10815	0.013	−19.35362	0.002
_cons	1729.146	0.000	1741.897	0.000
Number of obs	18			18
Number of groups	6			6
Wald	0.0000			0.0000
Hausman		0.8468		
Xttest		0.0001		
Method	FE			RE

Source: Own calculations

The impact of Moody's long-term issuer credit rating on the CDS premium was also analysed, indicating an infrequent change in this determinant With this in mind, only 7 changes in credit ratings across European counties were studied. The analysis of this limited group of observations provides different results. First, the strong negative impact of the investment notes on the cost of capital is observed. The application of the Arellano–Bond method suggests the influence of the one-month lags of the countries' credit ratings effect on the CDS premium. The financial market reacts more strongly to the previous notes given by Moody. In this context, as far as Moody's published estimates are concerned, only the notes that have been given earlier are important for the cost of capital. The negative relationship between the earlier and the current CDS premium can be explained by the change of risk from speculative to investment. These findings are very important for future borrowers and investors. Therefore, the Moody's credit rating change causes long-term shifts in the cost of capital (Table 3.10).

The same applies to S&P's, where changes of CDS premium are not only conditioned by changes of countries' credit ratings, revealing the strong impact of the constant variable. The influence of Moody's long-

Table 3.10 The impact of Moody's long-term issuer credit ratings on the CDS premium, using dynamic panel data models for the moment of countries' credit ratings change

	Arellano–Bond		Arellano–Bover/Blundell–Bond	
CDS	Coef.	P>z	Coef.	P>z
CDS				
L1.	−1.215715	0.044	.6538933	0.002
Moodys				
–.	−6.081323	0.362	.7028751	0.890
L1.	−12.83593	0.050	5.067003	0.059
lnwm	−58.01258	0.448	−126.8013	0.099
Number of obs	19		26	
Number of groups	7		7	
Wald	0.0000		0.0000	
Sargan	0.2279		vce(robust)	
AB1	0.7127		0.1924	
AB2	0.4308		0.2125	
Method	One-step		One-step	

Source: Own calculations

Table 3.11. The impact of Moody's long-term issuer credit ratings on the CDS premium by using static panel data models for the moment of countries' credit ratings change

CDS	Coef.	P>z	Coef.	P>z
Moody's	−8.976744	0.000	−8.994377	0.000
_cons	1188.924	0.000	1169.345	0.000
Number of obs	20		20	
Number of groups	7		7	
Wald	0.0000		0.0000	
Hausman		0.9645		
Xttest		0.0001		
Method	FE		RE	

Source: Own calculations

term issuer credit rating on the cost of the capital is quite similar, as shown by using static panel data models while taking into consideration dynamic panel data models (Table 3.11).

5 Conclusion

The risk assessment of countries' sovereign credit ratings is a significant determinant of CDS premiums across Europe. Credit rating agencies play an important role in taking investment decisions. According to previous research, the influence of notes assigned by particular agencies delivers different effects.

The basic goal of this article was to analyse the impact of the countries' credit ratings on the cost of capital, which is measured by the CDS premium. The analysis relates to European countries for the 2005–2013 time period. The sample studied was divided into sub-samples according to the group of risk (investment and speculative credit ratings) and the moment of change from speculative to investment degree or vice versa.

The results differ from those provided by others, confirming the significant influence of countries' credit ratings on the cost of capital. The important factor is the moment when the financial market responds to the changes in countries' credit ratings. According to Lee, Naranjo and Sirmans (2014) this takes 90 days; Ismailescu and Kazemi (2010, 2861–2873) imply that there is a 2-day lag. Monthly data are found to be useful in understanding this issue.. The findings of the presents research suggest that financial markets react during the current month to changes in credit ratings assigned by Moody's and by S&P's. But the sensitivity over g 30 days is observed only for the results from a study of the full sample. The analysis prepared only for the moment of changes of classification from speculative to investment degree produces different outcomes. The cost of capital on the financial market alters within 30 days in response to S&P's credit ratings modification, but within 60 days in response to Moody's. Thus Moody's position as first mover in up-growth is challenged while S&P's is shown to be more sensitive to the communication effect.

The study of full sample as well as sub-samples finds that CDS premium is more sensitive on S&P's credit ratings than those assigned by Moody's (nearly 40 and 20 basis points respectively). The cost of the capital reacts more strongly for speculative degrees (92 basis points for S&P's and 51 for Moody's by using ordinary last squares method; 40 basis points for S&P's and 20 for Moody's by using static panel data models; 42 basis points for S&P's and 6 for Moody's by using dynamic panel data models).

The analysis of changes from speculative to investment gives different results. Here the weaker impact of credit ratings on the cost of the capital is evident. One note risk assessment change given by S&P's reduces the cost of the capital by 200 basis points, and an additional 100 points for modification of the risk classification. A one note change by Moody's reduces the CDS premium by 60 points in the current and 30 in the next month, with an additional 58 points for change from speculative to investment group of credit ratings. The influence is weaker for findings received by using static panel data models.

Taken together these findings help in making decisions about investing in the European treasury bonds and credit default swaps.

Bibliography

Aizenman, J., Binici, M., & Hutchison M. M. (2013). Credit ratings and the pricing of sovereign debt during the Euro crisis. National Bureau of Economic Research Working Paper, No. 19125.

Alsakka, R., & Gwilym, O. (2010). Split sovereign ratings and rating migrations in emerging economies. *Emerging Markets Review, 11*, 79–97.

Ashcraft, A. B., & Santos, J. A. C. (2007). Has the CDS market lowered the cost of corporate debt?, Federal Reserve Bank of New York Staff Reports, No. 290.

Bergman, M., Hutchison, M., & Jensen, S. (2013, April). Do sound public finances require fiscal rules or is market pressure enough?, European Commission, Directorate – General for Economic and Finance Affairs, European Economy Papers, 489.

Boot, A. W. A., Milbourn, T. T., & Schmeits, A. (2006). Credit ratings as coordination mechanisms. *The Review of Financial Studies, 19*(1), 81–118, doi:10.1093/rfs/hhj009.

Callen, J. L., Livnat, J., & Segal, D. (2009). The impact of earnings on the pricing of credit default swaps. *The Accounting Review, 84*(5), 1363–1394, DOI: 10.2308/accr.2009.84.5.1363 2009.

Carr, P., & Wu, L. (2009). Stock options and credit default swaps: A joint framework for valuation and estimation. *Journal of Financial Econometrics, 2009*, 1–41. doi:10.1093/jjfinec/nbp010.

Chava, S., Ganduri R., & Ornthanalai C. (2012). Are credit ratings still relevant?, Working Paper, Georgia Institute of Technology and University of Toronto.

Chen, R., Cheng, X., & Wu, L. (2005). Dynamic interactions between interest rate, credit, and liquidity risks: Theory and evidence from the term structure of credit default swap spreads. http://www.risknet.de/fileadmin/eLibrary/Chen-Dynamic-Interactions-LiquidityRisks.pdf

Daniels, K. N. S., & Jensen, M. (2005, December). The effect of credit ratings on credit default swap spreads and credit spreads. *Journal of Fixed Income, 15*(3), 25–72, DOI: 10.3905/jfi.2005.605421.

Das, S. R., & Hanouna, P. E. (2009). Implied recovery. *Journal of Economic Dynamics and Control, 33*(11), 1837–1857, DOI: http://dx.doi.org/10.1016/j.jedc.2009.04.005.

Graham, J. R., & Harvey, C. R. (2001). The theory and practice of corporate finance: Evidence from the field. *Journal of Financial Economics, 60*, 187–243.

Greene, W. H. (2008). *Econometric analysis*. Upper Saddle River: Prince Hall.

Elkhoury, M. (2008, January). Credit rating agencies and their potential impact on developing countries. United Nations Conference on Trade and Development. Discussion papers, No. 186.

European Commission. (2013). New rules on credit rating agencies (CRAs) – Frequently asked questions, MEMO/13/13 Event Date:16/01/2013.

Ferri, G., Liu, L. G., & Stiglitz, J. E. (1999). The procyclical role of rating agencies: Evidence from the East Asian crisis. *Economic Notes, 28*(3), 335–355.

Flannery, M., Houston J., & Partnoy F. (2010). Credit default swap spreads as viable substitutes for credit ratings. *University of Pennsylvania Law Review, 158*, 2085–2123.

Hahn, T. K. (1993). Commercial paper. *Federal Reserve Bank of Richmond Economic Quarterly, 79*, 45–67.
Hull, J., Predescu, M., & White, A. (2004). The relationship between credit default swap spreads, bond yields, and credit rating announcements. *Journal of Banking and Finance, 28*, 2789–2811.
Ismailescu, I., & Kazemi, H. (2010). The reaction of emerging market credit default swap spreads to sovereign credit rating changes. *Journal of Banking & Finance, 34*(12), 2861–2873.
Jaramillo, L., & Tejada, C. M. (2011). Sovereign credit ratings and spreads in emerging markets: Does investment grade matter?, IMF Working Paper, WP/11/44.
Jorion, P., Liu, Z., & Shi, C. (2005). Information effects of regulation FD: Evidence from rating agencies. *Journal of Financial Economics, 76*(2), 309–330.
Kisgen, D. J., & Strahan, P. E. (2010). Do regulations based on credit ratings affect a firm's cost of capital? *Review of Financial Studies, 23*(12), 4324–4347.
Kliger, D., & Sarig, O. (2000). The information value of bond ratings. *The Journal of Finance, 55*(6), 2879–2902.
Lee, J., Naranjo, A., & Sirmans, S. (2014). Exodus from sovereign risk: Global asset and information networks in the pricing of corporate credit risk. Working Paper, University of Florida.
Lucas, A., Schwaab, B., & Zhang, X. (2013, May). Conditional euro area sovereign default risk. SvergiesRiskbank Working Paper Series, 269.
Micu, M., Remolona, E. M., & Wooldridge, P. D. (2006). The price impact of rating announcements: Which announcements matter?, BIS Working Paper, 207.
Millon, M. H., & Thakor, A. V. (1985). Moral hazard and information sharing: A model of financial information gathering agencies. *Journal of Finance, 40*, 1403–1422.
Patel, J., Evans, D., & Burnett, J. (1998). Junk bonds behaviour with daily returns and business cycles. *The Journal of Financial Research, 21*, 408–418.
Restrepo, F. (2013). Credit ratings and the cost of debt: The sovereign ceiling channel. https://www2.bc.edu/~restrepf/RESTREPO%20-%20Credit%20Ratings%20and%20the%20Cost%20of%20Debt.pdf
Schneider, P. G., Sögner, L., & Veza, T. (2010). The economic role of jumps and recovery rates in the market for corporate default risk. *Journal of Financial and Quantitative Analysis, 45*, 1517–1547.
Stiglitz, J. E., & Weiss, A. (1981). Credit rationing in markets with imperfect information. *American Economic Review, 71*, 393–410.
Villouta, C. (2006). *Empirical study of liquidity effects in the relation between corporate credit spread and credit default swaps*. London: London Business School.

4

Risk Analysis as an Instrument of Public Management

Marta Postuła

1 Introduction

Risk and uncertainty are an intrinsic element of human existence, covering all aspects of socio-economic lifethe entirety of determinants that influence human activities (despite the proverbial inevitability of death and taxes). According to the definition developed by F. H. Knight in the 1920s, uncertainty takes on a measurable as well as an immeasurable form; risk is measurable uncertainty, whereas immeasurable uncertainty remains an uncertainty in the true sense of the term.

Risk is created when decisions are taken concerning future events. An individual or someone acting in an official capacity, when taking any step, is not completely certain as to the development and final outcome of their operations. Phenomena that have an impact on the outcome of entrepreneurs' actions, and independent of their will, constitute 'uncer-

---

M. Postuła (✉)
Faculty of Management University of Warsaw, Director Centre of Entrepreneurship, Warszawa, Poland

K. Raczkowski (ed.), *Risk Management in Public Administration*,
DOI 10.1007/978-3-319-30877-7_4

tainty'. J. Zieleniewski and S. Szczypiorski (Zieleniewski and Szczypiorski 1963, 38; Kaczmarek 2010, 22) define risk as certain capacity for failure. More specifically, this implies the probability of the occurrence of events that completely, or to a certain extent, deprive the operations of the features of effectiveness, cost-effectiveness and benefit, in particular through increased expenditures and/or diminished useful outcomes. These events are independent of the operating entity, which is not able to accurately predict or fully prevent them.

The concept of risk may be traced back to the Italian term, *risicare*, meaning to avoid something current, whilst in Italian, *risico*, principally stands for a venture whose outcome is unknown or uncertain or whose successful outcome is impossible to predict (Kaczmarek 2010, 62).

The area of inquiry on the issues of risk in management science is immense. There is a plethora of definitions and criteria for dividing and structuring different types of risk. This chapter only identifies and discusses similarities between selected aspects of financial risk management in enterprises and entities across the public finance sector. Financial risk management in banks, insurance institutions and other companies across the broadly-understood 'financial market' form a separate and very expansive area of research and practical solutions. Financial risk can be measured using appropriate tools, the aim being to determine its impact on ultimate financial performance. Non-financial risk is barely measurable, and its impact on financial results is indirect.

Other classifications of risk are applied when constructing integrated systems for risk management or, broadly speaking, integrating risk management into an enterprise management system.

The majority of measurable risks are eventually reflected in financial performance, and thus high importance is given to the investigation of financial risk categories, as is totally appropriate for private business enterprise. However, in this chapter I argue that the motive for measuring risk is different in the public finances sector. In this context, it is worth citing the statement by Max Weber (made at the beginning of the twentieth century), which holds that administration of a financial enterprise differs from public administration. In a financial enterprise all significant parameters underpinning decisions may be voiced in monetary categories, effects, as well as expenditures. However, objectives in administration have a substantial nature, which suggests that they cannot be directly gauged in financial terms. Only expenditures are subject to calculations (Kamiński 2008, 55). This means a considerable narrowing of the area of financial risk as it relates to public administration.

There has been a notable paradigm shift in relation to state institutions, motivated by the desire to replace uncertainty with measurable risk, meaning that they now have to quantify the degree to which objectives pursued by an administration were accomplished within budget (defined by the term 'activity-based budget' in the Polish context). The requirement to add effectiveness to targets of public administration makes the following statement by W. Kieżun relevant: Management in its scope embraces not only traditional administration, but it also obliges an organisation to attain maximal performance while accomplishing strategic goals (…). Transformation of rigid public administration into flexible apparatus guided by private initiative, being an equivalent of business organisations subordinated to competition paradigm, requires appropriate preparation of the personnel (Kieżun 2002, 14).

The recent financial crisis has led to changes in risk management across both the business and the government sector in order to avoid future crisis or at least to attenuate its aftermath. The financial crisis exposed failures in risk management in large financial institutions. Particular emphasis has been placed on the fact that the function of risk management as well as the independent risk assessment conducted by government organizations failed. Investigations made by international organizations (Organization for Economic Cooperation and Development, and the World Bank) concluded that since the crisis, state authorities have stepped up regulation and supervision of risk management in financial institutions. These measures involve introducing or strengthening legislation and guidelines, placing greater responsibility for risk management on management boards, who are also expected to carefully assess the accuracy and utility of information provided, so as to fulfil their duties effectively. Additionally, governments in various countries intensively began to implement measures intended to assess the efficiency of risk management frameworks in an effort to ensure appropriate risk management in all business ventures.

In this paper I assess the impact exerted by financial risk management on entities across the public finances sector with regard to enhanced effectiveness (and its measurability), implementation of budgets and plans, undertaken to improve the quality of public finances. The objective is to show that financial risk in the public sector is systemic in its nature and is impacted by external forces to a higher degree than enterprises. In my analysis I shall draw on available literature, source materials on issues related to risk in the public sector, and on my own investigations. I decided to address the theme because management systems in public administration are in flux, and effectiveness in risk management tends to vary across specific countries, and is continually being honed. Control and financial risk management in entities across the public finance sector have significantly gained in importance, especially over recent years. Yet substantial differences of control and management persist in the organization of both private and public sectors – and therefore the system of financial risk assessment in public entities and enterprises is not uniform. Thus in the author's opinion it is crucial to address the topic of these differences.

1.1 Key Categories of Financial Risk Likely to Be Established in Relation to Enterprises

This section of the paper focuses on the explanation of essential categories of financial risk in business operations. A considerable impediment while handling these issues is the lack of a consistent designation by which specific types of risk in the literature can be classified, notwithstanding that definite designations for their division exist.

Meanwhile, the unquestioned principle holds that while managing a contemporary company, the bulk portion of risks identified have financial consequences. From among numerous existing ways of marshalling aspects of financial risk , the author recommends selecting one that takes into consideration essential types of financial risk: market, operational, liquidity, legal, business and events risks (Jajuga 2009, 18). Market risk applies to interest rates, exchange rates, stock exchange prices, goods prices and other prices that affect the financial bottom line of the enterprise, while credit risk refers to the fulfilment of obligations by business partners and their creditworthiness. Operational risk is related to internal processes in the enterprise: actions taken by personnel, the working of information systems and internal control as well as appropriate response to external events. Liquidity risk, of tremendous importance, is relates to matching maturities of assets and liabilities. A similar situation is represented by the term solvency risk, which is concerned with the market value surplus of assets over liability market value. Legal risk lies in amendments to legislation and in provisions contained in agreements concluded by the enterprise.

The 'business' group of risks pertains to overall economic settings for business operations, development of new products in the context of enterprise operations that translate into the financial standing. The last group of risks involves events that do not fall into other categories, including such things as extraordinary weather events, and natural catastrophes. These various types of risk must be viewed in the context of the public sector.

1.1.1 Key Categories of Financial Risk Likely to Be Established in Relation to Entities Across the Public Finance Sector

At first sight, the above catalogue of financial risk in the business sector would seem also to apply to individual entities of the public finance sector. However, there are fairly considerable differences, the objectives of public entities frequently being centred on providing public goods and the way their activities should be financed. These differences in perceiving financial risk may be accounted for by pointing to the typically lesser impact of risk on the financial situation and consequent differences in the manner by which risk is managed across public sector entities, as compared with private enterprises. Moreover, it should be noted that there is a different sort of influence of specific financial risks on the financial status of the whole sector and individual entities within it.

Financial risk for entities in the public finance sector is constituted mainly by operational risk, with marginally less significance attached to legal risk and risk from events. Also, liquidity risk has limited significance. The author claims that it is necessary to discount credit and business risk for public entities. However, it should be emphasized that this remark does not apply to public authority – after all the state is involved as a participant in the market of trade risk management i.e. with regard to the support provided by them for export trade credit insurance, which is tremendously vital in terms of trade with the East.[1]

The key type of financial risk faced by entities composing the public sector is functional, involving procedures, reliability in planning, reporting, accounting, and personnel—analogous to factors underpinning operational risk, described above in connection with commercial enterprises. To some degree, a legal risk could potentially arise from participation in supranational legal systems, e.g. membership in the EU, which entails the obligation to apply regulations/provisions stipulated by the legislative Community as well as the need to respect EU case law (though this aspect of risk is greatly reduced by active involvement and representation of the state in EU legislative procedure).

A specific type of legal risk occurs when devolving responsibility for accomplishment of public tasks from national government sub-sector to local government sub-sector, with their ambiguous appraisal, or non-alignment between the size of funding and actual needs and capacities to absorb support. It is also possible to identify risk perceived by local government entities with regard to changes in principles governing financing of their operations. As regards risk related to agreements and contracts, this is mitigated by the need to adjust their content to public procurement law and other laws regulating the operations of the specific entity. However, enhanced immunity to provisions of public procurement law by uncompetitive business entities can present a risk if they

[1] Assistance provided to exporters is part of economic policy pursued by the state. The purpose of such aid is to maximize the success of Polish companies that sell their goods and services abroad, particularly exporters that expand market outlets and execute innovative projects and investments. One form of such support is an insurance instrument made available to exporters that ensures safe trade throughout the world – especially in markets labelled as risky. The act on Export Insurance Guaranteed by the State Treasury of 7 July 1994 authorizes KUKE S.A. (Korporacja Ubezpieczeń Kredytów Eksportowych Spółka Akcyjna to provide insurance not available from private insurance companies. Thanks to this, Polish exporters may forge trade relationships with new business partners, e.g. from the Commonwealth of Independent States, and carry out complex, frequently long-term investment and trade projects. A prerequisite for benefitting from state-supported insurance is that the product should genuinely be of Polish origin , in compliance with principles set out in the Ordinance of the Minister of Economy of 19 December 2014. See the website of KUKE).

are awarded with a procurement contracts and find methods for only formal fulfilment of certain requirements, an eventuality which may be attributed to insufficiently dynamic or inadequate adaptation of regulations to actual situations and behaviours displayed by market actors. This type of risk may arise when experienced employees in units responsible for public procurement in public institutions move into employment in the private sector)

Another distinctive legal risk is the risk closely connected with potential irregularities occurring from regulatory decisionsrisk from unreliable regulation or deregulation of domains of business activity that fall within the remit of powers exercised by a specific entity within the public finance sector. In the context of the play of forces and balancing required, it is critical to retain optimal measures. In effect, the state may rein in abusive marketing practices by companies in the private sector through giving new powers to entities across the public sector whereas, conversely, excessive deregulation diminishes companies' expectations regarding public aid (and vice versa). As noted by Z. Staniek, the situation may vary depending on the type of business activities, and thus it is needful (and appropriate) to initiate increased regulation for some and deregulation for others. For instance, the functioning of the energy market, which is not typically competitive, is characterized by high entry barriers and extremely low supply flexibility in the short term (Staniek 2012, 194–195). Z. Staniek argues that An additional problem is high risk that causes that electricity markets subject to deregulation lack automatic market guarantees inducing them to investment in new production capacities and transmission. Basically, this hinders adequate regulation, thereby running the risk of creating the specific market of regulatory services with corrupt practices and strengthening interest groups (Staniek 2012, 194–195). Another problem includes risks of so-called regulation effects, in a lack of consistency in organization and financing legal norms, e.g. in the sphere of the environment it may stem from the concerns that other types of risk (not necessarily legal types) may arise with regard to other state functions (e.g. with regard to the function of the labour market in the form of surging unemployment) which are likely to emerge when these norms are overly strictly observed (if they are not adequately tailored to the economic situation of the country) (Staniek 2012, 84).

In this author's opinion, market risk principally affects the costs incurred by the sector entities, though the risk is diminished by existing reserves and shifts in levels of funding to particular budgets The need to take into consideration the consequence of possible changes in annual budgets and financial plans appears to be an additional factor for public entities. Risk of extraordinary events also influences public sector entities, though dealing with the consequences of such events may burden the finances of the state rather than the finances of the individual entity. Liquidity risk, if it occurs at all, emerges in a slightly different way than in a private enterprise. Generally, it involves delayed subsidies or other revenues, in which case. delays in the discharge of liabilities may occur.

In the author's view, credit and business risk may occur when making an investment or purchasing products or services from companies (this also relates to the issues of the optimal functioning of the public procurement system detailed above), though in the most cases mistakes in these activities do not automatically imply financial consequences (e.g. in relation to revenues) for the public sector entity. Even when a transaction does not work out as anticipated, this will not have such negative repercussions as in the case of relationships between private enterprises. Therefore, the author proposes that these types of risk for public sector entities may be categorized as operational.

A particular type of business risk resides in decisions taken in the public sector with regard to the privatization of public enterprises or the outsourcing of public services. In the first case, a good illustration of the resilience to the occurrence of this risk—frequently addressed in the reference literature—is typically the analysis of the privatization model leveraged for the railway market in a specific country. In this context, the risk refers to the change in the manner by which this type of services is delivered – though their complete liberalization makes it possible for external effects not to be considered. The maintenance of railway lines, though a burden on the state budget, suggests less ecological damage, actual (not formal retaining minimal service standard at the price acceptable for the society), as well as higher accessibility to places for study and work (in particular for poorer members of society). Nonetheless, the above comments do not imply that it is not reasonable to strive to reduce costs and maximize profits in providing freight and passenger rail services. Yet, when the privatization takes place, these operations should be performed in a well-advised and cautious manner while keeping in mind risks in the form of so-called external effects. (In such cases there are two principal manners for tackling the problem: subsidies for companies providing services to bring them up to an acceptable standard, or, preferably, subsidizing those rail users who are most in need (e.g. large families, the unemployed and those on low incomes, school-aged children and students, see Staniek 2012, 94).

Another operational risk also results from information asymmetry between public entities that provide subsidies and entities that fulfil a specific task—giving rise to a so-called moral hazard as a source of ineffectiveness. Typically, this problem largely lies in information asymmetry between an entity commissioning the accomplishment of a public task and its contractors. In the author's view such an effect is likely to partially constrain the instrument of an activity-based budget adequately applied for tasks, which through reliable measurement and evaluation of effects yielded by accomplishment of tasks provides a response to a question of whether and to what extent risk related to an indirect method for delivery of a specific type of public service by the state was restrained.

In this short chapter, as already mentioned, there is insufficient space for addressing the issues of risk across the whole private sector as regards the entities supervising them, adequate supervisory bodies, etc. A different situation applies to the public finance sector which is overseen by relevant bodies of the legislative and executive authority. Thus it is worth giving a brief view of the characteristics underlying financial risk on the macro scale in relation to the whole public finance sector.

At the outset, it is necessary once again to emphasize the relevance of operational risk linked to existing budgeting processes (planning, fulfilment of tasks, reporting, accounting), management procedures, IT system, personnel, alongside the market risk, which is to a degree determined by the inflation level (having implications for the size of expenditures as well as revenues). But the significant factor is the interest rate of Treasury and municipal bonds, and the exchange rate, which indicates the magnitude of the debt denominated in foreign currencies. Liquidity risk is, to a degree, related to the scheduling of implementation of revenues and expenditures, and to the performance attained by the sector. Thus, the focus should be on the substantial sizes of refinancing public debt, resulting in credits and debits on an annual basis being close to revenues and expenditures of the state budget. Taken together, on-going shifts in liquidity are correlated with the timing and sizes of these financial flows. Legal risk in relation to the whole sector may be regarded, as stated earlier, as minor, though it is possible, though not very likely that some risk may attach to deficient co-ordination of new legislative measures, high frequency of changing relations or exceeding the constitutional or statutory rules. Also, there is a certain degree of risk associated with new norms enshrined in EU legislation and implemented by domestic law. As previously noted, risk of extraordinary events mostly affects the finances of the whole sector, because the consequences of such events typically puts a burden on state liabilities across the board.

Given the public finance sector as a whole, it is possible to specify risk related to the use of resources from European funds. This risk is financial in nature, and significant because of the large sums involved, which will be allocated for co-financing entities across the domestic public sector, with these entities being charged with their appropriate deployment and settlement. The nature of that risk, though partly operational, resembles the business risk faced by companies.

To fully typify the settings in which entities across the public finance sector in Poland operate, we need to exemplify types of risk. The paper provides 5 examples to illustrate the grouping of risks, with 3 examples portraying financial risks. Principally, three different areas of financial risk in the entity were identified:

(a) those concerning controls of finances and use of entities capital (cost estimate, financial liquidity, investment, those associated with errors in accounting books, size of financial resources);
(b) budgetary, fraud and theft, those related to insurance, public procurement and task commissioning, responsibility;
(c) administration of funds coming from the EU budget, the size of subsidies received.

The form selected to determine financial risks is exemplary in its character, but fails to thoroughly encompass the whole possible catalogue, though the analysis of their content and scope reveals that it should be considered as the list of detailed risks directly connected with financial economy of the entity from the direct perspective. The instances outlined refer to the state budget, financial documents and financial flows. The review of the content of remaining groups of risk shows that some of them, in the case of previously discussed classifications of financial risk for companies were incorporated into this category of risk, have been separately identified. Specifically, this applies to such categories of risks included in guidelines beyond the financial risk such as: operational/activities risk, external and economic risk referred to economic drivers (inflation, exchange rates). For two examples illustrating groups of risk, the guidelines do not contain financial risk altogether. The selection of the grouping type in the risk management system within a given entity certainly remains optional. However, it should be underscored that the domain of financial risk is perceived in the considerably narrower sense than it happens for the enterprise, and it may be blatantly omitted by the entity – thus risk management remains in the area of organisational, personnel and systemic issues, negligibly treating financial analysis or effectiveness of operations. On the other hand, ignoring finances may suggest a marginal degree of autonomy enjoyed by the specific entity within the public finance sector in terms of budgetary planning. In the context of the arguments cited above, it is crucial to emphasize the specifics embedded in financial risk management in the public sector in relation to the process taking place in private enterprises.

Typically, of the various decisions taken by companies with regard to national and international exchanges involve risk and uncertainty. The achievement of set targets may require increased inputs and costs due to the occurrence of unforeseen events beyond companies' control.

While discussing risk, uncertainty must be mentioned, because both categories usually emerge concurrently, and are sometimes identified with each other, despite each having a distinctive significance. Risk and uncertainty define the propensity to deviations from the anticipated state. The difference is that uncertainty cannot be gauged, but risk can be pinned down, e.g. by using probability theory, and can be insured against. Distinctions between risk and uncertainty was a subject first investigated by A.H. Willett, who in *The Economic Theory of Risk and Insurance*

(Willet 1951, 6. after Kalinowski 2012, 8), depicted risk as the degree of uncertainty of the occurrence of a loss, which is distinguished from the probability of its occurrence. But this is only one of multiple meanings ascribed to the term uncertainty. Frequently, in works devoted to insurance the authors use the word uncertainty in order to define risk associated with psychological phenomena. According to H.S. Denenberg, risk is uncertainty of a loss. He presents it as mainly a psychological phenomenon due to human reactions and experiences (Denenberg 1964, 4. after Kalinowski 2012, 8).

F.H. Knight, when investigating the relationships between uncertainty and risk in his doctoral dissertation under the title *Risk, Uncertainty and Profit* (Knight 1921, 233. after Kaczmarek 2004, 23) disclosed the occurrence of two types of uncertainty: measurable and immeasurable. He claimed that uncertainty is unlikely to be subject to any mathematical calculations or reckoned by harnessing statistical methods. Only risk tends to be a measurable uncertainty.

The two first official definitions of risk were given in 1966, in a bulletin from The American Commission on Insurance Terminology. The first exhibits risk as uncertainty of the outcome of the event in the moment when two or more possibilities appear. The second maintains that risk is an individual or object covered by insurance (Kalinowski 2012, 8). Yet these definitions were not sufficiently accurate, thereby inspiring subsequent attempts to craft new definitions.

Relations between risk and uncertainty were depicted thus by I. Pfeffer in his *Insurance and Economic Theory*: Risk is a combination of elements of gambling and it is measured by the probability; uncertainty is measured by the belief level. Risk is the state of the world, uncertainty is state of mind (Pfeffer 1956, 42 for Dziawgo 1998, 14). Risk is inherently linked to gambling.[2]

[2] Similarly for international exchanges when experiencing failure in gambling, there is the probability of the occurrence of many types of risk. Essentially, gambling is closely related to the game theory, which as a mathematical branch is committed to examining optimal behaviour during the conflict of players' interests. It originates from the analysis of gambling games. Furthermore, the theory is applied in IT science (artificial intelligence), economics, biology and sociology. Any conflict situation is interpreted as a game and its participants all termed players. Every player makes use of his own conduct strategy, and then, depending on that and other participants, each player receives remuneration in utility units. These may be money or increased chances. Generally, utility

When addressing the issues of risk in international exchanges, M. Stalmaszczyk shows that it is tied to the eventual occurrence of a specific incident, damage by force majeure or accidents. The surrounding environment brings singular and unique phenomena. Most are scarcely anticipated. The probability of identifying underlying causes, effects and behaviours of some events would lead to elimination of risk and uncertainty from the specific operations. While monitoring the course of action, it is necessary to take into account extraneous factors which are unlikely to be avoided, yet having an impact on the given phenomenon and having the potential to produce unexpected effects.

S. Nahotko (2001, 38) shifts attention to the definition of risk in a sense of:

(a) venture: where the outcome is not known, i.e. there is a possibility of success or failure;
(b) function: risk is a function of quality and quantity of economic and socio-political information provided, non-conformity of external and internal conditions for operations, and the degree of variations;
(c) probability: risk of probability of suffering loss, connected with approval of the specific economic decision.

The occurrence of different types of risk with a particular intensity may be recognised in foreign trade, for which the risk indicator is far higher than for operations in the domestic market. This is attributed to the higher number and increasing volatility of forces that influence business entities, making their detection and forecasting problematic.

1.1.2 Types of Risk

The capacity to deploy various research approaches towards risk is demonstrated in the reference literature. Risk surfaces in different domains

units reflect the type of the game. Moreover, the game theory deals with strategies to be selected by players so as to gain highest possible profits. In effect, its adoption facilitates the recognition of rational solutions to problems.

of business operations and may be analysed on many fronts. The scheme below presents the classification of risk.

According to J. Rymarczyk, the primary types of risk occurring in international exchanges are illustrated in the scheme (Fig. 4.1):

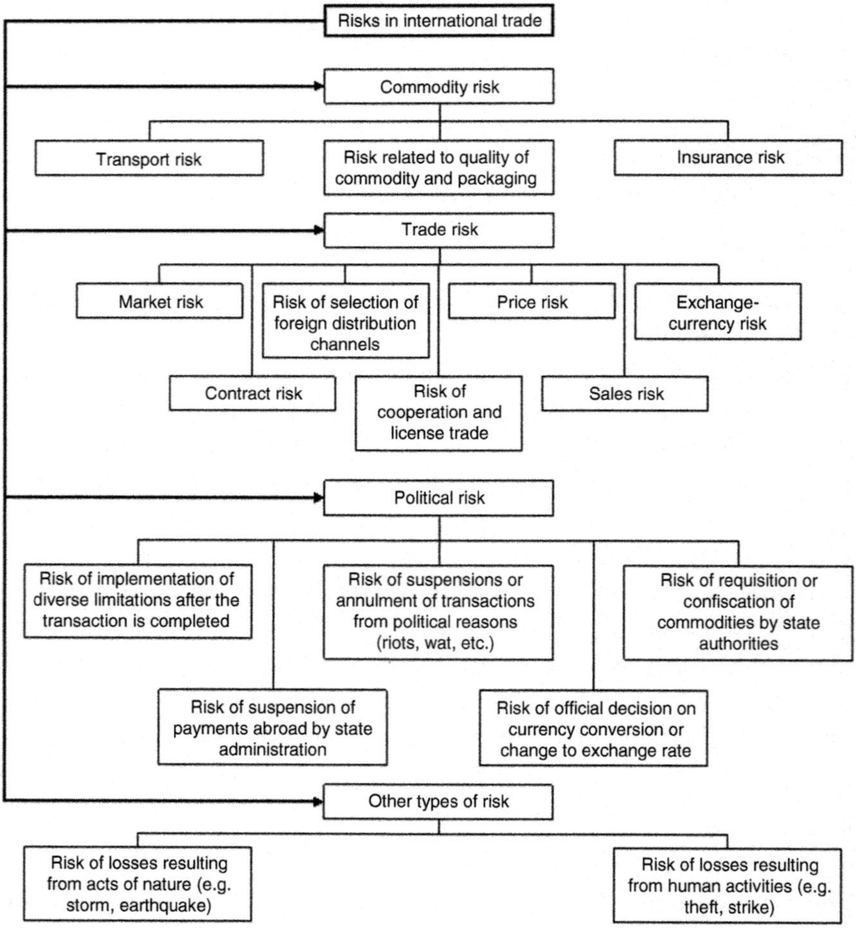

Fig. 4.1 Risk in international trade (*Source*: own study based on J. Rymarczyk, *Handel zagraniczny, Organizacja i technika*, PWE 2002, 2002 Warszawa, pp. 263 and 267)

Division and types of foreign risk are displayed in the figure below (Fig. 4.2):

The above figures reveals that when exploiting the division of risk given the number of potential victims, the collective and individual risk may be designated. The first implies all hazards occurred with regard to business entities operating in the specific national economy. It comprises legal and currency risk. Whereas individual risk explicitly refers to the position of the foreign business partner. It encompasses transport risk and risk of contract completion.

Entrepreneurship (including small and medium enterprises (SMEs) generating over 47 % of GDP in the country) is regarded as necessary and a central driver propelling social and economic growth. Therefore, it is critical to carry out in-depth analysis of risks connected with the operations conducted by SMEs, not only on the grounds of risks intrinsic to the private sector, but also risks associated with the involvement of the public sector – i.e.in pursuit of state policies directed to supporting small and medium-sized enterprises. Thus this is an exceptional area where the risks outlined above, both private and public, interact on one platform – in the field of public policies and state interference committed to stable and sustainable economic growth. Steps taken by the state in an effort to

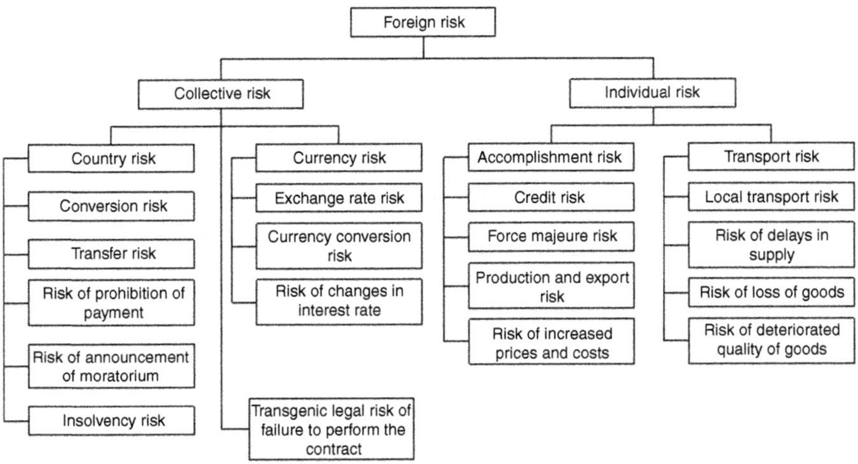

Fig. 4.2 Risks in foreign export (*Source*: own study based on T.T. Kaczmarek, *Ryzyko w handlu międzynarodowym*, wyd. cyt., p. 108)

improve operating conditions for SMEs contribute to increasing competitiveness of the national economy (and indirectly the wider competitiveness of the EU economy, which moreover was highlighted in The Treaty of EU membership), which will enable, in the long term, competition with stakeholders from outside (in the domestic, EU and third country markets), thereby enabling a catch-up with EU countries that have stronger economic growth and more advanced technology (Nahotko 2001, 38).

The need to offer support for certain activities budgets to support the SME sector stems from the need to mitigate the risk of a variable economic cycle, yet (as mentioned above) the socio-economic importance of these enterprises should also be taken into account. It should be recognized that such enterprises are particularly sensitive to the exigencies of dwindling economic growth linked to a global slow-down. These enterprises have relatively fewer opportunities for raising external sources of funding their growth, including, enhancing their innovations (*Growth trends for the SME sector in the assessment of entrepreneurs in the first half of* 2012, Ministry of Economy, No. 2/2012)), though at the present time there is disinclination to seek such external sources of funding because credit interest rates are low, and also potential investors are reluctant to take on financial risk. In the second half of 2011 30 % of surveyed companies applied for investment or working capital credits, and over half of them received the credit at the amount applied for, 8 % of entrepreneurs made use of the investment credit, the same percentage tapped the working capital credit, at the same time 65 % of investment expenditures made by enterprises are financed from own funds, in every hundredth case these are EU funds. In the view of C. Kosikowski: " Polish entrepreneurs do not know other more advanced funding instruments and forms and they are scared to use them. Such paths are only available to large and public entrepreneurs who have employees adequately educated in this respect or can afford to pay for independent services in this respect. … Unless this situation changes, Polish entrepreneurship will be, to a large extent, a source of public expenditure rather than of public revenues" (Kosikowski 2011, 231). There is also a problem, especially in times of economic contraction, with effective collection of debts, which is critical for maintaining SMEs' liquidity (risk of liquidity, risk of failure to receive payments or overdue payments) (Starczewska-Krzysztoszek 2012, 53–71).

Additionally, this sector (particularly in the context of launching and functioning of newly-established business undertakings) is tremendously sensitive to so-called 'barriers to entrepreneurship' which constitute not only 'objective' barriers to running existing operations, but also 'subjective' barriers related to deciding to take new business initiatives. A high level of support from various types of public services is required to make conditions conducive to enterprise.

Shifts in the public management system fit into the broad trend centred on the modernization of the state, labelled New Public Management (referred to as NPM), involving, among other things, introducing the management mechanisms that prevail in the private sector into state institutions, with the goal of ensuring 'effective state' or 'performing state' (Schick 2008, 23–48; Opolski and Modzelewski 2004, 35).This approach is along the lines by which efficiency and effectiveness of tasks in activity-based budget is measured (see Pogoda et al. 2010, 115–171).

On the whole, the specifics inherent to NPM (including activity-based budget) encourage the argument that such a philosophy behind state finance management, based on 'competitive' pro-effective mechanism intended primarily to support the measures, programmes or public services that prove to be the most efficient and useful for recipients, i.e. on public accountability of 'work' performed by state institutions through reference to demonstrable results—should be favoured by the private sector from which these methods were transferred. (Deputy Minister of Finance Mirosław Sekuła during the opening of training schemes devoted to management by objectives for administrative bodies in 2012/2013 informed participants that *'Management in* public *administration is archaic, governance in public* administration *is archaic. If private companies were managed in this way, we would have had a series of bankruptcies. I hope that during these meetings you will show* the *right course for Polish administration to recover from this ruin.'*, See website of the Social Insurance Fund: *www.zus.pl/warsztaty/materialy.asp?id=1*)

Given that growth of the public sector coupled with the private sector is—as underlined by J. Komorowski—the requirement for application of the principle of reasonability (Komorowski 2012, 18), it would be appropriate to tap all channels for the transfer of information between these two sectors, and, in consequence, to gain, to a larger degree than hitherto, directly from entrepreneurs, knowledge on the requirements for economic growth in the context of public finances, and ways in which state encouragement of conditions for entrepreneurial business should be financed.

As a result of the implementing such measures such as activity-based budget, the manner by which public tasks/services are delivered to entrepreneurs by the state—making use of funds coming from taxes paid by entrepreneurs and persons employed—could become (provided that assumptions underlying these innovations are consistently implemented) consumer-oriented, to a larger degree and more precisely. In addition, this kind of 'fine-tuning' of mechanisms leveraged to plan an activity-based budget correspond to the overall systemic assumptions of NPM, where the overriding principle embraced is 'an emphasis on learning from citizens what their needs and expectations are, team work with communities' (referring here to the community of SME entrepreneurs) (Krynicka, p. 7).

Moreover, while considering the quest for alternative and honed ways to boost performance and effectiveness of the state, in the context of forwarding the liberalization process of its mechanisms selected (public tasks) – adequately to capacities resulting from the specifics anchored in specific operations – it is private entrepreneurs that may become, in NPM theory, a executors of services contracted (privatization of public services) under circumstances ensuring fair competitive rules and robust institutional and social control with regard to the domains likely to be accomplished in the future more effectively and efficiently than that which takes place on an unexamined on-going basis (Najnigier 2008, 170) – also due to the results obtained from evaluation of the activity-based budget.

2 Conclusion

Financial risk management does not only receive attention exclusively from banks and other financial institutions. In general, this applies to all enterprises as well as entities across the public finance sector and the sector as a whole. Certainty, distribution of risk areas, the probability of its occurrence and instruments applied varies. Primary categories of financial risk with regard to the public sector and its entities include operational, legal and market risk as well as the risk of extraordinary events. Entities in the public finance entities across Poland expand management control systems where risk management proves to be an essential element. In parallel, the activity-based structure for planning, executing and budget reporting (and part of financial plans), containing targets and task measurements fosters the integration of effectiveness and financial information helpful in risk management. Financial risk management continues to encompass numerous key areas in which sector entities operate, including those related to the award and execution of public contracts. Taken together, the procedures guiding risk management, including financial risks, are used across the public finance sector as a whole (e.g. in public debt management) as well as with individual entities, thus reinforcing the achievement of the budget, and financial plans, along with projects and programmes. The incorporation of methods intended for financial risk management in the budgeting practice of the public finance sector improves the quality of public finances due to, *inter alia*, the increased measurability of the degree to which targets set for particular tasks are achieved(as well as providing an improved and unbiased way to measure budget tasks), through recognition of responsibility, and thus identifying and activating preventative measures against risk likely to effect the final outcome.

Bibliography

Bulletin of the Commission of Insurance Terminology of the American Risk and Insurance Association. (1966). 2(1).

Denenberg, C. H. S. (1964). *Risk and insurance.* Englewood Cliffs: Prentice Hall.

Deputy Minister of Finance Mirosław Sekuła during the opening of training schemes devoted to management by objectives for bodies in administration in 2012/2013 informed participants that "*Management in public administration is archaic…*", see a website of the Social Insurance Fund: http://www.zus.pl/warsztaty/materialy.asp?id=1

Dziawgo, D. (1998). *Credit-rating. Ryzyko i obligacje na międzynarodowym rynku finansowym* (p. 250). Warszawa: Wydawnictwo Naukowe PWN.

Growth trends for the SME sector in the assessment of entrepreneurs in the first half of 2012. Ministry of Economy, No. 2/2012.

Jajuga, K. (scientific ed.). (2009). *Zarządzanie ryzykiem*. Warszawa: Wydawnictwo Naukowe PWN.

Kaczmarek, T. T. (2004). *Ryzyko w handlu międzynarodowym*. Gdańsk: ODDK.

Kaczmarek, T. T. (2010). *Zarządzanie ryzykiem. Ujęcie interdyscyplinarne*. Warszawa: Difin.

Kalinowski, M. (2012). *Ryzyko walutowe zarządzanie ryzykiem w przedsiębiorstwie*, CeDeWu.pl, Warszawa, edition I.

Kamiński, A. Z. (2008). Administracja publiczna we współczesnym państwie. In J. Czaputowicz (Ed.), *Administracja publiczna. Wyzwania w dobie integracji europejskiej*. Warszawa: EIPA, Wydawnictwo Naukowe PWN.

Kieżun, W. (2002). Struktury i kierunki zarządzania państwem, "Nauka", No.1.

Knight, C. F. H. (1921). *Risk, uncertainty and profit*. Boston: Houghton Mifflin Company.

Komorowski, J. (2012). Budżet zadaniowy jako narzędzie racjonalizacji gospodarki budżetowej. In P. Albiński (Ed.), *Budżetowanie zadaniowe w kontekście sanacji finansów publicznych w krajach Unii Europejskiej*. Warszawa: Oficyna Wydawnicza SGH.

Kosikowski, C. (2011). Naprawa finansów publicznych w Polsce, Wydawnictwo Temida 2, Białystok.

Krynicka, H. (2006). Koncepcja zarządzania w sektorze publicznym (New Public Management), Prace Instytutu Prawa i Administracji w Sulechowie, Studia Lubuskie PWSZ w Sulechowie, nr 2.

Nahotko, S. (2001). *Ryzyko ekonomiczne w działalności gospodarczej*. Bydgoszcz: Oficyna Wydawnicza Ośrodka Postępu Organizacyjnego.

Najnigier, S. (2008). *Administracja, czy biznes?*. In: Administracja publiczna. *Wyzwania w dobie integracji europejskiej*, ed. Nauk. J. Czaputowicz, EIPA, PWN, Warszawa.

Opolski, K., & Modzelewski, P. (2004). *Zarządzanie jakością w usługach publicznych*. Warszawa: Wydawnictwo CeDeWu.

Pfeffer, I. (1956). *Insurance and economic theory*. Illinois: Richard. D. Irwin, Inc.

Pogoda, A., Chrzanowski, M., Marczewski, K. (2010). *Fundamentalne znaczenie miernika jako elementu ściśle skorelowanego z celami w ramach budżetu zadaniowego*. In: budżet zadaniowy w administracji publicznej, ed. nauk. M. Postuła, P. Perczyński, Ministerstwo Finansów, edition II, Warszawa.

Rymarczyk, J. (2002). *Handel zagraniczny, Organizacja i technika*. Warszawa: PWE.

Schick, A. (2008). Państwo Sprawne. Rozmyślania nad koncepcją, która nie doczekała się jeszcze realizacji, choć jej czas już nadszedł, in: Administracja publiczna. Wyzwania w dobie integracji europejskiej, red. nauk. J. Czaputowicz, Europejski Instytut Administracji publicznej, Wydawnictwa Naukowe PWN, Warszawa.

Staniek, Z. (2012). Mikroekonomiczna rola państwa. In M. Garbicz and Z. Staniek (Eds.), *Mikroekonomia. Problemy zawodności rynku*. Warszawa: Wydawnictwo Wyższej Szkoły Menedżerskiej w Warszawie.

Starczewska-Krzysztoszek, M. (2012). *Szanse i zagrożenia dla rozwoju mikro, małych i średnich przedsiębiorstw*. A report on the results from the research prepared by PKPP Lewiatan within the project "Monitoring pf the condition of the SME sector over 2012–2012" co-financed by the EU within the European Social Fund, Lewiatan/PARP, December, Warszawa.

Willet Cf, A. H. (1951). *The economic theory of risk and insurance*. Philadelphia: University of Pennsylvania Press.

Zieleniewski, J., & Szczypiorski, S. (1963). *Zasady organizacji i techniki handlu zagranicznego*. Warszawa: PWE.

5

Multidimensionality of Risk in Public Safety Management Processes

Barbara Kożuch and
Katarzyna Sienkiewicz-Małyjurek

1 Introduction

Public safety management is the part of public management which has the greatest exposure to risk. However, the scope of research in that particular field of public safety is modest (Tomasino 2011, 1350; Strömgren and Andersson 2010, 288; Industrial Development Report 2011, 10–12).

Public safety management extends from social policy through regional and crime policy, to emergency and disaster management (Williams et al. 2009; Tomasino 2011). The diversity of threats, activities and the large number of units held in a constant state of readiness demonstrates the complexity of this sector. This complexity and the nature of the performed activities are the sources of particular uncertainty and con-

B. Kożuch (✉)
Jagiellonian University, Kraków, Poland

K. Sienkiewicz-Małyjurek
Silesian University of Technology, Gliwice, Poland

K. Raczkowski (ed.), *Risk Management in Public Administration*,
DOI 10.1007/978-3-319-30877-7_5

tingency while planning for events and threats which cannot be fully predicted. Any threat may take a potentially differing course which requires taking various actions, involving a diverse group of units. Similarly a given type of threat would be different in every occurrence as regards its nature, intensity and location, and requires an approach appropriate to each particular situation. Existing procedures are never sufficient because of the irregular and dynamic nature of taking actions, so that public safety requires appropriate, flexible and agile management (Sienkiewicz-Małyjurek and Kożuch 2015). For this reason, the exercise of public safety management is burdened with a risk at every stage of its course. Therefore, there is a need for more explicit recognition of the importance of researching risk in this area and taking advantage of opportunities to reduce it. This chapter assumes that the appropriate starting point is to explore the multidimensionality of risk in public safety management, which enables a reliable description of its nature and sources, and the appropriate ways to minimize it, which is our primary purpose. Our investigations suggest that risk-based approaches to public management are the best method of improving the efficiency of all protective actions (Rothstein et al. 2013, 215; Johansson et al. 2009, 680). First, the main features of risk in public safety management are analysed. Next, there is an analysis of their specific features, such as: criteria of risk assessment, types of risk, risk vulnerability, consequences of risk, factors of risk minimizing and so on. Finally, the fundamental processes carried out in ensuring public safety and the main threats to be dealt with were examined. On this basis, a typology of risk dimensions in public safety management was developed.

2 Theoretical Background

2.1 Public Safety Management

Public safety management is an organized activity involving the deployment of human, financial, technical and information resources provided by multiple organizations, with the aim of mitigating potential threats, ensuing the undisturbed course of social life, and protecting human health and life, along with property and the environment. It also encompasses upholding the law and maintaining public order, with an emphasis placed on the fulfilment of public interest (Sienkiewicz-Małyjurek 2010, 124). To put it in other terms, it is a social process which is intended to safeguard an optimal level of security given existing opportunities and restrictions, and having regard to the environment dynamics. Groups of entities taking part in the process of public safety management include (Kożuch and Sienkiewicz-Małyjurek 2014a):

(a) Local government.
(b) Response and rescue units, including:
    - core unit, designed to deal competently with a specific type of hazard;
    - basic units, which mostly respond collectively and mutually collaborate in public safety management;
    - ancillary units, which supplement actions taken by a core unit and basic units, possessing knowledge and competences critical in a specific situation.
(c) Society: local communities and enterprises operating on the given territory;
(d) Media: radio, television, press, Internet;
(e) Non-governmental organizations;
(f) Research and development units.

The specified groups of entities constitute mutually complementary units whose role is continually modified to match the ever-changing requirements of the type of hazard encountered. These entities may execute actions in a parallel way, in compliance with their own procedures, or within an inter-organizational collaboration.

Fundamentally, public safety management, being in compliance with prevailing legal regulations, presumes that all ventures undertaken rely on collaboration (Waugh and Streib 2006; Berlin and Carlström 2011; Kapucu et al. 2010), and that the units involved carry out parallel activities that are complementary. Collaboration in this area evolves in a horizontal as well as vertical configuration. In effect, the vertical collaboration is principally the passage of instruction thereby providing the foundations for conducting undertakings. However, the horizontal collaboration that takes place at the district level is more significant(Kożuch and Sienkiewicz-Małyjurek 2015).

Inter-organizational collaboration is a mutually beneficial and well-defined relationship established by two or more organizations, which is intended to accomplish the common goals pursued by all these organizations (Mattessich et al. 2001; Payan 2007; O'Leary and Vij 2012). It is open in its character, it results from an evolution of inter-organizational relationships and it commonly applies to the private, public as well as non-governmental sectors. Overall, inter-organizational collaboration is diverse in scope, structure, form and goals. In each particular case, it has diverse proceedings typical to a given situation and hinges on current internal and external circumstances. Moreover, understanding and practical application of principles guiding inter-organizational collaboration depends on their interpretation and may differ substantially between organizations (Kaiser 2011, 5). A useful approach is to recognize the capability of organizations to enter into inter-organizational collaboration (Kożuch 2011, 122–126). Whether this is possible depends on both individual and organizational capability to collaborate (Lank 2007, 159–167). Individual capability means the potential of a member of an organization to collaborate effectively, which requires appropriate knowledge, skills and attitude. Organizational capability refers to basic operations, organizational competencies and organizational behaviour.

In essence, collaboration in the field of public safety tends to evolve based on applicable legal regulations and norms, safety programmes embraced and agreements concluded. The scope of joint operations includes: support for initiatives and co-ordination of activities designed to promote the issues of security; the organization and execution of operations aimed at preventing crimes and offences from being committed as well as other crime-related duties; the arrangement of activities facilitating the co-ordination of operations performed by fire brigades, medical rescue, protection of the populace, providing assistance to victims of naturally occurring disasters, provision and organization of material aid and physical assistance to families and persons facing difficulties, preventative measures against substance abuse and exploitation of addictions. Clearly, activities which are launched for public safety management are marked by their complexity, and they must be executed in an unanticipated and volatile environment. Therefore, they are susceptible to risk. Moreover, the inter-organizational nature underlying public safety management increases the multi-dimensional character of the risk.

2.2 Risk in Public Safety Management

Risk is the probability of the occurrence of harmful effects and resultant anticipated losses (e.g. deaths, injuries, property damage, disturbance to business activities, pollution of natural environment) in the wake of interactions between natural hazards and those triggered by a man and society's susceptibility to these hazards (UNISDR 2004). Basically, it originates from uncertainty which defines difficulties while unequivocally assessing the state and future evolution of phenomena, objects and processes given the shortage or inconsistency of information gained as well as paucity of opportunities for obtaining necessary information. Uncertainty tends to be a characteristic which is inherent to reality as typified by its subjectivity, and the lack of means to measure and specify it. On the whole, it is one of the reasons behind decisions and actions concerned with risk, which in turn emerges to be an unbiased, objective, tangible situation periodically cropping up where alternatives and chances for the occurrence of potential outcomes may be established (Dohn and Gumiński 2013; Jonek-Kowalska 2010). From the perspective of uncertainty, risk represents the uncertainty function and grows proportionally to it. The nature of the risk may be described in the following way:

- Risk is not a uniform concept, and thus it is not appropriate to provide one single universal and unambiguous definition of the term.
- Risks always come up in at least two aspects: objective and subjective.
- Risk may be examined in diverse contexts, e.g. as uncertainty, gambling, probability and peril.
- Risk is a variable and stage-based idea, this is a process rather than a state of the environment (Tarczyński and Mojsiewicz 2001, 14).

Every organization when executing its functions, copes with multiple categories of risk that may implicate and mutually affect one another. Therefore, the accurate identification of the sources of these risks appears to be critical to reduce them to the acceptable level.

Risk in public safety management stems from both external and internal drivers. External factors result from environmental circumstances (e.g. threats received, or legal requirements) and typically there are no options to eliminate these, it is only possible to adjust to them. Internal factors are various (e.g. communication, co-ordination of joint initiatives) and occur within units involved in the public safety management system. Risk occurring in the area of public safety and emergency management is illustrated by the following formula (UNISDR 2004, 6):

$$\text{Risk} = \text{Hazards} \times \text{Vulnerability}.$$

Vulnerability constitutes the function of exposure to the hazard and the potential to handle its consequences. Vulnerability proves to be a stronger determinant than hazard (Alexander 2006), since hazard alone is not able to stir up an emergency situation. Such a situation is created only when there is interaction between the society or infrastructure and environment.

Of primary importance is the identification of the site where the risk occurs, assessment of its scale, and the impact on activities and processes instigated, as well as the determination of ventures that reduce the risk to an acceptable level. Such measures, alongside optimal decisions taken, are termed as risk management (Jajuga 2007, 15), which involves a systematic management of decisions, organizations, competences and operational skills in order to pursue the policy, execute the strategy and provide the society with opportunities for handling any hazards (Mansor et al. 2004). Nevertheless, an appropriate strategy designed to effectively manage the risk only contributes to the diminished probability of the occurrence of hazards, because they cannot be eliminated altogether.

2.3 Specificity of Risk Management Safety in Public

The reference literature commonly defines risk management as all processes employed to identify, assess and judge risk, assign ownership, launch operations with the goal of reducing and anticipating risk as well as monitoring and reviewing the progress achieved (Orange Book 2004, 49). Risk management constitutes the foundation for the establishment of appropriate organizational order. Specifically, it rests on balancing a variety of correlated elements that mutually interact and need to stay in equilibrium with one another. Accordingly, one risk cannot be isolated from any others, because management of one risk may potentially exert an impact on other risks. Furthermore, sometimes there can be situations where operations can be only effective while simultaneously controlling a larger number of risks (Orange Book 2004, 13; Dohn et al. 2013). According to Dennis M. Woo and Kim J. Vicente, effective risk management requires the identification of all entities that participate in activities taken, clear formulation of their targets, effective feedback within the whole operation, contractors with adequate competencies and a proper security culture (Woo and Vicente 2003, 269).

Simply put, risk management is a cyclical and pro-active process used to assess the acceptability of events occurring in a specific context and environment (Jonek-Kowalska 2014). It comprises five phases (Mansor et al. 2004, 365): pinpointing the context for actions, identification, analysis, assessment and risk mitigation. These phases are accompanied by continual communication and consultations about actions as well as monitoring of the on-going situation. Thus, risk management emerges as a decision-making process that helps to deliver projected targets, through reducing the potential risk of hazard occurrence to the acceptable level. Overall, it is performed in a systematic and forward-looking manner. According to Margaret Woods 'within local authorities, the emphasis is on the provision of guidance rather than specific requirements in relation to risk management'" (Woods 2009, 71).

The risk management process in public safety is performed on the basis of efficient flow of information, because anticipation and analysis of perils requires continuous and swift collection of data so as to provide best opportunities for activating early warning systems. The initial phase involves setting the boundaries within which the process will be carried out. Also, the criteria for risk assessment will be formulated based on a broad array of information that includes (Kosowski 2006, 47–51):

(a) basic data: topographic data, hydrographic structure, demographic and sociological information, technical infrastructure, hazardous materials distribution, data concerned with agriculture and breeding, description of urbanized territories, medical security, rescue capacities, flood protection and historical data;

(b) aspects of hazard classification: environmental (e.g. scale, intensity, duration time) as well as legal and social (e.g. scope of the law impact, difficulty in scale of change, involvement of parties, social perception of changes implemented);
(c) catalogue of hazards occurring in the specific territory, in line with the outcome produced by their identification process.

In line with all this, a list of potential hazards is compiled, followed up by their underlying causes and consequences. Subsequently, the analysis and evaluation of risk is conducted using the existing methods or, if such a need occurs, a newly designed method. Analysis is needed to recognize the character of hazards identified and encompasses: determination of causes and outcomes, classification and investigation of potential for hazard duplication and escalation, and binding risk with aims and actions (Wang 2012). This is at the heart of risk assessment and involves designation of acceptable and unacceptable risks based on the specified limit values. In general, analysing and assessing risk in emergency management requires both qualitative methods (e.g. brainstorming, synectics, Delphi) and quantitative methods (e.g. event tree analysis, fault tree analysis, failure mode and effects analysis – FMEA). Their selection depends on the decision-maker. In practice the analysis of combination of the probability of an event and its consequence tends to be one of the most common methods designed to evaluate the risk. Primarily, it is conducted with the use of a risk assessment matrix. At the final phase of risk management, steps required to be taken in order to reduce the probability of a hazard occurrence are determined, and a plan to address the risk is prepared and put into place. Across all phases of the process monitoring and review take place so as to detect and remove errors and irregularities (Mansor et al. 2004; Williams et al. 2006). Effective and accurate risk analysis is core in safety management systems to develop and implement policy, procedures and practices that lead to efficient accomplishment of actions (Demichela et al. 2004, 185; Reiman and Pietikäinen 2012, 1997).

In the context of the holistic approach to risk management in public safety, consequences triggered by direct physical impacts (exposition and sensitivity) as well as indirect effects caused by potentially perilous events (social and economic instability and lack of resilience) are taken into account. Each individual category identifies vulnerability determinants and determines their level using the set of indicators and indices. Thus these measures produce the result that reveals the current risk level and potential social, economic and environmental consequences. As part of the feedback, control is carried out, thereby directly influencing the risk level through identification of improvements and implementation of new steps, among others, in terms of risk identification and its mitigation.

2.4 Vulnerability in Public Safety Management

Essentially, vulnerability is associated with exposure level, sensitivity to perturbations and adaptive capacity (Adger 2006). It is negative in its nature and related to losses and costs. Generally, it arises from a situation when a specific organization or system fails to handle hazards, and thus grows susceptible to changes that could previously be absorbed. It pinpoints the types of hazard to which the organization is likely to be vulnerable. In effect, the concept of vulnerability is grounded on three elements including: level of losses and damage caused by hazard impact, degree of exposure to hazards and resilience level (Al-Khudhairy et al. 2012).

Thus vulnerability refers to the human-environment system and embraces three basic categories: exposure, sensitivity and resilience (Turner et al. 2003). Exposure applies to threatened entities and includes core characteristics of hazard, i.e. frequency, magnitude and duration. Sensitivity implies the degree to which the socio-environment capital helps maintain resilience of the whole system, which in turn involves the capacity to adapt to volatile circumstances. The reference literature emphasizes that the following features underlie sensitivity (Birkmann 2013, 13):

(a) multi-dimensional and differential (vulnerability varies across physical space and among and within social groups);
(b) dependence (vulnerability depends on time, space and units subject to analysis);
(c) dynamic (characteristics and driving forces of vulnerability change over time).

Vulnerability is only slightly determined by the type of hazard. Its essential causes mostly lie in the society's standard of living, capacity to protect its own health, life and assets as well as its institutional settings. From that perspective, vulnerability involves legal, administrative and social aspects as well as management.

Vulnerability in public safety management has an open and interactive nature. It chiefly refers to current circumstances, portraying not only the level of exposure to hazards and deficiency of capacities for addressing them, but also relating to cultural, economic, environmental, physical, political, social and technological processes evolving during stability as well as execution of operations (Palliyaguru et al. 2014, 50; McEntire 2011). Potential hazards have complex, non-linear and diverse character, and they may be driven by both internal as well as external settings. For these reasons, vulnerability pertains to micro as well as macro factors (Turner et al. 2003). Additionally, it is a principal determinant of risk, and a tool and central requirement for effective assessment of that risk (UNISDR 2004, 14–15).

3 Methodology

Research for this chapter was carried out under the project entitled 'Coordination, communication and trust as a factors driving effective inter-organizational collaboration in the system of public safety management'. This project is financed by the National Science Centre based on decision no. DEC-2012/07/D/HS4/00537. Desk research and empirical investigations were the methods used. Desk research was based on the analysis of international scientific literature and also on the analysis of internal documents, ordinances and regulations of police, fire brigade and medical rescue in Poland.

There was also some participant observation, conducted from September to December 2013 on 16 shifts in the Province Headquarters of the State Fire Service in the Silesian Region. Observation covered principles underpinning the operations of the fire service as well as their response actions, meetings, training and exercises. The selection of the subject for observation was determined by to the possibility of carrying out research there, and dynamics anchored in the growth of that province. In general, this is the most urbanized region in Poland with the highest population density (Development Strategy for the Silesian Province 2010, 5), and one of the areas where the highest number of environmental hazards tend to emerge – over 12% across the whole country (Statistical data of KG PSP).

The results were complemented, using the hermeneutic process, in December 2014 in a focus group of scholars, namely a four-person group of researchers actively involved into investigating inter-organizational collaboration. Two persons carried out research in this field for over 10 years, and further two – for over 5 years. Discussions within Brainstorming sessions were held, focussing on practical instances and analyses of typical collaborative situations. These sessions helped characterize relational risk. More information on the subject of relational risk was obtained through structured interviews conducted with 54 employees from 4 emergency information centres in Poland (25% of all such centres).

Empirical investigations are presented with regard to the system and process of public safety management and the scope of risk in this area. The analysis identifies the dimensions of risk in public safety management.

3.1 Results

3.1.1 Public Safety Management Process

From the holistic perspective, the process of public safety management is a decision-making cycle based on the diagnosis of potential hazards, analysis of information and resources (human and tangible), which result in the transfer of these resources. Fundamental sub-processes carried out in public safety by the management function include: forecasting, programming, analysing and supplementing of resources, systemizing, preparing, informing, responding, verifying and evaluating (Kożuch and Sienkiewicz-Małyjurek 2014a). These are shown in Fig. 5.1.

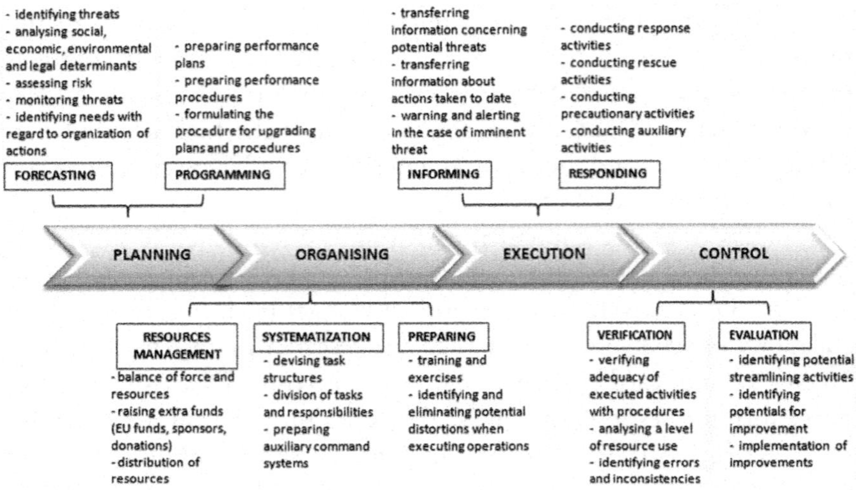

Fig. 5.1 Fundamental processes carried out in public safety by their management function (*Source*: Kożuch and Sienkiewicz-Małyjurek 2014a)

Public safety management is initiated by the identification of an occurrence, or specific hazard— social, natural and/or technical—, and the source(s) of its occurrence. At the same time, the ramifications generated by the specific hazard are analysed, and prevention and intervention measures are developed and executed. If the hazard seems almost impossible to avoid, steps are taken so as to eliminate it as quickly as possible. Meanwhile, during the inspection, activities executed are verified and evaluated with the goal of streamlining actions and ensuring readiness in the case of new incidents. However, mitigating the risk of this hazard occurring, or minimizing its consequences, are only the contractual part of the operation, they are followed up by verification and improvement of measures.

3.1.2 Dimensions of Risk in Public Safety Management Process

The objective of public safety management is to minimize the risk and combat social, technical and natural hazards. Accordingly, risk in this area is principally associated with the issues centred on the occurrence of these hazards. However, our analyses reveal that although risk management with regard to occurrence of social, technical and natural hazards is a highly important area for public safety and must be a high priority , there are many hazards of a different nature, such as organizational hazards, which affect the process of management. It is these hazards likely to occur in the course of risk management, vulnerability to these hazards and the probability of their occurrence which are significant factors, affecting all sub-processes carried out in the area researched. Primary hazards are summarized in Table 5.1.

Table 5.1 Primary hazards likely to occur in sub-processes of public safety

Function	Sub-process	Primary hazards
Planning	Forecasting	Faulty interpretation of hazards Inappropriate analyses of social, economic, environmental and legal determinants Ineffective monitoring of hazards Inappropriate identification of needs in terms of organization of actions
	Programming	Plans and procedures for actions inadequate to needs No update for plans and procedures
Organization	Analysis and replenishment of resources	Inadequate balance of forces and resources Resources possessed inadequate to needs Inappropriate distribution of resources
	Systematisation	Faulty development of task structures Faulty allocation of tasks and responsibilities
	Preparedness	No or incomplete preparedness of systems supporting the command No or only occasional trainings and exercises conducted Failure to identify and eliminate potential destruction while executing actions
Execution	Informing	No, disruptions or transfer of incomplete information about potential hazards and measures launched to date No response or delays in warning and raising the alarm in the case of imminent hazard
	Response	Response, rescue, safeguards and support measures carried out inadequately to needs Limitation to accomplishment of actions resulting from inadequate number of resources, inadequate coordination, etc.

(continued)

Table 5.1 (continued)

Function	Sub-process	Primary hazards
Control	Verification	Errors and omissions while verifying the correctness of actions performed Inappropriate identification of errors and inaccuracies
	Evaluation	No or inappropriate identification of potential improvement actions No or incomplete implementation of improvements

Source: Own study based on Kożuch and Sienkiewicz-Małyjurek (2015)

All in all, hazards emerging in the process of public safety management are problems occurring during the collaboration between numerous units with complementary competencies which operate in parallel. The operations of these organizations suffer from a risk of inappropriate analysis of external and internal forces, thereby entailing inadequate preparation of measures, which consequently adversely affects the course of these operations. Essentially, these hazards may be driven by errors, negligence, lack of imagination, awareness, knowledge and competencies or ventures incompletely executed, etc. This in turn generates risk for outcomes of activities in specific sub-processes in public safety management. Also, there may be other threats arising from the attitude to actions jointly performed only as a form of collaboration imposed by law. The interpretation of legal regulations and the manner in which operations should be executed may be problematic, making legal measures that seek to reinforce the collaboration a hindrance rather than a help. Moreover, the effectiveness of jointly accomplished actions may be diminished by pragmatism resulting from, among other thing: imbalanced dependence between organizations, non-functional control systems, or increased centralized co-ordination. Risk escalation by legal and organizational requirements may add to threats related to interpersonal, inter-group and inter-organizational relationships as well as circumstances embedded in operations. Therefore, our analysis allowed for the identification of the following types of risk dimensions in public safety management process: legal, organizational, relational, situational, and environmental.

The legal dimension has the strongest impact on the functioning of public organizations, because it establishes the framework in which public organizations have to operate. Risks in this context may come from incoherence between legal regulations and practice. Legal problems and limitations may hinder the execution of actions, thereby posing the risk of failure.

The organizational dimension constitutes the principal driving force of operations. It depends on the structure and organizational culture of specific organizations, as well as the structure underpinning the whole structure of institutions involved in public safety management. Basically, it encompasses the elements developed by the organizations themselves, based on their experience. It consists of: organizational structure, management methods, current relations, resources, personnel's competencies, trainings, leadership, decision-making, accountability of participants, communication, specialization of activities taken by specific organizations and transparency of activities. The organizational dimension also involves equipment, facilities and applied technologies that facilitate the performance of sub-processes in public safety management. These include: technical equipment, technologies used, IT and communication systems, auxiliary management systems, decision support system. The studies previously conducted with regard to organizational problems in execution of rescue activities indicate that the fundamental problems are as follows (Sienkiewicz-Małyjurek 2012b, 7):

(a) in the context of the quality of activities: deficiencies in rescue equipment, shortage of resources, forces and means, low headcount and frequent personnel exchange, lack of financial resources for extra exercises,
(b) in the context of operation duration: limited financial and equipment resources, breakdown of vehicles, hindered access to the emergency site (poor condition of road infrastructure, road congestion, territory topography), reliance on collaboration with other units,
(c) in the context of planning emergency actions and preparations if a hazard occurs: immense diversity of hazards likely to occur, insufficient financial resources, shortage of funds in order to supplement obsolete equipment, training schemes, courses, volatility and unpredictability of circumstances under which activities are carried out, manner and form of collaboration with other entities, personnel turnover and low headcount,

(d) in the context of organization and procedures for operations: rapid advancement of infrastructure, immense diversity of potential hazards likely to occur, and, by the same token, forms and methods for activities performed, personnel turnover, volatility and unpredictability of circumstances under which activities are carried out, paucity of financial resources for basic equipment and investments, inconsistency in rescue procedures in terms of fulfilment of tasks and provision of medical assistance (ambulance services and fire brigades),
(e) in the context of execution of operational, rescue and fire-fighting, evacuation and assistance activities: limited financial resources, paucity of specialist equipment outside the fire brigade units, necessity to use the equipment based on agreements concluded with business entities, personnel shortage and personnel turnover, diversity and unpredictability of hazards, diminished communication and connectivity capabilities among services that collaborate while performing activities,
(f) equipment: reduced financial potentials for the purchase of new equipment, limited funds in order to maintain an appropriate technical state of readiness (interim reviews, maintenance),
(g) operational costs: shortage of financial resources to maintain subsidiary units (funds necessary to maintain operational readiness, purchase of fire extinguishers and neutralising agents, inspection of equipment, retrofitting, uniforms, maintenance of technical facilities), high operating costs (attestation, maintenance services),
(h) control of own operations: diversity and unpredictability of hazards, which influences the specifics underlying the preparations for actions and potential controlling activities, limited time capacities.

Especially important is the relational dimension that encompasses organizational behaviours within and between organizations, formal and informal linkages between organizations and the level of collaboration between these organizations. to the relational dimension involves organizational culture, involvement of specific organizations in activities, previous experience gained by particular organizations, inter-organizational and public trust, awareness of the role performed in the given situation, expectations, goodwill, co-ordination of efforts, interdependence of activities across specific organizations, need for information sharing among organizations, need for using material resources of other organizations, and compatibility among systems used by various organizations. Problems in the relational dimension may constitute a source of risk and a reason for operational failure.

As regards the situational dimension, forces such as uncertainty, volatility and dynamics, exacerbate the level of risk arising from the mismatch between actions and needs, or from the taking of inappropriate decisions. The environmental dimension consists of the topography and qualities of the territory, buildings, transport system, population density, level of economic growth, industrial structure, unemployment level, social integration, social dysfunctional phenomena, as well as features inherent in previously experienced hazards. This dimension differs between territories, requiring a more individual approach.

It is worth taking into account the fact that the level of public safety is contingent on current economic and social processes. Economic crises, increased unemployment, ineffective social policies and climatic changes triggered by excessive exploitation of the natural environment ultimately impoverish society, diminishing standards of living, increasing levels of crime and presenting a direct threat to human life and health. Thus the situational dimension inhibits the potential for successful public safety management.

Our analysis indicated that all driving forces identified and shown above should be incorporated in the risk management process since risk in specific situations is an outcome of the impact exerted not by a single but by a multitude of factors.

3.1.3 Multidimensionality of Risk in Public Safety Management

This multidimensionality of risk is reflected in the reference literature. For example, poor response during hurricane Katrina was attributed to the paucity of appropriate planning efforts, preparation, co-ordination and collaboration as well as organizational fragmentation and poor inter-organizational communication (Waugh and Streib 2006, 136; Eikenberry et al. 2007, 164). Thus there was risk in organizational, situational and environmental terms. This risk was demonstrated in hazardous circumstances in which to operate, higher losses, and prolonged and chaotic operations (Sobel and Leeson 2006; Schneider 2005). Moreover, it is argued that secondary effects of hurricane Katrina could have been prevented by more effective risk management, including identification of capacity for accumulating hazards and appropriate organization of actions (Parker et al. 2009, 216). Likewise, in the case of the terror attacks on the World Trade Centre and the Pentagon, there was risk in organizational, situational and environmental terms. The organizational risk involved problems in co-operation, co-ordination, policy attainment, organizational fragmentation, and bureaucratic conflict (Parker and Stern 2005; Parker and Stern 2002). Whilst situational and environmental dimensions generated additional hazards in adjacent areas, risk related to inadequacy of steps taken, as well as they applied to social, economic and political consequences of attacks. Meanwhile, mass murders in schools are distinguished by organizational, legal, relational as well as situational and environmental risk (DeLisi 2002; Flannery et al. (2013). Hazards in this respect may arise from unacceptability and non-alignment of units to prevailing social and administrative systems, organizational inefficiency in operations performed by educational institutions, problems in relationships with other individuals, sudden difficulties in private life, and so on.

Our observations made during preparedness and control activities, execution of rescue activities and training reveal the multi-dimensionality underlying risk in public safety management. When observing technical rescue activities, including road accidents and removal of overturned fuel tankers carrying various kinds of cargo, it was argued that risk is concerned with:

(a) in legal terms: either excessive or insufficient regulations, inadequacy of legal regulations to the practice of operations;
(b) in organizational terms: inappropriate decisions, inadequate co-ordination of activities, faulty interpretation of information, lack of inter-organizational communication;

(c) in relational terms: experiences gained in previous inter-organizational relationships, related good will and involvement in actions;
(d) in situational terms: sudden extra hazards, maladjustment of activities to situations;
(e) in environmental terms: ability to accomplish activities and reach threatened individuals and incident sites.

Our analysis allowed for the statement that in an attempt to minimize risk, rescue activities, though requiring rapid action, should primarily be characterized by flexibility and creativity. Officers charged with command of rescue activities considered numerous strategies, took into account opinions and suggestions proposed by other organizations, and examined potential secondary effects. These efforts aimed at appropriate decisions and the best possible solution. All the rescue activities we observed were efficiently executed: hazards were resolved and a state of safety was restored in public places. Afterwards, during their debriefing, officers wondered what results could have been achieved had they made different decisions, and whether such decisions would result in more effective performance. These considerations contributed to the development of future strategies.

Units responsible for accomplishment of activities in public safety management are aware of the multi-dimensional nature of risk as an indispensable element of their work. They strive to minimize the various dimensions through training and inspections to check on operational readiness. During exercises designed to test out operational and rescue plans in an establishment that was in serious risk of industrial accidents, ways of minimizing the risk to life and health of employees, rescuers and local community were learnt. The rescue emergency action was tested and a simulated evacuation of inhabitants from threatened territories was performed. Our observations and analyses suggested that the magnitude of risk in public safety management relies on incident, vulnerability attributes and management level. Depending on the situation, all or some risk dimensions may feature. The model of risk multidimensionality is displayed in Fig. 5.2.

Our research made clear the many-faceted and multi-level nature of public safety management. For each case there are many possible lines of

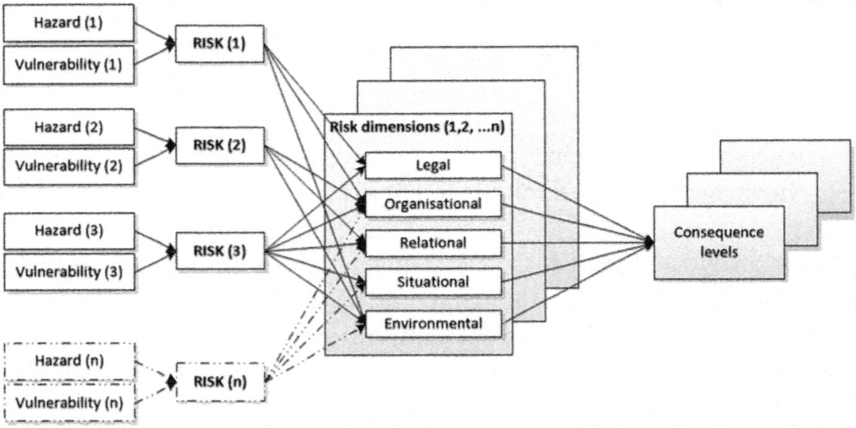

Fig. 5.2 Risk multidimensionality (*Source:* Own research)

action, and even the selection of the optimal solution does not guarantee success since further disruption may occur and hazards accumulate when following this optimal solution. Therefore, it is advisable to identify and interpret risk in the light of numerous dimensions on a continual basis, so as to mitigate potential, adverse repercussions of hazards.

Moreover, public safety management constitutes a complex structure of units, subgroups and modules, configured differently for each situation depending on needs (Kożuch and Sienkiewicz-Małyjurek 2014b). Thus, the fulfilment of activities in public safety management rests on collaboration which entails relational risk.

3.1.4 Relational Risk as the Main Factor of Effective Public Safety Management

In our inquiries on relational risk it was assumed that lack of conditions fostering effective inter-organizational collaboration in public safety management generates the risk of failure in any measures taken. This assumption is based on the fact that inter-organizational collaboration in this field stems from the complexity of contemporary hazards and the need for complementary of action by specific organizations. In public safety management, effective inter-organizational collaboration may achieve the following constructive results(Sienkiewicz-Małyjurek 2012a, 53):

(a) in the area of relations: transfer of information and knowledge, reduced risk of opportunistic behaviours, enhanced trust and partner relationships between network participants, improvement of learning processes,
(b) in the area of fulfilment of operations: reduced costs, mitigated risk of failure, bolstered efficiency and flexibility of operations, raising and more effective transfer of resources, quicker mobilization due to increased co-ordination of activities, limited competitors' access, diminished uncertainty by adaptation to turbulent environment,
(c) in the area of development: innovations, creation of knowledge, reinforced synergy effect, complementarity, increased value, improved collaboration processes.

Our continued inquiries draw on conclusions drawn from our systematic literature review, which identified drivers facilitating more effective inter-organizational collaboration. This was achieved through brainstorming based on actual incidents and analysis of typical collaboration situations. From such constructive discussions, we were able to construct a typology of factors that boost the effectiveness of inter-organizational collaboration in public management and their relative importance. Relational factors formed one of the groups, and the significance of specific factors in this group was evaluated using a three-level scale: 1 weak influence, 2 medium influence, 3 strong influence. Our findings are given in Table 5.2.

The factors summarized in Table 5.2 may constitute a trigger risk for disruptions in jointly executed actions. The existence of the negative factors listed in the said table leads to relaxed relations, disruptions in communication and thus problems in co-ordination of activities between numerous independent organizations. Thus relational risk is generated, encompassing probability and consequences resulting from unsatisfactory collaboration (Das and Teng 1996). The reference literature claims that the central reason for relational risk is opportunism in behaviour displayed by specific entities and related losses (Nooteboom et al. 1997,

Table 5.2 Impact of relational factors on relational risk

Influence on collaboration	Relational factors	Ability to create relational risk		
		Low	Medium	High
Strong	Specialization of collaborating organizations		+	
	Interdependence of the particular organizations			+
	Close links between organizations	+		
	Time of inter-organizational collaboration (time limits, cycles of collaboration)		+	
	Conflicts between organizations			+
	Uncertainty conditions of collaborative work			+
	Expectations of collaborating organizations			+
	Roles of particular organizations in collaboration (leader, co-ordination, assistance etc.)		+	
	Demands of collaborative tasks and their fulfilment	+		
Medium	Joint decision made by organizations	+		
	Constraints to inter-organizational collaboration			+
	Iteration of inter-organizational collaboration	+		
	Ability to compromise between organizations		+	
Weak	Shared mission, vision and goals	+		
	Equitable contributions to collaboration of each willing organizations	+		
	Balance between dependence and autonomy	+		
	Performance of inter-organizational collaboration	+		
	Support within collaborating organizations	+		
	Interest in collaboration in fellow partners		+	
	Management of inter-organizational collaboration (styles, transparency of decisions and guidance e.g.)			+
	Self-interest of individual organizations from collaboration			+
	Inclusiveness to collaboration of needed organizations	+		

Source: Own research

316). This opportunism arises from multiple internal and external conditions, including, among others: organizational cultures, trust, previous experience, prevailing procedures for operations.

Our analysis showed that the impact of relational factors on efficiency of inter-organizational collaboration does not automatically generate risk. Driving forces that weakly impact upon collaboration are marginally a source of relational risk. And the opposite applies. It was acknowledged that most of the strong factors are capable of creating relational risk. These factors include: interdependence of the particular organizations, conflicts between organizations, uncertainty in collaborative work, expectations of collaborating organizations.

Our research carried out in Emergency Information Centres in Poland during 2014 seeking to assess the significance of selected factors influencing the effectiveness of collaborative action in public safety management, enabled us to measure the implication of these forces for the occurrence of risk. Our findings, deploying a 5-level grading scale (1 = irrelevant; 5 = very important) are presented in Fig. 5.3.

As noted in our comments on Table 5 2, views on collaboration cannot be automatically ascribed to risk. The focus must be mainly on relational factors, including the sharing of information between organizations, commitment to shared activity, inter-organizational trust or interdependence of activities. Forces with the least impact on effectiveness of collaborative action in public safety management included: expectations towards other organizations, risk of failed activities, the need to tap resources of other organizations and government policy.

In-depth analysis revealed that each organization concentrates on fulfilling its statutory tasks (i.e. its portion of the joint venture) in compliance with applicable procedures, hoping that other organizations are similarly engaged. It should be underlined that in public safety management joint activities are the effect of specialization mastered by individual organizations, and it is commonly assumed that activities carried out by these organizations will complement rather than duplicate one another. It is generally believed that once mutual respect, good will, trust exist, relational risk will be minimized.

However, in practice these assumptions do not yield the expected results. The scope and structure of inter-organizational collaboration in public safety management make the process challenging, dynamic and

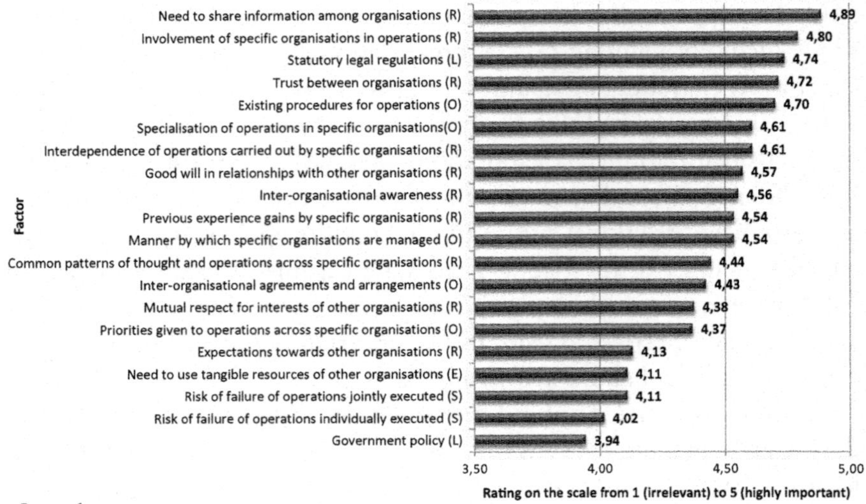

Legend:
L - legal dimension
O- organisational dimension
R - relational dimension
S- situational dimension
E - environmental dimension

Fig. 5.3 Assessment of the significance of factors that influence effectiveness of activities accomplished within collaboration in public safety management (*L* legal dimension, *O* organisational dimension, *R* relational dimension, *S* situational dimension, *E* environmental dimension. *Source:* Own description based on the analysis conducted in 2014)

complex. Interestingly, it is characterized by the organizational structure that is specific to the situation and rests on structures of particular organizations. Overall, representative of various organizations in appropriate number and configuration tailored to current circumstances and needs participate in the process. Progress is impacted by a host of factors related to the organization of initiatives, behaviours displayed by individuals in organizations, current environmental settings, and so on. This provides support to the research findings of Hélène Delerue, confirming that relational risk is multi-dimensional in its nature (Delerue 2004, 547). Multidimensionality intrinsic to relational risk in public safety management follows from its complexity as exhibited in the following characteristics (Kożuch and Sienkiewicz-Małyjurek 2014b, 475):

(a) Large number of components: the activities are performed by organizations from different sectors, which are complex systems themselves [....].
(b) Variation: a considerable quantity of resources in varying amounts and configurations is dispatched towards the activities—in every case differently, depending on the needs.
(c) Self-organization: system components are subject to continuous, spontaneous organizing. The structures are formed under the influence of relations between elements of the system and between the system and its surroundings.
(d) Diversity: the system is aimed at preventing and combating social, natural and technical risks. The scale and nature of the hazards are the basis of the diversity of the actions taken.
(e) Dynamism and liveliness: every event, even of the same type, is different [...].
(f) Adaptation to their environment: conditions for the implementation of activities create a need for an individual approach to each hazard, adequate to the emerging needs and requirements of the situation [...].
(g) Interactions: the units of a public safety system operate within the framework of cross-organizational collaboration built on the basis of formal and informal relationships.
(h) Non-linearity: It is never known what the outcome of actions will be, and the measures implemented are not directly proportional to the achieved results.
(i) Selection: in any case, there are many ways and strategies to perform actions [. . .].

From the perspective of complex system theory, the public safety management constitutes a complex structure of units, subgroups and modules, configured differently for each situation, depending on needs. The accompanying dynamics behind shifts in current settings give rise to relational problems. Hence, relational risk may be regarded as the main factor facilitating the effective public safety management, thereby demonstrating the specificity of risk management in this sector. In an attempt to maintain it at an acceptable level it is required to continually cultivate adequate conditions for the risk identification and its mitigation.

3.2 Discussion

The reference literature has highlighted the need for further research to give insight into risk issues in safety management across the public sector (Olsen et al. 2007). Attention is drawn to the myriad of risk factors, the interaction between them and the prevalence of a preventive approach over strategies used to respond to hazard (Tàbara et al. 2003; Strully and Conley 2004; Price and MacNicoll 2015). This paper attempts to bridge this research gap.

Our studies led to the identification of fundamental hazards likely to occur in sub-processes of public safety. It was recognized that this risk originates not only from environmental hazards, which have received considerable attention from literature devoted to safety in public sector and emergency management, but from other significant factors. Our discussions enabled the compilation of a typology of risk dimensions in public safety management containing legal, organizational, relational, situational and environmental dimensions. Generally our findings reflect those of studies carried out in Sweden, whereby risk in safety management at the local governmental level (Johansson et al. 2009, 683): identifies such factors as health and environment, traffic and transport, fires and extraordinary events, water, sewage and technical infrastructure, social problems, home and leisure, suicide. These factors include environmental hazards, but they also place an emphasis on the relevance of social aspects in safety management. Gudela Grote stresses that general organizational characteristics should be considered in safety management in high-risk domains. According to her research findings with regard to uncertainty management (Grote 2012, 1986), it is necessary to take into consideration such organizational features as: tasks and work processes (e.g., task complexity, types of task interdependencies); people (e.g., formal qualification, demographic and psychological diversity, tenure); organization structure (e.g., distribution of decision authority, specialization); technology (e.g., degree of automation, technical coupling of work processes); and external relationships (e.g., unionization, supply chain dependencies, outsourcing). The urgency of a broader approach to the issues of risk in safety management across the public sector is also seen by Joop T.V.M. De Jong, who argues that it is essential to understand the association between risk and protective factors (De Jong 2010). In the same way, Jens Rasmussen claims that risk management should be subject to interdisciplinary research, encompassing all possible correlations between social groups and hazard categories (Rasmussen 1997, 183).

Taken together, the risk dimensions identified during our research also underscore the significance of vulnerability in public safety management, which corroborates the results of studies presented in the reference literature (Lei et al. 2014; Jacobs 2005; Correia et al. 2014).Our analysis provided grounds for the statement that one hazardous incident comprises risk dimensions of diverse character. Clearly, such a situation calls for all-encompassing variety in approach to the task of public safety management.

Equally important, this paper typified the relational risk. It was stated that risk analysis should be carried out by all entities involved in activities relating not only to individual actions, but also to ventures jointly fulfilled. This helps to rein in the relational risk due to elimination of potential hazards and previous clarification of inaccuracies in inter-organizational collaboration. Thus, there is an increased solidarity, trust and goodwill in activities jointly performed (Liu et al. 2008). This leads to the conclusion that activities jointly performed in public safety management require constant supervision and cultivation. While our paper advances the research concept, with its typology of risk dimensions in public safety management, it also characterizes relational risk in this area. This investigation was essentially exploratory, as our field work could cover only one region of Poland. The scale of impact of specific risk dimensions on the process of public safety needs to be examined as do relations between the risk dimensions identified. Notwithstanding these limitations, the typology compiled has significantly improved understanding of key determinants underlying risk in public safety management, addressing the gap in theoretical and practical knowledge on the topic.

4 Conclusion

In summary, risk in public safety management is perceived as a negative phenomenon, which has an adverse impact on the attainment of targets set by institutions involved in this management. In this area of research, it is impossible to predict when, where and with what intensity a hazard occurs and exactly what its effects will be.

From the holistic perspective, risk is a function of physical damage and impact factor. These factors are predominantly dependent on the vulnerability of exposed elements, the hazards in respect to their potential intensity, as well as incidents occurring at a definite time. They are also determined by social fragilities and disruptions in the management of actions performed by collaborating organizations. Thus appropriate recognition and interpretation of dimensions of risk in public safety management has implications for prevention and rescue measures and for influencing the aftermath of incidents. There is a need to eventually integrate all potential disruptions, extra hazards and their accumulation and escalation into the way we actively deal with risk.

Bibliography

Adger, W. N. (2006). Vulnerability. *Global Environmental Change, 16*(3), 268–281.

Alexander, D. (2006). Trends, problems and dilemmas. *Journal of International Affairs, 59*(2), 1–22.

Al-Khudhairy, D., Axhausen, K., Bishop, S., Herrmann, H., Hu, B., Kröger, W., et al. (2012). Towards integrative risk management and more resilient societies. *The European Physical Journal Special Topics, 214*, 571–595.

Berlin, J. M., & Carlström, E. D. (2011). Why is collaboration minimised at the accident scene?: A critical study of a hidden phenomenon. *Disaster Prevention and Management, 20*(2), 159–171.

Birkmann, J. (2013). Measuring vulnerability to promote disaster-resilient societies and to enhance adaptation: Conceptual frameworks and definitions. In J. Birkmann (ed.), Measuring vulnerability to natural hazards: Towards disaster resilient societies. Tokyo: United Nations University Press.

Correia, W. F. M., Da Silva, S. X., Campos, F. F. C., Barros, M. L. N., & Soares, M. M. (2014). Design as a tool for managing risks and vulnerabilities regarding artifacts of public safety. In A. Marcus (Ed.), *Design, user experience, and usability. Theories, methods, and tools for designing the user experience, Lecture Notes in Computer Science* (Vol. 8517). Cham, Heidelberg, New York, Dordrecht, London: Springer International Publishing.

Das, T. K., & Teng, B. S. (1996). Risk types and inter-firm alliance structures. *Journal of Management Studies, 33*, 827–843.

De Jong, J. T. V. M. (2010). A public health framework to translate risk factors related to political violence and war into multi-level preventive interventions. *Social Science and Medicine, 70*(1), 71–79.

Delerue, H. (2004). Relational risks perception in European biotechnology alliances: The effect of contextual factors. *European Management Journal, 22*(5), 546–556.

DeLisi, M. (2002). The Columbine High School massacre and criminal justice system response: An exploratory case study. *Social Science Journal, 39*(1), 19–29.

Demichela, M., Piccinini, N., & Romano, A. (2004). Risk analysis as a basis for safety management system. *Journal of Loss Prevention in the Process Industries, 17*, 467–475.

Disaster Risk and Resilience (2012). Thematic think piece. UNISDR, WMO, http://www.un.org/en/development/desa/policy/untaskteam_undf/thinkpieces/3_disaster_risk_resilience.pdf. Accessed 12 June 2015.

Dohn, K., & Gumiński, A. (2013). Wykorzystanie Systemu Zarządzania Obiektami Wiedzy do wspomagania zarządzania ryzykiem w przedsiębiorstwie przemysłu budowy maszyn [Using management system of knowledge objects to support risk management in enterprise of machine-building industry]. *Journal of Management and Finance, 11*(4), t. 3.

Dohn, K., Gumiński, A., Matusek, M., & Zoleński, W. (2013). *Model wspomagania zarządzania w zakresie zarządzania wiedzą w polskich przedsiębiorstwach budowy maszyn* [*Model of management support of knowledge management in Polish enterprises of machine building*]. Warsaw: Difin.

Eikenberry, A. M., Arroyave, V., & Cooper, T. (2007). Administrative failure and the international NGO response to Hurricane Katrina. *Public Administration Review, 67*, 160–170.

Flannery, D. J., Modzeleski, W., & Kretschmar, J. M. (2013). Violence and school shootings. *Current Psychiatry Reports, 15*(1), 331–338.

Grote, G. (2012). Safety management in different high-risk domains – All the same? *Safety Science, 50*(10), 1983–1992.
Industrial Development Report (2011). Industrial energy efficiency for sustainable wealth creation, United Nations Industrial Development Organization. http://www.unido.org/fileadmin/user_media/Publications/IDR/2011/UNIDO_FULL_REPORT_EBOOK.pdf. Accessed 2 June 2015.
Jacobs, B. D. (2005). Urban vulnerability: Public management in a changing world. *Journal of Contingencies and Crisis Management, 13*(2), 39–43.
Jajuga, K. (2007). Teoretyczne podstawy zarządzania ryzykiem [Theoretical basis of risk management]. In K. Jajuga (Ed.), *Zarządzanie Ryzykiem [Risk management]*. Warsaw: PWN.
Johansson, A., Denk, T., & Svedung, I. (2009). The typology for allocations of societal risk and safety management tasks at the local governmental level – Framing the current directions in Sweden. *Safety Science, 47*(5), 680–685.
Jonek-Kowalska, I. (2010). Proces identyfikacji ryzyka operacyjnego w teorii i praktyce zarządzania przedsiębiorstwem [Identifying of operational risk in theory and practice of management]. *Zeszyty Naukowe Uniwersytetu Ekonomicznego w Poznaniu*, 142.
Jonek-Kowalska, I. (2014). Risk management in the hard coal mining industry: Social and environmental aspects of collieries' liquidation. *Resources Policy, 41*, 124–134.
Kaiser, F.M. (2011) Interagency collaborative arrangements and activities: Types, rationales, considerations, *Congressional Research Service* 7–5700, R41803.
Kapucu, N., Arslan, T., & Demiroz, F. (2010). Collaborative emergency management and national emergency management network. *Disaster Prevention and Management, 19*(4), 452–468.
Kosowski, B. (2006). *Prognozowanie działań na wypadek zaistnienia sytuacji kryzysowych [Forecasting actions in case of a crisis situations]*. Cracow: Szkoła Aspirantów Państwowej Szkoły Pożarnej.
Kożuch, B. (2011). *Skuteczne współdziałanie organizacji publicznych i pozarządowych [Effective collaboration between public and non-governmental organizations]*. Cracow: Instytut Spraw Publicznych Uniwersytetu Jagiellońskiego.
Kożuch, B., & Sienkiewicz-Małyjurek, K. (2014a, November). Collaborative performance in public safety management process, International Scientific Conference Lumen 2014, Transdisciplinarity and Communicative Action.
Kożuch, B., & Sienkiewicz-Małyjurek, K. (2014b). New requirements for managers of public safety systems. *Procedia – Social and Behavioral Sciences, 149*, 472–478.

Kożuch B., & Sienkiewicz-Małyjurek K. (2015). Mapowanie procesów współpracy międzyorganizacyjnej na przykładzie działań realizowanych w bezpieczeństwie publicznym [Mapping of inter-organisatonal collaboration processes on the example of the activities carried out in public safety]. *Zarządzanie Publiczne, 3*(31), 237–253.

Lank, E. (2007). *Collaborative advantage*. New York: Palgrave Macmillan.

Lei, Y., Wang, J., Yue, Y., Zhou, H., & Yin, W. (2014). Rethinking the relationships of vulnerability, resilience, and adaptation from a disaster risk perspective. *Natural Hazards, 70*, 609–627.

Liu, Y., Li, Y., Tao, L., & Wang, Y. (2008). Relationship stability, trust and relational risk in marketing channels: Evidence from China. *Industrial Marketing Management, 37*(4), 432–446.

Mansor, S., Abu Shariah, M., Billa, L., Setiawan, I., & Jabar, F. (2004). Spatial technology for natural risk management. *Disaster Prevention and Management, 13*(5), 364–373.

Mattessich, P. W., Murray-Close, M., & Monsey, B. R. (2001). *Collaboration: What makes it work*. Saint Paul: Amherst H Wilder Foundation.

McEntire, D. (2011). Understanding and reducing vulnerability: From the approach of liabilities and capabilities. *Disaster Prevention and Management, 20*(3), 298–313.

Nooteboom, B., Berger, H., & Noorderhaven, N. G. (1997). Effects of trust and governance on relational risk. *Academy Management Journal, 40*(2), 308–338.

O'Leary, R., & Vij, N. (2012). Collaborative public management: Where have we been and where are we going? *The American Review of Public Administration, 42*(5), 507–522.

Olsen, O. E., Kruke, B. I., & Hovden, J. (2007). Societal safety: Concept, borders and dilemmas. *Journal of Contingencies and Crisis Management, 15*(2), 69–79.

Palliyaguru, R., Amaratunga, D., & Baldry, D. (2014). Constructing a holistic approach to disaster risk reduction: The significance of focusing on vulnerability reduction. *Disasters, 38*(1), 45–61.

Parker, C. F., & Stern, E. K. (2002). Blindsided? September 11 and the origins of strategic surprise. *Political Psychology, 23*, 601–630.

Parker, C. F., & Stern, E. K. (2005). Bolt from the blue or avoidable failure? Revisiting September 11 and the origins of strategic surprise. *Foreign Policy Analysis, 1*, 301–331.

Parker, C. F., Stern, E. K., Paglia, E., & Brown, C. (2009). Preventable catastrophe? The Hurricane Katrina disaster revisited. *Journal of Contingencies and Crisis Management, 17*, 206–220.

Payan, J. M. (2007). A review and delineation of cooperation and coordination in marketing channels. *European Business Review, 19*(3), 216–233.

Pomarańczowa Księga. (2004). Zarządzanie ryzykiem – zasady i koncepcje [Orange Book. Risk management – Principles and concepts], Ministerstwo Skarbu Jej Królewskiej Mości, Crown, Colegate 2004.

Price, B., & MacNicoll, M. (2015). Multiple interacting risk factors: On methods for allocating risk factor interactions. *Risk Analysis, 35*, 931–940.

Rasmussen, J. (1997). Risk management in a dynamic society: A modeling problem. *Safety Science, 27*(2–3), 183–213.

Reiman, T., & Pietikäinen, E. (2012). Leading indicators of system safety – Monitoring and driving the organizational safety potential. *Safety Science, 50*, 1993–2000.

Rothstein, H., Borraz, O., & Huber, M. (2013). Risk and the limits of governance: Exploring varied patterns of risk-based governance across Europe. *Regulation & Governance, 7*(2), 215–235.

Schneider, S. K. (2005). Administrative breakdowns in the governmental response to Hurricane Katrina. *Public Administration Review, 65*, 515–516.

Sienkiewicz-Małyjurek, K. (2010). Rola samorządów lokalnych w kształtowaniu bezpieczeństwa publicznego [The role of local self-governments in shaping public safety]. *Samorząd Terytorialny, 7/8*, 123–139.

Sienkiewicz-Małyjurek, K. (2012a). Sieciowe ujęcie współpracy międzyorganizacyjnej w zarządzaniu kryzysowym [A network approach to interorganisational collaboration in emergency management]. *Współczesne Zarządzanie, 3*, 51–60.

Sienkiewicz-Małyjurek K. (2012b). Uwarunkowania i bariery w logistycznym wymiarze zarządzania kryzysowego [Determinants and barriers in the logistics dimension of crisis management]. *Logistyka, 6*, 5–8.

Sienkiewicz-Małyjurek, K., & Kożuch, B. (2015). System zarządzania bezpieczeństwem publicznym w ujęciu teorii złożoności. Opracowanie modelowe [System of public safety management in context of complexity system theory. *Development model], Bezpieczeństwo i Technika Pożarnicza, 37*(1), 33–43.

Sobel, R. S., & Leeson, P. T. (2006). Government's response to Hurricane Katrina: A public choice analysis. *Public Choice, 127*(12), 55–73.

Statistical data of KG PSP generated in the system SWD-ST (v. 1.24.9.0) as of 08.06.2011. http://www.kgpsp.gov.pl. Accessed 9 June 2015.

Strategia rozwoju województwa śląskiego. (2010). „Śląskie 2020." [Development strategy for the Silesian Province „Śląskie 2020"], Katowice, February 2010.

Strömgren, M., & Andersson, R. (2010). The usage of safety management tools in Swedish municipalities. *Safety Science, 48*(3), 288–295.

Strully, K. W., & Conley, D. (2004). Reconsidering risk: Adapting public policies to intergenerational determinants and biosocial interactions in health-related needs. *Journal of Health Politics Policy and Law, 29*(6), 1073–1107.

Tàbara, D., Saurí, D., & Cerdan, R. (2003). Forest fire risk management and public participation in changing socioenvironmental conditions: A case study in a mediterranean region. *Risk Analysis, 23*, 249–260.

Tarczyński, W., & Mojsiewicz, M. (2001). *'Zarządzanie ryzykiem: podstawowe zagadnienia' [Risk management: basic issues]*. Warsaw: PWE.

Tomasino, A. P. (2011). Public safety networks as a type of complex adaptive system. In H. Sayama, A. Minai, D. Braha, & Y. Bar-Yam (Eds.), *Unifying themes in complex systems, Proceedings of the Eighth International Conference on complex systems*. New England: Knowledge Press.

Turner, B. L., Kasperson, R. E., Matson, P. A., McCarthy, J. J., Corell, R. W., Christensen, L., et al. (2003). A framework for vulnerability analysis in sustainability science. *Proceedings of the National Academy of Sciences of the United States of America, 100*(14), 8074–8079.

UNISDR [The United Nations Office for Disaster Risk Reduction]. (2004). Living with risk. A global review of disaster reduction initiatives, Geneva, United Nations. http://www.unisdr.org/files/657_lwr21.pdf. Accessed 15 June 2015.

Wang, J.-J. (2012). Integrated model combined land-use planning and disaster management: The structure, context and contents. *Disaster Prevention and Management: An International Journal, 21*(1), 4–25.

Waugh, W. L., & Streib, G. (2006). Collaboration and leadership for effective emergency management. *Public Administration Review, 66*, 131–140.

Williams, R., Bertsch, B., Dale, B., van der Wiele, T., van Iwaarden, J., Smith, M., et al. (2006). Quality and risk management: What are the key issues? *The TQM Magazine, 18*(1), 13–29.

Williams, C. B., Dias, M., Fedorowicz, J., Jacobson, D., Vilvovsky, S., Sawyer, S., et al. (2009). The formation of inter-organizational information sharing networks in public safety: Cartographic insights on rational choice and institutional explanations. *Information Polity: The International Journal of Government & Democracy in the Information Age, 14*(1/2), 13–29.

Woo, D. M., & Vicente, K. J. (2003). Sociotechnical systems, risk management, and public health: Comparing the North Battleford and Walkerton outbreaks. *Reliability Engineering & System Safety, 80*(3), 253–269.

Woods, M. (2009). A contingency theory perspective on the risk management control system within Birmingham city council. *Management Accounting Research, 20*, 69–81.

6

Early Warning Concept in Identifying Risks in Business Activity

Katarzyna Dohn, Wojciech Zoleński, and Adam Gumiński

1 Introduction

Contemporary enterprises operate under conditions characterized by high complexity and very variable dynamics of changes (Brzóska 2014). In addition to foreseeable processes, surprises may also occur. Enterprise management means taking into account, analysing and interpreting, a lot of information. Information about a possible substantial loss, such as bankruptcy, liquidation of a large part of an enterprise, or a long-term, structural crisis, is particularly significant, and such phenomena are relatively common in business activity. Information about risks can serve as a warning if it has been obtained early enough and if there are possibilities to take preventive actions. Preventing irreparable, often sudden, destructive processes that can be initiated by a small stimulus is the essence of prevention. In such cases, preventive actions result in high economic

K. Dohn (✉) • W. Zoleński • A. Gumiński
Silesian University of Technology, Gliwice, Poland

K. Raczkowski (ed.), *Risk Management in Public Administration*,
DOI 10.1007/978-3-319-30877-7_6

effectiveness, which is not the case with every reaction to problems of this sort. Therefore, in early warning (EW), research information about low-level certainty may be useful.

EW constitutes a special and crucial way to identify risk. The value of EW information results mostly from its acquisition well in advance—the same information delivered later would be of little or no value. The identification of risks, in which promptness is vital and other factors are less important, is the essence of EW. Since all events and processes happen in time (even if they are not highly dependent on time), it is difficult to make a distinction between EW and the actual identification of risks. Nevertheless, three important scenarios, which virtually go beyond the concept of EW, can be distinguished:

(a) risks posed by actions taken at the initiative of an enterprise;
(b) risks for which benefits from rapid prevention do not compensate for the costs of acquiring the necessary information;
(c) risks associated with a low degree of information accuracy and reliability.

Studies were carried out in several enterprises located in the district of Silesia in Poland aimed at identifying the processes of the acquiring and processing information about possible endogenous and background risks for those companies, resulting in the following diagnosis:

(a) The identification of risks requires different kinds of information, including both qualitative and quantitative information, as well as realistic research and explanatory/interpretative information.
(b) The acquisition of warning information requires different methods, including:

  - methods for monitoring processes
  - index methods
  - extrapolative and non-extrapolative methods of strategic analysis
  - simulation studies of cause-and-effect models
  - heuristic methods
  - expert methods

(Despite the fact that these methods are not universal, each can be applied under specific conditions and in a specific scope.)

(c) There are various needs for EW information in enterprises. They depend on the specificity of an enterprise, and they also vary over time.
(d) The most frequent reason for limited implication of EW methods is the lack of systematised knowledge about risk identification.
(e) The successful application of EW methods will be hampered if there are no standardised procedures for efficiently gathering and processing a range of information.

The EW concept should become increasingly important in the widespread use of risk management in business activity. The higher the volatility of external and internal conditions of business activity, the higher the importance of both risk identification and quantification, as well as the importance of appropriate measures that counteract their negative effects.

This paper focuses on the analysis of potential use of EW concepts in the identification of risk factors in manufacturing, particularly in machine-building enterprises, which were the subject of research within the R&D project carried out over 2010–2013. In addition, this paper presents EW methods and tools, together with IT solutions that could support decision-making processes in strategic and operational risk management for the companies in this study.

1.1 Risks in Business Activity

Information, risks, risk management and other terms connected with business process management are often discussed since risks affect all daily activities conducted in connection with ensuring business processes (Černá 2012, 375–382).

Risk is an ambiguous and complex phenomenon, which is why in the literature there are numerous discussions and attempts to define risk itself. It may therefore be concluded that there are several perspectives to define the concept of risk (Aven 2008; Aven and Renn 2009; 12:1–11; Kożuch and Sienkiewicz-Małyjurek 2013, 316):

(a) defining risk in terms of probability of loss related to a particular economic decision that has been made (e.g. SO/IEC 2013, 3); (Moschandreas and Karuchit 2005, 168);
(b) defining risk as a hazard of potential failure in achieving objectives pursued while making a particular decision;
(c) defining risk as a negative deviation of achieved target value from a previously planned level;
(d) defining risk in terms of a threat of failure in achieving objectives.

Figure 6.1 shows different meaning of risk definition. Contemporary enterprises are exposed to various types of risk. Depending on the field of a given enterprise, some risks may occur more commonly than others. Buehler and Pritsch (Buehler and Pritsch 2003) recognise four basic categories of risk: operational risk, market risk, business-volume risk and credit risk. Operational risk, in accordance with Basel Committee of Banking Supervision (Basel Committee of Banking Supervision 2004), is defined as the risk of loss resulting from inadequate or failed internal processes, people or systems, or from external events. This definition includes legal risk, but excludes strategic and reputational risk. Market risk is related to changes in market prices, such as stock prices, exchange rates, interest rates and raw material prices. A way of reducing this risk is by hedging with the use of futures or options.

Business-volume risk is associated with the change in demand for products, caused by the change in customers' purchasing power, or the threat from new competition or new products on the market. The ability of a company to anticipate changes in product life cycle or in any other event is important here. In a free-market economy, credit risk is of great significance. It refers to potential financial liquidity problems for lenders and borrowers.

Banks and insurance companies are making efforts to categorise clients and identify risky or uneconomical clients. (Forland and Upadhyay 2011, 24).

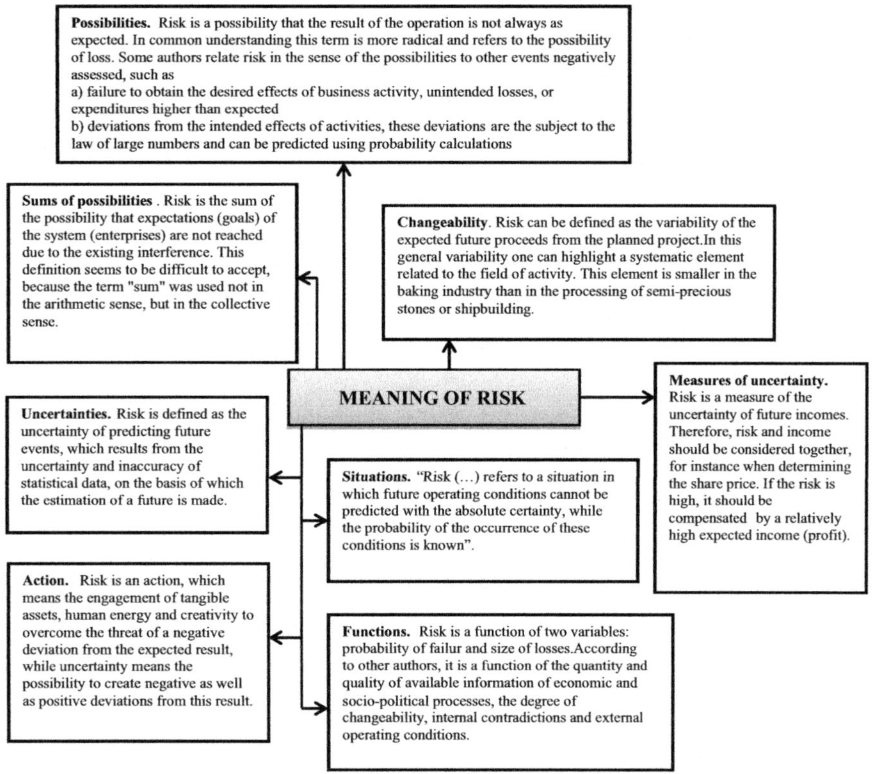

Fig. 6.1 Different meaning of risk definition (*Source*: Own study based on Kubińska-Kaleta 2008, 11)

From the point of view of the research subject it is important to identify risks in manufacturing enterprises. According to the literature (Kaczmarek 2006, 257), the source of risk for manufacturers is to be found in, among other things, lack of knowledge concerning the future state of an environment within which a given enterprise will operate. In the activity of manufacturing enterprises one can distinguish:

(a) operational risk—in time and scale which is difficult to predict, it is random, sudden, unexpected and irregular and usually related to production and distribution processes.
(b) risk to the whole enterprise (difficult to qualify)—generated by the enterprise environment, most likely the macro-environment. It may involve the poor condition of the economy, developments in rival techniques and technology, increased competition, and the possibility of losing important sales markets.

Taking into account different kinds of risk presented in this paper, three groups can be identified within a manufacturing company: production risk, logistics risk and research and development risk (due to the research project entitled: "Computer system supporting management in the area of knowledge management in machine building industry enterprise", realised in the years 2010–2013). Differentiating the probability of risk occurrence and the size of the potential hazards is particularly important for business activity. Strategic risk is maintained over a long period of time, and the scale and scope of its effects are relatively large. This is due to decisions taken at the strategic level of the enterprise (e.g. long-term investment plans and production programmes). Operational risk (Gleissner and Meier 2000, 87) refers to a shorter period of time and may relate to current disruptions of production processes that are difficult to predict, but are also of little significance.

It may therefore be concluded that, the higher an enterprise's vulnerability to macro-economic factors, the lower the possibility of influencing its active shaping and, as a result, its activity is characterised by a higher level of risk. An important reason for risk is the uncertainty of models used to determine business activity (a large number of parameters, their heterogeneity, of multistate parameters and random of changes).

Unfortunately, one may observe how ongoing changes limit the possibilities to qualify the scale, scope and assessment of effects. Hence, an objective evaluation of operations is difficult and, what is more, errors in the acquisition, sending and processing of information may occur (Gumiński 2013).

In managing enterprises of any type, particularly in manufacturing, it is necessary to consider the risk aspect, which in consequence obliges decision-makers to foresee various future scenarios and define the scope and scale of ongoing changes and their influence on business activity, including in particular the identification of actions that would reduce undesired effects. Thus, in recent years risk management has been defined as a crucial process for determining the growth potential of an enterprise (see more in Gordon et al. 2009, 301–327). Managing risk is a fundamental concern in today's dynamic global environment. In recent years, however, a paradigm shift has occurred regarding the way to view risk management. Instead of looking at risk management from a silo-based perspective, the trend is to take a holistic view of risk management. This holistic approach toward managing an organization's risk is commonly referred to as enterprise risk management (ERM) (Gordon et al. 2009, 301–327).

According to the literature (e.g., Barton et al. 2002; Lam 2003; Stulz 1996, 2003; COSO 2004; Nocco and Stulz 2006; Hoyt and Liebenberg 2009), the implementation ERM undoubtedly contributes to improving the functioning of modern enterprises. ERM may constitute a new concept of the management of portfolio risk, which poses a serious problem for enterprises. Furthermore, it may prove a source of competitive advantage for enterprises that show a strong capacity and discipline while implementing this concept. This concept is not completely unambiguous as in various studies it adopts slightly different, sometimes quite distinct, forms and contents. The essence of this method is an organized process of planning, organizing, leading, and controlling business activity to minimize the influence of risk on the entity's results. The Committee of Sponsoring Organizations of the Treadway Commission (COSO 2004) provided a model framework for enterprise risk management (ERM). That framework defines ERM as a process, effected by an entity's board of directors, management and other personnel, applied in strategy-setting and across the enterprise, designed to: identify potential events that may affect the entity; manage risk so that it is within its risk appetite; provide reasonable assurance regarding the achievement of entity objectives (COSO 2004).

Many organisations are implementing ERM processes to increase the effectiveness of their risk management activities, with the ultimate goal of increasing stakeholder value (Beasley et al. 2005 521–531). According to M. Power (Power 2009, 849–855), ERM is closely associated with the concept of integrated risk management at the firm level, an integration which promises more efficient use of scarce capital, the ability to charge business units according to the amount of capital they place at risk, and more coherent insurance strategies which recognize the natural diversification benefits at work in any large organization. Secondly, ERM also embodies an aspiration for enterprising risk management, namely a concept of risk management which is positive, entrepreneurial and explicitly in the service of wealth creation: 'risks are no longer the dark side of opportunities, they are also market opportunities' (Beck 1992, 46). From this it is easy to articulate a win–win logic of ERM; good risk management is good business.

ERM has become a necessity and it must be involved in the process of controlling and minimizing threats in order to achieve sustainable productivity, profitability and operation success. Both uncertainty and risk limit the discretionary powers and accuracy of choices, which is why they become the source of loss in an enterprise. Reduction of these factors aims at complex minimization of their influence on a decision-making process.

1.2 Identification of Risks as a Key Element of Decision-Making Processes in Business Activity

Managerial decisions which refer to actions determining the future of an enterprise are frequently taken when information is limited. As a result, despite a high level of competence demonstrated by decision-makers, serious disturbances may often occur in business activity. Information resources, often characterised by incompleteness and inconsistency, comprise a key element in preparatory processes for making a specific decision. The identification and quantification of risk factors introduce essential knowledge into the decision-making process. This knowledge helps to avoid or reduce decisions which could have serious consequences for the business. EW, throughout risk identification, has an impact on the quality of decisions, and it may reduce decision-making errors.

Manufacturing enterprises are particularly exposed to risks arising from both changes in the environment as well as responses to those disturbances. The majority of decision-makers in manufacturing companies have limited knowledge concerning the future development and use of new technologies, especially information and electronics technologies. In this context, identification of risk factors with the use of EW can significantly reduce decision-making errors, and particularly, minimize their negative effects. Above all, while analysing risk areas in manufacturing enterprises, three main areas should be distinguished: production, logistics, R&D (research and development). Despite the fact that logistics and R&D are supporting processes in the creation of a value chain, they are crucial to achieve objectives of manufacturing enterprises.

Decision-making is the process of evaluating and studying relationships between different solutions and choosing the one that a decision-maker defines as that of the highest usability (Flakiewicz 1978, 121). A decision-making process involves a series of operations between an input situation (system input) and an output situation (system output); it is therefore a process which transforms real conditions into desired or satisfactory conditions. What is more, this process takes place in the world of the abstract where the practical needs that occur in the real world are mapped (Gasparski 1976, 119–122).

In decision-making processes managers face various problems. They include problems which are easy or difficult to structure; short- and long-term effect problems; problems that have a weak or a strong influence on business processes; problems concentrated on a particular area of functioning or on the whole enterprise. Decisions can be divided according to the following criteria (Penc 1997, 147):

(a) kinds of problems—operational, tactical and strategic
(b) source—initiated by parent units, initiated by the manager, initiated by the employees

(c) scope of information—undertaken under certainty, risk and uncertainty
(d) activities they refer to—regulating, controlling, innovating, researching, allocating, executing, assessing, etc
(e) possibilities of quantification—possible to quantify, difficult to quantify and impossible to quantify
(f) relation to managing functions—planning, organising, motivating and controlling
(g) forms of decision-making—individual, collegiate, collective
(h) field of business activity—administrative, manufacturing, marketing, technical, transport, etc.
(i) period—current, short-term, medium-term, long-term
(j) importance of problems—key (essential), standard, marginal
(k) degree of repeatability—routinized, non-routinized, innovative
(l) structure of decision-making situations—programmable (made in accordance with prescribed rules), non-programmable (made in new or special cases)

The decision-making process involves the following stages:

(a) recognising and identifying the situation
(b) identifying optional choices
(c) analysing and assessing variants
(d) choosing the most suitable variant
(e) implementing the selected variant
(f) controlling and assessing the selected variant

Decisions should be rational. This means that rule of subjectively expected utility (SEU) should be implemented under risk (Kozielecki 1975, 78–80). In addition, at various stages, one must take into account all conditions resulting from the identification and quantification of risks with the use of EW methods and tools, which should reduce the possibility of negative decisions, and thus improve the efficiency of a decision-making process. Through four essential processes, one can indicate how the identified risks affect a given decision-making process:

(a) identification of a decisive situation (recognising and describing the decisive problem, collecting data and identifying reasons for the occurrence of the event)
(b) preparation for a decision (classification of the problem (research task), defining conditions for a solution, assessment of those conditions, and development of alternative solutions)
(c) decision-making (evaluation of solutions according to the criteria adopted for the selection, the choice of an option and its preliminary examination, acceptance of the solution)
(d) implementation of the decision (selecting the facilitator, determining measures for decision implementation, planning moves in case of emergencies during the implementation of the decision, controlling decision implementation, analysing and assessing decision effects and deviations from the assumed state)

Finally, the information about the existing risks, which will be acquired using EW in the decision-making processes, may potentially bring various effects. The most serious consequence may be the interruption of the decision-making process and rejection of the existing choices in order to establish new alternatives in the situation arising. Another possibility is a guarantee of increased resources and measures to minimize the adverse effects or strengthen the positive effects of the identified risk factors for future scenarios. Another consequence includes needs for an in-depth analysis of the impact of identified risks, and the consequent modification of the proposed decision-making alternatives.

The number of identified risk factors that influence business activity usually varies between tens and hundreds. The direct assessment of all factors simultaneously, including numerous evaluation criteria, goes beyond any one expert's abilities. Therefore, defining the relative importance of factors by means of an interactive comparison method with the use of SAP Infrastructure Project Plan (SIPP) system is justified. In many pairwise comparisons one of the factors is clearly more important (due to the Pareto principle, the '80–20 rule'), which can be determined directly, without taking into account all evaluation criteria. What is more, when comparing less important factors, usually a simplified evaluation, based on heuristic mental expert model, is sufficient.

Having identified the risk factors using EW methods and tools, the risks should be selected and initially estimated before including them in the decision-making process. This can be reached through the following stages:

(a) Defining the most crucial risk factors for an enterprise. This task aims at isolating a certain number of initial positions within a structured set. Among these, one should distinguish key security factors and critical threat factors, including not only an ad hoc activity, but also a long-term perspective.
(b) Creating indicators characterising the most important factors. An indicator is a feature (usually quantitative) characterising the factor and demonstrating a high information value. There are two groups of indicators: indicators characterising the overall condition of an enterprise and indicators characterising narrower areas of observation, important because of the nature of the enterprise. In order to describe the overall situation of an enterprise, financial and operating indicators are used. The application of EWS indicators shows that analysis of 4–6 indicators is sufficient to predict bankruptcy of a company, with an accuracy of 80–90 per cent, two to four years in advance. In practice, different sets of indicators of comparable diagnostic and prognostic value are used. An excessive expansion of the set of indicators is unjustified as it would complicate the assessment and, additionally, it does not provide any relevant information (Zaleska 2002). In the literature one can find lists of indicators used most frequently in EW systems for bankruptcy (Hunek 1989, 27–25). Indicators related to specific areas, important for business activity, should be used primarily to objectify, concretise and specify the description of these factors which have been identified as key or critical. Describing the factor using the quantitative indicators enables the comparison with values regarded as normative. Moreover, it allows the identification of statistical measures of the value range (average values, standard deviation, correlation) and the nature of trends, periodicity, predictability of changes, etc.
(c) The establishment of a set of references for factors and indicators. Identification of regulatory, relatively universal, EW indicators is

possible (to some extent, with many reservations) only for indicators that characterise the overall financial factors and efficiency of actions. For other factors, it is only possible to determine comparative references. Comparative references include: factor condition in the environment in similar enterprises in the sector. Factor condition in the environment can be described by various metrics, such as: average values; marginal values (characterising leaders and businesses at risk); standard deviations; values resulting from the plan forecasts; calculations; the balance sheet; world, national and sectorial standards; values from previous periods; current and cumulative values; extrapolated values (determined on the basis of a trend); values in previous seasons; and normative values determined heuristically. For numerous, especially qualitative and difficult-to-measure factors, an expert evaluation is the basic reference.

(d) The aggregation and interpretation of EW situation models. An EW situation may provide information of different importance and reliability. Some information is supplemented, some repeated, and some may be contradictory. For example, results of comparing the index value to the former state may be beneficial, whereas results of comparing values in the environment can be adverse. Some contradictions may be explained in the definition of a pattern. In case of factors shaping the competitiveness of enterprises, comparison with the environment is more important. However, in the case of factors characterising the growth potential, comparison with the former situation is of greater importance.

1.3 General Characteristic of the Concept of Early Warning System

Generally, EW systems (EWS) are specific IT systems to indicate key external and internal threats for the studied object. EW signs are transmitted in advance so that system user can undertake preventive actions to eliminate or reduce the effects of indicated risks (Ansoff 1985). As a result of analysing business processes in the environment, both opportunities and threats are recognized. An event can be perceived as an opportunity or a threat. The system analysing risks and opportunities is referred to as the early identifying system. In majority of cases the fundamental part of early identification is warning against threats concerning business activity.

The researchers distinguish three main categories of EWS:

(a) EWS for large economic systems, such as the economy of a given country and region or the global economy. The principle of inertia and continuity of changes is crucial in these systems (Siedlecka 1996). Quantitative, mostly statistical and econometrical, methods for identifying threats are used. To make these methods efficient, great accuracy and certainty of predictions are necessary. These expectations are difficult to achieve in ian mplemented IT system.
(b) EWS for prediction of bankruptcy in business activity— mostly in enterprises and banks. Such systems are extremely important for external entities, i.e. financial institutions, cooperating enterprises, potential investors and shareholders. EW information in these systems is formulated on the basis of many key financial and economic indicators (Zaleska 2002). Certainty of information should be relatively high. As a result, these systems are not adequate for an analysed entity to undertake effective preventive actions against the foreseen bankruptcy.
(c) EWS for enterprises. Such systems were defined by W. Klausmann in the 1980s. He distinguished three generations of these systems (Klausmann 1993):

    – first-generation systems, operating EWS, concentrating on periodic comparison of actual conditions with their planned values;
    – second-generation systems, indicative EWS, based on indicators with high predictive values and comparing them with the benchmark values;
    – third-generation systems, associated with the concept of Ansoff's weak signals (eak signals derive from the distinct enterprise's environment as well as from initial links of the cause-and-effect relationship chain and they may be informative about the coming strategic changes).

Advanced IT systems are being used more and more extensively. They include artificial intelligence and methods based on knowledge processing, primarily technologies of expert systems, enabling integration of various EW methods and concepts.

The development of new fourth-generation EWS can encourage the use of detailed analysis of cause-and-effect relationships and methods of systems theory, which include system dynamics. The concept of weak signals concentrates on warning about threats, emerging in distant environment, well in advance. Complicated interactions between an enterprise and its close environment often constitute a larger threat.

In order to take effective preventive actions, the following conditions should be simultaneously taken into consideration (Zoleński 2005, 365):

(a) Disadvantageous events and processes are conditioned by cause-and-effect relationships. It is possible to undertake preventive actions to influence their course.
(b) One can observe a strengthening in many cause-and-effect relationships. Serious consequences can derive from a relatively small effect. Preventive actions should be undertaken if the cost of removing a disadvantageous event is lower than the value of the expected loss.
(c) The effect is delayed in relation to the cause. Both disadvantageous events and processes and preventive actions similarly proceed. The delay in disadvantageous cause-and-effect relationships makes EW against threats more effective.
(d) Running processes are irreversible. If the occurred losses were recovered without any extra expenditures, it would be unnecessary to take preventive actions. Irreversibility of events and processes is a result of the principle of an entropy increase in real (non-ideal) isolated systems. The flow of time is a particular example of an irreversible processes.

Methods specific for systems of a single category can be applied—to a certain extent and with numerous reservations— to systems of a different category. However, it is necessary to check that the assumptions of the applied method are fulfilled in any such a situation.

EW methods and concepts could be used to a varying degrees to identify threats occurring in an enterprise:

(a) Methods for low-profile systems, e.g. EW in case of a fire, natural hazards, construction disasters (Feng Li-Jun 2006).
(b) Alert systems warning and informing about events pre-defined by the user and events that may have been overlooked. This type of EWS is along the lines of of a personal organiser.
(c) Time series analysis—examination concerning the loss of a trend predictability, the prediction of a trend collapse, the study of periodic components and cyclical trends, and realistic forecasts based on trend extrapolation (Zeliaś 1997).
(d) Methods based on econometric cause-and-effect models. The application of econometric models, which are regression models and empirical/inductive models, is limited to those cases in which, in the investigative processes, the structure of cause-and-effect relationships is not changed. This is because the objectives of the econometric forecast theory need to be achieved. This requirement also applies to studying time series. For this reason, econometric methods are not widely used in acquisition of EW information in an enterprise.
(e) Methods combining index analysis with econometric methods (e.g. Z models). These are tools used in systems of bankruptcy forecasting (Zaleska 2002), which are a specific case of EWS.
(f) EW operational systems. Within these systems actual, planned or predicted values, important to organise indicators, are compared. It is particularly important to monitor the implementation of specific schedule tasks, especially those on the critical path,
(g) EW indicator systems. In these systems, indicators of a significant prognostic value are identified. These, in turn, are compared with normative values. Financial indicators are used most frequently; however, to receive a warning well in advance other perspectives, such as customers, internal processes and perspective of company development (Kaplan and Norton, 2001), have to be taken into account. Controlling tools can be used in advanced indicator systems (Sierpińska and Niedbała 2004).

(h) Weak signal concept, in which the identification of EW information is based on the assumption that there are stable, long-term processes which start in a distant business environment, and are therefore beyond the standard area of observation. Weak signals may appear in reports on directions of research, dissemination of new ideas, views and positions of key individuals or political organisations, and in reports on new legal initiatives. The term 'weak' refers to the observability, not to the force of impact. (Strong signals refer to information about factors difficult to overlook, as they are constantly observed and constitute the centre of management's attention (e.g. financial results, value of sales, company's share price).

There are various reasons why weak signals are not recognized in time:

(a) Weak signals are scattered and their recognition requires observation and analysis of a wide chain of information (such interpretation of weak signals goes beyond the concept formulated by Ansoff).
(b) The influence of threats described by weak signals is revealed after a longer period, so it tends to be ignored in an ad hoc observation. When managing information, there is often a tendency for concentrating on ad hoc actions and effects,
(c) The set of factors which can have a significant impact in the future is really broad, therefore some factors may be omitted. It is difficult to foresee well in advance which of numerous factors could be significantly important for business activity in the future,
(d) Weak signals may be inaccessible to observers because of different reasons: the simple lack of possibilities for observation or measurement; or even as a result of hiding information that could give a competitive advantage or hiding information about a competitor's intentions.
(e) Weak signals may overlap with other signals (interference) and they can strongly affect the observers. The importance of signals does not always depend on their intensity.

Inadequacy of the weak signal concept involves the weak operationalization of methods for the identification and interpretation of information, which could be important for business activity in the future (Siedlecka 1996, 156).

The applied methods in EWS are as follows:

(a) Non-extrapolative methods of strategic analysis include: opportunities and threat analysis, strategic gap analysis, portfolio methods, life-cycle methods and scenario methods.
(b) Game theory methods (Kałuski 2002). Game theory represents formal models of interaction (of a conflict or cooperation nature) that may occur between an enterprise and other entities. These entities, in the pursuit of their own goals, can gain an advantage provided that they hide their actions and practices. Game theory offers methods for making optimal decisions under conditions of ambiguity.
(c) Artificial intelligence methods (Rutkowski 2005): expert systems; approximate logic, e.g. logic based on fuzzy sets; character recognition; artificial neural networks; genetic algorithms (especially self-learning systems) (Cytowski 1996; Goldberg 2003); analysis of turbulence and chaos theory (Mantegna and Stanley 2001).
(d) Catastrophe theory. This theory is not directly applicable to economic sciences, but the results led to the formulation of research hypotheses, which in some cases appear to be useful in EWS.
(e) Cause-and-effect models based on logical-deductive methods. In these models, in contrast to econometric models, it is possible to take into account not only changes in the structure of cause-and-effect relationships, but also model processes that did not occur in the past. However, the accuracy and reliability of mapping real objects are smaller. These methods are particularly useful in the formulation of research forecasts. System control theory has effective tools to create such cause-and- effect models of this type.
(f) Heuristic methods, particularly expert methods, are often used in long-term warning forecasts, (e.g. the Delphi method).

An important element of the construction of EWS is to design solutions that would integrate different methods and handle different EW information. This task was performed in two stages:

(a) Classification of EW information and specification of problems arising during its acquisition and processing.
(b) Integration of solutions occurring while operating information of different categories.

EWS can be divided into three basic categories of information (Fig. 6.2):

(a) Realistic EW information characterized by a high degree of certainty and relatively high accuracy (Cieślak 2005, 24). Realistic EW information relates primarily to uncontrolled, particularly inevitable, factors (strongly dependent on the passage of time and weakly dependent on other factors) or poorly controllable. This limits the ability to respond to such information. Realistic EW information can also—in a small area of variation for variables— describe cause-and-effect relationships. Realistic forecasts are mostly short-term forecasts. Due to

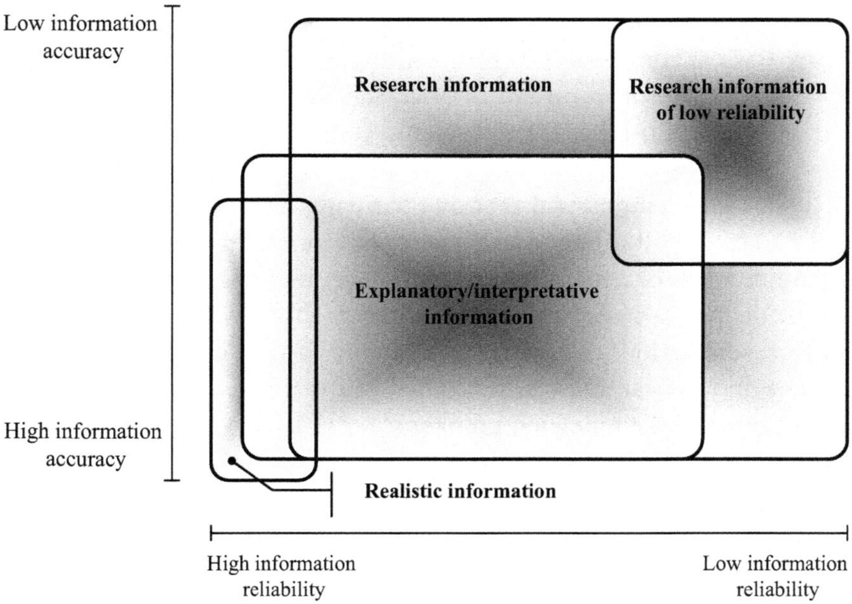

Fig. 6.2 Characteristics of EW information (*Source*: Own study)

the above mentioned factors, realistic EW information does not play a key role in EW systems.

(b) Research information of EW, which is responsible not only for comprehensive diagnosis of possible events and processes, but also for the presentation of numerous possible variants (Cieślak 2005, 23). Reliability and accuracy of research information, especially when one of many possible options is considered, are generally not large. In EW, research information of low reliability that warns about the possibility of significant loss plays an important role. In many cases, the cost of actions to prevent losses is much smaller than its expected value. Research information of EW may relate to controllable and uncontrollable factors and to observable and unobservable factors. Therefore, in some EW areas the only available information includes research information, particularly of low reliability,
(c) Explanatory/interpretative information of EW, which refers to cause-and-effect relationships, especially to complicated and unobvious relationships, which show system or logical-structural complexity. This type of information is crucial in advanced EWS. They can apply to both uncontrollable factors, which are, however, observable well in advance (Ansoff's concept of weak signals), and controllable factors (EW concepts based on control and system theory) (Senge 2004).

It should be emphasised that one particular EW method can constitute a source of information in different categories. For instance, depending on the time of a forecast, information arising from the trend analysis can be defined as realistic or research information. While operating EW information, various difficulties specific to a particular category of information may appear. Difficulties related to the use of realistic EW information involve the following problems:

(a) Development of reliable and accurate information is difficult. Generally, it requires a wide source information, which is not always available. In IT-based EWS it has been assumed that in order to obtain information difficult to access, external studies are recommended.

(b) Reliability and accuracy of EW information requires using reliable sources, which can be impossible at times.
(c) Realistic EW information is based on the idea of the structure of a problem being invariable. This assumption, however, needs to be verified.
(d) In the use of realistic EW information, problems with operating numerous collection of information do not occur because in a normally functioning enterprise not many real threats of major importance appear.

Difficulties in using research-based EW information are related to the following problems:

(a) Difficulties in obtaining a full collection of information including—at a certain level of significance—all possible threats.
(b) The lack of easily operable methods for the acquisition and evaluation of research information. In all methods an expert opinion plays a key role.
(c) Difficulties in managing numerous, difficult-to-organize, collections of diverse information. Research information is mostly qualitative; it may vary in terms of relevance, urgency, pragmatic values and other attributes. Furthermore, it is characterised by a diverse structure (numeric figures, text, graphs, etc.). In research information management, as well as in its acquisition, an expert opinion is of significant importance.

Difficulties in using the operating explanatory/interpretative EW information are associated with the following problems:

(a) Difficulties in forming the structure of a model which maps the actual cause-and-effect relationships.
(b) Difficulties in obtaining complete information necessary to conduct simulation research on a designed model. A large part of information necessary to determine model parameters, initial conditions and value of manipulated variables results from the evaluation made with the use of heuristic methods. Therefore, it is generally not possible to

obtain explanative/interpretive information of a high reliability and accuracy.

(c) Complexity of explanative/interpretive information, practical use of which in enterprise management requires specific skills.
(d) Acquisition, processing and use of explanative/interpretive information generally requires expert support, which, due to the cost and availability of expertise, constitutes a significant barrier in the use of such information.

Differences between categories of EW information according to the criterion of an information structure and its linguistic representation:

(a) realistic EW information is mainly quantitative information, represented by a numerical value;
(b) research EW information is primarily qualitative information, expressed by a verbal description,
(c) explanative/interpretive information is information about relationships that are represented graphically, by means of graphs, cause-and-effect relationships diagrams and charts.

Differences between categories of EW information according to the method of information acquisition:

(a) In order to obtain realistic information of EW, indicators relevant for the enterprise are determined. These, in turn, are compared with the values considered to be correct (standard). Standard values of indicators are determined on the basis of the experience, historical data, data characterising the environment and trend forecasting. Operational and index EWS and explorative methods are sources of realistic information,
(b) Acquisition of research EW information involves noting possible threats (initial EW information) and assessing their significance (size and probability of potential loss) for business activity. Specific methods for obtaining this kind of information include non-extrapolative methods of strategic analysis and expert methods (including also the concept of weak signals).

(c) Explanative/interpretive EW information results from simulation studies conducted on models mapping cause-and-effect relationships important for enterprises. To a certain extent, it is also possible to develop this type of information directly on the basis of mental expert models.

Differences between categories of EW information according to the criterion of information operating:

(a) The set of realistic EW information is relatively small, because all information is transferred to relevant services in order to take immediate preventive actions. However, in order to identify EW information as realistic, it is necessary to check that it has been acquired correctly, that the source data are reliable, and to check the context in which the information has been gathered.
(b) Research EW information is wide in range and it varies in terms of reliability, importance, urgency, pragmatic values and other attributes. Therefore, their processing and use must be preceded by evaluation (evaluating individual attributes and determining the potential addressees) and selection,
(c) Explanative/interpretive EW information is not wide in range, and is characterized by high complexity and a relatively high degree of certainty. Its use may require expert support. Such information is especially formulated to describe relationships and processes of strategic importance. For this reason, it is designed mainly for senior management.

The above analysis demonstrates that in order to integrate solutions while using various categories of EW information, it is necessary to:

(a) harmonise the risk description;
(b) adopt the concept of the acquisition of EW information;
(c) develop a procedure for handling information and integrating actions that can be found in the processing of realistic, research and explanatory/interpretative information.

An EW situation, i.e. one which constitutes a potential source of threats, enables a uniform description of various threats. In order to apply the universal concept for obtaining EW information, it is necessary to introduce the concept of an 'EW situation model'. It is an abstract model of a certain class of EW situation. The acquisition of EW information involves creating a set of EW situation models and comparing them to the present state of the company and its surroundings. Information about an enterprise and its environment derives mainly from the company's own sources. In justified cases, in order to obtain the missing information, appropriate research and expertise can be commissioned.

1.4 Methods and Tools of Early Warning in Risk Identification in Machine-Building Enterprises

The analysis of identified risk factors and assessing their importance for decision-making processes in an enterprise require a multi-criteria evaluation, which should include the following criteria:

(a) The size of losses for the company, which may be caused by a risk factor.
(b) The possibility of cumulating or compensating the adverse impact of the risk factor with the impact of other risk factors. Inability to compensate for the effects is a criterion for distinguishing critical and key factors. Factors which are particularly important include those that determine the occurrence of a synergy or that are elements of a serial cause and effect structure (the weakest elements in the chain, narrow sections, limitations).
(c) The interchangeability and liquidity of a risk factor. These properties are characteristic particularly for resources. What is beneficial for an enterprise's security is the structure of assets with a large involvement of resources of a good convertibility and liquidity, i.e. these which can be easily and quickly exchanged for other resources.
(d) The necessity to balance a factor with other factors. Factors of this type must be formed in an appropriate relationship with other factors. Even a small change in the absolute value of a factor can influence the positive or negative results of the balance sheet.

(e) The strength of risk factor's influence (intensity). Intensity depends on the factor's position in the cause and effect chain or whether it is present in the feedback loop.
(f) The dependence of a risk factor on other factors (reactivity). Factors strongly dependent on others should be regarded as less important, since their interaction is taken into account when assessing the importance of relevant intensive factors.
(g) The dynamics of interaction—relationships between the strength of the ad-hoc and long-term impact. In EW those risk factors are significant which, in the long term, can lead to significant losses, although on the ad-hoc basis they do not reveal the negative impact. In particular, it is important to observe and shape risk factors showing non-minimal phase impact (e.g. a short-term improvement before a long-term deterioration).
(h) The dynamics of risk factor shaping (dynamics asymmetry). An EWS requires a careful observation of risk factors whose conditions may change rapidly. Mainly intangible factors display such an attribute (e.g. legal regulations). Of particular importance, however, are risk factors of asymmetric dynamics for which improvement is of a long-term character and deterioration can occur within a short period of time.
(i) The cumulativeness of risk factor effects. Factors with a long-term accumulative impact are usually more important than factors which do not demonstrate this property (e.g. the impact effects are dispersed).
(j) The ability to buffer a risk factor.
(k) The heuristic determination of the importance of a risk factor based on intuitive expert evaluation.

The research and development project was conducted in the years 2010–104 to analyse different aspects of knowledge management in machine-building enterprises. The project concerns 38 selected Polish enterprises in the machine-building industry, located in Silesia, which were divided into four groups:

(a) enterprises manufacturing products general purpose (8),
(b) enterprises manufacturing products for the mining industry (15),

(c) enterprises manufacturing products for the defence industry (6),
(d) enterprises manufacturing products for the automotive industry (9).

The project determined specific characteristics of the sample group of machine-building enterprises as follows (Dohn et al. 2011; Dohn and Matusek 2012):

(a) The business processes are particularly sensitive to economic changes, with the sensitivity to depression being stronger and more violent than the reaction to economic growth.
(b) The production processes are highly complex and descrete.
(c) Production is mainly 'make to order', i.e. a response for individual customers' requirements.
(d) Business activity is characterized by a high degree of uncertainty and changeability in the medium term (due to the size and the structure of production capacity) and for this reason there is a production capacity surplus for machinery and equipment and a deficit in employment.
(e) Key factors in business activity include high technical and organizational competence of employees (design engineers, technologists, production workers).
(f) In make-to-order production, various factors of low stability influence the profitability level (parameters of orders, and of contracts with customers, suppliers and cooperators).
(g) In order to select profitable contracts and avoid unprofitable ones, it is essential to have knowledge of stock in hand and supply capacity, and to gain knowledge of manufacturing costs, production capacities, and of potential suppliers and co-operators (information about their reliability, prime costs, willingness to cooperate, negotiating potential).

At the initial stage of the project the following information concerning EW was studied in the analysed enterprises:

(a) general knowledge of EW issues
(b) methods and tools of EW used
(c) potential external and internal threats to business

As a result, with reference to EW issues, the following conclusions were drawn:

(a) Unfortunately, there are no formalised structures focusing on threats, which could be defined as EWS. The only warnings are against specific hazards, such as a fire or a construction disaster.
(b) Knowledge about EW, including information about external and internal risks, is insufficient for a proper evaluation of the benefits and expenditures associated with the implementation and use of EWS. The potential of EWS is generally overestimated and essential warning information that is completely certain, not trivial, is expected.
(c) The importance of system solutions are underestimated. In particular, it is not recognized that the desired features of warning information (certainty, non-obviousness, significance) derive from system acquisition, processing and from the use of a good deal of information that seems less important, relatively obvious and less certain.
(d) Information, including EW information, is only partly obtained and processed. Managers monitor the completion of the planned tasks, set quantitative indicators (especially financial and efficiency ones), comparing them with the previous values or benchmark values. What is more, in some situations, methods of a strategic analysis are also implemented—for instance, to prepare business plans or loan applications. These actions, however, are not systematic.

The results of the project research showed requirements that should be involved in an EWS determining risks to support decision-making processes in machine-building enterprises. The system should take into account the following aspects:

(a) The effective determination of external and internal risks requires a systematic and comprehensive storage, processing and distribution of information. Implementation of specific methods and tools for EW is crucial to meet these requirements. The system should integrate all categories of warning information and various methods and concepts of EW.

(b) The essential aspect of an effective early warning system is a knowledge base containing all necessary information concerning EW. System users should be provided with the following information:

   - complete information about an enterprise and its environment,
   - knowledge of EW methods, tools and models.
   - knowledge of expert interpretation and verification of EW information.

(c) The main element of the system should include IT tools supporting processing of qualitative knowledge of EW. Additionally, the opportunity to process quantitative information of EW should be taken into account in selected areas in business activity of machine-building enterprises.
(d) The system should be flexible i.e. implemented tools and methods should enable both to adjust to enterprise's individual requirements and to modify and currently adapt to changing needs.

The concept of the EWS determining risks to support decision-making processes in these enterprises is the result of the expectations of potential users, mainly production managers and technologists. The system should be suited to EW information and the general principles of the design of IT tools. The quantitative processing of EW information may use standard IT tools, but qualitative information is processed by dedicated EW tools. Prototypes of these tools were created on the MS Office platform with VBA programming language (Visual Basic for Applications). The creation of tools on a high-level computer platform is much easier, and means that even less advanced users can run system maintenance programs, introduce small extensions and perform minor modifications. Additionally, the use of a commonly known user interface facilitates system implementation and operation.

The integration of EWS tools with an enterprise information system and other standard computer tools is implemented at the level of data exchange. Virtually all computer systems allow data exchange with MS Office applications, at least in RTF (rich text format). Whereas, integration of dedicated EW tools is ensured by the mechanisms of MS Office.

The concept of EW tasks for identifying risks supporting decision-making processes is shown in Fig. 6.3. Four separate IT tools for executing these EW tasks were defined:

(a) hypertext knowledge system
(b) rule-based expert system
(c) interactive paired comparison system
(d) dynamic research simulation system

Hypertext knowledge system enables storing and organising knowledge about identified risks presented in the form of unified, standard elementary objects.

An elementary object of knowledge combines a single formal structure with the possibility of recording various types of information (text, graphic, numeric, and others, as well as those more complex, such as any object of MS Office package). Different attributes can be assigned to objects of knowledge, e.g. descriptive and interpretative attributes, classifying and evaluating attributes, as well as verbal and numerical attributes (e.g. ordinal number, updating date, a source of information, assessment of validity and reliability). Elementary objects of knowledge can be connected by superiority or inferiority relationships or relationships with any hierarchical or systemic structure (directed graph). It is also possible to register free objects which are not associated with other objects.

Rule-based expert system is designed to cooperate with small modules of knowledge that can be integrated to form a larger knowledge base. Knowledge within the expert system is based on standard Horn rules. These are implications with one conclusion, whose conditional elements are represented as statement conjunctions. In the rule-based expert system, the following solutions were used:

(a) The use of inference in three-valued logic (true, false, lack of knowledge). Such a solution ensures monotonicity of inference in case of developed knowledge bases (two-valued logic inference would be non-monotonic). A natural generalization of three-valued logic is approximate logic, such as fuzzy logic. A rule-based expert system enables inference in approximate logic.

Defining the areas of observation for risk determination

- Determination of potential observation areas in the environment and in the enterprise including:
  - safety key factors
  - critical risk factors
- Observation areas selection taking into account the possibility of implementing early warning

Applied IT tools: hypertext knowledge system, standard computer tools used in an enterprise

Creating a set of risk situation standards

- Overview of early warning for risk situation standards stored in the knowledge base
- Modification of archetypes and general early warning models, mainly the dynamics system models
- Generalization of risk situations in the past observed in production enterprises

Applied IT tools: hypertext knowledge system, dynamic research simulation system, rule-based expert system, standard computer tools used in an enterprise

Development of primary early warning information about risk situations

- Acquiring information about the company and the environment in the various risk patterns
- Comparison of the actual situation of the company with the situation defined by the standard
- Assessment of the reality of risks and the size of potential losses

Applied IT tools: hypertext knowledge system, rule-based expert system, standard computer tools used in an enterprise

Verification of primary early warning information about risk situations

- Checking the completeness of the information
- Formal and content verification of information:
  - examine the compatibility of information from independent sources and obtained by different methods
  - experts reliability assess

Applied IT tools: hypertext knowledge system, rule-based expert system

Developing a comprehensive early warning information concerning risks - interpretation

- Explanation and interpretation of complex early warning information concerning risks:
  - simulation research
  - presentation the complex relationships in a graphic form
- Structuring, organizing and selecting information concerning risks:
  - information ordering according to importance, urgency and other attributes
  - selection and compression of information
- Information distribution - the determination of the recipients of information

Applied IT tools: hypertext knowledge system, interactive paired comparison system, rule-based expert system, dynamic research simulation system, rule-based expert system,

Fig. 6.3 The concept of EW tasks for identifying risks supporting decision-making processes in a machine-building enterprise (*Source*: Own study)

(b) The concept of calculating and concluding expert sheets, combining spreadsheet capacities (algebraic models) with an expert system (logical models).
(c) The concept of a self-organising decision table for storing in the knowledge base (in the form of Horn rules).
(d) The technique of an interactive creation of graphical representation of knowledge.
(e) A graphical method for justifying the results, involving the visualisation of inference paths.
(f) Simulating processes of complex logical structure. A rule-based expert system can interpret EW information about risks of a complex logical structure and it can integrate different EW methods.

Interactive paired comparison system can support sequencing of knowledge objects on the basis of qualitative expert assessment. It involves comparing pairs combined with the current sorting of the set of objects. Implementation of interactive methods of paired comparison often reduces the number of comparisons. The interactive paired comparison system can be used to organise and assess the importance of EW information concerning external and internal risks.

Dynamic research simulation system can be used to study a system's dynamics of changing risks. The models refer to the concept of system diagrams (Senge 2004) that illustrate the typical structures and behaviours of systems (archetypes). Diagrams depict key features of the systems, especially the feedback loops (Forrester 1994). However, the level of simplification is often too high to explain accurately all the dependencies that are difficult for intuitive interpretation. The system of dynamic research simulations provides a precise and unambiguous representation of the test system structure. In particular, it may be used in the interpretation of an EW information system with a complex structure of determined risk factors. For the system of dynamic research simulations, the concept of a graphical representation of system models was developed. The graphical representation of the systemic model is a sequence (table) of consecutive objects and corresponding time graphs. Objects represent the dynamic relation (integration, derivative, delay) and the non-linear static relation (e.g. parabolic, exponential, sigmoidal, step). Objects can also represent external extraction controllers, especially the control size and interference. The system of dynamic research stimulators enables the creation of interactive graphical representation of system models and test simulation for different values of model parameters and various external excitations.

The proposed methods and tools can be applied in EWS for identifying and assessing external and internal risks. It can be of great importance to deliver the extra knowledge which is necessary in decision-making processes in machine-building enterprises. The EW information about risks can lead to:

(a) avoiding significant losses by determining different objectives within the whole period of enterprise existence;
(b) taking preventive, economically effective actions which would minimize the losses, (in other types of actions such high efficiency is unattainable).

The most important aspect of EW information is its adequate interpretation. Any misunderstandings in the analysis of predictable processes can lead to new threats and risks. Inefficient knowledge processing in EWS can result from:

(a) incomplete information about risks or possible responses;
(b) neglecting available information or failing to take appropriate actions in time;
(c) difficulties in the interpretation of complex information. This can arise from an overload of diverse information or from high complexity of cause-and-effect relationships, such as feedback, dynamic effects, and non-linear, complex logical structures.

The implementation of EW information in decision-making processes can result in positive effects, despite the fact that it is not often characterized by a high degree of certainty and accuracy. The primary aim of EW is not to develop a precise and realistic forecast, but to recognize the possibility of taking highly efficient preventive actions against forthcoming threats. In explaining and interpreting complex cause-and-effect relationships, the methods of system dynamics are very useful, in particular, research simulations carried out on simplified models that correspond with system archetypes. The proposed IT methods and tools based on knowledge provide the flexibility of EWS and enable its creation by means of evolutionary methods. In particular, it is possible to connect the familiar EW methods with the experimental solutions. Actions of an experimental and research nature are important in predicting risks and their influence on business activity.

One of the most effective information tools, supporting a logical aggregation of comparison results, is the rule-based expert system. In this system, one can also combine the logical aggregation with an algebraic aggregation. The model of EW situation includes (Fig. 6.4.):

(a) archetype of unfavourable properties and behaviour of a system;
(b) factors defining the company and its surrounding, corresponding to meta-features of the archetype.

This type of model provides above all the explanatory/interpretative information for EW. The archetypes of unfavourable properties and behaviour of the system can be found in the framework knowledge base. A large part of system archetypes refers to the theory of linear system control. In the description of linear systems there are primarily quantitative features (values). However, when defining the risk factors specific to the company, it is not necessary to be limited solely to the quantitative factors. One can also take into account factors which are valuated, such as product quality, quality of relationships with key customers and so on. The model of an EW situation determines the structure of a relationship between factors (attributes), but does not specify solid attributes, variables and parameters. For this reason, it is not possible at this stage to determine strictly potential adverse properties and behaviours which may occur in the studied enterprise.

In the study of results concerning risk factors, four basic directions can be identified:

(a) rejection of irrelevant information—flooding recipient with unimportant information may bring more losses than benefits;

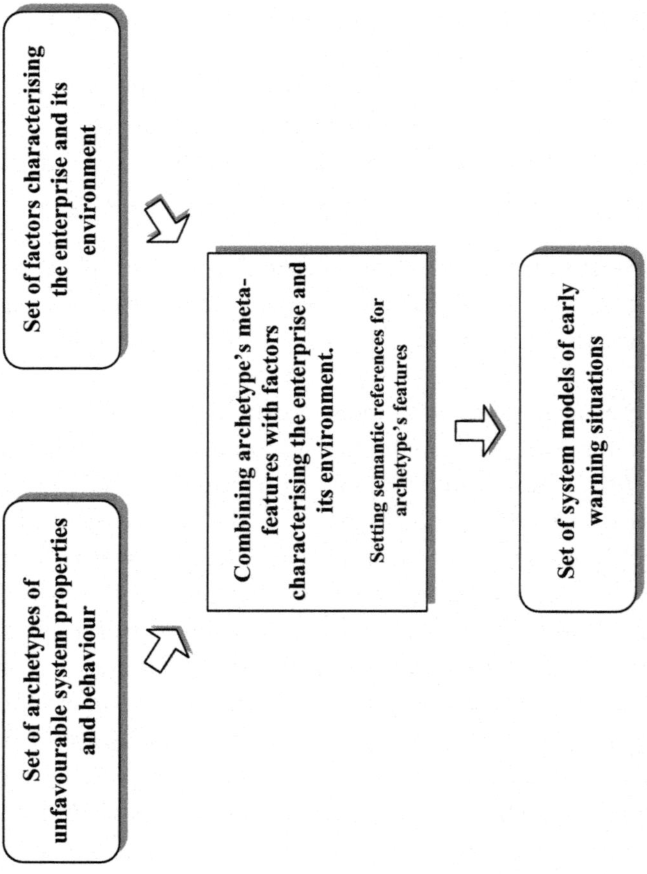

Fig. 6.4 Scheme for creating systemic models of EW situation (*Source*: Own study)

(b) spread of information among different audiences, according to needs and competencies;
(c) distribution of information transfer in time (not all information is equally urgent);
(d) adaptation of the form of information, e.g. structure, order, accuracy, language and way of transfer, perceptual skills and needs of recipients.

In a properly functioning enterprise, in which consistency between the objectives declared and all funds possessed is found, not many risks of significant importance occur. In the management of such a company too much information of high complexity referring to large risks is unlikely to occur.

In a short-term perspective, the development of EWS that use knowledge requires the gradual creation of knowledge libraries, describing potential risks and hazards, ways of their recognition and prevention. In a long-term perspective, the development of an EW model based on deep knowledge is intentional. In studies on the deep knowledge of EW, in addition to control theory and systems, different methods and concepts should be considered, e.g. the turbulence analysis and chaos theory. Important issues in further studies on the EW concept should include:

(a) theoretical and practical deepening of the key aspects of EW ideas;
(b) determination of limits of EW methods in decision-making processes.

2 Conclusions

The proposed concept of information tools was developed and dedicated to a specific group of enterprises, for which specific conditions and restrictions for the use of EW methods and tools to identify risks were defined. This complex proposal, however, requires adaptation to specific manufacturing environment and enterprises. What is particularly important for its application is to develop and implement software for creating database systems and to access the internal and external experts who will verify and add to the knowledge accumulated in these databases.

The expansion of these tools may constitute a starting point for creating a complex system for identifying risk factors to assist the decision-making process within the company. This system will require the creation and verification of direct knowledge libraries that contain the complete characteristics of potential risks. In the longer term, it is also desirable to develop EW models based on a deep knowledge. The effective use of large direct databases requires systematising this knowledge and creating searching rules. Meta-knowledge of EW, acquired in this way, will serve as an important source of information, indicating the directions of research on models of deep knowledge. In studies of deep knowledge of EW, in addition to the control and systems theory, different methods and concepts should be included, e.g. in the field of game theory, turbulence analysis and chaos theory. Important issues that should be raised in further research include deepening the concept of EW in the identification of risks and defining the limits of its usefulness.

The above considerations, for which machine-building enterprises served as the reference point, are universal in nature. This means that, after considering the nature of business in a particular industry, they can be applied to different enterprises.

Bibliography

Ansoff, H. I. (1985). *Zarządzanie strategiczne, [Strategic management]*. Warszawa: PWE.

Aven, T. (2008). *Risk analysis*. Chichester: Wiley.

Aven, T., & Renn, O. (2009). On risk defined as an event where the outcome is uncertain. *Journal of Risk Research, 12*, 1–11.

Barton, T. L., Shenkir, W. G., & Walker, P. L. (2002). *Making enterprise risk management pay off: How leading companies implement risk management*. Upper Saddle River: Financial Times/Prentice Hall PTR.

Basel Committee of Banking Supervision. (2004). *International convergence of capital measurement and capital standards*. A Revised Framework.

Beasley, M. S., et al. (2005). Enterprise risk management: An empirical analysis of factors associated with the extent of implementation. *Journal of Accounting and Public Policy, 24*, 521–531.
Beck, U. (1992). *Risk society: Toward a new modernity* (trans: Ritter, M. A.). London: Sage Publications.
Brzóska, J. (2014). *Innowacje jako czynnik dynamizujący modele biznesowe, [Innovations as a business model boosting factor]*. Gliwice: Wydawnictwo Politechniki Śląskiej.
Buehler, K. S., & Pritsch, G. (2003). *Running with risk*. New York: McKinsey.
Cieślak, M. (2005). *Prognozowanie gospodarcze, [Economic forecasting]*. Warszawa: Wydawnictwo Naukowe PWN.
Cytowski, J. (1996). *Algorytmy genetyczne, [Genetic algorithms]*. Warszawa: Podstawy i zastosowania. Akademicka Oficyna Wydawnicza PLJ.
Committee of Sponsoring Organizations (COSO). (2004). *Enterprise risk management – Integrated framework*. New York: COSO.
Černá, M. (2012). Information risks and their connection with accounting. *Proceedings of the European Conference on Information Management & Evaluation*, pp. 375–382.
Dohn K., & Matusek, M. (2012). Identyfikacja obszarów wiedzy w procesie realizacji zamówienia, [Identification of knowledge areas in order fulfillment processes]. *Logistyka [Journal of Logistics], 2*, 457–466.
Dohn, K., Gumiński, A., & Zoleński, W. (2011). Assumptions for the creation of a system supporting knowledge management in an enterprise of mechanical engineering industry. In P. Jałowiecki, P. Łukasiewicz, & A. Orłowski (Eds.), *Information systems in management XIII. Business intelligence and knowledge management* (pp. 19–27). Warsaw: Warsaw University of Life Science – SGGW.
Feng, L.-J. (2006). Study on early warning of building safety based on SVM. *Journal of Applied Quantitative Methods, 1*(2).
Flakiewicz, W. (1978). *Podejmowanie decyzji kierowniczych, [Making managerial decisions]* (p. 121). Warsaw: PWE [Polish Economic Publishing House].
Forland, S. I., & Upadhyay V. (2011, June). Risk – A cost to allocate? An emipirical study of business practice. Industrial Economics and Technology Management, Norwegian University of Science and Technology.
Forrester, J. W. (1994). System dynamics, system thinking, and soft OR. *System Dynamics Review, 10*(2), 245–256.
Gasparski, W. (1976). *Sytuacja problemowa w projektowaniu "Prakseologia", [Problematic situation in the designing process "Praxeology"]*, No. 2.

Gleissner, W., & Meier, G. (2000). *Wertorientiertes Risiko Management für Industrie und Handel. Methoden, Fallbeispiele, Checklisten, [Value-based risk management for trade and industry. Methods, case studies, checklists]* (p. 87). Wiesbaden: Gabler.

Goldberg, D. E. (2003). *Algorytmy genetyczne i ich zastosowania, [Genetic algorithms and their use]*. Warszawa: WNT.

Gordon, L. A., Loeb, M. P., & Tseng, C.-Y. (2009). Enterprise risk management and firm performance: A contingency perspective. *Journal of Accounting and Public Policy, 28*, 301–327.

Gumiński A. (2013) Identyfikacja czynników ryzyka w kluczowych obszarach działalności przedsiębiorstwa budowy maszyn, [Identification of risk factors in key business areas of machine building enterprises]. Scientific Papers, University of Szczecin.

Hoyt, R. E., & Liebenberg, A. P. (2009). The value of enterprise risk management. Working Paper.

Hunek J. K. (1989). Systemy wczesnego ostrzegania, [*Early warning systems*]. Przegląd Organizacji, nr 5.

Kaczmarek, T. T. (2006). *Ryzyko i zarządzanie ryzykiem Ujęcie interdyscyplinarne, [Risk and risk management, Interdisciplinary approach]* (p. 257). Warszawa: Difin.

Kałuski, J. (2002). *Teoria gier, [Game theory]*. Gliwice: Wydawnictwo Politechniki Śląskiej.

Kaplan, R. S., & Norton, D. P. (2001). *Strategiczna karta wyników, [Balanced scorecard]*. Warszawa: Wydawnictwo Naukowe PWN.

Klausmann, W. (1993). Betriebliche Frühwarnsysteme im Wandeln. *Zeitschrift Führung und Organisation, 1*, 39–41.

Kozielecki, J. (1975). *Psychologiczna teoria decyzji, [Psychological theory of decision]*. Warszawa, pp.78–80.

Kożuch, B., & Sienkiewicz-Małyjurek, K. (2013). Collaborative networks as a basis for internal economic security in sustainable local governance. The case of Poland. In K. Raczkowski & F. Schneider (Eds.), *The economic security of business transactions. Management in business,* (pp. 313–328). Oxford: Chartridge Books Oxford.

Kubińska-Kaleta, E. (2008). Zarządzanie ryzykiem w przedsiębiorstwach przemysłowych na przykładzie huty stali, [*Risk Management in Industrial enterprises on the basis of a Steel Plant*]. PhD Thesis, AGH, Cracow.

Lam, J. (2003). *Enterprise risk management: From incentives to controls*. Hoboken: John Wiley & Sons, Inc.

Mantegna, R. N., & Stanley, H. E. (2001). *Ekonofizyka, [Econophysics]*. Warszawa: Wydawnictwo Naukowe PWN.
Moschandreas, D., & Karuchit, S. (2005). Risk uncertainty matters: An engineer's view. *International Journal of Risk Assessment and Management, 5*(2/3/4), 167–192.
Nocco, B. W., & Stulz, R. M. (2006). Enterprise risk management: Theory and practice. *Journal of Applied Corporate Finance, 18*(4), 8–20.
Penc, J. (1997). *Decyzje w zarządzaniu, [Decisions in management]* (p. 147). Cracow: Wydawnictwo Profesjonalnej Szkoły Biznesu.
Power, M. (2009). The risk management of nothing. *Accounting, Organizations and Society, 34*, 849–855.
Rutkowski, L. (2005). *Metody i techniki sztucznej inteligencji, [Methods and techniques of artificial intelligence]*. Warszawa: Wydawnictwo Naukowe PWN.
Senge, P. M. (2004). *Piąta dyscyplina. Teoria i praktyka organizacji uczących się. [The fifth discipline. The art & practice of the learning organization]*. Kraków: Oficyna Ekonomiczna.
Siedlecka, U. (1996). *Prognozowanie ostrzegawcze w gospodarce, [Warning forecasting in an economy]*. Warszawa: PWE.
Sierpińska, M., & Niedbała, B. (2004). *Controlling operacyjny w przedsiębiorstwie, [Operational controlling in an enterprise]*. Warszawa: Wydawnictwo Naukowe PWN.
SO/IEC. (2013). International Organization for Standardization (ISO). Information technology – Security techniques – Information security risk management (ISO/IEC 27005:2011, IDT), p. 3.
Stulz, R. (1996). Rethinking risk management. *Journal of Applied Corporate Finance, 9*(3), 8–24.
Stulz, R. (2003). *Rethinking risk management: The revolution in corporate finance* (4th ed.pp. 367–384). Hoboken: Blackwell Publishing.
Zaleska, M. (2002). *Identyfikacja ryzyka upadłości przedsiębiorstwa i banku. Systemy wczesnego ostrzegania, [Identification of the bankruptcy risk of companies and banks. Early warning systems]*. Warszawa: Wydawnictwo "Difin".
Zeliaś, A. (1997). *Teoria prognozy, [Forecast theory]*. Warszawa: PWE.
Zoleński, W. (2005). Early warning systems in the enterprise. *Scientific Papers of Silesian University of Technology, Organization and Management*, No. 27. Gliwice, p. 365.

7

Risk Perception in the Activity of Social Enterprises

Martyna Wronka-Pośpiech, Aldona Frączkiewicz-Wronka, and Konrad Laska

1 Introduction

A fundamental problem faced by developed countries is to find practices for public funds management that will allow for the effective achievement of social goals defined in the process of political choices made by citizens. It is crucial that the final outcome—the service provided—should be economically sound, qualitatively satisfying and compliant with the rules of social fairness. As a consequence, many state governments undertake measures aimed at the reform of the public sector, implementing solutions developed as part of the concepts of New Public Management (NPM) or governance. In practice, it means not only the emphasis on measurable outcomes and the economization of the process of public and social service provision, but

M. Wronka-Pośpiech (✉) • A. Frączkiewicz-Wronka
University of Economics in Katowice, Katowice, Poland

K. Laska
University of Rzeszów, Rzeszów, Poland

K. Raczkowski (ed.), *Risk Management in Public Administration*,
DOI 10.1007/978-3-319-30877-7_7

also the reinforcement of mechanisms involved in codecision, cooperation and the application of democratic procedures to decisions about the hierarchy and fulfilment of the needs (Verhoest and Mattei 2010, 163–171; Pennings 2010, 180). The implementation of market mechanisms, decentralization and a wide application of management tools oriented towards management control has resulted in a new logic of the public sector, involving a shift from the traditional model of public funds management (which is based on the hierarchy characteristic of public administration and the hegemony of public service providers) to a networking model, and the granting of access to service provision to entities other than public institutions. As a consequence of initiatives launched both by the EU (European Union) and nation states, the actual processes involved in service provision are shifted from public entities to citizen and business sector entities, while the methods of service provision are also changing.

Both in theory and in practice, services are inherent in a state's social policy. T.H. Marshall argues that: "*social policy is government action having a direct impact on the welfare of the citizens, by providing them with services or income*", hence—by providing services—countries strive "*to eliminate poverty, maximize prosperity and achieve equality*" (Marshall 1967, 169). T.H. Marshall uses the term service without adding the adjective 'social'. However, the goals that are to be achieved by these services imply that only such services will be social that will be easily identifiable as being part of broader social support offered to individuals and social groups in the inclusion process. The author also differentiates between services and income and assumes that services (including social services) have a direct impact on well-being. As a consequence, we can presume that social services comprise such institutional actions taken by the state and its entities or financed from public funds and delivered by entities other than state institutions that directly contribute to a decrease in poverty levels and the reduction of social inequalities. The considerable role of social policy in forming the foundations of socio-economic growth and the services it provides is reflected both in the EU development guidelines and aid measures provided by the European Social Fund in order to support service provision.

The provision of high-quality public services, offered at affordable prices and meeting consumer and business needs, is an important element that contributes to the achievement of strategic goals, initially defined in the Lisbon Strategy (Lisbon Strategy 2000) and now part of Strategy Europe 2020 (Commission Communication 2010). Public services are now regarded as a key factor in boosting the competitiveness of the economy and ensuring social and territorial cohesion. The White Paper (*BiałaKsięga nt. usługużytecznościpublicznej. KomunikatKomisji do ParlamentuEuropejskiego, RadyKomitetuEkonomiczno-Społecznegoora zKomitetuRegionów*. Bruksela, 12.5.2004. COM (2004) 374 final) and the Green Paper (*Green Paper on Services of General Interest*, Brussels, 21.5.2003.COM(2003) 270 final) highlight the position of the EU as an institution promoting the necessity to develop high-quality public and social services and present the key elements of the strategy aiming to make these services available to all EU citizens and firms. Citizens expect access to high-quality services provided at affordable prices throughout the EU, as such services are an important component of the social model, and allow people to take full advantage of their human and civil rights. Firms, on the other hand, consider high-quality public services to be a necessary prerequisite to developing a competitive environment for business. The concept of public /social services attaches particular importance to their provision because:

(a) they are one of the most important pillars of the European social model, a key factor ensuring social order and economic, social and territorial cohesion in the European Union and a tool used to achieve the goals of the Lisbon Strategy and Strategy Europe 2020;
(b) they strive to implement the values accepted throughout Europe, including social fairness, equality, solidarity, the development of democracy and freedom and the respect of basic civil rights and human dignity;
(c) they cannot be regarded as a burden for public authorities—on the contrary, they yield positive results in terms of economic growth, prosperity, employment and social cohesion;
(d) they are provided in a dynamic environment, to which they have to adjust constantly in order to maintain high standards of quality and effectiveness;
(e) social services cannot be regarded as marginal, because due to the segment of the society to which they are addressed, as well as their spe-

cial nature from the point of view of the organization, financing and fulfilled tasks, should be treated as a separate and specific category of services with fundamental importance for society (Commission Communication 2010, 7–8).

Different views and perspectives of national and international public entities, described in The White Paper, contribute significantly to a discussion about the framework of society. The essence of implementing public and social services according to the EU, is that they reflect the values and objectives of the society, which were established on a number of common elements, such as: accessibility, continuity, quality and affordability, as well as user and consumer protection. Services as well as the environment in which they are provided, including the EU itself, are constantly evolving. The process will continue due to continuous changes in social structure. Changes are not limited to demographic ones but cover also political, sociological, and existential aspects of public life. On this basis, it is understandable that not only the public sector should deal with civic service. The progressive pressure on the effectiveness of the public sector creates the possibility of cooperating with the private sector as well as the social sector (third sector, non-profit, and so on). An important aspect is that, whether the provision of public services is organized in cooperation with the social sector or entrusted to private organizations, the definition of their mission, scope and supervision of implementation is still in the hands of public authorities with appropriate jurisdiction. This last statement directs our attention towards research studies about risk identification in the provision of public services. Final probe task, was to consolidate such management instruments, which if introduced, would benefit in increased effectiveness.

2 Social Services: New Service Providers, New Service Provision Methods

The development of the social policy concept, in particular the attempts to implement practical solutions characteristic of active social policies, influenced the emergence of new provision methods for social services. One such method, which has recently gained popularity, is the creation and growth of social economy entities. Social economy entities are a natural organizational response to the need for such pro-social solutions that, as their prime concern, pursue social goals while ensuring economic return on the invested public funds. By definition, the social economy is a system of enterprises and organizations, with respective legal regulations, which aim to support those at risk of social exclusion. The primary role of the social economy is to prevent social exclusion. The groups that are particularly threatened with social exclusion are the long-term unemployed, the homeless, the socially isolated, and addicts. From the practical perspective, the social economy bridges the private and public spheres, while its enterprises are entities of dual orientation, as they are both geared to the market and aiming at the integration of the socially excluded or the disadvantaged in the labour market. This dual orientation is manifested by the necessity to reconcile the efficacy and efficiency of business with the pursuit of social fairness goals. Social economy entities are a new socio-economic phenomenon in Poland. Their a priori attitude to support market activities of the disadvantaged groups is perceived both by citizens and researchers of economic processes with certain caution. Unfortunately, this negative association attached so far to social economy entities (including social enterprises) means that these organizations are not positioned in the national economy correctly. Moreover, it is unjustified considering the profits that they actually generate. Elinor Ostrom, a US political scientist, argues that the effectiveness of these organizations is particularly important in the driving forces behind national economies (Ostrom 2013, 10). It is fundamental that entrepreneurs and local communities should understand that profit maximization in terms of monetary value is not always the most important. Sometimes, long-run social goals, such as the integration of people excluded or at risk of exclusion from the labour market, can determine the economic potential and social cohesion of the entire country.

The growth levels and dynamics of social enterprises are related to the acceptance for and strengthening of manifestations of social entrepreneurship. Social entrepreneurship involves offering local communities benefits that they can reap as a result of economic initiatives taken in the conditions of risk stemming from business competition, while accepting the need to create public/social value as an inherent logic of the situation. The nature of social enterprises assumes fulfilling the needs of development, self-actualization and achievement of the economic effect that the participants of such enterprises have. This poses a new challenge for managers who are in charge of social enterprises, as they have to modify the existing management model and develop a new one that would account for the dual character of activity, so important in these entities. The necessity to reconcile contradictions on the continuum of market activity and public/social value creation is a particularly difficult task for managers, who are required to identify any risk involved in their actions

An important role of social entrepreneurship, which is a major force in business practice, has created the need for research on the phenomenon. In the literature, the issue of social entrepreneurship attracts considerable interest across the world. The seminal works were published by J.G. Dees (1998, 55–67, 1994, 54–58), A. Nicholls (2008, 2009, 755–769, 2010, 611–633), J. Thompson (2002, 412–431; Thompson et al. (2000, 328–338), F. Perrini (Perrini and Vurro 2006), C. Leadbeater (1997), P. C. Light (2008) and many others.

Researchers' interests and the scope of analysis are mainly determined by how they define social entrepreneurship and on what aspects and dimensions they focus. The literature identifies a number of separate research trends. One trend attempts to define social entrepreneurship as a scientific discipline and distinguish it from 'commercial' undertakings from an individual perspective. This school of thought is represented by K. Hockerts (2006), J. Mair and I. Martí (2006, 36–44, 2009, 419–435). In addition to these authors, it is worth quoting the research results and their analysis stemming from the formation of theoretical background by such scholars as J. Boschee (1998; Boschee and McClurg 2010), J. Weerawardena (Weerawardena and Mort 2006, 21–35) and G. Mort (Mort et al. 2003, 76–88). Another research trend, based on opportunity recognition theory, focuses on the assumption that entrepreneurs recognize social opportunities as worthy of exploiting. It is represented by such prominent scholars as J. Robinson (2006), E. Shaw (Shaw et al. 2002), S. Carter (Shaw and Carter 2007, 418–434) and S. Dorado (Dorado and Haettich 2011; Dorado 2006, 319–343). Although research on social entrepreneurs is still scarce, the existing examples indicate a number of distinctive features and skills. This research trend is pursued by such scholars as J. Thompson, G. Alvy and A. Lees (Thompson et al. 2000, 328–338), W. Drayton (2006, 80–96), J. Boschee (1998; Boschee and McClurg 2010). However, we still know relatively little about how business initiatives taken to pursue social goals are developed and implemented. Some researchers of social entrepreneurship, e.g. J. Defourny and M. Nyssens (2008, 202–228, 2010, 32–53), J. Kerlin (2010, 162–179) and C. Borzaga (Borzaga and Defourny 2001) also concentrate on the organizational level of social enterprises.

An increasing number of studies examine the impact that activity related to social entrepreneurship has on the local environment and, more broadly, the national economy. Among the scholars who study how social entrepreneurs perceive success and what indicators they use to measure performance, the most prominent places are occupied by H. Haugh (2005, 346–357, 2006), M. di Domenico (di Domenico et al. 2010, 681–703), C. Clark and L. Brennan (2012, 17–39) or R.D. Herman and D.O. Renz (Herman and Renz 1998, 823–838; Herman and Renz 2008, 339–415). The issue, which has attracted almost no research interest, is risk identification in social enterprises and a response to risk in their management practices. Hence, there is a noticeable knowledge gap in the area of risk perception in social enterprises.

The analysis of problems involved in risk perception and response in the management of a social economy entity does not only have a theoretical dimension, but, above all, it is of crucial importance for business practice. The study of emerging tendencies focuses researchers' interests on risk identification and minimization in social economy entities, as they have a significant impact on the effectiveness of social services provided by these organizations. Thus, it becomes particularly important for social entrepreneurs to develop the ability to use adequate financial and management tools, such as the recording and accounting of resources, performance reporting and measurement, and, finally, risk identification and the adoption of adequate response procedures. This is because economic performance is slowly becoming a basic indicator used to evaluate service-providing organizations, so their managers seek to make decisions that will win approval for the results of the enterprise from its customers and other stakeholders, and thereby legitimize its activity (Donaldson et al. 2008, 88–112). The issue that is crucial for the survival of the enterprise is that service providers have a variety of customers, whose interests are at best non-conflicting and whose assessment criteria may vary, or for whom the same criterion may have varying significance. This implies that the performance of a service-providing organization may be perceived differently by different stakeholders. The variability and vagueness of assessment criteria are a threat to the efficient operation of service providers and require research insight into what is perceived as risk by managers (Raczkowski et al. 2015, 14–55). Adequate risk identification contributes to the effective running of an organization. On the macro level, the development and existence of social enterprises are regarded as increasingly important for the foundation of socio-economic growth of the state, whereas on the individual level they improve the living conditions of people at risk of, or already suffering from, marginalization.

3 Characteristics of Social Enterprises

Considerable discrepancies exist as to the meaning of a social enterprise. First of all, it combines the characteristics of a non-governmental organization and a market entity, creating new jobs and setting additional goals of sustaining these jobs and providing services to local communities (Leś 2004, 7). Based on the proposal included in the UK government document, social enterprise can be defined as an institution that runs business activity, sets primarily social goals, and reinvests the earned surplus for those purposes in the business or in the community, rather than being driven by the need to maximize profits for shareholders and owners (DTI 2002). R. Dart argues that in order to fully understand the potential locked in social entrepreneurship, it is necessary to accurately define the concept of 'a social enterprise' (Dart 2004, 415). Generally, it is regarded as a basic institution of the social economy, a manifestation of new entrepreneurship, which pursues social obligations and is shaped by practices of the third sector. In the literature, some scholars perceive it as a more effective form of an organization in the non-for-profit sector, while others include it in the for-profit sector, emphasizing at the same time that it caters to the social needs emerging in the market (Harding 2004, 40–43). J. Pearce defines it as 'all the economic entities that have a social objective, are not oriented towards the generation and distribution of capital, and have a democratic and measurable structure based on joint governance' (Pearce 2003, 190). H. Haugh also sees a social enterprise as a collective term defining organizations acting for social objectives. They can adopt one of many available legal forms, but they share the commitment to finding solutions, based on commercial experiences, which will allow them to pursue social goals and reinvest profits from the operations for the benefit for the community (Haugh 2006, 5). M. Yunus points out that social enterprises are organizations aiming to maximize social benefits for people, but they are not interested in making particular individuals (shareholders) rich (Yunus 2008). J. Thompson and B. Doherty define them as organizations that apply business solutions to address social problems (Thompson and Doherty 2006, 403), while J. Hausner claims that they are part of the market economy that places their objectives and mission outside the market (Hausner et al. 2007).

Considering a great variety of approaches and classifications of social enterprises, the authors made a compilation of their existing definitions, which have emerged since 1994. In their majority, the definitions presented in Table 7.1 come from the articles published by the researchers interested in the issue.

The definitions presented in Table 7.1 were subsequently examined in terms of the frequency of particular logical constructs in each definition. This aimed to group repeat attributes of the term 'social enterprise' according to their frequency. The analysed texts yielded 29 attributes of the term, which were transcribed and reduced to keywords. The set of the identified qualities was quantitatively analysed with the use of the word cloud (Fig. 7.1). The word cloud highlights these key words that are the most frequent in the analysed text. The size of particular words forming a cloud corresponds with their frequency in the text. It is a quantitative method, which does not suffer from the weaknesses of interpretative examination (Klimas and Czakon 2010, 115). The application designed to create word clouds, available on http://www.wordle.net, established the frequency of the attributes in the definition for 'social enterprise'.

Table 7.1 Definitions of social enterprise

	Source	Definition
1.	J. G. Dees (1994)	Social enterprises are private organizations dedicated to solving social problems, serving the disadvantaged, and providing socially important goods that were not, in their judgment, adequately provided by public agencies or private markets
2.	J. Emerson and F. Twersky (1996)	Social enterprise is a revenue generating venture founded to create economic opportunities for very low income individuals, while simultaneously operating with reference to the financial bottom-line
3.	J. Pearce (2003)	A general term referring to all economic entities that have a social objective, are not oriented towards the generation and distribution of capital, and have a democratic and measurable structure based on joint governance
4.	OECD (2003)	Social enterprises are any private activities conducted in the public interest organised with an entrepreneurial strategy but whose main purpose is not the maximisation of profit but the attainment of certain economic and social goals, and which has a capacity of bringing innovative solutions to the problem of social exclusion and unemployment
5.	A. Ligane and S. Olsen (2004)	A seed-stage or early-stage venture that is designed to be profitable and that has an integrated social mission. The social impact of its operations is greater than the industry standard
6.	Dart (2004, 411)	Social enterprise differs from the traditional understanding of the nonprofit organization in terms of strategy, structure, norms, [and] values, and represents a radical innovation in the nonprofit sector
7.	R. Harding (2004, 41)	They are orthodox businesses with social objectives whose surpluses are principally reinvested for that purpose in the business or in the community, rather than being driven by the need to maximize profit for shareholders and owners
8.	H. Haugh (2006, 5)	Social enterprise is a collective term for a range of organizations that trade for a social purpose. They adopt one of a variety of different legal formats but have in common the principles of pursuing business led solutions to achieve social aims, and the reinvestment of surplus for community benefit. Their objectives focus on socially desired, nonfinancial goals and their outcomes are the nonfinancial measures of the implied demand for and supply of services

Table 7.1 (continued)

	Source	Definition
9.	J. Thompson and B. Doherty (2006, 362)	Social enterprises – defined simply – are organisations seeking business solutions to social problems
10.	K. Hockerts (2006, 145)	Social purpose business ventures are hybrid enterprises straddling the boundary between the for-profit business world and social mission-driven public and nonprofit organizations. Thus they do not fit completely in either sphere
11.	A. M. Peredo and J. J. Chrisman (2006)	Entails a community acting corporately as both entrepreneur and enterprise in pursuit of the common good
12.	R. L. Korosec and E. M. Berman (2006)	Organizations and individuals that develop new programs, services, and solutions to specific social problems and those that address the needs of special populations
13.	P. Hartigan (2006, 41)	They are orthodox businesses with social objectives "whose surpluses are principally re-invested for that purpose in the business or in the community, rather than being driven by the need to maximize profit for shareholders and owners"
14.	E. Leś (2004)	1. The subsector in the social economy, which is market-oriented and regarded as a separate, completely new institution of the social economy, the aim of which is to achieve economic balance through a successful combination of market and non-market sources of funding, non-financial resources (social labour) and income from private donors 2. The manifestation of the entrepreneurship of third-sector organisations, which combine classic solidarity with the spirit of entrepreneurship by developing business activity 3. The institutional response of third-sector organisations to the problems involved in the financing of non-profit organisations, stemming from the transformation of the post-war welfare state and a decrease in charitable donations
15.	J. Hausner et al. (2007)	A social enterprise is a specific piece of the market economy, placing its goals and missions outside the market. A social enterprise is the glue that connects attributes of the social economy of free-market principles

(continued)

Table 7.1 (continued)

	Source	Definition
16.	B. L. Masseti (2008, 7)	Social enterprise can be defined based on whether a business has a more market- or socially driven mission and whether or not it requires profit. The Social Entrepreneur Matrix combines those factors that most clearly differentiate social entrepreneurism from traditional entrepreneurism
17.	M. Yunus (2008)	Organisations oriented towards the maximisation of social benefits bringing value to people and completely uninterested in profiting particular individuals (shareholders)
18.	European Commission (2011)	Enterprises that (a) trade for the purpose of common good and have a strong element of social innovation, (b) reinvest profits for that purpose, (c) adopt a model (or a form of ownership) that reflects their mission with democratic or participatory procedures and the focus on social fairness
19.	J. Defourny and M. Nyssens (2012)	Social enterprises are organizations with an explicit aim to benefit the community, initiated by a group of citizens and in which the material interest of capital investors is subject to limits. They place a high value on their independence and on economic risk-taking related to ongoing socio-economic activity

Source: Own study

Fig. 7.1 Word cloud for social enterprise (Created with http://www.wordle.net)

As a result of the analysis of the word cloud made of the word-attributes of the definition 'social enterprise', the following conclusions may be risked:

(a) The scholars tend to agree that a social enterprise is regarded as an organization deliberately established or modified to fulfil particular objectives.
(b) The other identified attributes of the social enterprise are its perception as a quasi-economic activity, the inherent feature of which is that the profit made is allocated for statutory objectives—in other words, the profit is not paid out to shareholders, but reinvested in the business. The fact that these two attributes rank highly proves that although the social enterprise is defined as a business organisation, its most important imperative is the pursuit of the objectives socially perceived as important for local growth, in particular increased social cohesion. Accordingly, although in principle it should report a positive financial result (profit, surplus), two additional elements are emphasized: (1) the economic surplus earned by the enterprise is reinvested instead of being distributed among shareholders, and (2) the reinvestment area is defined by the enterprise's social mission and objectives. This hierarchy of goals highlights the primacy of social objectives over profit maximization and the reinvestment of profits in order to ensure the sustainable growth of the enterprise.
(c) The other qualities featuring in the definitions of the social enterprise are the following phrases: 'business solutions' and 'social problems'. They define both the focus and the method of operation. The focus, or the mission of the social enterprise, is to stimulate socio-economic growth by identifying, alleviating and preventing social problems. The strategy is the skilful implementation of social solutions in the actions taken by social managers. This involves the use of existing resources and the unlocking of the potential of the employees, according to both capabilities and needs, in order to maximize the intended effect. This approach is aligned with New Public Management (NPM), in particular its pro-efficiency approach, which, on one hand, highlights the necessity to implement business solutions, and on the other hand, stresses that these actions should be

based on the ideas of governance, which by definition values bottom-up participatory mechanisms and allows for the inclusion of stakeholders and local communities. It is notable that in addition to its social mission, the social enterprise should develop a business model accounting for the market realities. This explains why business-related aspects tend to emerge increasingly often.

(d) Further analysis of the definitions reveals that social enterprises are also characterised by innovation. This is particularly important in the light of a growing need for an innovative approach to identifying new areas of market opportunity. Social enterprises conduct innovative activity of social nature in the for-profit and non-profit sectors.

(e) The remaining identified attributes indicate that social enterprises operate in the area between the private and public sectors. It probably stems from the fact that, according to many researchers, they fill a gap in the economy that traditional enterprises do not want to enter due to insufficient profitability, while typical social organisations cannot run sufficiently effective operations there.

The compilation reveals a variety of applied criteria. Despite various legal forms and areas of operation, social enterprises share a number of features. Analysis of the definitions above reveals a few basic components of social enterprise:

(a) It makes a product or provides a service that involves business risk and it is verified in terms of the economic efficiency of this activity.
(b) It is driven by social integration objectives on the scale of a given local community.
(c) It gives primacy to stakeholders' interests over shareholder relations.
(d) Its management culture is based on partnership and participation.
(e) Democratic control comes from stakeholders.
(f) The earned surplus and accumulated capital are not owned individually, but they are used to pursue a particular social mission (Germak and Singh 2010, 86–89; Mair and Marti 2006, 38; Kelly 2003, 35; OECD 2003, 27; Mason 2012, 125–138).

A review of the literature provides a more detailed explanation, which argues that social enterprises are the initiatives that fulfil specific criteria. When J. Defourny presented the study conducted by the EMES network that aimed to identify the criteria distinguishing social enterprises, he defined two groups of criteria. The EMES definition comprises 9 criteria distinguishing social enterprises: four economic and five social ones. They are formulated in a relatively conservative way, which makes them more universal, but on the other hand limits their applicability and raises numerous interpretation-related concerns. The authors of the definition argue, however, that the criteria should not be regarded as necessary 'conditions' that each organization has to fulfil to earn the label of the social enterprise, but they might rather serve as a description of 'the ideal type' of such an enterprise (Defourny and Nyssens 2008, 210; Defourny and Develtere 2009; Defourny and Nyssens 2010, 33–36). The systemization of the features of a social enterprise comprises a number of criteria (or indicators) used to identify and evaluate such organizations, ranging from their business aspects (the attribute of entrepreneurship) to their social dimensions (the attribute of socialization). Accordingly, a social enterprise is any initiative that fulfils particular business and social criteria. The fulfilment of all the above criteria characterizes the ideal social enterprise; in practice, however, enterprises operating within the social economy possess only some of the discussed socio-economic qualities (Szot-Gabryś 2008, 126). As a consequence, a given entity can be regarded as a social enterprise provided it meets most of the criteria.

4 Identification of Rrisk in the Activity of Social Enterprises

This part aims to introduce some fundamental considerations about risk in the social economy literature. For much of human history, risk and survival have gone hand in hand. Analysis of secondary resources gives an additional insight about potential risks that may be encountered by organisations operating in the third sector.

Nowadays our lives are changing at an unprecedented pace. Transformational shifts in our economic, environmental, political and societal systems offer unparalleled opportunities, but the interconnections among them also imply enhanced systemic risks. Stakeholders from across government and civil society face an evolving imperative in understanding and managing emerging risks which, by definition, respect no boundaries. Risk by definition is a probability or threat of damage, injury, liability, loss, or any other negative occurrence that is caused by external or internal vulnerabilities, and that may be avoided through pre-emptive actions. Approach to delimiting the risk in social enterprises consists of identifying the main internal and external adversities. The conditions associated with the existence and stability of their functioning has been a leading concern of many scholars. In this chapter the problem is analysed from a multiple standpoint, by presenting a number of risk factors concerning social entrepreneurs, and by discussing some of the available data.

A key insight encapsulated in the literature was that of difficulties in defining social enterprise (Waśniewska 2012, 6; Wygański and Frączak 2006, 32). Many problems arising from running social activity relates to its hybridity. Bogacz-Wojtanowska described this as the necessity to combine social and economic requirements, which in fact increase the risk associated with confusion and inconsistency in key organisational assumptions (Bogacz-Wojtanowska 2012, 40). Amin argues that threat of risk reduces organizational goals in many ways, internally and externally, making standard operations not entirely predictable (Amin 2002, 13). This leads to the idea of risk identification. Social capital does not wear out with use, but rather with disuse (Ostrom 1999, 172); lack of local initiatives increase the risk of social exclusion and dysfunction, making it impossible to increase the wealth of society (Będzik 2008, 28). Less attracted in career and own development individuals (disabled or marginalized) with learned helplessness syndrome (Wygański, Frączak 2006, 33) seek for other than work opportunities, to make for living. Demanding attitudes and rising requirements for government support weaken the functionality of social initiatives. Following that it is appropriate to remember, how important the human factor is in social economy. Whenever there is a core element with limited or no possible substitutes (alternatives), the potential risk is higher. The following are good examples of potential internal risks: lack of competences and skilled professionals; poor marketing skills

(Bogacz-Wojtanowska 2012, 39; Raport ROPS... 2013, 32–35); neglected control function of management (Bogacz-Wojtanowska 2012, 38); lack of trust and social skills (Wygański, Frączak 2006, 34; Będzik 2008, 28); high individualism of involved people, making it difficult to combine efforts (Będzik 2008, 29); lack of commitment.

The generation coming of age in the 2010s faces high unemployment and precarious job situations, hampering their efforts to build a future and raising the risk of social unrest. In developing countries, an estimated two-thirds of the youth are not fulfilling their economic potential. Dees, Emerson and Economy, basing their argument on empirical evidence, suggest that social enterprises face a host of external problems, i.e. government cuts, rising demands, new forms of competition from the business sector, and rising requirements about their effectiveness (Dees et al. 2001, 67). There is no model of best practice (Amin 2002, 14) and no best method for conducting social activities. Different types of potential risks, make it hard to distinguish a best model of practice. Further examples of limiting factors are: a small number of projects and limited volume of permanent employees; financial limitations (Bogacz-Wojtanowska 2012, 35); regulations that are meant to support social cooperatives, but instead bring confusion and start-up difficulties; rigorous provisions for obtained resources from the Labour Fund to start the business; local authorities failing as a potential incubator of social initiatives; unresponsiveness of officials (Dąbrowska 2013, 56); overvaluation through excessive demand, which the Polish social economy cannot currently meet; chaotic growth of social economy (Wygański and Frączak 2006, 32–34); particularism, exclusive benefits for members of certain communities (ethnic, religious, cultural)—Weber's manifestation of social closure (Szarfenberg 2006, 6).

The Regional Social Economy Centre, based on data gathered from 15 social cooperatives actively working in north-east Poland, presented a list of the highest ranked problems affecting social initiatives. These are: lack of understanding and interest in social cooperatives among representatives of local authorities; market competition; difficulties in new projects acquisitions; complicated legal regulations; obstacles in obtaining the funds; limited access to supporting organizations. In response to a question about the most important internal problems of cooperatives, respondents most often pointed to: lack of knowledge about available governement help, or uneven involvement in organizational activities of members. Every third social cooperative pointed out the difficulty in balancing relations between the social reintegration mission and the desire to achieve economic efficiency (Raport ROPS w Białymstoku 2013, 32–35).

Threats emerging in the environment of the organization are risks for the effective functioning of a social enterprise, which in turn requires identification and quantification of risk factors in order to take actions to mitigate the impact and/or probability of the risk to an acceptable level. Risk identification is understood as recognition of the source of specific forms of risk that may appear in the organization. Risk analysis is understood as the quantitative and qualitative analysis of risks in organisation, while responding to risk is connected with minimizing the impact of previously detected threats. In this section, risks encountered by social enterprises have been identified. As presented research results concern so-called managerial perspective, what is presented here are views and opinions of social enterprises managers.

In order to study risks in the activity of social enterprises, a modified questionnaire proposed in the Canadian social enterprise guide was used (Enterprising Non-Profits Program 2005)[1]. Measure used in research consists 26 statements related to potential risks. The questionnaire was used to collect data in the form of the subjective opinions of respondents. Prior to this research, a thorough examination of secondary data sources (foreign and domestic literature, published studies) was conducted. On this basis, the research tool was created making it possible to collect the information about respondents' perception of potential risk factors. The target group in this research were representatives of top management (social entrepreneurs, managers of social enterprises). Managers of social enterprises (social entrepreneurs) received the questionnaire directly, as variables used in the study require information to be provided by people who have a good knowledge of the functioning and development of the whole organisation. The respondents assessed a series of 26 statements,

[1] The Canadian Social Enterprise Guide, Enterprising Non-Profits, 510 – 815 West Hastings Street, Vancouver, BC V6C 1B4, www.enterprisingnonprofits.ca, Most up to date copy available at: http://www.socialenterprisecanada.ca/en/learn/nav/canadiansocialenterpriseguide.html

declaring the degree to which the statements accurately describe perilous situations. Responses range along a seven-point scale (1, 'strongly disagree' to 7, 'strongly agree'). The research was conducted in social enterprises operating in the formula of social cooperatives based throughout Poland. The sample was selected randomly and comprised 160 social cooperatives (which equals 19 % of the total population); thus our sample formally meets the criteria of representativeness. Research took place in the period from 1 May 2015 to 30 June 2015.

The research indicates that 10 out of 26 surveyed risk factors can be considered as critical. Table 7.2 displays the weighted averages, standard deviations, and variances of the highest ranked variables included in our study (Table 7.3).

The study helped to identify a hierarchy of risks in the activity of social enterprises. The analysis of the overall evaluation of the distinct areas (calculated as the mean of each respondent's rating of the items in the areas) demonstrated that, according to the respondents, the following risks are the most crucial for the organisation: (1) the lack of employee involvement, (2) damage to the brand and reputation, (3) a decrease in the income (revenue), (4) a failure to comply with, or a violation of, terms and conditions of the contract, (5) the responsibility we bear for the quality of goods/services, (6) a deterioration of market conditions, (7) intentional or unintentional actions to the detriment of customers, (8) a failure to comply with or a breach of the contract by the operators and organizations we work with (partners), (9) a theft of cash earned by the organization (10) the loss of funding.

The respondents rated the lack of employee involvement as the highest risk in the activity of social enterprises (the mean of 6.2298, the standard deviation of 0.963). The importance of this risk factor is crucial for every organisation, but in the case of social enterprises its importance increases due to the socio-economic characteristics of people employed. Creating workplaces for people at the risk of social exclusion and professional marginalisation leads to employing long-term unemployed, people with disabilities (physical or mental), women returning to the job market after maternity leave, former inmates of prisons or pupils from orphanages. In addition to the difficulties that these groups face on the labour market, they might also pose a certain risk for an organisation—for example they

Table 7.2 Table of responses regarding risks in the activity of social enterprises

		Strongly disagree	Disagree	Somewhat disagree	Neither agree or disagree	Somewhat agree	Agree	Strongly agree	Wt. average	Stand. deviat.	Rank
1.	Injuries and accidents in the workplace	20	24	25	24	36	8	24	3.9441	1.911	26
2.	Death, retirement or resignation of key employees	12	16	16	20	28	24	45	4.7888	1.963	23
3.	Lack of employee involvement	0	0	4	4	24	48	81	6.2298	0.963	1
4.	Damage or destruction of property at organizations' headquarters	8	20	16	16	28	45	28	4.7578	1.830	21
5.	Loss of organizations' headquarters	0	16	36	20	21	20	48	4.8509	1.797	15
6.	The risk associated with the theft of equipment necessary for the operation of the organization	8	20	12	12	32	40	37	4.9130	1.862	17

7.	Theft of materials/ resources necessary to operate the organization	12	20	12	8	32	32	45	4.8882	1.997	18
8.	Theft of cash earned by the organization	12	16	24	8	4	40	57	5.0124	2.104	9
9.	Loss of critical organizational information	16	4	20	36	40	13	32	4.5342	1.792	25
10.	Theft or threat to intellectual property (e.g. imitating well-selling product)	4	12	16	44	12	44	29	4.8385	1.650	16
11.	Damage to the brand and reputation	4	4	4	12	32	48	57	5.7081	1.421	2
12.	Intentional or unintentional actions to the detriment of the customers	0	4	12	28	28	28	61	5.5342	1.454	7

(*continued*)

Table 7.2 (continued)

		Strongly disagree	Disagree	Somewhat disagree	Neither agree or disagree	Somewhat agree	Agree	Strongly agree	Wt. average	Stand. deviat.	Rank
13.	Intentional or unintentional actions to the detriment of cooperating entities and organizations (partners)	4	4	20	20	40	28	45	5.1863	1.586	12
14.	Intentional or unintentional actions to the detriment of the local communities in which organization exists	4	8	24	36	28	36	25	4.7640	1.571	22
15.	The responsibility we bear for the quality of goods/services	0	16	0	12	40	36	57	5.5590	1.520	5
16.	The possibility of damage to other persons or other organizations' properties	8	12	20	44	29	36	12	4.4286	1.564	20

17.	Failure to comply with, or violation of, terms and conditions of the contract	4	8	0	12	44	57	36	5.4783	1.397	4
18.	Failure to comply with or a breach of the contract by the operators and organizations we work with (partners)	0	8	12	16	40	53	32	5.3292	1.368	8
19.	Loss of funding	8	12	8	20	29	56	28	5.0497	1.687	10
20.	Loss of other income, e.g. grant from LGU	8	4	8	36	25	56	24	5.0497	1.548	11
21.	Decrease in the income (revenue)	0	4	0	28	32	44	53	5.6832	1.237	3
22.	Losses resulting from fire, flood or other random events	0	20	4	28	29	44	36	5.1242	1.600	14
23.	Deterioration of market conditions	0	8	4	36	36	57	20	5.1801	1.264	6

(*continued*)

Table 7.2 (continued)

		Strongly disagree	Disagree	Somewhat disagree	Neither agree or disagree	Somewhat agree	Agree	Strongly agree	Wt. average	Stand. deviat.	Rank
24.	Poor knowledge of employer's legal obligations	4	12	28	24	20	53	20	4.7578	1.642	13
25.	Poor knowledge of the applicable legislation (requirements, norms and standards of running the business)	8	12	20	20	24	49	28	4.8571	1.757	19
26.	Deliberate circumvention of the statutory obligations (e.g. social security contributions payment—including NHS, improper record of sales)	12	16	20	12	28	32	41	4.7888	1.963	24

LGU: Local Government Unit.

Table 7.3 Main risks in the activity of social enterprises

		Wt. average	Stand. deviat.	Rank
3	Lack of employee involvement	6.2298	0.963	1
11	Damage to the brand and reputation	5.7081	1.421	2
21	Decrease in the income (revenue)	5.6832	1.237	3
17	Failure to comply with, or violation of terms and conditions of the contract	5.4783	1.397	4
15	The responsibility we bear for the quality of goods/services	5.5590	1.520	5
23	Deterioration of market conditions	5.1801	1.264	6
12	Intentional or unintentional actions to the detriment of the customers	5.5342	1.454	7
18	Failure to comply with or a breach of the contract by the operators and organizations we work with (partners)	5.3292	1.368	8
8	Theft of cash earned by the organization	5.0124	2.104	9
19	Loss of funding	5.0497	1.687	10

may have incomplete qualifications, lack of work habit, potentially high morbidity and absenteeism, poor discipline, or lack of motivation due to low wages (Tworek 2014, 832; Haltiwanger et al. 2010). Current legislation adopted in Poland, regarding the social economy sector, requires that the contract of employment is entered with a social cooperative's member only after one year probation, which considering the above mentioned risk factors is sometimes a difficult task. Therefore, in order to minimise the risk, the manager of a social enterprise needs well-developed social skills embracing diversity management, conflict resolution and the ability to cooperate in a multicultural environment. Proper management skills are in the best interest of every enterprise because in the long run loyal and competent staff is a critical success factor. As the vast majority of Polish social enterprises are involved in the provision of services, their staff is the first and often the only source of an image built by an organisation to communicate with different stakeholders (customers, beneficiaries, and so on). Interestingly, one of the critical success factors of a social enterprise is, in fact, the motivation and commitment of employed people (Wronka 2012), which can be explained by the fact that profit not being the main motive for activity in the social sector is largely offset by a high degree of motivation shaped in particular by an effective and charismatic manager.

The risk factor rated second by the respondents is the loss of the brand and reputation (the mean of 5.7081, the standard deviation of 1.421). The choice of this factor can be explained by the fact that the success of non-profit organizations is often a consequence of how the organization is perceived in the public space. As the effectiveness of a social enterprise (in terms of not only performance itself, but also created value) is sometimes financially immeasurable and the results of its operation are visible only in the longer term (Kirby 2003, 20), it is necessary to present the activities of the enterprise in such a way that it is recognized and appreciated by stakeholders. The latter is of particular importance, as the social enterprise's employees may be perceived as stigmatised due to their previous labour market issues. This implies the need to take measures aimed at creating and strengthening key personal qualities for front-line service delivery, such as good manners, openness and communication skills, in order to create the positive image of an organisation. Neglecting such actions may result in less successful operations in the market.

The third risk factor in the activity of social enterprises is the decrease in income (the mean of 5.6832, the standard deviation of 1.237). Organisations that operate across sectors, for example as social enterprises, are different in terms of their 'defining source' of revenue (i.e. grants from various sources, such as a state government, foundations, companies, private sponsors, as well as the results of their own market activity) (O'Neill and Young 1988). The multiplicity of potential sources of financing is both an opportunity and a threat (Moore 2000, 183–186). The initial phase in the development of a social enterprise is often associated with a significant dependence on both the amount obtained as grants from public funds and the way of using it. One of the biggest risks in the activity of social enterprises is the moment when the organization stops using grants and starts relying solely on income resulting from its market activity. Personnel-related risks indicated earlier may build up at this moment and adversely affect the decrease in income, contributing in turn to the discontinuance of the social enterprise. In order to lower the level of that risk, social enterprises' managers must be able to identify, analyse and interpret financial performance indicators, while keeping in mind the priority social goals. Moreover, they need to approach the question of owned financial resources in a pro-active manner and configure them appropriately to the needs and realities of the social enterprise (Vladeck 1988, 71–81).

The factors that rank fourth and fifth in the hierarchy of risks subjectively perceived by the respondents are the responsibility that a social enterprise bears for the quality of goods/services (the mean of 5.5590, the standard deviation of 1.520) and the failure to comply with or the violation of terms and conditions of the contract (the mean of 5.5590, the standard deviation of 1.397). These factors are strongly associated with the most important risk factor in the organisation, which is the human factor. Both the responsibility for the quality of goods/services and the failure to comply with or the violation of terms and conditions of the contract can be variously interpreted—for example as the fear that the level of employee involvement in the work process is not high enough and this results in the poor execution of contracted tasks (or performing those tasks on a lower level than expected or not within certain time constraints). This may lead to reluctance to subcontract other tasks. Another potential risk associated with these factors is whether employees fully accept working conditions in the organization. Sometimes employees' ideas regarding potential income or the nature of the job are incompatible with the reality, a consequence of which may be rejection of organizational norms and values as well as a tendency to act in an opportunistic way. The ultimate result on the individual level may be the withdrawal from the social enterprise, while at the organizational level it may even involve problems with maintaining the established social cooperative (the activity of which in Poland is related to the number of people who received financial support at the beginning of its functioning).

According to the respondents, another threat to the development and operations of the social enterprise is a deterioration of market conditions (the mean of 5.1801, the standard deviation of 1.264). Unfavourable market changes lead to a reduced demand for goods and services as well as greater rivalry between competitors. For social enterprises, adapting quickly to changing conditions and acute competition is a challenging task. It is especially difficult in small local markets, where the fundamental idea of the social economy—bringing pro-employment activities among the marginalized in the labour market and thus the creation of public/social value—may not be fully appreciated by consumers. Customers often seek a cheaper product/service or one of better quality rather than focus on supporting pro-employment activities through their market choices.

Another factor identified as a risk is intentional or unintentional actions to the detriment of customers (the mean of 5.5342, the standard deviation of 1.454), which might be interpreted as a consequence of the poor understanding of job descriptions by employees. While intentional actions are rare, unintentional ones can be encountered more often owing to the psycho-social status of employees. This is particularly evident in organizations employing people with mental disabilities. As indicated earlier, in order to operate effectively, it is essential for the social enterprise to maintain good relationships in the micro-environment. Hence, the risk ranked just below being the failure to comply with or the breach of contract by the operators and organisations (partners) (the mean of 5.3292, the standard deviation of 1.369). The selection of this factor is determined by the specificity of social enterprises and the need to obtain institutional support from organizations and entities with whom they work (i.e. funders, clients, volunteers, public authorities, pressure groups, local communities, private donors, citizens, other social enterprises or even for-profit organizations). Since the survival of the social enterprise largely depends on its ability to preserve liquidity, which, due to combining economic activities with social objectives, is not an easy task, thoughtful partnering organizations, which can understand the temporary difficulties of social enterprises, are crucial. What is undoubtedly another challenge is the fact that stakeholders and partners perceive social enterprise through the prism of their particular needs (Herman and Renz 1997, 190–192). Therefore, pro-employment and pro-social objectives of social enterprises are not always taken into consideration. Inevitably, the inability to manage partner relationships can affect the survival of social enterprises.

The ninth factor identified as a risk by respondents is the theft of cash earned by the organization (the mean of 5.0124, the standard deviation of 2.104). This choice may be determined by the fact that most enterprises involved in the sale of products/services are exposed to risks associated with theft of profits. The more problematic the contact of social enterprises' employees with potential customers, the greater that risk becomes. The above-mentioned difficulties may arise from a lower level of social skills being the consequence of mental or physical dysfunctions.

The tenth factor identified as a risk to the social enterprise is the loss of funding (the mean of 5.0497, the standard deviation of 1.687). In recent years, Poland has reported an increase in the number of social enterprises (mainly social cooperatives), being a consequence of financing activities related to active (or activating) social policies (ASP) pursued by the EU member states in the framework of the European Social Fund. Unfortunately, financial support for newly created social enterprises is limited to one year, after which it is possible to receive bridge financing to ensure that an organization is able to cover mandatory fees. Following this period, an organization should become independent and financially self-sufficient, which, as shown in many statistics, is not always the case. Therefore, some social enterprises experience difficulties in the market, often having to close down. The loss of funding and the lack of market mechanisms cause problems on both the individual (as the employment of people previously working in social enterprises may be terminated) and the local community (as growing numbers of the unemployed result in greater income inequalities, lack of cohesion and social problems) level.

5 Conclusions

In sum, social services underlie a certain quality and standard of living. Regulations, that stands behind social services, guaranteed by amended European Social Card and Universal Declaration of Human Rights, secure the society in respecting their rights to social justice, bringing social cohesion. Public authorities have a general responsibility for the efficient operation of social services. Not only do additional funds maintain a high level of quality but they also maintain the provision of knowledge and expertise. Hence the need for special attention to potential risks, which may destructively affect continuous growth in the social sector. In fact, their precise identification might help prepare a suitable management tool, which may increase the effectiveness of social enterprises in fulfilling their organizational objectives. Social services in all EU countries are provided by a wide range of organizations from the social sector. The largest proportions of them are those with objectives to help society, increase welfare, but gain no profit from operations (associations, cooperatives, foundations). Derived from various initiatives (public, charitable, philanthropic, religious, private, etc.) they fulfil an important role—the more so, because the nature of the socio-economic behavioural characteristics of the people forming them, can hamper their smooth functioning on the open market.

Contemporary organisations, functioning in a turbulent environment, with a limited number of professionals and poor knowledge about regulations, face the need to meet many complex requirements and it is necessary for them to adjust to constant changes. The current situation requires social enterprises to be innovative and to shift their orientation towards achieving results in terms of efficiency and effectiveness (Kieżun 2000, 32). The shift in attitudes to entrepreneurship has been noticeable recently. Entrepreneurship is not only an economic but also a social activity that influences society (Steyart and Katz 2004, 82), and positive outcomes are not the necessary condition of entrepreneurship (Shane 2003, 57, Dey and Steyaert 2010, 89–93). Therefore, the identification of risks in the activity of social enterprise should be one of the fundamental tasks of their management, as these risks may determine the areas in which strategic decisions are to be placed, as well as the areas, procedures and processes which need to be facilitated. These issues are crucial especially for social enterprises, which nowadays face significant difficulties regarding the efficiency of their activities.

Risk identification is the first step in pro-active participation in the social environment. Understanding root causes can help to identify additional, related risks. Analysis of emerging trends directs the attention to risk identification, an ability that is of particular importance, especially for social entrepreneurs as it is essential for the effectiveness of the services they provide. It is commonly recognised that risk identification and assessment have the largest impact on the accuracy of judgments.

The results of our study show how social entrepreneurs perceive risks. As such, these findings provide a glimpse into the composition of factors associated with threat, tied up to fundamental facets of operating social enterprises. Such knowledge provides an additional tool for social entrepreneurs to actively run their businesses in a rapidly changing environment. We feel that the description of factors presented in this study provides some useful directions for those who manage social cooperatives thereby fostering a deep understanding of possible risks. It provides the opportunities, indicators, and information that allow social entrepreneurs to predict major risks before they adversely affect operations.

The twenty-six risk related factors proposed in the questionnaire were, broken into two separate groups—internal and external. Out of the ten with the highest results, three were external (decline of market conditions; failure to comply with or breach of contract by the operators and organizations we work with (partners); loss of funding) while the remaining seven were internal causations (lack of employee involvement; loss of brand and reputation; decrease of income; failure to comply with, or violation of terms and conditions of the contract; the responsibility we bear for the quality of goods/services; intentional or unintentional actions to the detriment of the customers; theft of cash earned by the organization). It means that more internal aspects are higher risk ones, which supports the opinion that proper relations, communication and the identification of employees' needs, problems, dysfunctions and disabilities, are at the heart of the prosperity of social cooperatives.

Risk identification and risk awarness may provide a rationale for actions taken on other grounds, to prevent, and be prepared to provide a surrogate for social, ideological and economic ailments. Risk communication and risk identification efforts are destined to fail unless they are structured as a two-way process. Each side, entrepreneur and employee, has something valid to contribute. Each side must respect the insights and dysfunctions of the other.

Perhaps the most important message from this research is that there is a wisdom as well as error in attitudes towards and the perceptions of social economy. People sometimes lack certain information. The challenge is stimulating and motivating a group of people who are estranged form society. Managers need proper skills as well as guidelines to facilitate smooth operations, i.e. how to increase the involvement of co-workers and improve their sense of responsibility for their actions.

Proper knowledge may reduce the amount of social cooperatives closures. Based on study findings, 33 % of social cooperatives record a loss, 44 % report that their organizational revenues offset organizational costs, and only 23 % confirm their profitability. From the economic point of view, it is important to decrease the amount of businesses that suffer lack of stability and liquidity, mainly because of the continuous growth of the social economy, and the increasing needs of society. The average number of employees working in social cooperatives examined during our research, numbered up to 10. It means that up to 10 individuals per initiative received a chance to return to and assimilate with society. This measure could be presented in quantified economic values, but this may possibly be the domain of future studies (such as SROI).

Bibliography

Amin, A. (2002). *Placing the social economy*. New York: Routledge.

Będzik, B. (2008). Bariery i możliwości generowania kapitału społecznego na obszarach wiejskich w Polsce [Barriers and abilities to generatesocialcapital in ruralareas of Poland]. *Oeconomia, 7*(4), 27–34.

Bogacz-Wojtanowska, E. (2012). Problemy organizacji pozarządowych przekształcających się w podmioty ekonomii społecznej [Problems of non-governmentalorganizationsconvertingintosocialcooperatives]. *Ekonomia społeczna, 1*(4), 33–42.

Borzaga, C., & Defourny, J. (Eds.) (2001). *The Emergence of Social Enterprise*. London: Routledge.

Boschee, J. (1998). *Merging mission and money: A board member's guide to social entrepreneurship*. Washington, DC: The National Centre for Nonprofit Boards.

Bosehee, J., & McClurg, J. (2010). Toward a better understanding of social entrepreneurship: Some important distinctions. http://www.se-alliance.orgf-better_understanding.pdf

Clark, C., & Brennan, L. (2012). Entrepreneurship with social value: A conceptual model for performance measurement. *Academy of Entrepreneurship Journal, 18*(2), 17–39.

Commission Communication. (2003). Green Book on Services of General Interest (2003) Brussels, 270 Final.

Commission Communication. (2004). White Book on SGI (2004) Brussels, 374 Final.

Commission Communication. (2007). Services of general interest, including social services of general interest: a new European commitment (2007), 725 Final.

Commission Communication. (2010). EUROPE 2020 A strategy for smart, sustainable and inclusive growth (2010) Brussels.

Dąbrowska, E. (2013) Uwarunkowania rozwoju spółdzielczości socjalnej osób bezrobotnych w Polsce. EkonomiaspołecznadlarozwojuSpołecznościlokaln ych [Conditions for development of social cooperatives in Poland. Social economy, development of local communities], (red. A. Ejsmont, J. Ruszewski) Suwałki.

Dart, R. (2004). The legitimacy of social enterprise. *Nonprofit Management & Leadership, 14*(4), 411–424.

Dees, J. D. (1998) The meaning of 'social entrepreneurship'. Centre for Advancement of Social Entrepreneurship (CASE), Fuqua School of Business, Duke University, Durham. www.fuqua.duke.edu/centers/case/articles/0805/corner

Dees, J. G. (1994). Social enterprise: Private initiatives for the common good. *Harvard Business Review, 76*, 54–58.

Dees, J. G., Emerson, E., & Economy, P. (2001). *Enterprising nonprofits: A toolkit for social entrepreneurs*. New York: John Wiley and Sons.

Defourny, J. (2004) Przedsiębiorstwo społeczne w poszerzonej Europie koncepcja i rzeczywistość [Socialenterprise in anenlarged Europe, the concept and the reality], referat zaprezentowany podczas II Europejskiej Konferencji EkonomiiSpołecznejwKrakowie/paperpresentedatIIEuropeanSocialEconomy Conference in Cracow, ZLSP.

Defourny, J., & Develtere, P. (2009). The social economy: The worldwide making of a third sector. In J. Defourny, P. Develtere, B. Fonteneau, & M. Nyssens (Eds.), *The worldwide making of the social economy. Innovations and changes*. Leuven & The Hague: Acco.

Defourny, J., & Nyssens, M. (2008). Social enterprise in Europe: Recent trends and developments. *Social Enterprise Journal, 4*(3), 202–228.

Defourny, J., & Nyssens, M. (2010). Conceptions of social enterprise and social entrepreneurship in Europe and the United States: Convergences and divergences. *Journal of Social Entrepreneurship, 1*(1), 32–53.

Defourny, J., & Nyssens, M. (2012). The Emes approach of social enterprise in a comparative perspective, WP no. 12/03, EMES European Research Network.

Dey, P., & Steyaert, C. (2010). The politics of narrating social entrepreneurship. *Journal of Enterprising Communities: People and Places in the Global Economy, 4*(1), 85–108.

di Domenico, M., Haugh, H., & Tracy, P. (2010). Social bricolage: Theorizing social value creation in social enterprises. *Entrepreneurship Theory and Practice, 34*(4), 681–703.

Donaldson, C., Bate, A., Mitton, C., Peacock, S., & Ryta, D. (2008). Priority setting in the public sector: turning economics into a management process. In J. Hartley, C. Donaldson, C. Skelcher, & M. Wallace (Eds.), *Managing to improve public services*. Cambridge: Cambridge University Press.

Dorado, S. (2006). Social entrepreneurial ventures: Different values so different processes of creation, no? *Journal of International Development, 11*(4), 319–344.

Dorado, S., & Haettich, H. (2011). Social entrepreneurial ventures: Worth a careful look? Working paper, Colledge of Mangement, UMASS-Boston.
Drayton, B. (2006). Everyone a changemaker: Social entrepreneurship's ultimate goal. *Innovations, 1*(1), 80–96.
DTI. (2002). Social enterprise: A strategy for success. www.seeewiki.co.uk/~wiki/images/5/5a/SE_Strategy_for_success.pdf
Emerson, J., & Twerksy, F. (1996). *New social entrepreneurs: The success, challenge and lessons of non-profit enterprise creation.* San Francisco: Roberts Foundation, Homeless Economic Development Fund.
Enterprising Non-Profits Program. (2005). The Canadian Social Enterprise Guide. Vancouver. http://vibrantcanada.ca/files/social_enterprise_guide.pdf
European Commission. (2011). COM(2011)0682 final. http://ec.europa.eu/internal_market/social_business/docs/COM2011_682_en.pdf
European Council of Lisbon (2000). *The Lisbon strategy*. Lisbon: European Council of Lisbon.
Frączkiewicz-Wronka, A. (eds.) (2009). Zarządzanie publiczne – elementy teorii i praktyki [Public Management – Elements of theory and practice], Wydawnictwo Uniwersytetu Ekonomicznego w Katowicach.
Germak, A. J., & Singh, K. K. (2010). Social entrepreneurship: Changing the way social workers do business. *Administration in Social Work, 34*(1), 79–95.
Haltiwanger, G., Landaeta, R. E., Pinto, C. A., & Tolk, A. (2010). Understanding the relationship between risk management and knowledge management. *International Journal of Knowledge Management Studies, 4*(3), 281–300.
Harding, R. (2004). Social enterprise: The new economic engine? *Business Strategy Review, Winter*, 39–43.
Hartigan, P. (2006). It's about people, not profits. *Business Strategy Review, 17*(4), 42–45.
Haugh, H. (2005). The role of social enterprise in regional development. *International Journal of Entreperenurship and Small Business, 2*(4), 346–357.
Haugh, H. (2006). Social enterprise: Beyond economic outcomes and individual returns. In J. Mair, J. Robinson, & K. Hockerts (Eds.), *Social entrepreneurship*. Basingstoke: Palgrave Macmillan.
Hausner, J., Laurisz, N., & Mazur, S. (2007). Przedsiębiorstwo społeczne – konceptualizacja [Social enterprise – Conceptualization]. In J. Hausner (Ed.), *Zarządzanie podmiotami ekonomii społecznej [Managing social economy entities]*. Kraków: Małopolska Szkoła Administracji Publicznej.
Herbst, J. (2008) Wstęp – pole przedsiębiorczości społecznej. Od trzeciego sektora do przedsiębiorczości społecznej – wyniki badań ekonomii społecznej w Polsce [Introduction – The field of socialentrepreneurship. From the third

sector to social entrepreneurship – Social economy in Poland, StowarzyszenieKlon/Jawor.
Herman, R. D., & Renz, D. O. (1997). Multiple constituencies and the social construction of non-profit organization effectiveness. *Non-profit and Voluntary Sector Quarterly, 26,* 190–192.
Herman, R. D., & Renz, D. O. (1998). Nonprofit organizational effectiveness: contrasts between especially effective and less effective organizations. *Nonprofit Management & Leadership, 9*(1).
Herman, R. D., & Renz, D. O. (2008). Advancing nonprofit organizational effectiveness research and theory: Nine theses. *Nonprofit Management & Leadership, 18*(4).
Hockerts, K. (2006). Entrepreneurial opportunity in social purpose business ventures. In J. Mair, J. Robinson, & K. Hockerts (Eds.), *Social entrepreneurship*. Basingstoke: Palgrave Macmillan.
Kelly, S. (2003). In T. Kaźmierczak & M. Rymsza (Eds.), *Ekonomia społeczna i przedsiębiorczość społeczna w Unii Europejskiej [Socialeconomy and socialentrepreneurship in the European Union], W stronę aktywnej polityki społecznej.* Warszawa: Fundacja Instytut Spraw Publicznych.
Kerlin, J. A. (2010). A comparative analysis of the global emergence of social enterprise. *Voluntas: International Journal of Voluntary and Nonprofit Organizations, 21*(2), 162–179.
Kieżun,W.(2000).Transformacjaadministracjipublicznejwświetleteoriiorganizacji i zarządzania [Transformation of public administration in the light of the theory of organization and management], MBA no. 1.
Kirby, D. A. (2003). *Entrepreneurship*. London: McGraw Hill Education.
Klimas, P., & Czakon, W. (2010) Sieci oraz firmy kotwice – ich znaczenie w gospodarce opartej na wiedzy [Networks and anchor firms – their importance in the knowledge economy], Zarządzanie. Informatyka. Dylematy i kierunki rozwoju, Uniwersytet Ekonomiczny w Katowicach, Centrum Badan i Ekspertyz, Katowice.
Korosec, R. L., & Berman, E. M. (2006). Municipal support for social entrepreneurship. *Public Administration Review, 66*(3), 448–462.
Leadbeater, C. (1997). *The rise of social entrepreneur*. London: Demos.
Leś, E. (2004). Przedsiębiorczość społeczna [Social entrepreneurship]. *Nowe Życie Gospodarcze, 15.*
Leś, E. (2007). Rola trzeciego sektora w polityce społecznej [The role of third sector in social economy]. In G. Firlit-Fesnak & M. Szylko-Skoczny (Eds.), *Polityka społeczna*. Warszawa: PWN.
Ligane, A., & Olsen, S. (2004). Guidelines for social return on investment. *California Management Review, 46*(3), 116–135.

Light, P. C. (2008). *The search for social entrepreneurship*. Washington, DC: Brookings Institution Press.

Lipka, A. (2002). Ryzyko personalne. Szanse i zagrożenia zarządzania zasobami ludzkimi [Personal risk. Opportunities and threats of human resources management], Poltext.

Mair, J. (2011). Social entrepreneurship: Taking stock and looking ahead. In A. Fayolle & H. Matlay (Eds.), *Handbook on social entrepreneurship*. Cheltenham: Edward Elgar.

Mair, J., & Martí, I. (2006). Social entrepreneurship research: A source of explanation, prediction, and delight. *Journal of World Business, 41*(1), 36–44.

Mair, J., & Martí, I. (2009). Social entrepreneurship in and around institutional voids. *Journal of Business Venturing, 24*(5) 419–435.

Marshall, T. H. (1967). *Social policy*. London: Hutchinson University Library.

Masseti, B. L. (2008). The social entrepreneurship matrix as a "tipping point" for economic change. *Emergence: Complexity and Organization, 10*(3), 1–8.

Miżejewski, C. (2006). Polityka społeczna wobec sektora ekonomii społecznej [Social policy towards the socialeconomy]. *Polityka Społeczna, 7*, 1.

Moore, M. (2000). Managing for value: Organizational strategy in for-profit, nonprofit, and governmental organizations. *Nonprofit and Voluntary Sector, 20*(1), 183–186.

Mort, G. S., Weerawardena, J., & Carnegie, K. (2003). Social entrepreneurship: Towards conceptualisation. *International Journal of Nonprofit and Voluntary Sector Marketing, 8*(1), 76–88.

Nicholls, A. (2006). Social entrepreneurship. In S. Carter & D. Jones-Evans (Eds.), (second edition), *Enterprise and small business: Principles, practice and policy*. Harlow, Essex: Pearson Education.

Nicholls, A. (2009). We do good things, don't we?: Blended value accounting in social entrepreneurship. *Accounting, Organizations and Society, 34*(6–7), 755–769.

Nicholls, A. (2010). The institutionalization of social investment: The interplay of investment logics and investor rationalities. *Journal of Social Entrepreneurship, 1*(1), 70–100.

OECD. (2003). *The non-profit sector in a changing economy*. Paris: Organisation for Economic Co-operation and Development.

O'Neill, M., & Young, D. R. (1988). *Educating managers of nonprofit organizations*. New York: Praeger.

Ostrom, E. (1999). Social capital: A fad or a fundamental concept. In P. Dasgupta & I. Serageldin (Eds.), *Social capital: A multifaceted perspective* (pp. 172–214). Washington, DC: The World Bank.

Ostrom, E. (2013). *Dysponowanie wspólnymi zasobami [Governing the commons]*. Warszawa: WoltersKluwer.

Pearce, J. (2003). *Social enterprise in anytown*. London: CalousteGulbenkian Foundation.

Pennings, P. (2010, March). Exploring variations in the political discourse on public sector reforms, 1981–2005. *Public Management Review, 12*(2), 173–190.

Peredo, A. M., & Chrisman, J. J. (2006). Toward a theory of community-based enterprise. *Academy of Management Review, 31*(2), 309–328.

Perrini, F., & Vurro, C. (2006). Social entrepreneurship: Innovation and social change across theory and practice. In J. Mair, J. Robinson, & K. Hockerts (Eds.), *Social entrepreneurship*. Basingstoke: Palgrave Macmillan.

Raczkowski, K., Noga, M., & Klepacki, J. (2015). *Zarządzanie ryzykiem w polskim systemie finansowym [Risk management in polish financial system]*. Warszawa: Difin.

Regionalny Ośrodek Polityki Społecznej w Białymstoku [Regional Center of Social Policy] (2013). *Raport: Diagnoza stanu i potrzeb spółdzielni socjalnych z terenu województwa podlaskiego [Diagnosis of the condition and needs of socialcooperatives from across the region of Podlasie]*. Białystok: Obserwatorium Integracji Społecznej.

Robinson, J. (2006). Navigating social and institutional barriers to markets: How social entrepreneurs identify and evaluate opportunities. In J. Mair, J. Robinson, & K. Hockerts (Eds.), *Social entrepreneurship*. Basingstoke: Palgrave Macmillan.

Rymsza, M. (2005). Stara i nowa ekonomia społeczna. Polska na tle doświadczeń europejskich [Old and new social economy. Poland appraisal base on European experiences]. *TrzeciSektor, 2*, 2.

Shane, S. (2000). Prior knowledge and the discovery of entrepreneurial opportunity. *Organization Science, 11*, 448–469.

Shane, S. (2003). *A general theory of entrepreneurship: The individual-opportunity nexus*. Cheltenham: Edward Elgar, 448–469.

Shaw, E., & Carter, S. (2007). Social entrepreneurship: Theoretical antecedents and empirical analysis of entrepreneurial processes and outcomes. *Journal of Small Business and Enterprise Development, 14*, 418–434.

Shaw, E., Shaw, J., & Wilson, M. (2002). *Unsung entrepreneurs: Entrepreneurship for social gain*. Durham: University of Durham Business School.

Steyaert, C., & Katz, J. (2004, May). Reclaiming the space for entrepreneurship in society: Geographical, discursive, and social dimensions. *Entrepreneurship & Regional Development, 16*.

Szarfenberg, R. (2006) Słabości trzeciego sektora i partnerstwa publiczno-prywatnego [Weaknesses of the third sector and public-privatepartnerships], Instytut Polityki Społecznej, Uniwersytet Warszawski.

Szot-Gabryś, T. (2008). Koncepcja ekonomiczna przedsiębiorstwa społecznego – studium przypadku [The economicconcept of socialenterprise – Casestudy]. *Problemy Zarządzania, 2*(21), 126.

Thompson, J. L. (2002). The world of the social entrepreneur. *The International Journal of Public Sector Management, 15,* 412–431.

Thompson, J., & Doherty, B. (2006). The diverse world of social enterprise: A collection of social enterprise stories. *International Journal of Social Economics, 33*(5/6), 399–410.

Thompson, J., Alvy, G., & Lees, A. (2000). Social entrepreneurship – A new look at people and the potential. *Management Decision, 38*(5/6), 328–338.

Tworek, P. (2014). Behavioural aspects of risk management in investment processes in construction. In M. Čulik (Ed.), *Managing and modeling of financial risks* (Part III). Proceedings from 7th International Conference, VŠB – TechnickáUniverzita Ostrava, Ostrava.

Verhoest, K., & Mattei, P. (2010). Welfare governance reforms and effects in the post-Golden Age. *Public Management Review, 12*(2), 163–171. March.

Vladeck, B. C. (1988). The practical differences in managing nonprofits: A practitioner's perspective. In M. O'Neill & Y. D.R (Eds.), *Educating managers of nonprofit organizations.* New York: Praeger.

Waśniewska, A. (2012). Problemy rozwoju Ekonomii Społecznej (na podstawie badań) [Problems in developing sociale conomy (based on research)]. *Zeszyty Naukowe Akademii Morskiej w Gdyni, 72,* 1–15.

Weerawardena, J., & Mort, G. S. (2006). Investigating social entrepreneurship: A multidimensional model. *Journal of World Business, 41,* 21–35.

Weerawardena, J., Mort, G. S., & Carnegie, K. (2003). Social entrepreneurship: Towards conceptualisation. *International Journal of Nonprofit and Voluntary Sector Marketing, 8*(1), 76–86.

Wronka, M. (2012). Analyzing the success of social enterprises – Critical success factors perspective. In V. Dermol, N. TrunkŠirca, & G. Dakovic (Eds.), *Active citizenship by knowledge management & innovation.* Proceedings of the management, knowledge and learning international conference. MakeLearn, Cejle 2013.

www.ekonomiaspołeczna.pl – Serwis ten służy tym organizacjom, które interesują się ekonomią społeczną, czyli np. przedsiębiorstwami społecznymi, spółdzielniami socjalnymi, działaniem na rzecz bezrobotnych itp. [This service serves organizations that are interested in the social economy, i.e. social enterprises, social cooperatives and any other activities focused on social integration of society.

Wygański, K., & Frączak, P. (2006). Ekonomia społeczna w Polsce – definicje, zastosowania, oczekiwania, wątpliwości [Social Economy in Poland – Definitions, applications, expectations, doubts]. *Ekonomia Społeczna, 1,* 1–40.

Yunus, M. (2008). *Creating a world without poverty: Social business and the future of capitalism.* New York: Public Affairs Books.

8

Identification of Risks Related to the Operations in the Internet

Sylwia Wojciechowska-Filipek and Zbigniew Ciekanowski

1 Introduction

Dynamic growth of information and communication technologies has long affected the manner in which a human being, organization, society or state operates. Nevertheless, the Internet triggered a genuine revolution, as it allowed for a shift from the traditional market into the so-called electronic market. It was possible to move the operations to cyberspace and carry them out on an unprecedented scale while minimizing costs. Networks and mutual interdependence became the common protocols designed for organizing collaboration that ensured effective exploitation of resources as well as high flexibility and quick response to shifts in the market. Hence, enterprises beginning to move

S. Wojciechowska-Filipek (✉)
University of Social Sciences, Warszawa, Poland

Z. Ciekanowski
Cardinal Stefan Wyszyński University, Warszawa, Poland

K. Raczkowski (ed.), *Risk Management in Public Administration*,
DOI 10.1007/978-3-319-30877-7_8

part of their operations to the Internet and depart from traditional business forms. Currently, for today's organizations, the connection with the complex environment such as the Internet is no longer a choice, but a necessity. An organization that fails to have at least a simple website practically does not exist in the market and is not able to compete there. Business operations conducted in cyberspace yield multiple gains to all market participants, yet it is necessary to keep in mind that it also generates completely new threats, not experienced in the traditional business model.

The objective of the paper is to characterize new potentials for organizations' operations in cyberspace as well as to analyse risks created by the transfer of the business operations to the Internet.

2 Functioning of the Organization on the Internet

Dynamic changes occurring in the organization's environment encourage the taking of decisions that would make it possible to carry out operations in a more flexible manner aligned to new requirements. This refers to both commercial enterprises as well as public organizations and indeed the whole state. Changes not only include the implementation of new technologies into products and services, communication processes and management systems, but they also apply to the manner and culture in which the operations are conducted. Basically, the adoption of virtual solutions by organizations is determined by multiple factors likely to be structured into three basic groups (Wojciechowska-Filipek 2014, 98):

a) External factors related to macro-economy, legislation, operations conducted by agencies, progress of technology and telecommunication infrastructure, digital education, and so on. They have an immense impact on modelling other groups of factors, because they define the opportunities for their potential development.
b) Factors dependent on the organization—those which are affected by the organization itself and its management. These include, e.g. cre-

ation of its own website or application of information and communication technologies by employees to execute their work and business contacts.

c) Social (human) factors—concerned with transformations emerging in society (e.g. development of information society) and humanity itself (personal predilections, education, age, risk propensity, and so on).

The forming of these factors affects the swiftness and scope of the application of new solutions by organizations. The literature distinguishes four elementary phases for service development in the Internet that reflect the primary phases through which electronic distribution channels were exploited for organizations' operations (Wojciechowska-Filipek 2010, 67–69; Rorissa et al. 2011, 355):

a) *First phase—online presence.* A website at this phase only contains statistical data. A key element and the core of the first phase of transformation is to provide the customer with the largest amount of information about the organization's operations.
b) *Second phase—initiation of the interaction with customers.* The second phase suggests introduction of certain elements of interaction with a customer. In essence, a reciprocal communication occurs. The website includes functions such as forms to be downloaded, a search facility and simple data collection.
c) *Third phase—possibility for performing transaction.* The website offers processing of tasks online which makes it possible to handle business without the need to get to the physical agency or enterprise. An organization provides its customers with a full array of services through the Internet. This phase involves the connection of the external organization's systems to the global Internet, and thus it is far more complicated as compared to previous phases. An organization has to integrate the electronic channel (Internet) with the back-office system, thereby ensuring a reliable security system that guarantees safety to users while performing Internet transactions.
d) *Fourth phase—integration and strategic use of the Internet.* Only very few organizations succeed in harnessing the Internet in this rigorously strategic manner. In this phase of Internet system advance, the adop-

tion of cutting-edge technological measures takes place, thereby frequently revolutionizing previous techniques designed for contacts with customers. In effect, a single point portal is created which, as in the case of e-administration, integrates all services for all government branches across all levels.

The first two phases are relatively easy to be achieved: provision of information, forms and email addresses in the Internet does not require much effort or any changes to existing procedures and systems. The development of actual transaction services is far more challenging, because it calls for substantial investment in the systems *back-office*.

The operations by an organization over the Internet are closely connected with the concepts of e-state and e-economy, in particular:

a) *e-administration*: defined as, among other things, the use of information and communication technology (ICT) and its application by the government to provide information and public services to the populace (Rorissa et al. 2011, 355).
b) *e-business*: any forms of transaction related to the commercial use of individual and institutional business entities when relying on digital processing and data transmission. This is business carried out over computer networks such as the Internet, including its related infrastructure (Chmielarz 2007, 16).
c) *e-health*: effective, safe and frugal use of information and communication technologies to shore up any activities devoted to health protection, encompassing provision of health services, monitoring systems related to health, health education, scientific research, and the advancement of professional expertise and literature (Szewczyk 2007, 106).
d) *e-banking*: all products and banking services based on data processing and transferring in the digital form, including texts, audio and images (Pilawski 2000, 191). Overall, this is a set of services and tools with varying financial and organizational nature, made available to a broadly understood customer from the banking sector, resting on cutting-edge information and communication technologies, integrated with a conglomerate of traditional IT systems supporting bank management (Chmielarz 2007, 16).

It should be highlighted that the literature already features a concept that goes considerably beyond basic definitions such as e-voting, e-management, e-democracy (Weerakkody et al. 2012, 67), e-payments, e-stores, e-offices, and so on.

3 Benefits Delivered by Operating Online

The moving of operations to the web produces benefits to both the organization itself as well as its stakeholders. Typically, the top benefits to the organization are as follows (Kisielnicki 2008, 72):

a) Financial savings—due to diminished need for office space, a company reduces its rental fees, electricity consumption, administrative costs, and so on; costs for maintaining infrastructure are likely to be shrunk by 35 % (Major et al. 2008, 680).
b) Real, global impact.
c) Potential to exploit the Internet as a platform for marketing activities. The Internet also operates dispatch and the info-line, but with the advantage of ensuring direct, two-way and instantaneous contact between a potential customer and an organization (Porebska-Miąc 2001, 70). Essentially, this allows an organization to prepare and offer current customers the customised products and/or standard products they do not possess.
d) Opportunities for collaboration between partners who would not collaborate under circumstances of the traditional organization. Territorial distance between partners no longer presents a problem. It is possible for employees based in other cities, countries or even continents to collaborate successfully.
e) Improved access to the labour market: the web enables teleworking, which in turn, makes it possible to attract employees from any regions, including territories where labour tends to be cheaper. Besides, the search for specialists is not confined to the local market, as collaboration may be established with top-notch experts in the specific domain throughout the world.
f) Increased competitiveness, through more rapid response to shifts in the environment.

g) e-health shrinks costs and enhances the performance of health care, boosts and supports the quality of health care through better monitoring of patients, increased data and information exchange among health care employees. Moreover, it increases the number of medical services to patients, bolsters the performance and decreases costs for health care by eliminating duplicates and redundant diagnoses or therapeutic intervention (Dünnebeil et al. 2012, 747).

Meanwhile, the gains brought to customers through an organization's operations over the Internet include (Wojciechowska-Filipek 2014, 201):

a) 24/7 access throughout the year;
b) liquidation of geographical barriers (an organization ceases to be a specific place, the store is always with the customer);
c) opportunities for using products and services that the customer would otherwise be unlikely to purchase;
d) opportunities for accessing a substantially larger number of offers—not only domestic but also worldwide;
e) opportunities of comparing goods and services from various suppliers;
f) in general, financial savings (products purchased online are typically cheaper than those in traditional stores);
g) saving time when shopping or using services from home, the workplace or other locations (not necessary to travel and wait for an employee to complete the transaction);
h) frequent possibility of returning the product within 14 days without giving reasons;
i) possibility of reading comments on products and suppliers left by other customers, which facilitates choice;
j) easy use of the offer proposed by another company—when dissatisfied with services provided by one supplier, it is possible to move, without problems, to another competitive supplier whose offer is a mouse click away.

4 Development of e-organization

Due to a wide range of benefits to both organizations and their customers by moving operations to the Internet, every year sees a surge in the number of organizations that make their products and services available over the web as well as an increasing number of individuals accessing products and services over the Internet (Fig. 8.1).

On the whole, e-business, specifically e-commerce, has gained robust momentum. According to reports by Eurostat, across the European Union (EU28) the number of individuals shopping online (at least once over 12 months) totalled 30 % in 2007, 40 % in 2010 and 47 % in 2013.

Also, e-administration is now on an equally healthy course. In line with current trends, the use of information and communication technologies together with changes in working practices to maximize the performance of services has resulted in cost savings (Weerakkody et al. 2012, 71). State institutions worldwide strive to make all contact with them available on the Internet (ABW 2011, 16). According to reports compiled for the purposes of the European Union, Scandinavian countries had the highest shares of Internet users harnessing the services provided by e-administration across Europe (Fig. 8.2).

However, the exploitation of e-health care services across the European Union appears to look slightly different. Clearly, health information systems have the potential to improve the quality of health care significantly, by reducing the frequency of undesirable incidents such as the application of incorrect medications, the number of hospitalizations and expenditures for health care. Even though the majority of physicians confirm the potential benefits, the degree to which e-health solutions are deployed is rated as low (Dünnebeil et al. 2012, 747).

With regard to the development, implementation and promotion of potentials yielded by e-health, larger hospitals and public hospitals enjoy a clear advantage. This does not come as a surprise because such institutions have economies of scale and profound expertise in terms of e-health deployment. Large hospitals (including public hospitals) utilize superior Internet connections. Furthermore, they seem to have better data protection rather than small and medium-sized hospitals, and they tend to be

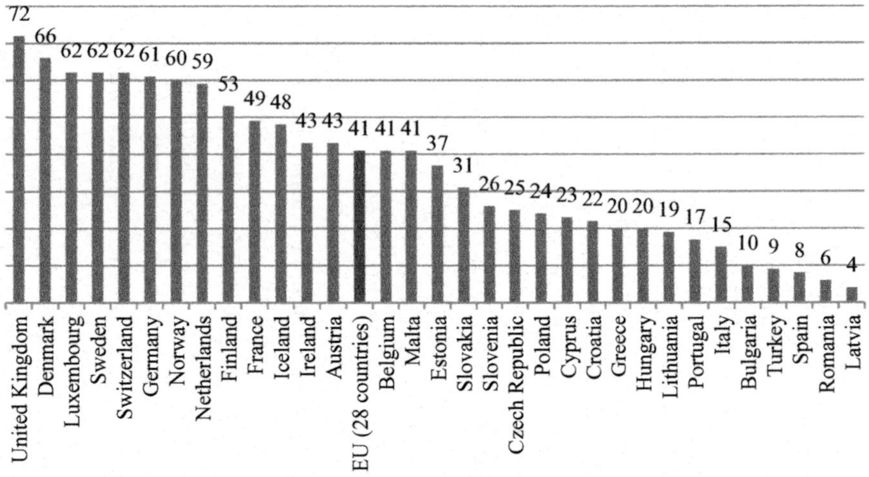

Fig. 8.1 Individuals (% of population) having ordered/bought goods and services for private use over the Internet in the last three months of 2014 (*Source*: own study based on http://ec.europa.eu/eurostat/tgm/table.do?tab=table&init=1&language=en&pcode=tin00067&plugin=1; 31.03.2015)

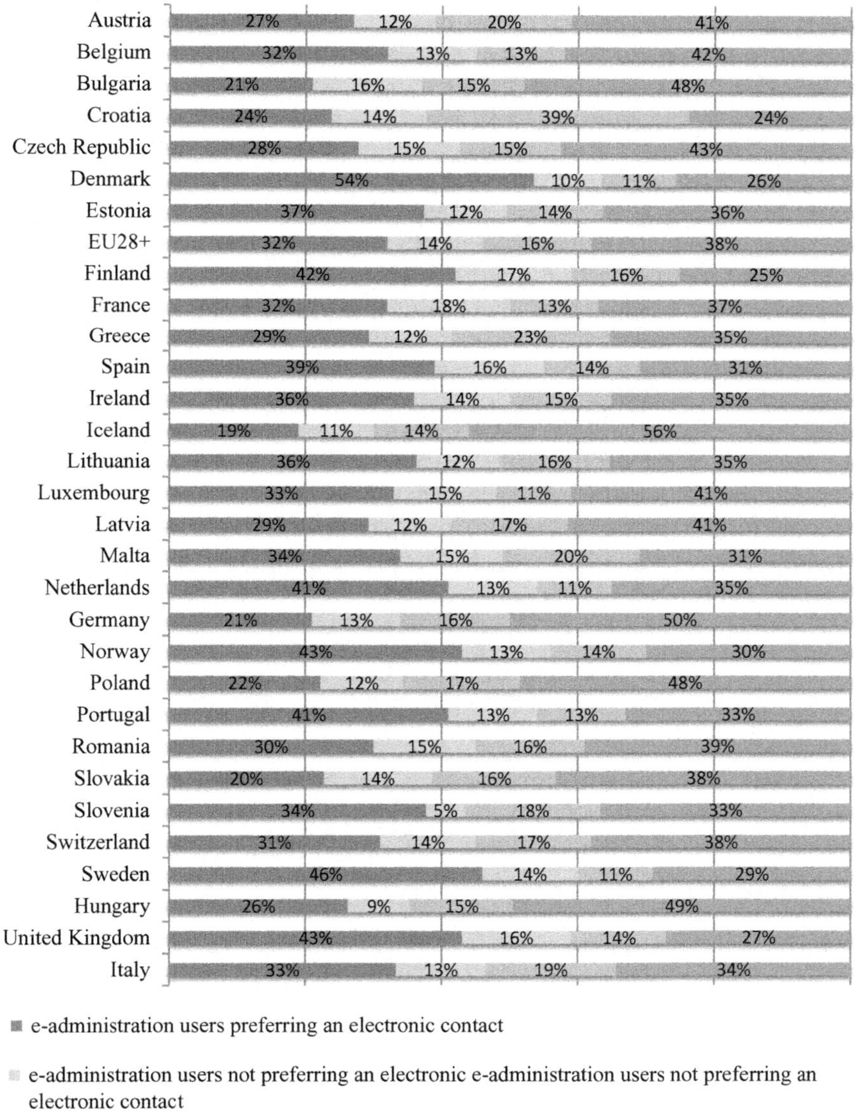

Fig. 8.2 Users of e-administration in Europe in 2014 (*Source*: own study based on https://ec.europa.eu/digital-agenda/en/news/scoreboard-2014-country-factsheets-e-government; 3.03.2014)

more inclined to embrace cutting-edge IT systems and share their information more willingly with other facilities.

Scandinavian countries are the best performers regarding e-health deployment across the European Union (EU-27(+3)).

However, advanced functionalities embedded in e-health are not widely used across hospitals, but, when available, they become very popular. For instance, digital archiving of radiology images is made available in only 53 % of EU hospitals, but in almost all of these (92 %) it is fully tapped.

Meanwhile, connectivity of e-health measures among entities continues to lag behind, as most hospitals fail to share medical information electronically. Finally, the vast majority of hospitals do not allow their patients to access their health records online (PWC 2014, 10).

Another dynamically growing area of virtualized operations is e-banking. The number of individuals taking advantage of remote access to banking services continues to rise, irrespective of shifts in economic standing. It is facilitated by declining prices of devices designed for this form of banking as well as stable progress of the infrastructure supporting mobile phones, the Internet or other devices for handling payments. Moreover, legal regulations that facilitate the expansion of electronic banking prove to be immensely important (Wojciechowska-Filipek 2014, 260) (Fig. 8.3).

Given the benefits from operating via the web, it may be assumed that virtual solutions will be increasingly cropping up every year, and the development of virtual projects implemented by institutions (including public ones) will bring a totally new quality of life.

5 Basic Risks

Alongside manifold unquestioned benefits produced while moving at least a portion of business and service operations to the Internet, it should be emphasized that operating over the web generates varied risks that had not been previously faced in traditional ways of operating. Risk is defined as a venture of unknown or uncertain outcome or possibility that something may fail (Zaleska 2007, 275). Business risk may be defined as a measurable uncertainty in business operations, reliant on

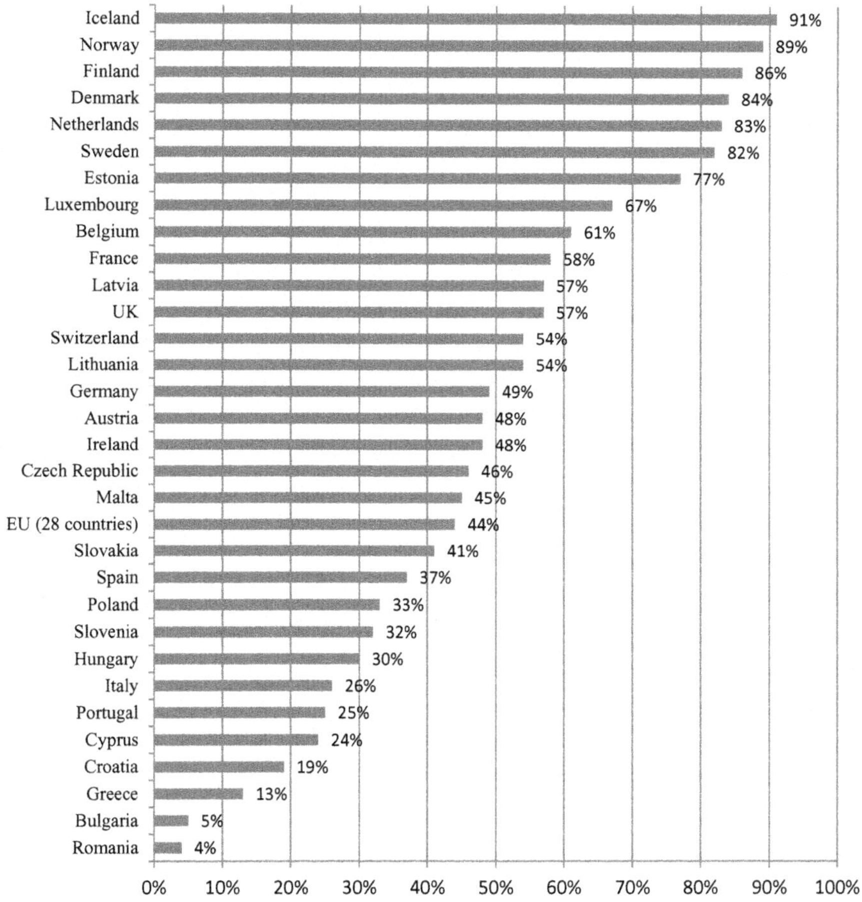

Fig. 8.3 Online banking penetration in 2014 (*Source*: own study based on The Statistics Portal; http://www.statista.com/statistics/222286/online-banking-penetration-in-leading-european-countries/; 16.05.2015)

a propensity interpretation of incidents by a decision-maker, within occurring frequencies and probabilities of conditional social and economic processes (Raczkowski et al. 2015). The concept of risk is closely related to multiple aspects of life, and its significance may be discerned while executing ventures where required information is not possessed. Shortage of current data as regards the shaping of the specific phenomenon, their limited utility or accuracy entails the impossibility of precisely predicting developments that are the results of any decisions that have been made. Research into electronic transactions suggest that the sense of risk or uncertainty about using the product or service, and worry about possible negative consequences, are hampering the development of a positive attitude to online trading, and thus ultimately triggering users' reluctance to embrace or utilize electronic services (Beldad et al. 2011, 860). It should be noted that alongside 'traditional' threats to consumers, such as financial, psychological and social threats, electronic contacts are vulnerable to perils instigated by an electronic channel for selling products and services. Deployment of the Internet as a purchase channel poses threats to transactions, because transactions are remote without any face-to face contact between a seller and consumer (Hong and Cha 2013, 928).

The major risks related to online operations are as follows:

a) risk of data security breach
b) supply risk
c) product risk
d) payment risk
e) shopping time risk
f) privacy risk
g) seller risk
h) risk of contradictory regulations

Research corroborates that the majority of customers regard the data security risk as the top risk category (Grant et al. 2014, 105).

5.1 Risk of Information Security Breach

Security is a primary driver behind the growth of e-commerce, specifically remote-access channels for products and services (Ganesan and Vivekanandan 2009, 117). It should be noted that current telecommunication and IT resources help to carry out attacks on remote systems within organizations even operating in other parts of the globe. Such activities are termed asymmetric activities by computer networks. Threats may be generated by an organization as well as a single criminal or a criminal group. Technological development sparked off the emergence of numerous dysfunctional phenomena, including broadly understood ICT crimes (computer frauds, computer espionage, hacking, balance sheet manipulations, etc.) to cyberterrorism or cyber fight (covering both civil as well as military systems) (Wojciechowska-Filipek 2015, 205). Cybercrimes involve, among others, the use of the global web for actions aimed to destroy or distort information sent, processed and stored in ICT systems. In general, they may be carried out by multiple diverse entities, may come with varying scale and intensity, and may bring various implications (Ciekanowski and Ulijasz, 2015, 192). The information security breaches may be broken down into (Kopczewski 2011, 575–578):

a) *Attacks on information:* data processed and stored in the computer system are the target of the attack. Given the goal behind obtaining illegal access to information, two subcategories may be distinguished:
   - The asset which the criminal targets is the credibility of the system and users' trust in the system. This will take the form of, e.g. entering new information into the computer system or modifying the existing operation, which will manifest itself by dysfunctionality of the device or process controlled by the system;
   - Classic theft of computer data from the system.

b) *Attacks on the system:* Activity aimed at the operational system of the computer or/and its software, with the goal of taking over control of its functionalities or rendering it non-functional.

When ensuring security, frequently the focus is on technical issues (such as e.g. encryption) without devoting equally sufficient attention to non-technical issues (for instance: ethical or legal). Technical issues revolve around technically oriented knowledge and tools required to safeguard and protect information. Typically, these issues confine themselves to technical departments and employees with adequate technical expertise. Non-technical issues concern all employees and encompass such

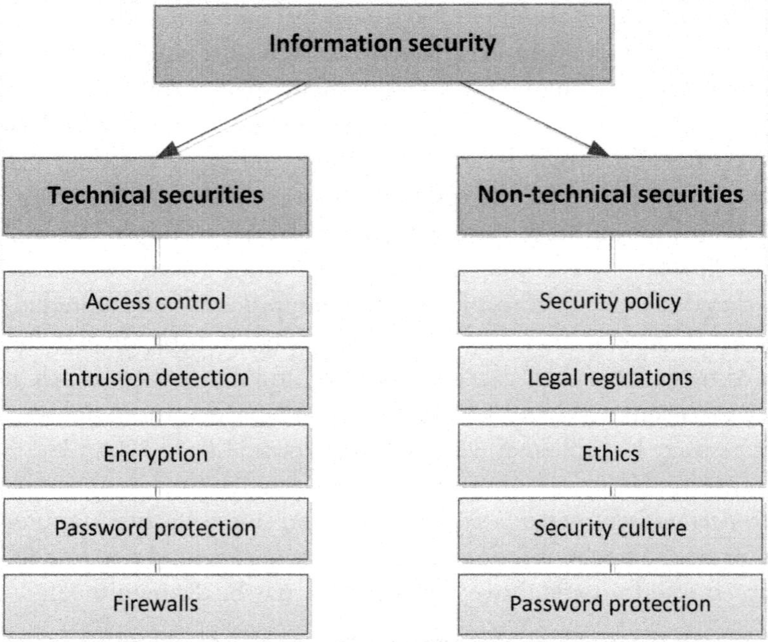

Fig. 8.4 Technical and non-technical information securities (*Source*: Own study)

topics as: ethics, security culture or legal matters. Some issues may be analysed in both technical as well as non-technical terms. For instance, password protection may be perceived as a technical matter if it regards installing software that governs the password use. Conversely, it may be seen as non-technical aspect if it applies to the selection of safe password by the user (Kritzingera and Smith 2008, 225) (Fig. 8.4).

The safeguarding of information stored, processed and transferred through information systems proceeds at several levels. These include (Gospodarowicz 2002, 190):

a) *Personal computer* (*terminal, customer*) *and its operational system:* security through the use of access passwords and designation of tasks for individual computers connected with the networks across the specific organization;

b) *Network operational system:* includes access passwords, access rights, tracking programs, programming-device mechanisms such as *firewall* and cryptographic methods;
c) *Database management system:* should contains extra mechanisms in relation to the operational system reinforcing the security level;
d) *Application software:* mechanisms designed for identification and authentication, limitation of access rights, settlement mechanism;
e) *Physical level:* mostly any solutions that prevent incidents from affecting the system;
f) *Organizational level:* appropriate performance of activities.

Growing reliance of any activities on information prompts the need to apply a wide spectrum of technical as well as non-technical safeguards so as to ensure security for information, information systems, and thus for an organization and its customers.

5.2 Supply Risk

Apart from the purchase of digital products likely to be delivered through the Internet, any other purchase via the Internet requires the supply process, which implies that a recipient has to wait for accomplishment of the goal. Above all, the supply process generates the risk of non-compliance between a product ordered and that delivered. Moreover, the dispatch may be lost or delivered to the wrong address. Additionally, the dispatch may arrive later than expected. Failure to deliver the product purchased on time tops the list of complaints filed by Internet customers. What is interesting is that e-shops are blamed for delays rather than direct suppliers, e.g. a shipping company. Even though, e-shops and suppliers of product delivery services are partners, it is e-shops that are service providers in online transactions and hence they are assessed by end customers (Ju et al. 2015, 104). Currently, customers expect the product purchased to be delivered within a few days (Table 8.1), but with the growth of Internet trade, the customers' expectations soar, and in the near future it is anticipated that they will expect the delivery to be completed within a few hours from the order placement (Kostecka 2015).

Table 8.1 Acceptable delivery time for the product purchased online

	UK (%)	Germany (%)	Nordics (%)	France (%)	Benelux (%)	Spain (%)	Italy (%)	Poland (%)
1–2 day(s)	12	14	4	11	18	13	9	16
3–5 days	76	77	64	72	62	62	73	72
6 days and over	10	8	24	16	17	22	18	12

Source: Own study based on Postnord: *E-commerce in Europe. 2014.* http://www.postnord.com/globalassets/global/english/document/publications/2014/e-commerce-in-europe-2014.pdf; 17.04.2015

5.3 Product Risk

Principally, product risk is a concern that a product will differ from that displayed in the Internet. This concern stems from impossibility of physical examination of the product ahead of its purchase by the buyer. Due to advanced photography technologies, the image of the item offered may be distorted, e.g. the garment in the photo seems to be made out of excellent fabrics, whereas the fabrics actually have a different texture and colour (Wojciechowska-Filipek 2014, 203). Product risk increases when required information on the product is limited, the price is overly high, or a consumer cannot adequately assess the product (Aghekyan-Simonian et al. 2012, 326). Some surveys put the spotlight on the role of Internet shops as a source of perceived risk in transactions. Some sellers have a propensity for opportunistic behaviour, failing to ensure an appropriate product in a timely fashion in line with the promise, or simply deceiving a customer. This results from, among others, information asymmetry where a seller possesses more information than consumers on the quality of products (Hong 2015, 323).

For some industries, e.g. the clothing industry, the most valuable factor that mitigates the product risk is a known brand (Aghekyan-Simonian et al. 2012, 330). For other cases, the biggest impact on mitigation of the product risk is exerted by opinions provided by other customers: 62 % of consumers consult customers' opinions ahead of the purchase, whereas feedback has an influence on purchasing decisions for 82 % of consumers (Benedicktus et al. 2010, 311). Customers' opinions provide an analysis of a company's operations in the past, based on the accumulated experiences of other customers, and they refer to the product, sales process, or both. Suppliers receiving the opinions usually encourage consumers to assess their experiences with the company or products, and then they illustrate aggregate information for potential customers in various formats, such as result tables, histograms and ratings in the form of stars. Customers' opinions are viewed as an important indicator of attitudes and behaviours, as 'social proof for seller's credibility'. This information leads to persuasion through concluding that opinions held by the majority must be appropriate, and thus a consumer should agree with the majority. The outcomes from opinions may provide consumers with a direct indication of a company's credibility (Benedicktus et al. 2010, 312). Some shops, despite their display of customers' opinions, provide discussion forums on their websites so that consumers are able to spontaneously share their remarks, opinions or recommendations about the products (Hong and Cha 2013, 930). Product risk substantially declines when shopping in so-called trusted shops. This is the case for 96 % of Poles. The most popular recommendation system for online shops in Poland is the program 'ZaufaneOpinie Ceneo.pl'. Overall, the system rests on online questionnaires filled out by the customers who made an actual purchase in the specific Internet shop. Since the program inception in 2009, almost 3.5 million credible opinions were collected. Customers willingly share their views with around 4000 new opinions popping up on a daily basis (Ceneo.pl 2014).

Importantly, Internet communities play a huge role in reducing the product risk. They offer swift responses to inquiries on information, which follows from their direct communication possibilities. Consumers receive support from other consumers' experiences. The establishment of online communities and like-minded consumers leave customers feeling more comfortable and safe (Tsai and Pai 2012, 24).

5.4 Payment Risk

The survey found that 42 % of Europeans worry about online payment security (European Commission 2015, 24). Payment risk is principally concerned with fears of disclosing the credit card number over the

Internet. Diverse surveys revealed that Internet users are increasingly anxious about the fact that information regarding the credit card used for payments may be intercepted and exploited by hackers, or even by Internet marketers without the cardholder's consent (Hong and Cha 2013, 928). On the whole, these fears are reflected in payment methods preferred by customers. In Poland the most commonly used payment methods for online shopping include payment services (such as PayU, Dotpay, PayPal, Przelewy24) (used by 37 % of online shoppers), bank transfer (28 % of shoppers) and cash on delivery (21 %). Credit cards are used for payment for online shopping by merely 7 %. Cash is particularly popular among older e-customers (aged above 50), transfer among the youngest ones (below 24), whereas payment services are more popular for persons aged 25–34 (Gemius 2014, 118) (Table 8.2).

The high popularity of payment services is attributed to two basic factors: convenience and security. The most popular payment services ensure comfort to users, as all data required for the transfer are filled out automatically, so that there is no need to complete the order forms or write dispatch details. Further, services provide higher security than other payment methods. Fundamentally, this stems from the fact that in accordance with requirements set by payment organizations, companies offering online payments should comply with strict

Table 8.2 Preferred payment methods for online shopping in 2014

Method	UK (%)	Germany (%)	Nordics (%)	France (%)	Benelux (%)	Spain (%)	Italy (%)	Poland (%)
Debit or credit card	58	14	44	55	27	34	25	10
Bank transfer	1	9	22	2	23	1	5	43
Payment services (PayPal or similar)	38	38	6	36	29	49	55	21
Cash on delivery	1	1	2	2	4	13	13	24

Source: Own study based on Postnord: *E-commerce in Europe. 2014.* http://www.postnord.com/globalassets/global/english/document/publications/2014/e-commerce-in-europe-2014.pdf; 17.04.2015

security standards set out in the Payment Card Industry Data Security Standard (PCI DSS). This is a worldwide standard set by payment organizations (Visa, MasterCard) to protect cardholders' personal data and information related to transactions carried out using these payment cards. Data transmission on services is carried out through the SSL EV (Extended Validation Secure Sockets Layer) certificate, which provides the highest standard for communication security. When paid by a card in the service, a shop that enables identification of the cardholder in 3DS[1] (3-D Secure) protocol is protected against any potential fraudulent transactions , no matter whether the card used for payment is registered in 3DS or not. In addition, customers are covered by the special purchaser protection programme. For example, the Purchaser Protection Programme in PayU allows for the recovery of up to PLN 10,000 (Polish złoty) (http://www.payu.pl/dla-sklepow/jakosc-i-bezpieczenstwo; 17.04.2015):

a) In the event where the product is not received, a customer is entitled to reimbursement of 100 % of its price.
b) In the event when an item significantly differs from the description, a customer is entitled to reimbursement of 50 % of the paid amount.
c) In addition, reimbursement of shipping costs up to PLN 100 is ensured.

Meanwhile, for on-line transfers, Polish banks deploy two-step security level—the first for logging onto an account, the second for transaction confirmation. For security reasons, banks apply a combination of various authentication methods. These include passwords (static and masked), scratch cards, text messages (with a one-off password or a one-off password related to the transaction), tokens (devices generating one-off passwords) or electronic signatures (program and equipment) (http://www.bankier.pl/static/att/68000/2034334_RaportBankier.pl.pdf; 17.04.2015).

In the case of a debit card used for payment in the electronic transaction, standard 3DS enhances the security level. This is additional

[1] 3DS (3D-Secure) –transaction security standard through cardholder's identification using an extra, mostly one-off password generated by token or received in the text message.

protection that involves the need to provide, alongside with the card number, expiry date and CVV2/CVC2 code, an extra, mostly one-off, password generated by the token or received in a text message. The password is not used in any transactions that require the physical presence of the card, and therefore there is no risk of it being seen while shopping in any sales outlet (Polish Financial Supervision Authority 2014).

In February 2015, Visa Europe announced its plans to implement tokenization services attuned to the needs of the European market. Tokenization technology is regarded as one of the best presently available methods for data protection and fraud prevention. The tokenization service safeguards the customer's data through replacement of information placed on the debit card by a sequence of digits which may be subsequently used for payment authorization without disclosing card details. In doing so, e.g. when making proximity payments in shops using a mobile device, thanks to such a solution, only a so-called token (sequence of digits) is transferred rather than card details (Visa Europe 2015).

Surveys show that in addition to online payment security methods that are applied, the payment risk may be further mitigated when shops provide their customers with security guidelines on their websites (Aghekyan-Simonian et al. 2012, 327). They inform users that security for transactions also depends on them, and the outlets communicate elementary principles to be observed when performing transactions over the Internet as well as demonstrating the most common mistakes.

5.5 Shopping Time Risk

This covers the time loss caused by difficulties in navigation while placing an order through websites. It should be underlined that for electronic communication, the efficiency of the channel designed for information transfer as well as skills of the user have become most important. When assessing the Internet skills of potential users, six fundamental internet-related activities are taken into account: use of search engines to find information; sending emails with files attached; posting messages to chat rooms, newsgroups, or any online discussion forum; use of the Internet to make phone calls; use of *peer-to-peer* file sharing for exchanging films, music, etc.; and setting up web pages. The accomplishment of only 1 or 2 activities suggests a low level of basic Internet skills, 3 or 4 an average level, and

5 or 6 high (http://ec.europa.eu/eurostat/tgm/table.do?tab=table&init=1&language=en&pcode=tsdsc470&plugin=1; 1.04.2015). The level of Internet skills across the European Union states is portrayed in Table 8.3.

Table 8.3 Level of Internet skills among EU citizens in 2013 (% of citizens aged 16–74)

	Low level (1–2 activities)	Average level (4–5 activities)	High level (5–6 activities)
Austria	35	36	**10**
Belgium	29	40	**13**
Bulgaria	22	22	**15**
Croatia	29	27	**11**
Cyprus	22	37	**8**
Czech Republic	32	38	**8**
Denmark	23	50	**21**
Estonia	24	35	**21**
EU (28 states)	30	35	**12**
Finland	27	45	**19**
France	34	37	**12**
Germany	46	33	**5**
Greece	21	30	**12**
Hungary	20	39	**16**
Iceland	18	43	**34**
Ireland	35	36	**7**
Italy	19	28	**15**
Latvia	23	35	**19**
Lithuania	12	27	**32**
Luxembourg	32	49	**12**
Malta	26	31	**11**
Netherlands	31	41	**21**
Norway	37	42	**15**
Poland	23	32	**10**
Portugal	21	32	**13**
Romania	29	23	**5**
Slovakia	26	46	**12**
Slovenia	28	31	**15**
Spain	28	33	**14**
Sweden	25	42	**26**
Turkey	27	15	**5**
United Kingdom	31	44	**14**

Source: Own study based on http://ec.europa.eu/eurostat/tgm/refreshTableAction.do? tab=table&plugin=1&pcode=tsdsc470&language=en; 1.04.2015

Websites offering products and services are often seen as overly complicated, and finding the necessary information presents difficulties even to individuals with high Internet skills. Websites often contain excessive amounts of information, do not include categorizations or their categorizations prove to be needless or ambiguous, or they fail to deliver expected navigation options (Kraaijenbrink 2007, 1370). Paucity of adequate tools intended for a quick search of necessary information causes delays likely to provoke a feeling of time pressure, stress or dissatisfaction. Delays lead to more selective obtaining of information, fewer alternative comparisons, and most importantly a switch to simpler decision-making rules, which may result in a decrease in the decision quality (Dennis and Taylor 2006, 812). Moreover, on-line services should streamline the procedures rather than frequently reiterate excessively complex traditional methods in which matters are handled. Unfortunately, even in countries that are developed in terms of the Internet, such as the UK, e-administration services are embroiled in too many complicated formal procedures. The electronic systems offer as many as 61 diverse forms that mostly gather the same information. As a consequence, an ordinary citizen needs to prove their identify as many as 11 times every year (Budgol 2011, 130).

Easy of use, simple, intuitive and standard navigation, and adequate technical quality maintenance, contribute to diminishing the shopping time risk (Dutko 2013, 43). Additionally, design for the shop or institution needs to be explicit, whereas websites should be honed in order to facilitate tracing and understanding information as well as navigating through the service to seek out required information and to carry out necessary activities for executing transactions (iStore.pl 2013).

5.6 Privacy Risk

Primarily, privacy risk involves fears that personal data will be collected without consent. The risk is the effect of leaving traces in the web, thus allowing for collection of information about users, their preferences and behaviours. The analysis of these details may be harnessed to create a user's personal profile that quite precisely illustrates their behaviours over the Internet. It should be noted that for online transactions, a customer has hope that an enterprise will not use its advantage (information, financial and technical) against them. In the case of electronic transactions, we may be dealing with a customer's expectations that an Internet seller will act in a generally acceptable manner, whether the customer has checked the seller's credentials or not (Grudzewski and Hejduk 2007, 129), and that if there are risks, the seller will not take advantage of the customer's weaker position (Beldad et al. 2011, 860). The process behind trust establishment in electronic transactions is not a result of long-standing relationships as in traditional contacts. Trust is a dynamic concept. We may talk about trust ahead of the utilization of technology (*pre-use-trust*) which affects the adoption of the new business form, and trust following the employment of the electronic channel (*post-use-trust*) which affects further use of electronic services (Hernandes-Ortega 2011, 523–538). In the meantime, EU citizens are becoming anxious that their personal data will be abused. These fears rose from 37 % in 2013 up to 43 % in 2014 (European Commission 2015, 23). Transaction security and privacy protection is a driving force in stoking trust or distrust in e-economy, whilst adequate trust levels in transactions executed through the Internet is critical for their advance. Therefore, websites where a customer enters and edits data have to be properly protected by the system (Xiaohan and Junzhuo 2011, 5642). Importantly, works on new legislation devoted to privacy protection on the Internet are currently underway in the European Union (Ministry of Administration and Digitization 2015).

5.7 Seller's Risk

Seller's risk arises from the fact that in electronic contacts a customer cannot see a virtual seller, has scant information about the seller and does not necessarily know the company's performance (Dutko 2013, 43). Also, difficulties with establishing the actual location of provider of products and services, unclear proprietary structures or obscure authority structures, cause concerns (Perechuda 2005, 19). A lack of direct interactions, geographical dispersion, and often short-term collaboration do not help to nurture trust. The need for trust in electronic transactions results from the risk, uncertainty and dependencies between partners. Only partners that trust each other are capable of effective collaboration. The driving forces fostering trust include rational characteristics such as reliability, skills, sense of duty, and integrity, as well as emotional and social skills such as care and concern about the welfare of participants involved in the transaction (Leede and Kraan 2008, 22–46). In the customers' eyes the companies that offer their products and services through both channels—both traditional and electronic—earn more credibility. Thus, as many as 71 % of online consumers search for evidence of the physical presence of the company ahead of shopping online. Although this fails to reveal the company's potential to deliver on the promises, it does give consumers an insight into the company's trustworthiness (Benedicktus et al. 2010, 321). Essentially, psychological and cultural drivers tend to gain more significance in electronic contacts than traditional transactions (Warner and Witzel 2005, 181). Differences in trust offline and online come to light. In the traditional business model a person or an organization typically appears to be the trusted object, whereas in the internet context it is the technology and an organization implementing this technology. From the marketing perspective, contrary to traditional trading where a seller or an enterprise is a trusted object, in Internet trade customers largely trust a website, and then the underlying organization. (Beldad et al. 2011, 860).

Seller's risk may be reduced by such activities as:

a) *Presentation of the seller/shop:* placing registration data, regulations or privacy policy on websites.
b) *Organization's reputation:* in electronic commerce it may be interpreted as a collective measurement of credibility based on references and ratings prepared by the recipient, or as an indication of credibility resulting from comparison between what the company promises and what the company delivers. Placing certificates, awards, mentions from neutral sources on websites boost customers' trust (Ma et al. 2012, 769).
c) *Perceived organization's size:* surveys found that the perceived size of an e-seller has an impact on building trust in that seller.

d) *Presence in the actual world:* trust conferred on the company in traditional transactions enhances trust in it in on-line transactions. Companies that have physical facilities are better positioned to promote their credibility in the Internet (Benedicktus et al. 2010, 321).
e) *Experiences and familiarity with the on-line company:* surveys show that customer satisfaction with previous transactions with the specific Internet company determines trust in the company. People usually tend to trust those with proven credibility.

Surveys conducted by PwC across 15 countries on 5 continents reveal that purchasers worldwide display behaviours indicating loyalty to Internet sellers, because 43 % shop at no more than 5 e-sellers, whereas 27 % shop at no more than 10 (PwC 2015).

5.8 Risk of Contradictory Regulations

Conducting business operations over the Internet requires convergence of norms and standards across countries. Legal regulations need to state with a certain degree of flexibility so as not to stifle growth. There is no room for discrimination, as all participants have to reap benefits. Legal solutions should formulate: whether and to what degree content from cyberspace should be rationed, in what manner copyright protection should be ensured, how to protect citizens' privacy, and at the same time how to safely and effectively authorize electronic transactions (Szpringer 2005, 32–34). Legislative changes implemented refer to (Niedźwiedziński 2004, 64):

a) consumers' protection
b) terms and conditions for concluding the agreement
c) personal data protection
d) intellectual property rights protection
e) regulation of tax issues
f) regulation of customs laws
g) security guarantee

Internal laws across countries as well as guidelines as to the operations on the EU market tend to proliferate. Those carrying out operations on-line have to catch up with new legislation—which is not easy (Dutko 2015, 8). For instance, for e-health – regulations are misleading and contradictory, thereby directly affecting organizational management, business rules and virtual environment for the care of patients. Health care is managed in public and private sectors, which requires application of varied standards and laws, with those applicable for administering health care in the private sector being different to those that govern health care in the public sector. Additionally, there is significant diversity and incompatibility in formats and standards used in the provision of health care services that use information and communication technologies across the whole EU, which creates barriers that hinder the provision of cross-border health care and might mean potential peril to health protection (Fernando and Dawson 2014, 142–143).

6 Conclusion

The expansion of technologies, specifically the Internet, has resulted in organizations moving their operations to the web and offering their customers new electronic access channels to products and services. Operations on-line alongside unchallenged benefits, however, generate certain risks that do not occur in traditional business. The most widespread include: risk of information security breach, supply risk, product risk, payment risk, shopping time risk, privacy risk, seller's risk or risk of contradictory regulations. Overall, these risks effectively discourage some customers from deployment of electronic communication forms and hinder the growth of an e-state; therefore it is necessary to launch a wide range of activities likely to mitigate these risks. The following may be specified: application of both technical as well as non-technical securities; enhancement of Internet skills among citizens; standardization of data formats; streamlining procedure for using e-services or alignment of legal regulations. All these measures should amplify the level of trust in electronic contacts and organizations operating in the Internet, without which dynamic growth of the e-economy would fall short.

References

ABW. (2011). *Standardy bezpieczeństwa dokumentów państwowych, materiały konferencyjne*. Warszawa

Aghekyan-Simonian, M., Forsythe, S., Kwon, W., & Chattaraman, V. (2012). The role of productbrand image and online store image on perceivedrisks and online purchaseintentions for apparel. *Journal of retailing and Consumer Services, 19*(3), 325–331.

Beldad, A., Jong, M., & Steehouder, M. (2011). I trust not therefore it must be risky: Determinants of the perceived risks of disclosing personal data for e-government transactions. *Computers in Human Behavior, 27*(6), 860.

Benedicktus, R., Brady, M., Darke, P., & Voorhees, C. (2010). Conveying trustworthiness to online consumers: Reactions to consensus, physical store presence, brand familiarity, and generalized suspicion. *Journal of Retailing, 86*(4), 322–335.

Budgol, M. (2011). *Zarządzanie jakością w urzędach administracji publicznej*. Warszawa: Difin.

Ceneo.pl. (2014). Polak lubi zakupy w Internecie, Raport 2014. http://ranking.ceneo.pl/wp-content/uploads/ raport-zaufane-opinie-2014.pdf; 23.04.2015.

Chmielarz, W. (2007). *Systemy biznesu elektronicznego*. Warszawa: Difin.

Ciekanowski, Z., & Ulijasz, B. (2015). *Zwalczanie terroryzmu w Unii Europejskiej*. Jarosław: Państwowa Wyższa Szkoła Techniczno-Ekonomiczna.

Dennis, A., & Taylor, N. (2006). Information foraging on the web: The effects of "acceptable" Internet delays on multi-page information search behavior. *Decision Support Systems, 42*(2), 810–824.

Dünnebeil, S., Sunyaev, A., Blohm, I., Leimeister, J. M., & Krcmar, H. (2012). Determinants of physicians' technology acceptance for e-health in ambulatory care. *International Journal of Medical Informatics, 81*(11), 746–760.

Dutko, M. (2013). *E-biznes, poradnik praktyka*. Gliwice: Helion.

Dutko, M. (2015). Prawo w e-biznesie. Onepress.

EuropeanCommision. (2015). Cybersecurity. http://ec.europa.eu/public_opinion/archives/ ebs/ebs_423_en.pdf; 25.04.2015.

Eurostat. (2015). http://ec.europa.eu/eurostat/statistics-explained/index.php/Information_society_statistics_at_regional_level#E-commerce, 31.03.2015.

Fernando, J., & Dawson, L. (2014). The natural hospital environment: A socio-technical-material perspective. *International Journal of Medical Informatics, 83*(2), 140–158.

Ganesan, R., & Vivekanandan, K. (2009). A secured hybrid architecture model for internet banking. *Journal of Internet Banking and Commerce, Ottawa, 14*(1), 117.

Gemius. (2014). E-commerce w Polsce 2014. Gemius dla e-Commerce Polska. http://www.infomonitor.pl/download/e-commerce-w-polsce-2014.pdf; 16.04.2015.

Gospodarowicz, A. (2002). *Technologie informatyczne w bankowości*. Wrocław: Wydawnictwo Akademii Ekonomicznej we Wrocławiu.

Grant, K., Edgar, D., Sukumar, A., & Meyar, M. (2014). 'Risky business': Perceptions of e-business risk by UK small and medium sized enterprises (SMEs). *International Journal of Information Management, 34*(2), 99–122.

Grudzewski, W., & Hejduk, I. (2007). *Zarządzanie zaufaniem w organizacjach wirtualnych*. Warszawa: Difin.

Hernandes-Ortega, B. (2011). The role of post-use trust in the acceptance of a technology: Drivers and consequences. *Technovation, 31*(10–11), 523–538.

Hong, I. (2015). Understanding the consumer's online merchant selection process: The roles of product involvement, perceived risk, and trust expectation. *International Journal of Information Management, 35*(3), 267–406.

Hong, I., & Cha, H. (2013). The mediating role of consumer trust in an online merchant in predicting purchase intention. *International Journal of Information Management, 33*(6), 927–939.

Jakość i bezpieczeństwo. (2015). http://www.payu.pl/dla-sklepow/jakosc-i-bezpieczenstwo; 17.04.2015.

Ju, J., Subramanian, N., Ning, K., & Edwards, D. (2015). Product delivery service provider selection and customer satisfaction in the era of internet of things: A Chinese e-retailers' perspective. *International Journal of Production Economics, 159*, 104–116.

Kisielnicki, J. (2008). *Systemy informatyczne zarządzania*. Warszawa: Placet.

Komisja Nadzoru Finansowego. (2014). Usługi bankowości elektronicznej dla klientów detalicznych. Charakterystyka i zagrożenia. https://www.knf.gov.pl/Images/ Raport_Bankowosc_elektroniczna_tcm75–24666.pdf; 17.04.2014.

Kopczewski, M. (2011). Elementy infrastruktury krytycznej państwa (organizacji) jako obiekty narażone na ataki cyberterrorystyczne. In R. Knosala (Ed). *Komputerowo zintegrowane zarządzanie*. Polskie Towarzystwo Zarządzania Produkcją, Opole, s.575–578

Kostecka, A. (2015). E-commerce zmienia łańcuch dostaw; http://www.log24.pl/artykuly/e-commerce-zmienia-lancuch-dostaw,5339; 20.04.2015.

Kraaijenbrink, J. (2007). Engineers and the web: An analysis of real life gaps in information usage. *Information Processing and Management, 43*(5), 1368–1382.

Kritzingera, E., & Smith, E. (2008). Information security management: An information security retrieval and awareness model for industry. *Computers & Security, 27*(5–6), 224–231.

Leede, J., & Kraan, K. 2008. Conditions for innovation behaviour of virtual team members a "hight-road" for internationally dispersed virtual teams. *The Journal of E-working, 2*, 22–46.

Ma, Z., Liu Sheng, O., Pant, G., & Iriberri, A. (2012). Can visible cues in search results indicate vendors' reliability? *Decision Support Systems, 52*(3), 768–775.

Major, D., Verive, J., & Joice, W. (2008). Telework as a dependent care solution: examining current practice to improve telework management strategies. *The Psychologist-Manager Journal, 11*, 65–91.

Ministerstwo Administracji i Cyfryzacji. (2015). https://mac.gov.pl/aktualnosci/dzien-ochrony -danych -osobowych-konferencja-giodo; 27.04.2015.

Najbezpieczniejsze banki internetowe w Polsce. (2015). http://www.bankier.pl/static/ att/ 68000/ 2034334_ RaportBankier.pl.pdf; 17.04.2015.

Niedźwiedziński, M. (2004). *Globalny handel elektroniczny*. Warszawa: Wydawnictwo Naukowe PWN.

Perechuda, K. (2005). *Dyfuzja wiedzy w przedsiębiorstwie sieciowym*. Wrocław: Wydawnictwo Akademii Ekonomicznej im. Oskara Langego we Wrocławiu.

Pilawski, B. (2000). Bankowość elektroniczna – zagrożenia, ograniczenia i bariery rozwoju. In A. Gospodarowicz (Ed.), *Zastosowania rozwiązań informatycznych w bankowości*. Wrocław: Wydawnictwo Akademii Ekonomicznej im. Oskara Langego we Wrocławiu.

Platforma iStore.pl. (2013). Buduj swoją wiarygodność. Poradnik. http://istore.net.pl/pliki/pdf/iStore_blog_-_buduj_swoja_wiarygodnosc.pdf; 14.07.2013.

Porębska-Miąc, T. (2001). E-marketing bankowy. In A. Gospodarowicz (Ed.), *Zastosowania rozwiązań informatycznych w instytucjach finansowych*. Wrocław: Wydawnictwo Akademii Ekonomicznej im. Oskara Langego we Wrocławiu.

Postnord. (2014). E-commerce in Europe. http://www.postnord.com/globalassets/global/english/document/publications/2014/e-commerce-in-europe-2014.pdf; 17.04.2015.

PWC. (2014). Raport: EuropeanHospitalSurvey: Benchmarking Deployment of eHealth Services (2012–2013); p.10. http://ec.europa.eu/digital-agenda/en/news/european-hospital-survey-benchmarking-deployment-ehealth-services-2012–2013; 12.04.2014.

PWC. (2015). Globalny raport PwC: rosną obawy przed zakupami internetowymi.http://mensis.pl/globalny-raport-pwc-rosna-obawy-przed-zakupami-internetowymi/; 25.04.2015.

Raczkowski, K., Noga, M., & Klepacki, J. (2015). *Zarządzanie ryzykiem w polskim systemie finansowym*. Warszawa: Difin.

Rorissa, A., Demissie, D., & Pardo, T. (2011). Benchmarking e-government: A comparison of frameworks for computing e-government index and ranking. *Government Information Quarterly, 28*(3), 354–362.

Szewczyk, A (2007). *Społeczeństwo informacyjne – problemy rozwoju*. Difin

Szpringer, W. (2005). *Prowadezniedziałalnościgospodarcezj w Internecie*. Warszawa: Difin.

Tsai, H., & Pai, P. (2012). Positive and negative aspects of online community cultivation: Implications for online stores' relationship management. *Information & Management, 49*(2), 111–117.

Warner, M., & Witzel, M. (2005). *Zarządzanie organizacją wirtualną*. Kraków: Oficyna Ekonomiczna.

Weerakkody, V., El-Haddadeh, R., Sabol, T., Ghoneim, A., & Dzupka, P. (2012). E-government implementation strategies in developed and transition economies: A comparative study. *International Journal of Information Management, 32*(1), 66–74.

Wojciechowska-Filipek, S. (2010). *Technologia informacyjna w usługach bankowości elektronicznej*. Warszawa: Difin.

Wojciechowska-Filipek, S. (2014). *Funkcjonowanie organizacji zhierarchizowanej w wirtualnym świecie*. Warszawa: CeDeWu.

Wojciechowska-Filipek, S. (2015). *Zarządzanie jakością informacji w organizacjach zhierarchizowanych*. Warszawa: Wydawnictwo CeDeWu.

Visa Europe. (2015). Visa Europe wdraża usługę tokenizacji umożliwiającą tworzenie nowej generacji bezpiecznych płatności. https://www.visa.pl/o-nas/aktualnosci/visa-europe-wdra-a-us-ug-tokenizacji-umo-liwiaj-c-tworzenie-nowej-generacji-bezpiecznych-p-atno-ci; 24.04.2015.

Xiaohan, H., & Junzhuo, Z. (2011). E-commerce network security technology research and implementation. *Energy Procedia, 13*, 3381–3389.

Zaleska, M. (2007). *Współczesna bankowość*. Warszawa: Difin.

9

Intellectual Capital Risk Management for Knowledge-Based Organizations

Jolanta Jurczak

1 Introduction

Modern companies are in a very changeable and rapidly developing market where competition is one of the constant elements of the market. In such an environment, enterprises have to continuously adjust their strategy to suit the current situation in the market and forthcoming threats and opportunities. Therefore, we can observe increasing attention focused on problems connected with Intellectual Capital (IC) management over recent years, e.g. N. Bontis, M. Bratnicki, N. Brennan, A. Brooking, P.N. Bukh, W.R. Bukowitz, R.L. Williams, B. Connell, M. Dobija, L. Edvinsson, J. Guthrie, R. S. Kaplan, E. Kwiatkowski and J. Strużyna, D. P. Norton, H. Itami, I. Nonaka, H. Takeuchi, B. Lev, M.S. Malone, K. Perechuda, G. Roos, J. Roos, P. Sullivan, T.A. Stewart, K.E. Sveiby, B. Wawrzyniak. These authors claim that, first of all, the true

J. Jurczak (✉)
Helena Chodkowska University of Technology and Economics,
Warsaw, Poland

K. Raczkowski (ed.), *Risk Management in Public Administration*,
DOI 10.1007/978-3-319-30877-7_9

value of organizations resides in the 'power of the mind' of their members and concerns the IC of the organization.

The position of the organization on the competitive market depends strongly on the proper strategy of management of IC and the ability of the organization to limit risk connected with it. So organizations should create an individual, specific strategy of IC risk management to create added value, and increase their competitive advantage on the market.

Therefore, the author focuses on empirical research concerning identification and verification of factors which create IC capable of gaining competitive advantage and can still eliminate the IC risk in an organization. This will make the more efficient development of the organization possible. As a result, the author shows the practical model of IC's ability to gain competitive advantage on the market. The model used has been estimated on the basis of research and verified statistically by Confirmatory Factors Analyzing (CFA). Thanks to this model, it is possible to evaluate the influence of each factor in creation of added value and competitive advantage of the company on the global market. So, from that point of view, it is possible to manage IC risk in a proper way.

Summing up, if any organization wants to build up a competitive advantage in the long term, it should identify areas and types of risk connected with IC resources properly and try to manage them in a rational way that can lead to controlling risk in the entire organization. Organizations which introduce and perform this kind of policy can be treated as intelligent organizations, which are able to manage their risk and gain competitive advantage on the market.

2 The rule of Intellectual Capital to Gain a Competitive Advantage On the Market

IC has become a dominant factor, which boosts company development and determines the success or failure of modern enterprises. It is regarded as an asset that can generate a company's competitive advantage and value. So it is important to learn how to recognize and reduce the risk connected with IC, and its components and the way it is managed.

The literature on IC phenomena demonstrates that the difference between the market organization value and book value depends on IC resources that are difficult to copy and imitate – they should be '*invisible*' and long lasting. IC can be regarded then as a hidden value of the organization. Additionally, organizational value increases if the IC is used and managed properly in an elastic and dynamic way. Therefore, in numerous companies all around the world, managers see and understand the importance of IC, and its market opening, especially in companies that want to dominate the market, rather than just effectively compete with others. In a survey conducted by The Economic Intelligence Unit for Accenture (Roos et al. 2005, 1), 94 % of CEOs agreed that it is essential to understand and manage IC. Out of these, 50 % stated that IC management is one of the three most important challenges for managers nowadays, and 13 % stated that it is *the* most important challenge.

Proper management of IC has an influence on business performance. Thus, companies have to focus on their IC resources and their proper usage if they want to compete on the market and gain competitive advantage. Finally they should also understand and be aware of risk connected with IC in order to reduce its negative results.

The ability of IC to gain a competitive advantage and eliminate risk allows the enterprise to be more efficient in the market, and also has an impact on the relationship between business partners and their involvement during the development process. Although intangible assets may represent a value in an organization, managers do not have complete and clear information on the role IC plays and its potential nor on what and how many risks it generates. IC's ability to gain a competitive advantage is difficult to measure and requires information about the IC structure and risks that occur. It is therefore necessary to identify the determinants responsible for the development of individual components of intellectual capital. This approach allows us to create a complex view of an organization and make proper decisions as a result.

For an illustration of the potential of IC to gain a competitive advantage as a result of such attributes us: innovation, creativity, openness, uniqueness, acquisition of knowledge, worth, variety of occurrence, changeability, rareness, continuous development, continued, and accomodation (adaptation), see Fig. 9.1.

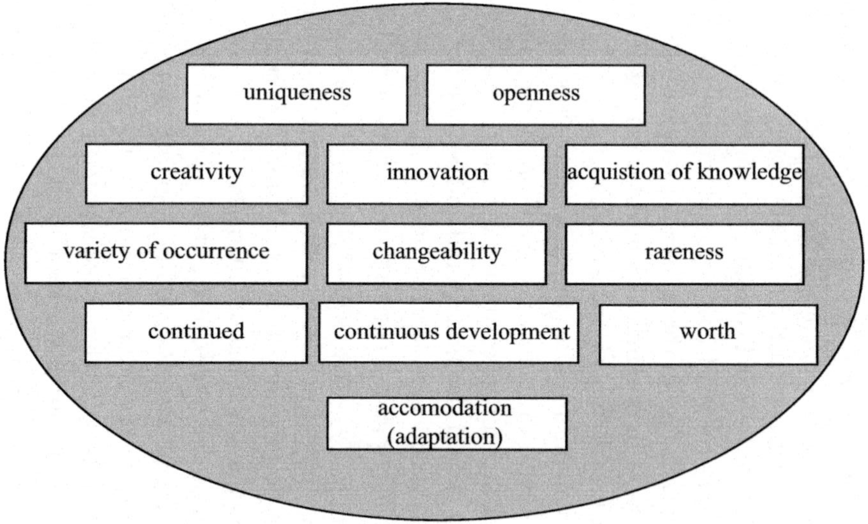

Fig. 9.1 Features of Intellectual Capital in the context of competitive advantage (*Source*: Szara and Pierścieniak 2007, 255)

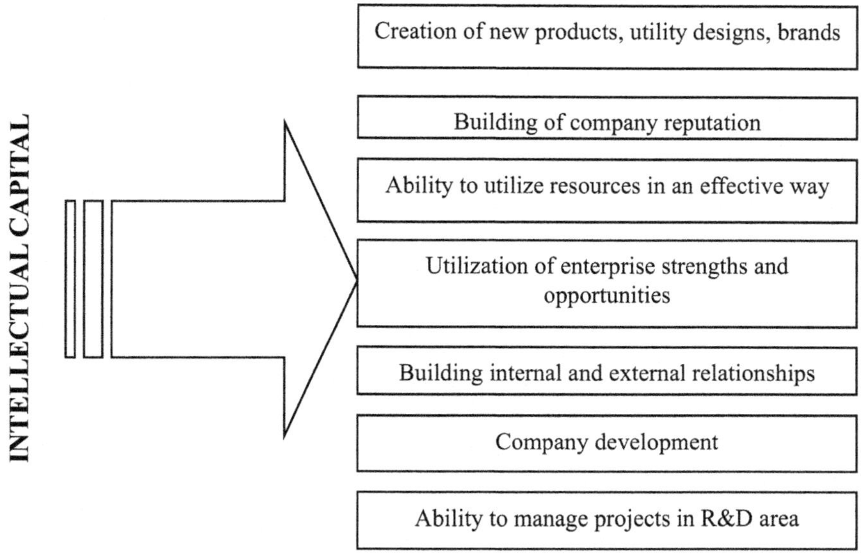

Fig 9.2 Chosen fields of competitive advantage generated by Intellectual Capital (*Source*: Szara and Pierścieniak 2007, 256)

These influence the competitive power of IC and its ability to gain a competitive advantage. So, there are also a lot of fields of competitive advantage generated by IC, some of them are presented in Fig. 9.2.

Fields of competitive advantage generated by IC can be regarded as important areas in which risk can occur.

3 Risk of Intellectual Capital in Knowledge: Based Organizations

Knowledge-based organizations (Perez-Bustamante 1999, 6–17, in Königová et al. 2012, 129–142) are organizations applying a knowledge-based approach to the organization. This approach perceives organizations as a means for the development, integration, preservation, sharing and application of knowledge. Wu et al. (2008, 541–549 in Königová et al. 2012, 129–142) add that knowledge-based organizations allocate resources to intangible assets in the rapidly changing and highly competitive business environment in order to gain competitive advantages. From this point of view IC is the main assets of the knowledge – based organization.

Among the many descriptions of IC, some are quite specific and created by individual companies for use within a specific industry (Grudzewski and Jurczak 2007, 392). In the literature IC is defined as:

(a) 'all nonmonetary and nonphysical resources that are fully or partly controlled by the organization and that contribute to the organization's value creation' (Roos et al. 2005, 19);
(b) the intelligence of the organization, which is not only a sum of the intelligence of its employees, but is also a result of existing synergy. The intelligence of the company consists of different elements such as: communication, technological, innovative, marketing, organizational, social and finally ecological intelligence (Grudzewski and Hejduk 2004, 58);
(c) the value of economic assets accumulated in structural and human resources (Dobija 2003, 27);
(d) the total knowledge of the company's employees and translation of this knowledge into IC components (Bratnicki and Strużyna 2001, 69–72);
(e) 'knowledge that can be converted into value' (Edvinsson and Sullivan 1996, 358).

However, the issue of IC should be defined in a wider context, by taking into account its measurable benefits. IC can be described simply as: 'All connected each other Knowledge Resources (tangible or intangible) that are inter-connected, and which the organization makes use of to gain a long-term competitive advantage.' (Jurczak 2006, 39–46)

In the literature IC is divided into different categories such as: Human Capital, Organizational (Structural) Capital and Relational Capital. So, it includes created knowledge of the organization as well as knowledge of its individual members (their experience, abilities and creativity). Additionally any technological invents and tools that boost efficiency of work in the organization (software, organization structure, patents, trademarks, licenses, methods, techniques) compose a part of IC. Finally, relationship with established between stakeholders and the organization is an important part of IC (Grudzewski and Jurczak 2007, 392). All IC components combine and interact with each other in a unique way to create added value, which causes personal, organizational or relational risk for all the company.

Risk is present in every organization and human situation. It has a dynamic character and requires human perception to evaluate (Raczkowski et al. 2015, 13). So to gain competitive advantage companies should try to manage IC in the proper way in order to reduce risk connected with it.

The definition of risk has changed from "*the chance of something happening that will have* an *impact on objectives*" to "*the effect of uncertainty on objectives*" (AS/NZS ISO 31000:2009 2010, 1). However, "*risks are usually defined by the adverse impact on profitability of several distinct sources of uncertainty*" (Bessis 1998, 5).

Enterprises should realize and pay attention to all types of risk, which can occur, especially risk connected with IC assets. Decision-making in the IC area and also the IC management process could generate the main potential of risk and uncertainty. Taking the risk, the enterprise can increase its chances forcefully, not only on surviving, but in development in the long term also.

Detailed classification of risk associated with IC has been presented in Table 9.1

Risks related to IC can be either financial or non-financial risks and can cause losses in various ways (Put Your Enterprise Knowledge to Work. A Guide to IC Management, 11), such as:

(a) resignation of key knowledge workers
(b) loss of business reputation due to bad staff practices or poor quality control
(c) theft of company data
(d) destruction of key data that had not been backed up
(e) infringement of intellectual property

Table 9.1 Classification of risks associated with Intellectual Capital in organizations

Categories of IC risk	Types of IC risk
Human capital risk (Lipka 2002, 57–167; Kierner 2008, 160; Król 2010, 54)	Risk of unsuitable amount of human capital in organization (deficit or **surplus of** human capital) – identical with planning human resources
	Risk of **surplus of** human capital competencies (**surplus of** qualifying employees) – identical with risk connected with process of recruitment and selection
	Risk of competency gap in organization (too low or unsuitable competencies of employees)
	Risk of information security for which employees have access (risk of security leak)
	Risk of human error
	Risk connected with development of human capital (risk of investing in trainings, bringing up of qualifications and competencies)
	Risk of knowledge loss arising from employee leaving organization
	Risk of employees' conflict
	Risk of poor communications skills
	Risk of employee's segmentation
Organizational capital risk	Risk of unsuitable amount of structural and innovational capital
	Risk of deficiencies, lack or **surplus of** information and communication technology (MRP, ERP, CRM, SAP, www, e-mail, e-commerce)
	Risk of deficiencies, lack or **surplus of** methods, techniques and management styles
	Risk of deficiencies, lack or **surplus of** systems (Knowledge Management Systems, SWD, ISO, TQM)
	Risk of incorrect application of personal process in organization
	Risk of selection or forming of unsuitable organizational structures
	Risk of lack of properly organizational culture initiating learning process, elasticity and readiness for changes
	Risk that enterprise is relying on out-dated communications technology
	Risk that old team structure is not fitted to new team challenges

(continued)

Table 9.1 (continued)

Categories of IC risk	Types of IC risk
Relational capital risk	Risk of unsuitable creation of relational capital (image, brand, reputation, loyalty, mission, vision, goals) Risk of lack of or unsuitable build of cooperation and trust with stakeholders Risk of loss or decrease of customers' satisfaction and loyalty Risk of incorrect forming of marketing policy Risk of lack market operation, such as: marketing action, advertising campaigns, charitable action, cultural performance

Source: Jurczak (2015, 3–4)

4 Process and Principles of Effective IC Risk Management in Knowledge-Based Organizations

In the literature, there are many accepted definitions of risk management. It can be defined as an activity which integrates recognition of risk, risk assessment, developing strategies to manage it, and mitigation of risk using managerial resources. Also, risk management is defined as a process consisting of following the steps in Fig. 9.3 (Heinz-Peter Berg 2010, 82–89).

In order to apply risk management effectively, it is crucial to understand the importance of the process in building the success of the organization. In knowledge-based organizations, the risk management process should refer to intellectual resources involved in value creation. These organizations should create their own individual IC risk management process.

We should understand IC risk management (ICRM) as a process that consists of human risk management, organizational risk management and relational risk management. We should try identifying, measuring, assessing, monitoring and controlling risk in every area which generates Intellectual Capital in the organization. The most important stage during the ICRM process is the identification of IC risk, because the correct recognition of its elements has a huge impact on proper measurement, estimation and control of IC risk. The second stage – the measurement of

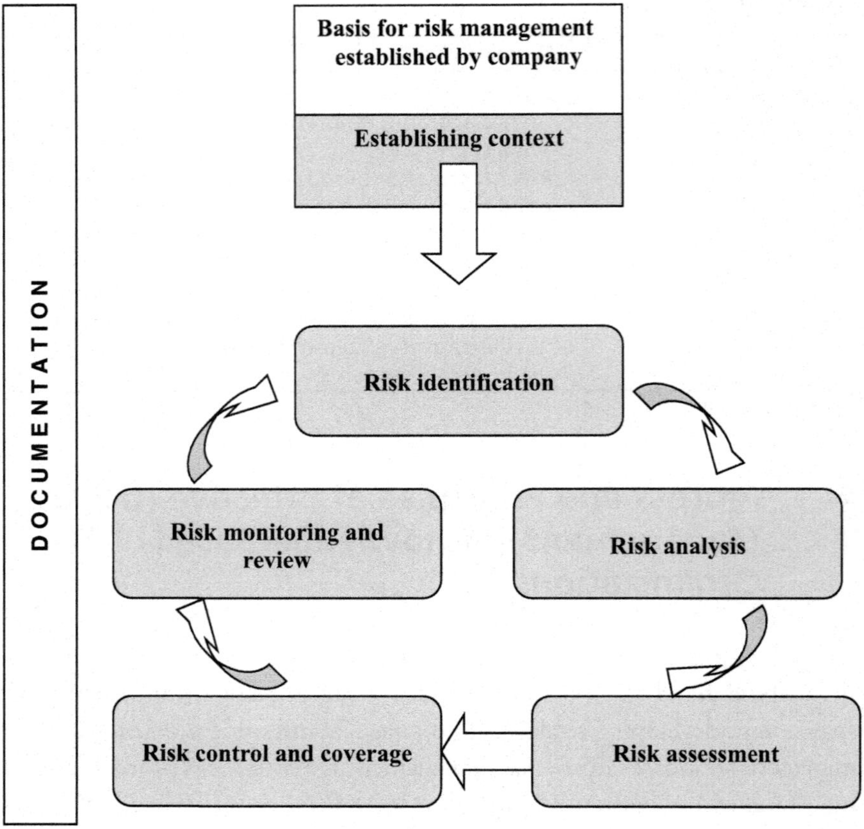

Fig. 9.3 Risk management process (*Source*: Heinz-Peter Berg 2010, 83)

IC risk – is the most difficult in the whole process because of numerous quantitative and qualitative indicators used to measure risk in intellectual assets. A proper measurement of IC risk leads to working out a strategy of monitoring and controlling it, and this can be an effective tool to increase the competitiveness and efficiency of the company on the global market.

The effective process of ICRM should be determined by some main principles (see Table 9.2). ICRM is a complicated process which enables realizing long-term objectives of organizations in competitive advantage area. Such a process depends on the particular type of enterprise, its size and scale of activity and also quality of IC gathered in organization. An economic environment favourable to enterprise activity is also very important. Each company should consider its own individual approach to ICRM.

Table 9.2 Principles of ICRM

Principles of ICRM	Characteristics
Creates and protects value	Proper management of IC risk contributes to the achievement of an organization's objectives through the continuous review of its processes and systems
Be an integral part of organizational processes	Management of IC risk needs to be integrated with a firm's management framework and become a part of its planning processes, at both the operational and strategic level
Be part of decision-making	The process of ICRM should help decision makers to make informed choices, identify priorities and select the most appropriate action
Explicitly address uncertainty	By identifying potential risks of IC, firms can implement controls and treatments to maximize the chance of achievements or minimize the chance of loss
Be systematic, structured and timely	The process of ICRM should be consistent across the firm to ensure efficiency, consistency and reliability of results
Based on the best available information	To effectively manage IC risk it is important to understand and consider all available information relevant to an activity and to be aware that there may be restrictions on that information. It is then important to understand how all this information informs the process of ICRM
Be tailored	A firm's ICRM framework needs to include its risk profile, as well as taking into consideration its internal and external operating environment
Especially take into account human factors	ICRM needs to recognize the contribution that people make to achieving a firm's objectives
Be transparent and inclusive	Engaging stakeholders, both internal and external, throughout the ICRM process recognizes that communication and consultation are key to identifying, analyzing and monitoring risk
Be dynamic, iterative and responsive to change	The process of managing IC risks needs to be flexible. The challenging environment we operate in requires organizations to consider the context for managing risk as well as continuing to identify new risks that emerge, and make allowances for those risks that no longer exist
Facilitate the continual improvement of organizations	Firms with a mature risk management culture are those that have invested resources over time and are able to demonstrate the continual achievement of their objectives

Source: Own work based on: AS/NZS ISO 31000:2009 (2010, 1–2)

IC risk management is an integral process of good management and decision-making at all levels of an organization. All departments in an organization should manage IC risk continuously and systematically in order to improve their effectiveness in gaining competitive advantage.

5 Model of Intellectual Capital's Ability to Gain Competitive Advantage and Reduce Risk

The ability of IC to gain a competitive advantage in the market is difficult to observe, describe, and it is all the more difficult to measure its effects. Up to now, in the literature dealing with IC issues, there is no well-defined or complete definition characterizing this ability without ambiguity. It can be understood intuitively, as something that generates a supplemental value of the organization. So, the author suggests her own definition of this concept and characterizes the ability of IC to gain a competitive advantage as: 'The readiness and willingness of an enterprise to introduce rapid changes in knowledge deployment and improvement of employees skills, to build relationships based on mutual trust and cooperation, to take care of the agile communication process, and to promote the positive image and reputation of the enterprise in the marketplace.' (Jurczak 2012, 77) This definition includes some basic factors which create the ability of IC to gain a competitive advantage, such as: knowledge and skills of employees, mutual trust and cooperation in the communication processes in the company, the public image and reputation of the company, which can, on the other hand, cause threats for the organization.

Continuous changes in the enterprise, the generation or absorption of a new knowledge, improvement of skills by employees, improvements in the proper utilization of IC resources, all have the desired result in creating a competitive advantage in the market. Mutual trust and cooperation between stakeholders, and careful communication during the creation of relationships, make use of the workforce's potential. All of these elements contribute to a positive image and better reputation of the enterprise in the market. On this basis, a model of IC's ability in gaining competitive advantage consists of factors and variables has been formulated. The model of ability of IC to gain competitive advantage in the market, its component factors and variables, is visualized in Fig. 9.4.

The model includes four of the above-mentioned factors needed to create this ability. First factor: 'Knowledge and skills of employees' can be characterized by three variables: learning by experience, participating in training, and motivating development. These variables express the possibility of improvement of knowledge and skills, as well as the encouragement applied in companies in order to increase the professional development of employees.

Second factor: 'Mutual trust and cooperation' is composed of three variables: team spirit', 'intensity of direct contact between employees' and 'positive atmosphere in relations between employees'.

Third factor: 'Communication processes in the company' is represented by only one variable: condition of communication processes. This variable expresses the variety of means of communication, which can improve knowledge and information flow in an organization.

The last factor named: 'Public image and reputation of the company' is characterized by two variables: building of positive client experience and diversified product offer. These variables concern development cooperation with clients.

The proposed model has been verified by using CFA on results of empirical research. Survey research included consulting enterprises in Poland (sample size 186) (Jurczak 2012, 148). To characterize the model given above, a detailed, basic and particular hypothesis was formulated. The basic hypothesis resulted directly from theoretical considerations concerning gaining competitive advantage by using IC factors. The basic hypothesis constitutes a base during the formulation of particular hypotheses, which in turn, were the base for matching variables. Variables characterize the structure of factors in the model. Such an approach allows us to define the individual positions of measuring instrument for each variable.

The basic hypothesis describes the proposed model of IC's ability to gain a competitive advantage in the market. The particular hypothesis concerns the structure of individual factors which create IC in gaining competitive advantage. A list of hypotheses and variables is presented in Table 9.3.

The model includes four of the above mentioned factors creating this ability and IC risk can be reduced by proper utilization of these factors. The factors have been characterized by the use of variables and positions, reproducing the character of this phenomenon (see Table 9.4).

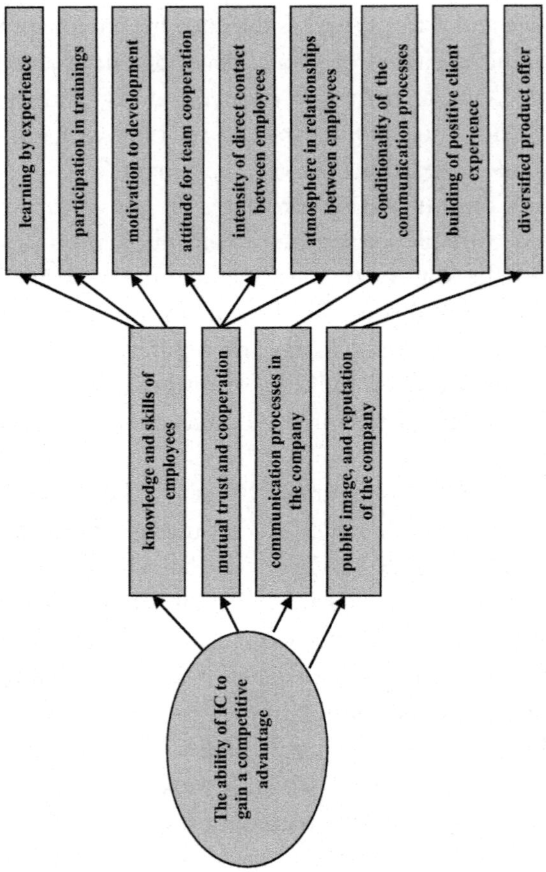

Fig. 9.4 The model of ability of IC to gain a competitive advantage on the market (*Source*: Jurczak 2012, 134)

Table 9.3 Listing of hypotheses and variables

Factor	Basic hypothesis	Particulars hypothesis	Variables
Knowledge and skills of employees	H1: The higher the value of knowledge and skills of employees, the higher the ability of IC to gain a competitive advantage in the market	H1_1: The faster employees deepen their knowledge and improve their skills, the higher the value of the knowledge and skills of the employees	**Learning by experience** **Participating in training**
		H1_2: The more employees are motivated to individual development and skills improvement, the higher the value of knowledge and skills of the employees	**Motivating development**
Mutual trust and cooperation	H2: The higher the value of relations based on mutual trust and cooperation, the higher the ability of IC to gain a competitive advantage in the market	H2_1: The more team-building is appreciated in a company, the higher mutual trust and cooperation	**Team spirit**
		H2_2: the more intensive the direct contact between employees, the higher the mutual trust and cooperation	**Intensity of direct contact between employees**
		H2_3: The better the work atmosphere in a company, the higher the mutual trust and cooperation	**Positive atmosphere in relationship between employees**

(continued)

Table 9.3 (continued)

Factor	Basic hypothesis	Particulars hypothesis	Variables
Communication processes in the company	H3: The more efficient the communication processes in the company, the better the ability of IC to gain a competitive advantage in the market	H3_1: The more an information system fosters spontaneous communication, the higher the quality of communication processes between employees	**Condition of communication processes**
		H3_2: The more differentiated means of communication are used in a company, the higher the quality of communication processes between employees in the company	
Public image, and reputation of the company	H4: The more the company takes care of its public image and reputation, the stronger the ability of IC to gain a competitive advantage in the market	H4_1: The more the marketing department builds positive experiences between clients and the organization, the easier it is to take care of the company's public image and reputation	**Building of positive client experience**
		H4_2: The more diversified the product offer, the easier it is to take care of the company's public image and reputation	**Diversified product offer**

Source: Own work based on Jurczak (2012, 134–139)

Table 9.4 List of variables and positions examining the ability of IC to gain competitive advantage in detailed factors

Factors	Variables	No	Positions
Knowledge and skills of employees	**Learning by experience**	1	Less experienced employees are mobilized to observe the practices of more experienced employees
		2	More experienced employees are trainers and advisers for less experienced employees
		3	Switching occupations in the enterprise to deepen knowledge and develop the skills of employees
	Participating in training	4	Training on occupational skills
		5	Discussion within team
		6	Case study
		7	Lectures
	Motivating development	8	Tackling different and complicated tasks
		9	Awarding bonus for improving processes and products of the enterprise
		10	Participation in formulating the purposes of enterprise
Mutual trust and cooperation	**Team spirit**	11	Cooperation within team helps employees achieve complicated daily tasks
		12	Cooperation can lead to breakthrough in thinking
	Intensity of direct contact between employees	13	Employees of enterprise permanently and systematically contact each other about problems concerning product development and services
		14	Big accent is putting in the enterprise on development of interpersonal contact
		15	Informal rules and norms of operations dominate in the enterprise
	Positive atmosphere in relationship between employees	16	Lack of involvement/involvement
		17	Lack of trust/trust
		18	Stagnation/orientation on development
		19	Secrecy/openness

(continued)

Table 9.4 (continued)

Factors	Variables	No	Positions
Communication processes in company	**Condition of communication processes**	20	Informal flow of information and knowledge exists in the organization
		21	Development of dialogue and discussion between employees is encouraged in the company
		22	Flow of information and knowledge between employees is intensive and easy
		23	Channels of communications are used intensively
		24	Channels of communications for passing information are used extensively
		25	Channels of communications to do with direct communication and interpersonal relations are used extensively
		26	Different ways of communication which boost knowledge and reach large numbers of people are used widely in the enterprise
Public image, and reputation of the company	**Building of positive client experience**	27	Aspiration of the enterprise to get the highest quality of offered products and services is visible
		28	Systematic growth of cooperation with clients (also potential clients) is practised to satisfy wishes and requirements
		29	Aspiration of the enterprise to get the highest quality of client service is visible
	Diversified product offer	30	Efforts of the enterprise to develop products and services most often concentrate on building innovative products and services
		31	The enterprise is perfect in creating new kinds of product and services for clients
		32	The enterprise's strategy to give clients the best product relies on numerous and dynamic changes in the offer of products and services

Source: Own work based on: Jurczak 2012, 177–178

Each factor of the model is characterized by the use of detailed variables. These variables include specific IC behavior, which takes into consideration the character of the examined phenomena and can generate plenty of different risks in an organization. To control and limit the risk we should analyse and monitor the variables of examining the ability of IC to gaining competitive advantage. Proper analysis and utilization of IC variables and positions can increase the efficiency of a whole company and improve its position in the market.

6 IC's Ability to Gain Competitive Advantage and Reduce of Risk: Verification Model

The empirical verification of a complete model of the ability of IC to gain a competitive advantage was carried out by using CFA and employing generalized least squares (GLS) and maximum likelihood (ML) approaches. The verification of individual factors was done first, and then a complete verification of the model was done. The verification method of suggested model has been based on A. Zgrzywa-Ziemak's method (Zgrzywa-Ziemak and Kamiński 2009, 139–172).

The following fit indices were used to measure how well the a priori model reproduces the sample data:

(a) $\chi 2/ss$ (measurement of the accuracy of the proposed model),
(b) RMSEA Steiger – Lind's (root mean square error of approximation),
(c) GFI Joreskog's (goodness of feet index),
(d) AGFI Joreskog's (adjusted goodness of feet index).

The proposed model was verified in terms of accuracy and reliability of fitting characterized by Cronbach's α – rate of reliability. The accuracy and consistency of the model was supported by a high score of fitting of particular factors as well as in the complete model.

Table 9.5 presents the fit index values of particular factors assumed in the model, while Table 9.6 shows the fit indices of the complete model of IC's ability to gain competitive advantage.

Table 9.5 Statistics of fit indices for individual factors of IC ability to gain a competitive advantage

Measure	Description	Variable	Factor
X^2/ss	The X^2/ss parameter measures an accuracy of fitting	0,848	Knowledge and skills of employees
	$X^2/ss < 2$ – it means that the model is of a perfect fitting	1,059	Mutual trust and cooperation
		0,964	Communication processes in the company
	$2 < X^2/ss < 5$ – it means that the model is acceptable	1,355	Public image and reputation of the company
RMSEA	RMSEA (root mean square error of approximation) evaluates an average error result from misfit a model	0,000	Knowledge and skills of employees
	RMSEA < 0,05 – it means that the model is of a perfect fitting	0,021	Mutual trust and cooperation
	0,05 < RMSEA < 0,08 – it means that the model is acceptable	0,000	Communication processes in the company
	RMSEA > 0,1 – it means that the model should definitely become rejected	0,039	Public image and reputation of the company
GFI	The GFI parameter is an index of goodness of fitting and it accepts value from 0 to 1	0,975	Knowledge and skills of employees
	GFI > 0,9 – it means that the model is acceptable	0,973	Mutual trust and cooperation
	GFI = 1 – it means the model is of a perfect fitting	0,983	Communication processes in the company
	GFI < 0,9 – it means that the model should be modified	0,983	Public image and reputation of the company
AGFI	The AGFI parameter is an corrected index of goodness of fitting. It accepts value from 0 to 1	0,957	Knowledge and skills of employees
		0,949	Mutual trust and cooperation
	AGFI > 0,9 – it means that the model is acceptable	0,964	Communication processes in the company
	AGFI < 0,9 – it means that the model should be modified	0,956	Public image and reputation of the company

Source: Jurczak (2012, 179)

Table 9.6 Statistics of fit indices for complete model of IC ability to gain a competitive advantage

Measure	Value	Model
X^2/ss	0.711	The ability of IC to gain a competitive advantage on the market
RMSEA	0.000	
GFI	0.876	
AGFI	0.857	

Source: Jurczak (2012, 180)

Statistical analyses of particular factors that are assumed in the proposed model show that the fitting quality is relatively high in every case. The basic $\chi 2$/ss index shows that the proposed model fits polling data very well. For each of the analyzed factors, $\chi 2$/ss indices are lower than the commonly accepted value of 2 ($\chi 2/ss < 2$). Furthermore, the RMSEA index is approximately about 0.05 and does not exceed 0.1, the lowest of which is treated as a critical value for the quality of the model. The results show that there is a very good fit between assumed factors and gathered data. Moreover, even the most sophisticated and challenging indices, such as: GFI and AGFI, exceed a value of 0.9, and suggest acceptability of the model.

The fitting quality of individual factors in the model should therefore be assumed as satisfying.

Basic statistical indices which show the fitting quality of the complete model are equal 0.711 ($\chi 2$/ss) and < 0.001 (RMSEA), and it is concluded that the proposed model is acceptable. Advanced GFI and AGFI indices in this case do not exceed the recommended value 0.9. However, such a situation is rather common during the analysis of complex models with many parameters and does not immediately attest to the poor quality of the model. The calculated value of GFI and AGFI indices (0.876 and 0.857) are at an acceptable level and in this case, the result suggests that the complete model can be regarded as satisfying and fulfilling basic criterions of fitting.

Summing up, calculated empirical results have confirmed the accuracy of the proposed model of IC ability to gain competitive advantage. This means that the ability of IC to gain competitive advantage can be measured accurately by use of the aforementioned factors that create such ability.

A detailed analysis of the results provided by the model shows that the second factor, 'mutual trust and cooperation', seems to be the main factor in the model of IC ability toward gaining competitive advantage on the market. That factor has the highest load with a value of 0.9, which means the best fitting with proposed model. The first factor in the model, 'knowledge and skills of employees', with a load equal to 0.85 also has a very high value and very good fitting. It is therefore justified to claim that both of the factors mentioned above have the most important effect on IC ability to gain competitive advantage on the market.

The load factor statistics of the model are presented in Fig. 9.5. Factor meaning: 1 – Knowledge and skills of employees, 2 – Mutual trust and cooperation, 3 – Communication processes in the company, 4 – Image and reputation of the company on the market.

Empirical analysis shows that the phenomenon of IC's ability to gain competitive advantage can be successfully measured by the use of four factors that form that ability.

Therefore, the greater IC's ability to gain competitive advantage, the lower the risk generated by IC. IC risk can also be controlled and reduced by verifying variables and positions of examining the ability of IC to gaining competitive advantage.

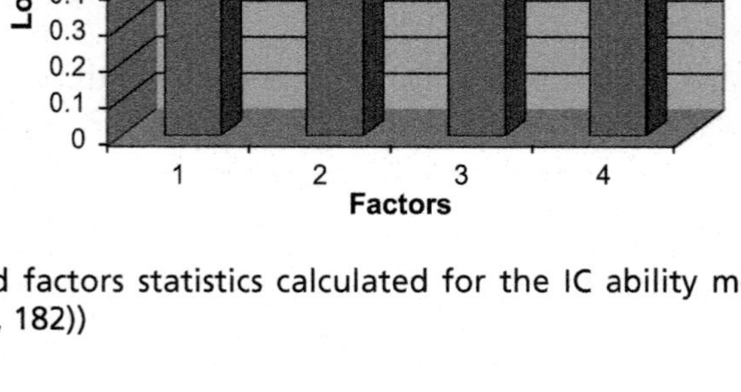

Fig. 9.5 Load factors statistics calculated for the IC ability model (*Source*: (Jurczak 2012, 182))

7 Conclusions

IC is a main factor that greatly pushes forward development of the company, which is able then to gain and sustain competitive advantage in the present. However, in the literature dealing with IC, there is a lack of research into how to use it in order to minimize the level of risk and increase the value of the company in the process of market activity.

The ability of IC to gain a competitive advantage has an important meaning for modern organizations since it affects development, market expansion, and value of the company in the long view. On the other hand, it is very difficult to identify and diagnose the ability of IC and all that complex phenomena, as well as devoting the attention required to monitor IC factors in enterprise continuously.

In fact, the real problem concerning IC is connected with the measurement of its components and reduction of the level of risk generated by it. To reduce the complexity of the problem, four IC factors were selected i.e.: knowledge and skills of employees, mutual trust and cooperation, communication processes in the company, and image and reputation of the company on the market. Proper usage of these factors could limit risk of the whole company.

CFA was used to analyse and to verify empirically chosen factors. The analysis has confirmed the importance all of these factors in the forming of IC ability to gain competitive advantage in the market. In particular, two of these factors – mutual trust, and cooperation and knowledge and skills of employees – play a main role in the process of forming the potential of IC. So, such results show that the building of mutual relationships based on trust and cooperation integrates human actions to maximize market effects and to minimize IC risk. Also, the improvement of staff knowledge and skills make for value of the organization. Therefore, both factors possess main importance for the ability of IC to gain a competitive advantage on the market and can limit the IC risk.

In-depth analysis of IC phenomena shows current directions of its development and future goals. Here, some of them are presented:

(a) the need to form modules, models and even whole systems of IC risk management and its ability to gain a competitive advantage and reduce the level of risk in different companies, and economic sectors
(b) unambiguous, and unique principles, and rules to measure IC risk
(c) evaluation, and measurement of costs, and benefits of IC assets investment

There are a lot of problems and barriers related to IC usage, but the most important is a lack of awareness concerning the possibilities of IC and its crucial role in the future. If any organization wants to achieve a competitive advantage in the long term by use of its IC assets, it should also be aware of risks that can be generated by this kind of capital. Thus, managers have to know how to identity, evaluate, and later measure, and manage the company's own intellectual potential and the risks connected with it, in order to reduce risks to the whole company. Moreover, it is most important to identify the specific IC resources which could generate risk during the process of building and gaining competitive advantage in the market. Limiting of IC risk contributes to increasing the quality of operations and the growth of efficiency, and the energy of the decision-making process, that will result in effective growth of the enterprise's market value.

In conclusion, organizations could achieve a competitive advantage in the long term only by using its IC resources and by controlling the IC risk in a proper way. Additionally, it is very important to identify and monitor IC factors and independent variables (such as learning by experience, participation in training and courses, employees' working relationships) which create the ability of IC to gain a competitive advantage in the market. Organizations which introduce and conduct that kind of policy can be treated as intelligent organizations, which manage their risk properly.

Bibliography

AS/NZS ISO 31000:2009. (2010). Risk management – Principles and guidelines. http://www.finance.gov.au/sites/default/files/COV_216905_Risk_Management_Fact_Sheet_FA3_23082010_0.pdf. Accessed 5 June 2015.

Bessis, J. (1998). *Risk management in banking* (p. 5). Chichester: Wiley.

Bratnicki, M., & Strużyna, J. (2001). *Przedsiębiorczość i kapitał intelektualny, Wyd.* Katowice: AE w Katowicach.
Dobija, D. (2003). *Pomiar i sprawozdawczość kapitału intelektualnego przedsiębiorstwa, Wydawnictwo Wyższej Szkoły Przedsiębiorczości i Zarządzania im.* Warszawa: L. Koźmińskiego.
Edvinsson, L., & Sullivan, P. H. (1996). Developing a model for managing intellectual capital. *European Management Journal, 14*(4), 358–363.
Fischer, T. M., & Vielmeyer, U. (2004). Analyse von Risk Disclosure Scores: Risikoorientierte Unternehmenspublizität der DAX 100-Unternehmen. *KoR*, p. 11.
Grudzewski, W. M., & Hejduk, I. K. (2001). *Przedsiębiorstwo przyszłości* (p. 356). Warszawa: Difin.
Grudzewski, W. M., & Jurczak, J. (2007). Intellectual capital of companies in gaining competitive advantage on global market. In W. M. Grudzewski, I. K. Hejduk, & S. Trzcieliński (Eds.), *Organizations in changing environment. Current problems, concepts and methods of management* (pp. 391–400). Poznań: IEA Press.
Heinz-Peter Berg. (2010, June). Risk management: Procedures, methods and experiences, RT&A # 2(17) (Vol. 1). http://m.gnedenko-forum.org/Journal/2010/022010/RTA_2_2010-09.pdf. Accessed 14 June 2015, pp. 82–89.
Jurczak, J. (2006). Kapitał intelektualny w organizacji przyszłości. *Ekonomika i Organizacja Przedsiębiorstw, 11*, 39–46.
Jurczak, J. (2012). Czynniki kształtujące kapitał intelektualny w osiąganiu przewagi konkurencyjnej. Doctoral thesis, Wrocław, pp. 134, 177–178.
Jurczak, J. (2015). Ograniczanie ryzyka kapitału intelektualnego – perspektywa systemowa. *Przedsiębiorczość I zarządzanie, 16*, nr 8, cz. 3 – *Zarządzanie ryzykiem w gospodarce*, pp. 275–286.
Kasiewicz, S., Rogowski, W., & Kicińska, M. (2006). *Kapitał intelektualny. Spojrzenie z perspektywy interesariuszy*. Kraków: Oficyna Ekonomiczna.
Kierner, G. (2008). Bezpieczeństwo osobowe. In I. Staniec & J. Zawiła-Niedźwiecki (Eds.), *Zarządzanie ryzykiem operacyjnym* (pp. 159–178). Warszawa: C.H. Beck.
Königová, M., Urbancová, H., & Fejfar, J. (2012). Identification of managerial competencies in knowledge-based organizations. *Journal of Competitiveness, 4*(1). http://www.cjournal.cz/files/90.pdf. Accessed 2 June 2015.
Król, M. (2010). Elastyczność zatrudnienia a ryzyko personalne, Współczesne zarządzanie nr 3/2010, *Kwartalnik Środowisk Naukowych i Liderów Biznesu*, p. 54.

Lipka, A. (2002). *Ryzyko personalne. Szanse i zagrożenia zarządzania zasobami ludzkimi* (Vol. 192, pp. 57–167). Warszawa: Poltext.

Perez-Bustamante, G. (1999). Knowledge management in agile innovative organisation. *Journal of Knowledge Management, 3*(1), 6–17. http://dx.doi.org/10.1108/13673279910259358. In Königová, M., Urbancová, H., & Fejfar, J. (2012). Identification of managerial competencies in knowledge-based organizations. *Journal of Competitiveness, 4*(1). http://www.cjournal.cz/files/90.pdf. Accessed 2 June 2015.

Put your enterprise knowledge to work. A guide to intellectual capital management. http://www.ipd.gov.hk/eng/ICM/guide_icm_e_txt.pdf. Accessed 28 May 2015.

Raczkowski, K., Noga, M., & Klepacki, J. (2015). *Zarządzanie ryzykiem w polskim systemie finansowym*. Warszawa: Difin.

Roos, G., Pike, S., & Fernstrom, L. (2005). *Managing intellectual capital in practice*. New York: Butterworth-Heinemann.

Steward, T. A. (2001). *The wealth of knowledge: Intellectual capital and the twenty-first century organization*. London: Nicholas-Brealey.

Szara, K., & Pierścieniak, A. (2007). Kapitał intelektualny jako obszar konkurencji przedsiębiorstw (wybrane aspekty teoretyczne). In M. G. Woźniak (Ed.), *Nierówności społeczne a wzrost gospodarczy. Gospodarka oparta na wiedzy* (pp. 249–258). Rzeszów: Uniwersytet Rzeszowski.

Wu, L. Ch., Ong, Ch. S., & Hsu, Y. W. (2008). Knowledge-based organizations evaluation. *Decision support systems, 45*. http://dx.doi.org/10.1016/j.dss.2007.06.013. In Königová, M., Urbancová, H., & Fejfar, J. (2012). Identification of managerial competencies in knowledge-based organizations. *Journal of Competitiveness, 4*(1). http://www.cjournal.cz/files/90.pdf. Accessed 2 June 2015.

Zgrzywa-Ziemak, A., & Kamiński, R. (2009). *Rozwój zdolności uczenia się przedsiębiorstwa*. Wrocław: Difin.

10

Regulatory Risk in the EU Banking Sector

Stanisław Kasiewicz and Lech Kurkliński

1 Introduction

The purpose of this chapter is to present the degree of suitability of the category of regulatory risk in the banking sector. It is widely known that banks are public trust institutions; they manage depositors' savings, ensure financing for business operations and support the functioning of households. Their activity is largely decisive for a high level of economic development and the living standard of society. In the conditions of increasing globalization, the provision of banking services and pursuit of a radical change in the post-crisis financial architecture banks are subject not only to national regulations, but also to international (regional) and world regulations. Since nearly all the aspects of business operations are subject to regulations and the external supervision of not only national but, in the case of the EU, also new, centralized EU institutions, it is

S. Kasiewicz (✉) • L. Kurkliński
Warsaw School of Economics, Warsaw, Poland

K. Raczkowski (ed.), *Risk Management in Public Administration*,
DOI 10.1007/978-3-319-30877-7_10

necessary and justified to introduce to the analyses a new type of risk, namely regulatory risk.

Formulated in this way, the main purpose of the chapter has determined its substantive structure. It consists of three sections. Section one presents factors supporting the implementation of regulatory risk analysis and management in the banking sector. This section contains a definition of regulatory risk, refers to its origins and describes potential benefits of more advanced regulatory risk management, particularly in banking legislation. A new element subject to deliberation is the presentation of cultural factors; this element is often ignored, although it is important, especially in the light of significant diversity across Europe. Section two contains the presentation and critical assessment of major publications dedicated to regulatory risk management in the financial sector. They were assessed in terms of the prioritization of regulatory objectives, regulatory risk measurement and the system of communicating ex-ante and ex-post regulatory effects for key stakeholders. Section three discusses the most important issues relating to the implementation of regulatory risk in the practice of enacting and implementing banking regulations.

The major findings obtained include a statement that, so far, attempts at using regulatory risk in the banking sector have been very sparse and these efforts did not take into account the specific character of the functioning of financial institutions. The vast part of the literature focuses on regulatory risk relating only to the phase of regulatory enforcement from the sectoral perspective, ignoring other important aspects and stages of the regulatory process. Consequently, the proposal to keep work in this area is natural; in this way, the analysis of regulatory risk in the financial sector will be included both in theoretical discussions and in practice.

This chapter is based on the descriptive research method related to the critical analysis of available literature about regulatory risk and practical experience. The authors have reviewed several cases of the regulatory impact assessment in the Polish and European banking sector. In particular, the analytical works have been focused on the legislative procedures carried out since 2006. The results have been achieved due to the cooperation with Polish institutions such as: ALTERUM Centre for Research and Analysis of Financial System, the Polish Bankers Association, the

Bank Guarantee Fund, the Credit Information Bureau and the Warsaw Institute of Banking.

2 Factors Supporting the Implementation of Regulatory Risk in the Banking Sector

2.1 Essence and Origin of Regulatory Risk

Risk may be defined differently in law, economics, and management sciences because it is highly disputable problem. That's why there are different definitions presented in scientific and research papers, depending on the discipline. From the regulatory point of view, a more important issue is whether risk is included in legislative theory and practice. Although in economic disciplines risk is a commonly useful, analysed and applied category, the theory of law notices benefits arising from risk management (administration) to a far smaller degree. It can easily be shown that the extent to which this is included in the legal framework is small or very small. Consequently, it can be concluded that the theory of law, especially economic law, could benefit to a much greater extent than at present from the accomplishments of other sciences in order to enact law of high quality.

In the long-term process of research development, two main streams of defining risk have emerged (Kasiewicz and Rogowski 2014, 7). The first perceives risk as a future threat that can have adverse consequences for the decision-maker. This definition prevails in the financial sector (for instance, it is applied by banking institutions, insurance institutions, and stock-market investors). This approach is termed as a negative risk. The second stream defines risk as a deviation from the expectations of the decision-maker as to the scale of future (planned, intended) events. These deviations can be either negative or positive, therefore this perspective is termed as a neutral approach to defining risk.

From among various proposals of defining regulatory risk, in this chapter the definition of the OECD (Organisation for Economic Co-operation and Development) is adopted: 'Regulatory risk covers a systematized framework of control or supervision, developed by the government or its regulatory agencies, and does not relate to achieving regulatory objectives.' This definition of regulatory risk is classified among the so-called negative definitions, because it emphasizes threats related to a given draft regulation or regulatory programme (Black 2010b, 187). It is a direct reference to the concept of risk-based regulation, according to which the greatest importance is attached to risk, rather than compliance with typical law-making rules (Hutter 2005; Baldwin and Black 2007; Black 2010a). In line with this idea, regulatory risk is used to assess threats (unfavorable or harmful events) in the planned decision-making process, by implementing the regulations being developed. It covers any actions and procedures related to setting priorities and rules of resource allocation to ensure effectives of draft regulations. It is thus a result of uncertainty as to the anticipated effects of achieving objectives of a given normative act, which are assumed in the proposed legislation and which can manifest themselves in negative or positive deviations (Kasiewicz 2010, 9). In the OECD publication of 2010, J. Black considers three possible definitions of regulatory risk (Black 2010b, 187). The first definition relates to the public sector, the second one relates to the internal model of risk used in the financial sector (mainly banks and insurers) and the third one can be termed as institutional. The author opts for the third definition; namely it is a risk borne by the regulator when developing and implementing draft regulations in business practice. In general, it can be asserted that regulated entities bear legal risk. In view of the above, legislative risk covers two layers: one is connected with the regulator's perspective and the other one is connected with risk generated for regulated entities. The latter approach is a good supplementation for the definition of regulatory risk adopted in this chapter, and the following deliberations will be presented in the spirit of that approach.

Should it be considered that regulatory risk is a threat for the implementation of the assumed regulatory objectives, then, first of all, its objectives must be determined explicitly, which is very rare. Secondly, it is required to present them in figures; it is not possible to confine oneself only to asserting intentions, for instance, that it is important for us to increase the access of young people to apartments, to provide increased customer safety or to strengthen the stability of the financial sector.

In the regulatory process that gives rise to an administrative intervention of the legislator, government or other state agencies in the functioning of institutions, organizations, companies or citizens, by using different tools, including, in particular, legislation, the key role is performed by the regulator (regulators) and regulated entities. As a result, an issue arises whether to use an unified perspective-singular risk of a given legislation or whether to assume and analyse separately the risk of the regulator (regulators) and the risk of the regulated entities (an binary perspective). The holistic approach to the issue would suggest the second solution, which emphasizes these two perspectives of legislative risk, so necessary for drafting, implementing and enforcing regulations. Thus this type of risk has two faces: one assesses threats and opportunities from the regulator's perspective, and the other assesses threats and opportunities from the regulated entities' perspective. Therefore it is important to justify why diagnosing and a separate treatment of regulatory risk is so important for the legislative practice.

Regulatory risk can be used for many important reasons, in particular in the case of the financial sector. The regulator is the main element of the legislative process, certainly as a contractor, process organizer and principal representative of the institution responsible for regulatory quality, but additionally the regulator's professionalism, involvement and motivation are decisive for effectiveness and efficiency of the final result. Moreover, the regulator has a legislative power (creating regulation), and then an executive power (proceeding legislation) in one hand. Both stages and functions require different regulatory tools. Additionally this situation is weakening a self-control of the regulator. As compared to regulated entities, the regulator usually has much greater funds, tangible resources and, above all, information. It seems also that it is easier to reach a consensus on the shape of regulations at the level of the regulator, rather than among numerous regulated entities that differ in interests, business situation, financial standing, and stage of development. An important argument in favour of including regulatory risk is the fact that more and more countries use this category in the legislative process (for instance, Great Britain, Canada, and Australia). And all the more so, because these authorities assume responsibility for the development of environmental protection, the natural environment, education, etc., which are affected, directly or indirectly, by regulations concerning the economic sphere. The importance of regulatory risk can be observed by increasing number of the research and analysis, new concepts how to incorporate this category and improve legislation procedure. This approach does not result from a short-lived vogue for creating legislation, but from the need arising from the present conditions, even bearing in mind the fact that regulations are becoming global or international to an increasing degree. In this situation, the national regulator, when implementing our own legislation, which is manifestly noticeable in the case of highly globalized financial markets, cannot ignore economic, social or environmental effects that go beyond traditional state borders.

Interest in the issue of managing risk in the financial sector's legislation is owed to P. Hampton. He critically assessed the weaknesses of the existing approaches to law-making, in particular with regard to using risk assessment (measurement), which, in his opinion, is fragmentary (Hampton 2005, 4; Eccles and Pointing 2013, 78). An undoubtedly important role, not only in the creation of the concept of risk-based regulation, but also in its development, should be attributed to the Institute Centre for Assessment of Risk Regulation (CARR). The CARR employees, Baldwin, J. Black and B. Hutter, through numerous publications, research and participation in conferences, have popularized the concept in the European Union and worldwide. According to P. Hampton, risk assessment is to serve as the basis for allocation of resources directed to these areas, which should prove most effective in limiting risk. It thus allows avoiding necessary involvement of forces and means of the regulator, and thereby allows the releasing of resources, for instance, by the provision of advisory services. For instance, from the research it can be concluded that during 2002–2003 in the UK only 60 % of high-risk factors were found in 35,000 inspections, and 10 % of low-risk factors were found in 72,000 controls. In spite of the fact that the risk assessment process is covered by much research, it turned out that from among 63 analysed national regulators only 36 conducted partial risk assessments. (Hampton 2005, 4). Major weaknesses of risk assessment include lack of comprehensiveness and consistency. Consequently, resources are not allocated to the highest risk areas. What is more, lack of exhaustive risk assessments creates, according to P. Hampton, excessive inspections at the local level, which also affect the quality of regulatory management.

Consequently, it is worth looking into the contemporary role of regulatory risk management in the financial sector, in particular in the banking sector.

2.2 Meaning of Regulatory Risk for the Banking Sector

An unquestionable benefit of regulatory risk measurement is that it can (Kasiewicz 2014, 27–36):

(a) define precisely the regulator's responsibility, not only for the implementation of a given regulation, but, first of all, for comprehensive economic and financial, social and environmental effects of its enactment. As a result, legislative activities can be monitored and controlled not only by regulated entities, but also by 'third parties', including society. All the parties may exert effective pressure on enacting good law, which is particularly important for banking institutions involved in financing business entities and households, since they affect macro-economic growth and the living standards of society.

(b) protect the regulator effectively against making decisions burdened with a high level of risk, namely against accepting regulations that have minute chances of success. Moreover, unsuccessful drafts are characterized by a very low efficiency, low social effects net; they cause loss of reputation of economic and political authorities, and create passive attitudes or hostile approaches from the regulated entities and managers. Regulatory risk measurement may be also favorable for allocation of resources to the identified risk levels and, in this way, may avoid wasting limited resources.

(c) hierarchize the adopted priorities, assess alternative solutions, identify critical areas for obtaining the planned objectives, allocate tasks, resources and responsibilities—in other words, regulatory risk measurement covers the issues that affect the quality of the whole regulatory drafting process.

(d) facilitate the regulatory implementation process through the system of monitoring and control of its course, in particular by responding quickly to new types of risk that emerged during their implementation. The quality of regulatory risk management dynamizes thus the whole legislative process and may be treated as an important assessment tool of regulatory intelligence of the regulator's activities.
(e) provide experience in drafting regulations that should be largely focused on generating high social benefits net, rather than resigned to favorable fate and undergoing continuous experiments (groping for optimal solutions).

The above list of benefits resulting from professional regulatory risk management, in spite of being incomplete, indicates that ignoring or excluding these issues in the legislative process is highly inadvisable and too costly, not only for the regulators, regulated entities, but, above all, for society.

The application of the concept of regulatory risk for enacting law in the banking sector seems particularly important when it results, for instance, from the fact that banks belong to sectors that are highly regulated and sensitive to this type of administrative intervention. After the crisis, this sub-prime sector has largely lost the trust of society; as a result, the issue of the way of bringing back its ancillary role becomes the key problem. However, these are not all the factors indicating that regulatory risk should be implemented in business practice.

After the outbreak of the financial crisis in 2007, numerous regulatory reforms were conducted that, as a result of their large number, objective scope and accumulation in time, made economists and managers believe commonly that the banking was over-regulated. It is worth emphasizing that the European Union alone introduced more than 40 drafts (5th Report of Session 2014–15 2015, 5); moreover, global and international organizations were also active in this area, not to mention existing national regulations, for national regulators were working very intensively. Almost any regulatory change causes an avalanche of adaptation activities, training sessions, modification of IT systems, creation of new organizational units and even institutions, which is reflected in growing costs, decreasing efficiency and negligence in developing corporate strategies, business models and the building of competitive advantages. When this wave of regulations covers larger and larger the areas of banks' activity, frustration grows, new types of risk are generated and pressure is exerted on the swing of the regulatory pendulum. In spite of common awareness of increasing encumbrances for banks, it is still necessary to continue the implementation of the Basel III requirements and the project of the Banking Union; moreover, at the same time, a new project has been undertaken: structural reform of the banking sector. Additionally, intensive activities are announced for developing the Basel IV principles. Another important problem the European financial sector is grappling with is its excessive over-banking as compared to other world markets. It is proved in the publication by the ESRB Advisory Scientific Committee (Is Europe Overbanked? 2014). The publication presents numerous facts concerning excessive sizes of the European banking sector, its accumulation and leverage ratio. In addition, it shows that the dynamics of development of banks were too high with regard to growth in their balance sheets. Banks had too large a share in the financial system and had a large scope of risky investment and non-banking activities (inter alia, trading). Superfluous over-banking generates high sensitivity of the whole economy to disturbances in this sector and creation of system risk, hence various propositions regarding scenarios of economic and regulatory policies that would allow the dangerous dominance of banks to be reduced, and which would be introduced mainly through the introduction of new financial regulations. However, it should be noted that the above comments are suitable for highly developed European economies. The situation in the Central and Eastern Europe is completely different. The degree of banking is lower and it can be even concluded that these countries are under-banked; it creates a significant problem in the European Union. Given such significant structural differences, the impact of uniform EU regulations has essentially different results. The anti-crisis regulations inhibit the development of the banking sector in countries with overbanked economies, as intended by the regulator, but this impediment also affects countries where banks should develop intensively.

Account should be taken not only of the latest crisis, but also of important developing changes in the conditions of the external environment of the EU, in particular the political environment (for instance, the stronger and stronger position of China, transatlantic negotiations, instability in the Middle East, and mass immigrations from instable countries, particularly those affected by armed conflicts, and threats resulting from the actual, albeit undeclared war between Ukraine and Russia). In the EU alone there have been many changes: strong disintegration trends have emerged; nationalist, populist and Eurosceptic views have grown in popularity, discrepancies with regard to the directions of the common foreign and economic policy have been intensifying (the crisis in Greece, the UK exiting the EU, problems with taking a stance on Russia, and heightened structural disproportions: after 2004, the EU became a system of countries with a highly diversified economic levels). Uncertainty, instability, discontinuity, a highly variable external environment bringing about the need to create some stable foundations for the functioning of business entities and the society—in this area, the financial sector, for which risk management is of key importance, performs a particularly important role. At this point, several risks could be listed—inter alia, insolvency risk of banks, and currently of nation states, credit risk, market risk, reputation risk, system risk, and regulatory risk.

The decreasing competitiveness of the economy etc' means that it is a fact and this fact is alarming. The report by the World Bank *Doing Business* states that the EU average in terms of competition ranks it 36th out of 189 analysed countries (Doing Business… 2014). It proves significant diversity of our group and present disproportions. Therefore, a fundamental question arises: how to increase competitiveness of the old continent as compared to more and more developing and aggressive global competition?

It seems that one of the main reasons for the weakening competitive position of the European Union is regulations that are insufficiently adapted to the changes taking place in international and external arenas: they do not eliminate the huge structural discrepancies among the member countries. Therefore, the regulators should use the principle of proportionality to a greater extent and address EU regulations to the areas that decrease structural disproportions and barriers for entrepreneurship at the micro level. Legislative restrictions and decreasing share of private investments call for another approach to creating the regulatory policy in the EU.

An important feature of the present condition of the European banking services market is the continuing revolutionary change in the architecture of the financial system's supervision and functioning. Projects already in operation, such as the CRD IV Directive, the CRR Regulation, and the Banking Union, or projects being prepared, such as the Capital Markets Union, will radically change the rules of attitudes and behaviors of the European banking institutions. It is worth emphasizing that although by 2007 the dominating approach to banking risk management was at the micro-economic level, in the following years it was concluded rightly that it was necessary to include the system (macro-economic) level.

In general, it can be concluded that legal and regulatory factors perform a more and more important and even key role in determining banks' competitiveness. Therefore, the category of regulatory risk should become a more and more important tool used in the regulatory policy, and this approach has been already implemented in some countries. The recent proposals of the European Commission towards improving the quality of enacted law are a step in the right direction, but the issue of risk has not been noticed sufficiently, yet. (Better Regulation for Better Results… 2015).

2.3 Cultural Factors

The cultural context of the regulatory process plays the important role for creating regulation and then for compliance with regulation. It varies among societies. Additionally, regulations are influenced by more or less different approaches to risk, also determined largely by national cultures. In short, cultural aspects are one of major groups of factors that explain diversity in the emergence and perception of regulatory risk.

When analysing the banking sector in terms of attitudes towards the law, banks' ownership structure should be taken into account. In many countries, in particular in Central and Eastern Europe, foreign capital and transnational financial corporations are dominating, which further complicates the image of the meaning of cultural aspects of law-making and enforcement. In each country, the main role for legislation process is performed by national culture of a domestic regulator. But entities with local and foreign capital respond to the issued regulations in different way. Moreover, in the case of the EU, regulations are created in the intercultural (mixed) community, and they are binding across the whole of a structurally diverse, multinational organism.

Cultural conditions emerge in the long run, lasting even for centuries. From among them, the leading position is taken by religious factors. The literature includes many publications on the impact of religion on economic growth, although with regard to the financial sector this literature is far less numerous. From among sparse publications, the paper by R. Stulz and R. Williamson of 2003 can be quoted; it presents the impact of religion on the position of financial institutions (mainly banks) to a degree larger than natural openness to foreign trade (Stulz and Williamson 2003, 313–349). On the other hand, J. Houston and his collaborators emphasize the following dependence: stronger (formal and informal) authority of lenders (mainly banks) is translated into their increased tendency to taking risks, and, further, the likelihood of crisis (Houston et al. 2010, 485–512). However, in this area the most quoted example refers to Islam and its role in shaping the principles of action and shaping banking institutions. From this paper's perspective, attention should be focused on analysis and comparison of the impact of Protestantism and Catholicism. In particular, a lively discussion, still ongoing, was provoked by the views of M. Weber, presented in his paper of 1905 *The Protestant Ethic and the Spirit of Capitalism* (Weber 1905). Opinions on the role performed by Protestantism in the development of the capitalist economy as compared to Catholicism are divided. Nevertheless, it is worth reflecting on whether certain traditions prove true in this matter when considering attitudes to the law, especially in the economic sphere. On the whole, the Catholic Church is distinguished by quite a strong catalogue of dos and don'ts of conduct, and these are guarded by a hierarchical organization. However, in practice, the key role is performed by priests with their arbitrary, subjective assessments, whereby they serve as confessors, for the Catholic Church has the convention of confession and penance. Thus, absolution is possible, which, in a sense, opens the door to accepting (since we are all imperfect) behaviours considered as a venial or mortal sin. On the other hand, in the case of Protestant religions, there are no conventions of individual confession and absolution. Each follower bears the burden of despicable behaviour for the rest of their life (Kurkliński 2013, 18). Available statistics, for instance referring to the USA or the UK, would indicate a higher level of crime among people who declare themselves as Catholics, rather than Protestants. For instance in the UK (England and Wales), Catholic prisoners accounted for 17.5 %, while Catholics accounted for 8 % of the whole population. Statistics were apparently more favourable for Protestants (Leyshon 2004, 8). The situation is similar in the USA where, for instance, the example of Italian or Irish gangs might be mentioned.

Proceeding to the level of secular economic regulations, it can be pointed out that societies dominated by the Catholic Church are characterized by a prevailing pursuit of regulating possibly large areas of the functioning of the economy, and, on the other hand, by frequent tendency to default on the binding provisions. The above division is noticeable also in the legal systems—Catholic countries have enacted law (based on standards adopted by the legislator), and the Protestant countries have case law (which gives a greater freedom and flexibility of action), or mixed law (Scandinavia) (Kurklinski 2015). From another point of view, the essence of such a conduct is reflected in a high level of cultural UAI (Uncertainty Avoidance Index), proposed by the Dutch researcher G. Hofstede (Hofstede and Hofstede 2005). The index defines a tendency of a given society to reduce uncertainty related to the future, which can take place within three main spheres of community life (Boski 2009, 109):

(a) development of science and technologies which, inter alia, enable better forecasting and control of natural phenomena (for instance, meteorological, seismographic forecasts, etc.);
(b) religions/ideologies related to faith concerning our future, from the earthly and transcendental perspective;
(c) rights, being precisely a catalogue of norms (dos and don'ts) of conduct, on the basis of which we can foresee future events (a driver exiting a side road will stop to let pass a car driving on the main road, behaviour resulting from the rules of the road).

In the context of this paper, the last sphere is of particular importance. There is gerat diversity in the way particular countries and societies perceive and respect the law. It has direct effects for conducting business activities (including, inter alia, banking), such as, for instance, the level of corruption acceptance (Boski 2009, 109).

G. Hofstede defined UAI openly as 'a degree of threat felt by members of a given culture in connection with certain familiar or unfamiliar situations' (Hofstede 2001, 161). If the level of this risk is high it will result, as in the case of Catholic societies, in a tendency to regulate by law almost all the main areas of society, including the economy, on the one hand, and, on the other hand, a paradoxical phenomenon of a culture of ignoring and questioning the established rules. As a result, the rules are excessive, unfriendly and obscure; they strongly limit freedoms, and create the possibility of making arbitrary decisions; they are often changed, and they force extemporization; at the same time they have many gaps, and, as a result, they cause chaos (Boski 2009, 112). Therefore the issue of regulatory risk gains in importance; however, interestingly, Protestant countries with low UAI lead the way in implementing legislative solutions that are based on that concept. From this perspective, the specification included in Table 10.1 is highly meaningful. However, it should be noted that, in terms of the discussed issues, societies with dominant Christian religions, based on the Greek rite, are similar to Catholic countries.

Table 10.1 UAI by G. Hofstede for selected countries

Country	UAI	Country	UAI	Country	UAI
Denmark	23	Holland	53	Turkey	85
Sweden	29	Switzerland	58	France	86
China	30	Finland	59	Spain	86
Great Britain	35	Germany	65	Romania	90
Ireland	35	Austria	70	Japan	92
USA	46	Czech Republic	74	Poland	93
Canada	48	Italy	75	Belgium	94
Norway	50	Brazil	76	Russia	95
Australia	51	Hungary	82	Portugal	104
Slovakia	51	Bulgaria	85	Greece	112

Source: Prepared by the authors on the basis of 'Strategy – Culture – Change', The Hofstede Center http://www.geert-hofstede.com (access on 20.03.2015)

The experiences of Greece, leader of the above ranking, show the effects of the combination of the global crisis with internal chaos and non-compliance with the rules (both national laws, for instance, regarding the payment of taxes, and EU rules, for instance, regarding the falsification of state statistics). In the final result, the country experiences social and economic collapse. Other countries which were strongly affected by the crisis, like Portugal and Spain, also ranked highly, probably not without a reason.

Cultural conditions also result in diversity in the way risk is perceived by particular societies and so, in combination with diverse approach to regulations, the attitude to regulatory risk is determined in different ways. On the basis of the descriptive theory of decision-making in the conditions of uncertainty by D. Kahneman and A. Tversky, termed as prospect theory (Kahneman and Tversky 1979, 263–291), E. Hens and C. Wang formulated four main aspects decisive for the approach to risk (Hens and Wang 2007):

(a) The way of choosing the point of reference. The point of reference relates to what is already regarded as loss and what is not. For instance, whether return on investment in shares smaller than profit on safe treasury bonds is loss or not. From the accountant's perspective it is not a loss, but for majority of stock-market investors it probably is a loss.
(b) The attitude to risk in the context of profits and losses. Usually, negative perception of loss is greater than satisfaction with a profit of the same amount.
(c) The level of risk aversion. It is a reverse attitude to risk appetite.
(d) The way of assessing and weighing likelihood of a given risk. The assessments of risk likelihood are diverse and relate to various expectations of a potential compensation for taking risks.

All the above factors are very culturally determined. So far, they have been analysed mainly when making decisions on financial markets. However, they have also a reference to regulatory risk, and the regulator's conduct (motivation) should be at the centre of attention. In the end, the adopted provisions of legal acts are a result of the work of specific people who cannot be separated from the cultural conditions in which they are living.

The findings of the research carried out by the consulting company PricewaterhouseCoopers, conducted along with the Economist Intelligence Unit, still in the first phase of the last crisis, that is in May 2008, can be interpreted as an emphasis of the meaning of the cultural aspects of law, risk, and the functioning of financial markets. When asked for reasons for the deteriorating situation in the financial markets, the respondents pointed to culture and an aggressive approach to risk-taking (73 % of the answers), whereas the so-often mentioned impact of monetary policy was indicated only by 31 % of those surveyed, and inappropriate supervision by 58 % of those surveyed (Gosling and Terry 2008, 11).

3 Regulatory Risk: Assessment of the State of Research

This section presents major findings of the research on regulatory risk relating to the financial sector, prioritization, risk measurement and communicating regulatory objectives and results.

P. Hampton was not dealing much with the issues of regulatory risk in the financial sector in his publications (Hampton 2004, 2005). He reports that the British supervisory authority, Financial Service Authority (FSA), was established in 2000; its scope of activities covered financial institutions and integrated the work of 9 existing regulators (The FSA's risk… 2006). The scale of the FSA was shown by annual average operating costs amounting to more than GBP 200 million and employment amounting to approximately 1000 workers who were involved in preparing and enforcing financial regulations. The FSA had quite unlimited possibilities of imposing penalties on financial institutions. In spite of the establishment of this super supervisor and regulator, it did not prove completely successful in the light of the crisis: its reorganization was necessary. Instead of the FSA, two offices were established: the Prudential Regulation Authority (PRA) and the Financial Conduct Authority (FCA). The task of the PRA, embedded in the central bank structure, is to protect the stability of institutions operating on the financial services market, inter alia, of banks, whereas the FCA is involved in customer protection.

According to Hampton, limited resources of the regulator should be allocated for the areas that betoken the biggest benefits directly connected with risk reduction. It results from the belief that, when preparing, implementing and enforcing regulations, attention should be focused on the most risky areas. In turn, in the areas with lower risk the imperative is to favour consulting and support to obtain more unanimous responses of regulated entities (Hampton 2004, 2). The report does not recommend any specific regulatory risk measurement methods, but specifies methodical requirements (Hampton 2004, 3, 41). It stresses that risk assessment is a base for regulatory effectiveness; it should be complex and lead to reduction in administrative burdens (Hampton 2005, 7).

Although P. Hampton notices in his reports the importance of communication with regulated entities, much more attention is paid to cooperation between specific regulators, in particular to arising communication problems in the conditions of complex character of the regulatory structures (Hampton 2004, 43).

From the conducted research it can be concluded that the principles proposed by P. Hampton were adopted in the regulatory practice, in particular in the works of the regulator responsible for environmental protection (Regulatory quality… 2008, 2; Effective inspection… 2008, 5). His report was, undoubtedly, an important breakthrough in regulatory enactment; it contributed to the development of the concept of risk-based regulation and became an important tool in the Better Regulation policy, developed and executed by the European Union.

The issue of regulatory risk management is visible in the publications by J. Black. Her numerous papers include publications on the financial sector (Black 2010, 2012; Black and Baldwin 2012). In 2004, she published a publication that presents implementations of the concept of risk-based regulation with regard to key regulators of the financial market—the UK, Canada, and Australia (Black 2004).

The main area of research interest of J. Black was to examine the way the national regulators of financial markets identify risk, assess and rank risk, and communicate the final results. As far as risk diagnosis is concerned, two approaches can be distinguished: the first one addresses inter-

Table 10.2 Identification of regulatory risk in the financial sector

Elements	British regulator	Canadian regulator	Australian regulator
Environment-specific risk	Political/legal Social/demographic Technological Economic Competition Market structure	Risk is not identified; it depends on the supervisor's decision	Risk is not identified; it depends on the supervisor's decision
Company-specific risk	*Business risk*: Financial standing Market Credit risk Strategy Features of customers/ products Further disaggregation into 15 risk types *Control risk*: Customer services Organization Internal controls Management board and employees Legal culture	*Internal risk*: Credit risk Market risk Insurance risk Operational risk Liquidity risk Legal and regulatory risk Strategic risk *Management and control*: Operational management Financial analysis Compliance analysis Internal audit Risk management Personnel management	*Internal risk*: Partner going bankrupt Balance sheet and market risk Insurance risk *Operational risk* *Liquidity risk* Legal and regulatory risk Strategy risk Risk of infection *Management and control*: Company authorities Personnel management Operational management IT systems management

Source: Prepared by the authors on the basis of Black (2004, 55)

nal risk related to companies' operations (inherent risk), and the other one addresses risk of control and management by the regulator. On the basis of the conducted interviews, J. Black obtained the following findings of risk identification (Table 10.2) and risk measurement (Table 10.3).

The regulatory risk measurement concept presented by J. Black shows, in general, the assessment of regulatory compliance by financial institutions: compliance with all the requirements binding upon banks. This approach is quite complicated but feasible on the basis of the research

Table 10.3 Measurement of regulatory risk

Elements	British regulator	Canadian regulator	Australian regulator
Regulator's objectives	Insolvency Poor management Lack of customer understanding Frauds/dishonesty Market abuse Money laundering Market quality	Insolvency	Insolvency
System of weights and ranks	Weights are not applied Qualitative assessment: High risk Medium Medium low Low	Weights are not applied Qualitative assessment: High risk Moderate risk Low risk	Score of risk in the 0–4 point scale Each risk component is assessed from the point of view of its percentage impact
Method for arriving at final probability assessment (risk ranking)	Aggregation of scores for each risk element (the role of IT) – score grouping Supervisory over-ride Assignment of group scores to overall risk ratings based on supervisory judgement	Aggregation of inherent and control risks separately based on judgement of supervisor Risk judgment of each significant activity— risk matrix (Net Risk Method) Net risk is offset against available capital to arrive at Composite Risk Rating	Aggregation of inherent and control risks separately based on judgement of supervisor Score for management and control averaged with inherent risk score to arrive at Net Risk Capital Support score averaged with Net Risk score to assess Overall Risk of Failure (ORF) Score for ORF translated into a probability index; non-linear relationship between the score and the index

Source: Prepared by the authors on the basis of Black (2004, 56, 57)

carried out. On the other hand, it is not consistent with the proposed definition of regulatory risk, since the key is the assessment of regulatory risk relating to a specific regulation, rather than generally binding (obligatory) provisions. This concept can be better used for comprehensive assessment of the regulator's work. In addition, the described method is exclusive of all significant stages of the regulatory process—for instance, formulated regulatory objectives, development of draft legislation or verification of the quality of social consultations; nor does it assess the degree of the regulator's involvement and sufficiency of the resources held for development, implementation and enforcement of the adopted requirements.

The system of communication and relationship building between the regulator and the regulated entities is in the sphere of interest of J. Black and R. Baldwin. They indicate a very poor use of the possibilities offered by 'third parties' (e.g. NGOs)—their power, motivation and activities (Baldwin and Black 2007). Presently, pressure exerted by social networking sites and the mass media may perform an important role, not only in the regulatory enforcement process but, more importantly, in the final shape of regulations.

The risk-based concept introduces several important methodological instructions affecting the approach and course of the regulatory development and implementation process. It should be emphasized that the whole legislative process is dominated by regulatory risk management. Risk level affects draft legislation and its amendments in relation to the identified types and sizes of risk. Depending on these determinations, legislative tools and rules are selected, and these, in turn, affect regulatory implementation. The identified symptoms and effects of regulations result from the attitudes and behaviours of regulated entities and the impact of other factors. The regulator has information on the course of risk adjustments or extending the risk portfolio to cover its new types. All the legislative process participants take up activities that include risk, namely they bear in mind pursuit of desired objectives set by the regulator.

Another important achievement of the concept of risk-based regulation covers two classes of regulatory risk management models (Bartle 2008, 2). The first model is described as scientific and technocratic; in this model, the term regulatory risk is an objective category that can be quantified through mathematical, scientific or technical analysis. What is more important, responding to the risk identification and measurement is based on assessing risk that is acceptable for society. The key role in the model is performed by technocrats. Moreover, many useful analyses are conducted using results obtained by the cost-benefit analysis method.

The second model of regulatory risk management is described as socio-political. The risk category is not quantified and recognized easily any longer. It combines risk with the phenomenon of uncertainty, and risk perception with objective risk. The model is characterized by huge scepticism as to the possibility of identifying and quantifying risk. Moreover, it is ascertained that made mistakes result from the excessive role attributed to the results obtained by means of quantified techniques. In the process that assumes democratization of the legislative process (participation of various groups of stakeholders) the main role is played by the elite of experts, whereas the process participants have a small room for action.

Undoubtedly, a big achievement of the concept of risk-based regulation is differentiation of regulatory risk management depending on risk level. Two polar risk levels are distinguished: low and high. The essence of a different regulatory risk management process depends on the hierarchy of resource allocation, granted by the regulator to a specific risk type (Black and Baldwin 2012). A risk can assume different features, inherent or net, static or dynamic, systemic or non-systemic. The nature of risk and activities related to the regulator's action plan are decisive for the regulatory risk management method. The adopted way of conduct also includes assessments of the nature of regulated entities, in particular the level of their involvement (determination) and ability to implement a specific regulation. At this point two options are possible: an option with regulated entities willing to accept regulations and having adequate regulatory potential (resources and sufficient information) and an option with a low level of motivation and low regulatory ability. For this issue J. Black and R. Baldwin (2012) propose the Good Regulation Intervention Design (GRID) method. Its stages are presented on Fig. 10.1.

The GRID method consists of four, logically connected key components. It is supported by an autonomous assessment of regulatory

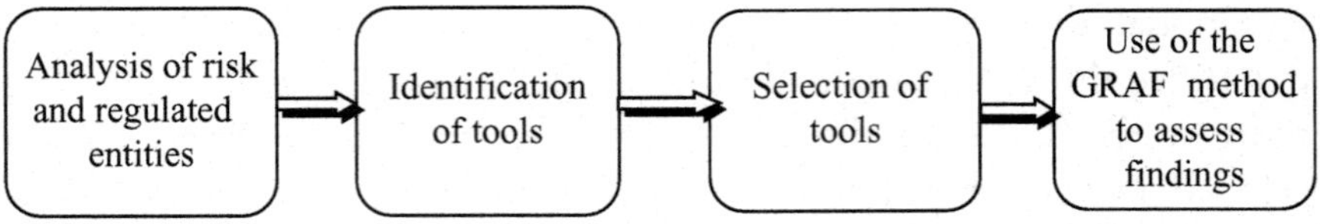

Fig. 10.1 GRID method elements (*Source*: Prepared by the authors on the basis of Description of regulatory… 2011, VII)

implementation using the Good Regulatory Assessment Framework (GRAF) method. It consists in asking the regulator questions and assessing fulfilment of different criteria related to the implementation of a given regulation. As in the case of GRID, the 1–5 point scale is used. As a result, weaknesses and strengths of the regulation being analysed are identified as simply as possible.

Table 10.4 presents the essence of the GRID method in relation to a draft environmental regulation.

The vast number of regulatory instruments that can be used in the assessment of draft regulations is surprising. Under the framework of three regulatory risk management strategies, 22 regulatory tools are used, including 4 in research, 14 in monitoring strategies and 4 tools in involvement strategies (Description of regulatory… 2011).

The third important contribution of the concept of risk-based regulation to the developing use of regulatory risk is the issue of risk measurement. J. Black and R. Baldwin do not present a clear stance on regulatory risk quantification (Baldwin and Black 2007; Black 2004). The proposals regarding its measurement come down to using qualitative measures. A clear description of this approach is included in publications on Implementation and Enforcement of Environmental Law (IMPEL) (de Gier and Kramers 2012, 22–29). Three regulatory risk calculation methods are proposed: linear, weighted average, and maximum. In the linear method risk is the average of points granted to all the adopted risk factors, i.e. total score divided by the number of the included criteria. In the weighted average method, apart from a score related to a specific criterion, its likelihood is also taken into account. In the maximum method, regulatory risk is a criterion (factor) to which the maximum score is granted. The use of the latter method is justified by experience

Table 10.4 System of regulations in the conditions of law risk for a draft regulation on municipal waste utilization

Character of regulated entities	Features (nature) of regulatory risk	Regulator's activities and their intensity
	Pure risk – may change and cumulate	
Regulated entities show low motivations and low ability of adapting to regulations	Situation when waste limit is exceeded	Research tools
	Thematic monitoring in sensitive geographical regions	*Monitoring tools*
	Monitoring with low frequency	
	Strategies of mandate (water sampling)	
	Independent monitoring and certification	
	Exchange of information and control	
	Information campaigns	
	Dialogue with concerned parties	
	Introduction of industrial solutions (design and installation)	
	Multi-agency approach	
	High risk	*Involvement and stimulation mechanisms*
		Regulatory intensity

Source: Prepared by the authors on the basis of Black and Baldwin 2012, 140

gained in the practice of conducting regulatory compliance controls. Thus risk relates to the number of conducted inspections of compliance with implementing requirements contained in the regulations.

When measuring regulatory risk, the way of choosing risk factors and the system of weighting is important: thus, on the one hand, the effects of impact of a given risk factor and, on the other hand, the meaning of a factor are both important.

The idea of risk-based regulation seems the most complex and widely used in numerous works carried out for the public sector, as compared to alternative proposals of regulatory development (for instance responsive regulation or self-regulation). The philosophy of this concept, developed so successfully in CARR, based in London, is adequate for the present operating conditions of companies, in particular of the banking sector. Its maturity is high. Nevertheless, the regulatory risk measurement method should be assessed as simple, or rather as over-simplifying the reality as compared to the present theoretical accomplishments, in particular in finance. It gives rise to a temptation to search for more advanced techniques of regulatory risk identification and measurement. All the more so, because particular requirements to be fulfilled by experts and their work styles are not analysed, whereas they perform the key role. Attention is focused on regulated entities' attitudes and behavior, and their regulatory potential is assessed, whereas the regulator's attitudes and resources are ignored. It is a certain inconsistency, since regulatory risk relates directly to the regulator.

4 Major Problems Related to Regulatory Risk Management

When considering how to implement regulatory risk in the legislative process, it is necessary to be aware of several major problems that will affect the quality of this process management and, in the final result, the quality of legislation. These problems include:

(a) The role to be attributed to regulatory risk management. Various solutions are possible: taking a stance that this category is the main driving force of drafted, implemented and enforced regulations or ignoring partially or completely regulatory risk management. The range of choices of the legislative policy from among these alternatives is vast. On the whole, it should not be aimed at adopting extreme, most desired solutions immediately, because when some element fails, it is possible to abandon highly effective tools, instruments and methods; this is confirmed to be the case by a successful examination of this in other countries.

(b) The definition of regulatory risk to be adopted in regulatory assessment. It is reasonable to start from the negative definition and then proceed to using the neutral definition of regulatory risk or focusing on its positive effects (Kasiewicz 2015). This approach results from the already accumulated knowledge, gained experience and results of widely conducted research.
(c) Usually the creation and implementation of regulation are based on the theoretical concepts developed and well-known in the discipline of Law & Economics. Their brief overview is included in the publication concerning the SME sector and in the report by K. de Weers (Kasiewicz 2014, 27–36; de Weers 2011). These are the following concepts: hierarchical, horizontal, intelligent, reactionary concept or regulatory risk-based concept.
(d) Ensuring consistency between definition, assumptions and statements of the adopted theoretical regulatory concept and the applied risk measurement method. It is a methodical problem whose solution is the most difficult, for it uses a thorough analysis of features of regulations, assessment contexts, and selective choice of methods and data to determine the risk level. The regulatory risk quantification process features few studies that transparently present all the actions related to ensuring consistency. Table 10.5 as per thecontent concept affects regulatory risk identification and measurement.
(e) Building adequate, institutional support for the legislative process. Unless the regulatory process is adequately supported by numerous institutions that, on the one hand, will help in developing draft legislation, foster its implementation, monitor its quality through the control and monitoring system, the adoption of a final version of a normative act, e.g. a bill, does not guarantee its effectiveness and efficiency.

It can be concluded from the table that each of these concepts leads to a different way of identifying regulatory risk factors and has a strong impact on the regulatory risk measurement process.

Table 10.5 Adopted concept of regulation and elements of the regulatory risk management process

Regulatory concept/ risk management elements	Role of risk	Typical risks (risk factors)
Vertical regulation	Low	Risk of lack of trust Risk of control effectiveness Risk of ignoring major risks Risk of applying inadequate system of penalties and tools Risk of ignoring effects of synergy Risk of narrowing the scope of regulatory impact on entities directly connected with a regulation
Horizontal regulation	Moderate	Risk of non-achievement of objectives Operational risk Risk of choosing stimulating tools Risk of behaviors inconsistent with expectations
Reactionary regulation	Low	Risk of stimulating penalties Risk of stimulating incentives Operational risk Risk of including too narrow regulatory scope
Intelligent regulation	Moderate	Risk of lack of sufficient control Risk of lack of trust Risk of non-achievement of objectives Risk of using too many tools
Risk-based regulation	High	Risk of non-achievement of objectives Process risk Macro-prudential risk Risk of ignoring hardly likely threats

Source: Prepared by the authors on the basis of Kasiewicz (2014, 33)

5 Directions of Searching for Regulatory Risk Measurement Methods

The regulator may determine the risk of a given regulation in the form of a qualitative or numerical opinion. In the first case, the risk may be: minute, low, moderate, high or very high. In the second case, the risk may be characterized by quantitative measures: likelihood and value of exposure (assessment of economic and financial effects in monetary units).

Regulatory risk requires not only specifying its size, but also specifying substantive premises for a given risk level.

The aspects of measuring and managing regulatory risk are considered in many publications which relate to such important issues as: risk identification process, data collection, performing risk assessments or building risk management systems (Black and Baldwin 2012). It is worth considering the method of qualitative risk management already mentioned—GRID—which concerns risk assessment on the basis of the potential and activities of the regulator and approaches and behaviors of regulated entities (Baldwin et al. 2013). After simplifying this approach, the regulator should take into consideration two components: regulatory potential and planned activities along with their intensity.

Regulatory potential depends on the regulator's involvement. It depends on such factors as the quality of the conducted consultations, the power of political pressure, the interest (participation) of the mass media in the regulatory preparation process, and the interest of society. It is also important to include the available resources of the regulator (funds, organizational resources and information).

Planned activities are related to a given regulation depending on the type and quality of the intended (anticipated) instruments and the intensity of their use. Typical actions that can be included in the regulator's repertoire include:

(a) tools of assessment and selection of alternative draft regulations
(b) method of monitoring and controlling the implementing of draft regulations
(c) mechanisms of motivation in the drafting and implementation process
(d) means of responding to unforeseen changes in draft regulation (for instance, a reporting system, regulatory risk analysis, budget reserves)

Intensity of the actions taken is decisive for their effectiveness; they can be assessed at a general and partial level. To simplify, three intensities of action can be adopted: low, moderate and high. The greater the degree and the scope of their use, the greater the chances of achieving the anticipated regulatory effect (objective).

6 Conclusions

The purpose of this chapter is to prove whether the category of regulatory risk can be a useful tool in enacting financial regulations in the banking industry. In particular, the references to three issues are presented: the system of regulatory priorities hierarchization, regulatory risk assessment, and the system of communication with stakeholders. At the present stage of legislative practice, it would be useful to acknowledge regulatory risk as a threat for achieving quite precisely defined objectives set by the regulator when enacting a given legal act. This statement results from an analysis of a large group of theoretical premises (the concept of risk-based regulation), practical premises (the programme and policy of the European Union, better regulation, studies by particular national supervisory and regulatory institutions, auditors), radical changes in external conditions, the inclusion of cultural factors and the need for a suitably rapid transition from prudential regulations to regulations that generate a higher competitiveness of the EU banking sector and economy.

The main result of this part of the paper is a statement that qualitative approach prevails for regulatory risk assessment. It is slightly delayed in relation to the present state of development, in particular in finance sciences, which can be a stimulus to take up research in this field.

With regard to regulatory priorities, the adoption of the concept of conducting the legislative process, first of all, on the basis of the category of legislative risk, allows a chance that under the broadly understood European legislation, work will focus on draft regulations generating the lowest risk in the conditions of obtaining net benefits. So far, the communication system with stakeholders has covered building relations with regulated entities. In the present conditions, the opinion of the remaining group of stakeholders is not taken into account; this applies in particular to stakeholders representing the European society (for instance, NGOs, local and industry communities, social networking sites).

The need for institutional support for efficient implementation of regulatory risk in the regulatory practice, in particular with regard to the banking sector, has been noted. These institutional aspects of the legislative process, taking account of ex-ante and ex-post approaches, concern the reporting system as well as correct recognition of political factors that accompany financial regulations.

Undoubtedly, our main conclusions should include paying attention to the adequate simplicity of conduct when developing, implementing and enforcing legislations. However, it cannot be too primitive, as is often the case when diagnosing and measuring risk (including regulatory risk); on the other hand, too complex procedures may result in their avoidance or uncontrolled simplification. For instance, the latest instruction on assessing the effects of EU regulations, *Better Regulation "Toolbox"*, contains as many as 414 pages, but it largely corresponds with the postulates formulated in this chapter, including those concerning risk recognition, measurement and management (Better Regulation "Toolbox" 2015). The most recent initiatives of the Juncker Commission towards improving the quality of regulations, incorporating the European Parliament and the Council in this process, institutional reinforcement, etc. should be praised. According to the declarations, they will be given priority status, although implementation practice raises doubts, since this priority is listed as one of the last on quite a long list.

Bibliography

5th Report of Session 2014–15, Post-crisis regulatory EU reform framework: Do the pieces fit? (2015). London: House of Lords, HL paper 103.

Baldwin, R., & Black, J. (2007). Really responsive regulation. LSE Law, Society and Economy working papers no 15. London: London School of Economics. https://www.lse.ac.uk/collections/law/wps/WPS15-2007BlackandBaldwin.pdf. Accessed 16 June 2015.

Baldwin, R., Black, J., & O'Leary, G. (2013). Regulating law risk: Innovative strategies and implementation. LSE Law, Society and Economy working papers no 9. London: London School of Economics. http://www.lse.ac.uk/collections/law/wps/WPS2013-09_Baldwin.pdf. Accessed 16 June 2015.

Bartle, I. (2008). Risk based regulation and better regulation in the UK: Towards what models of risk regulation, the 2nd Biennial Conference of the ECPR Standing Group on Regulatory Governance, Utrecht University, The Netherlands.

Better Regulation "Toolbox". (2015). European Commission. http://ec.europa.eu/smart-regulation/guidelines/docs/br_toolbox_en.pdf. Accessed 12 June 2015.

Better Regulation for Better Results – An EU Agenda. (2015). Strasbourg: European Commission. http://ec.europa.eu/smart-regulation/better_regulation/documents/com_2015_215_en.pdf. Accessed 30 May 2015.

Black, J. (2004). *The development of risk based regulation in financial services: Canada, the UK and Australia*. London: A Research Report, ESRC Centre for the Analysis of Risk and Regulation London School of Economics and Political Science.

Black, J. (2010a). *Risk-based regulation. Presentation to the Future of Legal Regulation Conference*. London: Birkbeck College.

Black, J. (2010b). Risk and regulatory policy. Improving the governance of risk. OECD Reviews of Regulatory Reform. In *Risk-based regulation: Choices, practices and lessons being learnt*. Paris: OECD.

Black, J. (2012). Paradoxes and failures: 'New governance' techniques and the financial crisis. *Modern Law Review, 75*(6), 1037–1063.

Black, J., & Baldwin, R. (2012). When risk-based regulation aims low: Approaches and challenges. *Regulation and Governance, 6*(1), 2–22.

Boski, P. (2009). *Kulturowe ramy zachowań społecznych. Podręcznik psychologii międzykulturowej [Cultural dimentions of social behaviour. Manual for crosscultural psychology]*. Warsaw: PWN.

de Gier, M., & Kramers, R. (2012). *Doing right things for waste shipment inspections (DTRT – TFS)*. IMPEL. http://www.impel.eu/projects/doing-the-right-things-for-waste-shipment-inspections/. Accessed on 28 May 2015.

de Weers, K. (2011). *Towards a European regulatory toolkit on the enforcement of Union Law by national regulatory authorities*. Utrecht: Utrecht University.

Description of regulatory approaches to assessing the effectiveness, of regulatory activities at low risk sites and proposed good practice framework: Phase 1 report. (2011). SNIFFER April, p. VII. www.lse.ac.uk/.../Sniffer%20ER%2013%20final%20r. Accessed on 09 June 2015.

Doing business 2015. Going beyond efficiency, Regional Profile 2015. (2014). Washington, The World Bank. http://www.doingbusiness.org/~/media/GIAWB/Doing%20Business/Documents/Annual-Reports/English/DB15-Full-Report.pdf. Accessed on 12 June 2015.

Eccles, T., & Pointing, J. (2013). Smart regulation, shifting architectures and changes in government. *International Journal of Law in the Built Environment, 5*(1), 71–88.

Effective inspection and enforcement: implementing Hampton vision in the Environment Agency. (2008). London: National Audit Office.

Gosling, T., & Terry, J. (2008). Reward: A new paradigm? PWC, p. 11. http://www.pwc.lu/en_LU/lu/hr/docs/pwc-publ-reward-a-new-paradigm.pdf. Accessed on 15 June 2015.

Hampton, P. (2004). *Reducing administrative burdens: Effective inspection and enforcement*. Norwich: H.M Treasury.

Hampton, P. (2005). *Reducing administrative burdens: Effective inspection and enforcement*. Norwich: H.M Treasury.

Hens, T. & Wang, M. (2007, April 24). *Does finance have a cultural dimension*. National Centre of Competence in Research Financial Valuation and Risk Management, Working Paper No. 377.

Hofstede, G. (2001). *Cultural consequences. Comparing values, behaviors, institutions and organizations cross nations*. Thousand Oaks: Sage.

Hofstede, G., & Hofstede, G. J. (2005). *Cultures and organizations: Software of the mind* (2 ed.). New York: McGraw-Hill.

Houston, J., Lin, C., Lin, P., & Mae, Y. (2010). Creditor rights, information sharing, and bank risk taking. *Journal of Financial Economics, 96*(3), 485–512.

Hutter B. (2005). *The attractions of risk-based regulation: Accounting for the emergence of risk ideas in regulation*. Discussion paper no. 33. London: London School of Economics and Political Science. http://www.lse.ac.uk/accounting/CARR/pdf/DPs/Disspaper33.pdf. Accessed on 15 June 2015.

Is Europe Overbanked? Reports of the Advisory Scientific Committee. (2014). No. 4, European Systemic Risk Board. https://www.esrb.europa.eu/pub/pdf/asc/Reports_ASC_4_1406.pdf. Accessed on 16 June 2015.

Kahneman, D., & Tversky, A. (1979). Prospect theory: An analysis of decision under risk, econometrica. *The Econometric Society, 47*(2), 263–291.

Kasiewicz, S. (2010). 'Ryzyko regulacyjne – narzędzie stanowienia lepszego prawa' [Regulatory risk – A tool for better regulation]. *Nowe Życie Gospodarcze, 2*, 8–9.

Kasiewicz, S. (2014). Koncepcje regulacji sektora MŚP a pomiar ryzyka regulacyjnego [Regulatory concept for SME versus regulatory risk measurement. In R. Sobiecki (Ed.), *Gospodarka w sieciach relacji [Economy in relation network]*. Lublin: KUL.

Kasiewicz S. (2015). Ryzyko regulacyjne projektu "Unia Bankowa". Polska perspektywa [Regulatory risk of Banking Union Project. Polish perspective], the paper not published.

Kasiewicz, S., & Rogowski, W. (2014). Ryzyko we współczesnym biznesie [Risk in the contemporary business]. In *Nowoczesne zarządzanie biznesem [Modern business management]*. BIK: Warsaw.

Kurkliński, L. (2013). Kulturowe i behawioralne uwarunkowania regulacji sektora MSP [Cultural and behavioral determinants of SME regulations]. *Ekonomika i Organizacja Przedsiębiorstwa, 7*(762), 17–28.

Kurkliński, L. (2015). Rola regulacji ostrożnościowych sektora bankowego w świetle kulturowego postrzegania prawa w Polsce [The role of prudential regulation of the banking sector in the context of the cultural perception of law in Poland]. Nałęczów, UMCS conference proceedings.

Leyshon, G. (2004). *Catholic statistics. Priests and population in England and Wales, 1841–2001*. Wonersh: St John's Seminary.

Regulatory quality: How regulators are implementing the Hampton Vision. (2008). London: National Audit Office, p. 2.

Strategy – Culture – Change. The Hofstede Center. http://www.geert-hofstede.com/countries.html. Accessed 20 Mar 2015.

Stulz, R., & Williamson, R. (2003). Culture, openness, and finance. *Journal of Financial Economics, 70*, 313–349.

The FSA's risk assessment framework. (2006). Financial Services Authority.

Weber, M. (1905). *The Protestant ethic and the spirit of capitalism*. Chicago: London, Fitzroy Dearborn Publishers.

11

The Financial Distress of Public Sector Entities, Causes and Risk Factors. Empirical Evidence from Europe in the Post-crisis Period

Magdalena Ziolo, Małgorzata Porada-Rochon, and Elżbieta Szaruga

1 Introduction

The phenomenon of financial distress is widely discussed in the literature, especially in the context of corporate finance. Based on a literature review, the study of financially distressed public sector entities is still rare compared to research carried out on financially distressed companies. In comparison to the private sector, it is more meaningful to consider the risk of financial distress in the public sector in terms of its aftermath and consequences. Public sector entities, especially self-governments, are responsible for providing crucial and basic public services such as public safety, water, sewage, health care, education, etc., which are necessary for the local community (Trussel and Patrick 2012, 620). The risk of financial distress in the public sector is worth researching and diagnosing because

M. Ziolo (✉) • M. Porada-Rochon • E. Szaruga
University of Szczecin, Szczecin, Poland

K. Raczkowski (ed.), *Risk Management in Public Administration*,
DOI 10.1007/978-3-319-30877-7_11

of the public sector's role in the economy and the quality of public services it provides to local communities. Financially distressed public entities are unable to adequately fulfil their tasks, which may result in crimes, rebellions, increased social disparity, and other kinds of civil unrest because the main functions of public finance such as macro-economic stabilization, income redistribution, and efficient allocation of resources cannot be performed properly.

The risk of financial distress, along with its factors and causes, is a common topic of research in the aftermath of a financial crisis or after an economic slowdown. There is usually a need for an in-depth analysis of a financial crisis and its outcomes, and such work takes up the challenge of identifying the fundamentals of the crisis and explaining the reasons for their existence. Based on such analysis, researchers try to create financial models and early warning systems that may be useful in predicting future financial distress, thereby mitigating it in advance and providing a means of immediate reaction when it does occur. The financial crisis of 2008 revealed the weaknesses of systemic solutions and the present way of financing public entities, especially those at local government level, which are strongly affected by the conjunctural cycle (tax-based financing). The limits of public debt, public debt measurements, and procedures to stabilize public finance (e.g. the excessive deficit procedure) have not been good enough to reduce the risk of financial distress in EU countries.

Public sector entities both at the local and central government level have responded differently to the risk of financial distress and its consequences. One strategy has been to reduce operating costs and capital spending while the other has been to make financial cuts or outsource services (Trussel and Patrick 2012, 620). This study investigates the factors and causes of financial distress risk in order to diagnose the entities that are much more prone to financial distress. For the purposes of research and this article, financially distressed entities are defined according to two criteria: they are places where (1) the entity has maintained a deficit over a three-year period, and (2) the entity has declared a five per cent cumulative deficit in relation to revenue over the same period (three years).

The above-mentioned criteria coincide with some of the criteria defined by the Financially Distressed Municipalities Program (1997, 1) of the state of Pennsylvania, USA, as seen below:

(a) the municipality has maintained a deficit over a three-year period, with a deficit of at least 1 % in each of the previous fiscal years,
(b) the municipality's expenditures have exceeded revenues for a period of at least three years,
(c) the municipality has defaulted in payment of principal or interest on a bond or note, or in payment of rentals due to an authority,
(d) the municipality has missed a payroll for thirty days,
(e) the municipality has failed to make required payments to judgment creditors for thirty days beyond the date of the recording of the judgment,
(f) the municipality, for a period of at least thirty days beyond the due date, has failed to forward taxes withheld on the income of employees, or has failed to transfer employer or employee contributions for Social Security,
(g) the municipality has accumulated and has operated for each of two successive years a deficit equal to at least 5 % of its revenues,
(h) the municipality has failed to make the budgeted payment of its minimum municipal obligation,
(i) a municipality has sought to negotiate resolution or adjustment of a claim in excess of 30 % against a fund or budget, and has failed to reach an agreement with creditors,
(j) a municipality has filed a Municipal Debt Readjustment Plan; or
(k) the municipality has experienced a decrease in a quantified level of municipal service from the preceding fiscal year, which has resulted from the municipality reaching its legal limit in levying real estate taxes for general purposes.

Using the definition of a financially distressed entity provided by the Pennsylvanian program, public sector entities in the study have been classified as either financially distressed or non-financially distressed. Several financial risk factors have been examined while considering different financial variables, such as revenue concentration, budget balance, debt usage, and intergovernmental transfers at different levels of government. Very few studies so far have used the GDA to predict financial distress; instead, a prognosis is usually based on absolute and relative models. Therefore, the use of the GDA is this article's contribution to the literature. The second contribution is the research scope, which is wider than average as it encompasses local and central government levels across EU countries. The period the research covers is also of significant value, because it provides a post-crisis perspective.

The study is organized into the following sections: Section 1 introduction, Section 2 theoretical background and consists of two coherent parts entitled: part 1 Financial distress versus fiscal distress and its determinants and part 2 Risk factors, causes and financial distress risk management. Section 3 empirical evidence that presents methodology and variables, and section 4 conclusion and future work. Section 1 describe the research problem and provide general picture of the financial distress phenomenon. Section 2 presents a literature review, the main thesis, and the goals of the study. Conventional wisdom is discussed and the major factors that might increase financial distress risk are separately identified. Section 3 provides an analysis of fiscal distress at the general government sector and subnational government level. In the last part of this section, a model that can predict the likelihood of financial distress is presented. The model makes it possible to forecast how financial distress factors may impact a country's financial distress risk. At last, Section 4 contains concluding remarks and provide information about future work.

2 Financial Distress Versus Fiscal Distress and Its Determinants

The post-crisis period is a perfect time to assess specific characteristics of financial distress, first, because of the time (two, three, or four years after a crisis depending on the country), and second, because of the scale of financial distresses occurring all over the world and their consequences. Although the events themselves are regrettable, they provide good empirical material for researchers.

It should be noted that financial distress is identified both on the macro- and micro-level; however, it is more difficult to recognize such an event on the macro-level. Financial distress from macro-perspectives is connected with the conjunctural cycle. It can therefore be assumed that the occurrence of financial distress is an integral part of the business cycle and that financial disorder leads to crisis. Given the history of crises (including financial) and their morphology, financial distresses should be attributed to the cyclical nature of the economy, in varying intensity and duration. Financial distress at the macro-level has a major impact on the incidence of financial distress at the micro-level. In a sense, events on the macro-level determine their own creation through the transmission and impact of macro-economic factors as well as other factors that occur as a consequence of the financial distress that is happening at the macro-level.

The literature does not present much research regarding the evaluation of the disorder on a macro-scale and/or concerning disturbances at the micro-level. However, recent economic literature on finance has paid significant attention to the changes and effects of the macro-economic environment on business failure and company insolvency. Moreover, researchers such as Gilchrist et al. (2009); Duca (1999); and King et al. (2007) have explored the relationship between conditions in the bond market and the real economy. In contrast, the relationship between conditions in the banking sector and real economic activity has received less attention. Concerning the banking sector, the conditions of the banks themselves have garnered special interest but, overall, it seems likely that the relationship remains less researched because it is somewhat more complex than the relationship between the bond market and economic activity.

Carlson et al. (2008) take into consideration the connection between the Financial Health Index and the real economy. Their results indicate that deteriorations in the Financial Health Index are associated with tighter lending standards and higher interest rates on bank loans, and that they precede declines in employment rates and industrial production. The researchers argue that such outcomes highlight how financial institutions act as an independent source of macro-economic variability, one that is distinct from traditionally accelerating mechanisms.

However, it is unquestionably noted that their existence at the macro-level intensifies their impact on the micro-level, which in combination with the contagion effect, causes a spiral of financial difficulties to occur at the micro-level. There are various channels through which the effects of financial distress can be transmitted among countries, economies, institutions, and private companies, thus increasing their overall intensity and range.

Post and Moon (1988), Wadhwani (1986), and Platt and Platt (1994) have all done some work from varying perspectives on the correlation between different macro-economic factors that influence financial distress on the micro-level. Therefore, the diagnosis of financial distress has turned out to be crucial in the context of identifying its sources, causes, and consequences, which may be multidimensional in nature and have also been observed in financial crises and recessions. Many studies in the field of finance support the value of being able to predict the occurrence of a financial distress.

Financial distress is also considered in regard to both public- and private-sectors entities. Without any doubt, there is some differentiation between the causes, determinants, scale, and risk factors associated with the public and private sectors, but the general approach is the same. Any financial distress detected in a private enterprise may have effects on and consequences for a public entity and vice versa.

There are many existent definitions for financial distress and many words are used interchangeably when it is being referenced. This situation is primarily the result of the different perspectives adopted by various researchers who have examined financial turmoil, along with a given study's objectives and methodology. In the context of a private company, financial distress is used as a synonym for a disruption, crisis, or threat that is imprecise and often inappropriate. This understanding is different from the usage of 'financial distress' in a public entity, where the term is used interchangeably with 'fiscal distress' or a 'fiscal emergency situation' because it does not have other divergent meanings. Table 11.1 presents examples of financial distress according to public and private entities.

Bradbury (1982) contributed to the field by dividing fiscal distress into budgetary fiscal distress and citizen fiscal distress: budgetary fiscal distress describes a situation where municipalities face difficulties with balancing their budgets, while a citizen fiscal distress happens when

Table 11.1 Definition of financial distress in public and private entities

Public entities	Private entities
Financial distress occurs when the entity, municipality or province, is no longer able to perform its essential functions and deliver due services, or when it is no longer able to meet debt with third parties through the ordinary means of restoring fiscal balance or the debt instrument with a balance sheet. (D. Lgs. 267, art. 244)	Financial distress is a state in which a fall in a corporation's earning power will at some point create a non-trivial probability that it will not be able to pay the interest and principal on its debt. Its bonds sell at yields materially above the interest rates at which financial institutions are willing to extend credit to otherwise similar corporations. (Gordon 1971)
Fiscal distress reflects short-term considerations, such as a local government's ability to meets its payroll and generally make payments in a timely manner, and long-term considerations, encompassing trends in a local government's tax base relative to its expenditures and commitments Kloha et al. (2005)	Financial distress is a sobering economic reality reflecting the uniqueness of the American way of corporate death. (Altman 1983)
Financial stress are episodes where economic agents are subjected to extreme uncertainty and varying expectations of loss in financial markets. (Illing and Liu 2006)	Financial distress is when the liquidation value of a firm's assets is less than the face value of the firm's liabilities. (Asquith et al. 1994)
Fiscal distress describes a municipality that experiences a significant and persistent imbalance between revenues and expenditures. (Trussel and Patrick 2012)	Financial distress means having operational, managerial, and financial difficulties. (Adeyemi 2011)
	Financial distress is a stage in the complex and dynamic process of deterioration, as a result of the impact of a significant external determinant, and causes significant deterioration of the financial condition so that enterprises require an informed choice in the configuration of a turnaround model. (Porada-Rochoń 2013)

Source: Own elaboration based on John M. Trussel and Patricia A. Patrick. (2012). 'A Survival Analysis of U.S. Municipalities in Fiscal Distress', *International Journal of Public Administration, 35(9)*, 620–633; U.S. General Accounting Office. (1990). *Distressed Communities: Public Services Declined in California as Budget Pressures Mounted*. Washington, DC: Author. (HRD-90-95); and Adeyemi, B. (2011). 'Bank Failure in Nigeria: A Consequence of Capital Inadequacy, Lack of Transparency and Non-Performing Loans', *Banks and Bank System, 6(1)*, 99–109 M. Porada-Rochoń, Modele decyzji finansowych MŚP w wybranych krajach Europy środkowowschodniej w warunkach zaburzeń finansowych. Wydawnictwo PTE. Szczecin 2013, Altman, E. I. (1983). 'Exploring the Road to Bankruptcy', Journal of Business Strategy 4(2): 6. Asquith et al. (1994). 'Anatomy of Financial Distress: An examination of junk-bond issuers', Quarterly Journal of Economics 109(3): 34, M.J. Gordon, Towards the Theory of financial distress. *Journal of Finance*, 1971, vol. 26, issue 2, pages 347–56.

citizens are levied high taxes and fees for municipal services or when the quality of the municipal services they are paying for is low. Capalbo et al. (2010) pointed out that the meaning of financial distress in terms of local government may be related to structurally distressed local authorities or financially destabilized local governments, even though overall a local government's understanding of a financial distress is the same.

Due to the fact that the aim of this paper is to study financial distress in public entities, the next section addresses them only. Knowing the determinants of financial distress enables their early identification and the application of tools to mitigate the risks and costs associated with their occurrence. Above all, however, such information makes it possible to prevent financial distress from happening in the first place. In the literature, there currently exists a wide distribution of determinants for financial distress. One existing classification distinguishes between macro- and micro-determinants, and between external and internal determinants.

Rossi et al. (2012) propose a 'socioeconomic-decline approach' and a 'local-management approach' for the analysis of financial distress. The 'socioeconomic-decline approach' perceives external factors to be the dominant players in financial distress while the local-management approach emphasizes the roles of management and politics. Capalbo et al. (2010) point out that external factors can be acknowledged in the changes seen in national legislative framework concerning taxation tools and expenses that have originated from non-recurrent events (such as defeats in judicial controversies). The researchers conclude that factors of financial distress can be categorized more as 'bad habits' than as a 'pathological status'.

From a macro-economic perspective, the following can be said to distinguish the determinants that relate to the theory of business cycles (McNamara et al. 2011):

(a) Supply or cost-push theories focus on changes in business costs, net profits, and the cost of labour and other factors of production.

(b) Monetary theories focus on the cost and availability of credit. Variables identified by these theories include a range of interest rates and money supply indicators.
(c) Savings and investment theories have their origin in nineteenth-century general equilibrium models. As the name suggests, these theories promote variables such as gross savings, change in business investment, industrial production, and so on.

According to the Advisory Commission on Intergovernmental Relations (ACIR), the causes and factors that influence financial distress are:

(a) changes in economic conditions, such as population growth, the rate of unemployment, or the rate of new business development;
(b) changes in socio-economic conditions such as per capita income, poverty, or education;
(c) changes in physical conditions such as the state of infrastructure assets; and
(d) changes in financial factors such as dependence on intergovernmental revenue, debt financing, and tax revenues (Advisory Commission on Intergovernmental Relations, 1985, after Trussel and Patrick 2012).

In this regard, fiscal distress is the result of cyclical and structural forces.

According to Lavigne (2006), the framework used to organize factors that influence fiscal distress should include the following:

(a) Political factors

  - government stability
  - majority government
  - executive elections
  - plurality

(b) Socioeconomic factors

  - the Gini coefficient
  - subsidies and transfers
  - the population over the age of sixty-five
  - ethnolinguistic fractionalization

(c) Institutional factors

- democratic accountability;
- rule of law

Park and Mercado (2013) studied the factors that determine the domestic condition. Their work indicates that there may be a common regional factor influencing domestic financial stress. Additionally, the shock emerging from one country may affect other countries in the same region more than those in other regions due to geographically similar fundamentals, integrated regional trade, the financial and investment network, and/or similar responses from international investors.

Trussel and Patrick (2013) proved that fiscally distressed districts have more diverse revenue sources, lower capital expenditures, higher debt usage, and are larger in size than non-distressed districts. In a more recent study, Borge and Hopland (2015) investigated three indicators of fiscal distress. Rainy day funds were found to be very significant and associated with the expected positive sign, i.e. local governments with small funds cut down on maintenance relative to other expenditures. Two other indicators of fiscal distress, lagged surplus and the ROBEK (Register for State Review and Approval of Financial Obligation) dummy, were also found to relate to their expected signs; however, they were not significant at conventional levels. As indicators of financial distress, the effects of local government revenue and the effective number of parties were largely observed to remain stable.

From a macro-economic perspective, Balakrishnan et al. (2011) discovered that the domestic Financial Stress Index in an emerging economy is influenced by the following factors: financial stress in advanced economies, global GDP growth, and interest rates–as well as country-specific factors such as degree of financial and trade linkages and other domestic macro-economic vulnerabilities.

Financial distress prediction models are widely discussed in the literature but little attention is paid to the associated costs. One of the most frequently cited results is the acknowledgment that financial distress costs are almost the same as the costs of bankruptcy. The financial literature has traditionally differentiated two types of financial distress costs: direct and indirect. The problematic issue is the selection of appropriate tools for measuring these costs, especially in the case of indirect costs. Pindado and Rodriquez (2005) have pointed out that financial distress costs are determined by both the probability of a financial distress occurring and the ex-post financial distress costs experienced. They found that financial distress costs are positively related to the probability of a financial distress happening, and that the costs are negatively related to the leveraging and holding of liquid assets.

The existent literature places great emphasis on minimizing the costs of financial distress and on the process of their elimination. Local governments must embrace the concept of prioritizing expenditures, maintaining fiscal transparency, and developing multi-year financial forecasts. Managers, policy makers, and department heads alike must undertake new and creative strategies in order to provide services in times when there is a perceived scarcity of resources (Powell 2013). One of the most important factor in budget proces is long-term forecasting. In particular, managers should see the consequences of today's decisions in the future (Bahl and Schroeder 1984).

Another important consideration was pointed out by Trussel and Patrick (2012), who assert that stakeholders play a primary role in avoiding financial distress. They argue that stakeholders can monitor the fiscal health of municipalities in order to prevent and mitigate fiscal distress but that they need reliable and efficient ways to do so. The problem in this regard arises from the lack of appropriate quantitative methods for predicting the likelihood of a fiscal distress occurring, which leads to late detection or no pre-emptive detection at all.

3 Risk Factors, Causes and Financial Distress Risk Management

Taking into account the specific characteristics of public entities and the nature of public finance, the risk of financial distress in the public sector is usually determined by weighing a variety of factors that are classified into four groups: economic, socio-economic, physical, and financial.

According to Trussel and Patrick (2012, 622), fiscal distress can be the result of varying conditions, such as:

(a) population growth, the unemployment rate, or the new business development rate (economic factors);
(b) per capita income, poverty, or education (socio-economic factors);
(c) the state of infrastructure assets (physical factors); or
(d) dependence on intergovernmental revenue, debt financing, or tax revenue (financial factors).

Today, determinants of new and old social risks play a crucial role as factors increasing the threat of fiscal distress in the public sector. Two social risks are particularly important: an aging society and decreasing or negative fertility rates (Cerami 2008, 1090). In such a scenario, as the number of people who use social public benefits systematically rises, there will be an increase in public expenditure that is met with a decrease in the tax base, thus strongly influencing the budget balance in a negative manner. Trussel and Patrick (2009, 586) have created a list of risk factors that indicate when fiscal distress is likely to occur in the public sector. They started their research in 1973 and have analysed not only risk factors but also measures for calculating the risk as well. Their analysis provided the fundamental base for this study's classification of financial distress risk factors (Table 11.2).

Based on the literature review, it is worth mentioning the most commonly attributed causes of fiscal distress at the local level: transitory economic shocks in the short term and structural budget imbalances in the long term (Fiscal Stress … 2010, 2). Economic shocks are responsible for a weak economic condition and significantly impact supply and demand at the local, regional, and state levels. Decreasing demand for goods and services will influence the level of taxes paid to the regional and central budgets. Due to the tax revenue structure, the central budget is much more prone to economic shocks than local ones as local budgets usually consist of property taxes, which are not sensitive to changing economic conditions (recessions and slowdowns). Economic shocks have an especially large influence on the level of indirect taxes being levied. For example, value-added tax is closely related to current economic condi-

Table 11.2 Risk factors of financial distress based on literature review

Risk factor	Study/year	Measure
One-year operations	ACIR (1973)	Revenues – expenditures
Continuous operations	ACIR (1973); Congressional Budget Office (1978)	Revenues – expenditures over time
Working capital	ACIR (1973)	Current assets – current liabilities
Short-term operating loan balance	ACIR (1973)	Current debt
Property tax delinquency	ACIR (1973)	Property taxes delinquent/total Property taxes
Property valuation	ACIR (1973); Congressional Budget Office (1978)	Assessed value of real property
Coverage of expenditures	Congressional Budget Office (1978)	Cash + Securities/total expenditures
Debt burden	Congressional Budget Office (1978)	Total debt/total revenues
Population	Congressional Budget Office (1978)	Population
Per capita income	Congressional Budget Office (1978)	Net income/population
Own source revenue	Congressional Budget Office (1978); Brown (1993)	Total revenue – revenue from federal and state government (Total revenue – revenue from federal and state government) Total revenues
Per capita long-term debt	Congressional Budget Office (1978); Brown (1993); Raman (1982)	Long-term debt/population
Per capita revenue	Brown (1993)	Revenue/population
Other source revenue	Brown (1993)	Revenue from federal and state government/total revenue
Operating expenditure ratio	Brown (1993)	Operating expenditures/total expenditures
Revenues to expenditures	Brown (1993)	Total revenues/total expenditures
Unreserved general fund ratio	Brown (1993)	Unreserved general fund balance/ general fund revenues
Liability coverage	Brown (1993)	(Cash + securities)/total liabilities

(*continued*)

Table 11.2 (continued)

Risk factor	Study/year	Measure
Debt to revenue ratio	Brown (1993)	Total liabilities/total revenues
Debt service to revenues	Brown (1993)	Debt service/total revenues
ST Debt to revenue	Raman (1982)	ST debt/total revenues
Working capital change to debt	Raman (1982)	Change in working capital/total debt
Cash change to debt	Raman (1982)	Change in cash/debt
Population growth	Kloha et al. (2005)	Year to year percentage change in population
Real taxable value growth	Kloha et al. (2005)	Year to year percentage change in assessed value of real property
General expenditures to taxable value	Kloha et al. (2005)	General expenditures/assessed value
Operating margin	Kloha et al. (2005)	(Revenues – expenditures)/ revenues
General fund balance to revenues	Kloha et al. (2005)	General fund balance/total revenues
Fund balance	Kloha et al. (2005)	Assets – liabilities
LT debt to taxable value	Kloha et al. (2005)	LT debt/taxable value
Revenue	Groves et al. (1981); Grove and Valente (1994)	Per capita revenues, restricted revenues, intergovernmental revenues, property tax revenues, Uncollected property tax revenues
Expenditure	Groves et al. (1981); Grove and Valente (1994)	Per capita expenditures, employees per capita, fixed costs, and fringe benefits
Operating position	Groves et al.(1981); Grove and Valente (1994)	Operating deficits, enterprise losses, fund balances, and liquidity
Debt	Groves et al. (1981); Grove and Valente (1994)	Current liabilities, long-term debt, debt service
Unfunded liabilities	Groves et al. (1981); Grove and Valente (1994)	Unfunded pension liability, pension assets, and accumulated employee leave

Table 11.2 (continued)

Risk factor	Study/year	Measure
Capital plant	Groves et al. (1981); Grove and Valente (1994)	Capital expenditures
Community needs and resources	Groves et al. (1981); Grove and Valente (1994)	Population change, median age, personal income per capita, poverty households, property value, residential development, vacancy rates, employment base, business activity

Source: Own elaboration based on: J. M. Trussel, P. A. Patrick, (2009), 'A Predictive Model of Fiscal Distress in Local Governments', Journal of Public Budgeting, Accounting & Financial Management, 21 (4), pp. 578–616

tions (Fiscal Stress … 2010, 2). The second important cause of fiscal distress is a structural budget imbalance, usually arising from political issues. It is often very difficult to arrange a budget when two drastically different political bodies are responsible for it. In such a scenario, a deficit may occur as the result of political manoeuverings (Fiscal Stress… 2010, 2). Other factors that increase the likelihood of a structural budget imbalance include demographic shifts or a lack of adequate budgetary or financial controls.

There exist a variety of risk factors and indicators that facilitate the measurement of financial distress risk; however, the key concern is to select a group of indicators that will be suitable for short- and long-term analysis and that have the most significant value for the government tier and country in question. Fiscal federalism and the government model determine the risk of a financial distress occurring as they vary across the EU countries. Taking into consideration short- and long-term approaches to fiscal distress measurement, the variables are separated into two categories (Table 11.3):

For European public sector entities, two financial distress risk factors are especially important and common: revenue concentration and debt usage. There is a positive association between revenue concentration and fiscal distress, and a positive association between debt usage and fiscal distress (Trussel and Patrick 2009, 593). Although there are many

Table 11.3 Extended approach to indicators used in fiscal distress analysis

Indicator	Perspective
Persistent negative cash balance	ST
Cash coverage ratio	ST
Bad debts as percentage of billable revenue	ST
Borrowing as percentage of total assets	ST
Asset renewal and repair and maintenance as a percentage of total municipality expenditure	ST
Opening balance plus receipts to payment ratio	LT
Medium-term expenditure review framework	LT
Operating expenses to own revenue ratio	LT
Own revenue to total population ratio	LT
Budget deficit/surplus	LT
Operating deficit ratio	LT
Per capita income	LT
Per capita expenditure	LT

ST short-term indicator, *LT* long-term indicator
Source: Measuring Fiscal Distress in South African Local Government (2014) 'Chap 10, Submission for the 2014/15 Division of Revenue'118. PART 3, www.fcc.co.za access data 28.06.2015, M. Ziolo (2014) 'Predicting Municipalities' Fiscal Distress. The Empirical Analysis of West Pomeranian Municipalities after the Crisis 2008, SGEM Conference on Political Sciences, Law, Finance, Economics & Tourism, Conference Proceedings, Volume II, International Multidisciplinary Scientific Conferences on Social Sciences & Arts, 3–9 September 2014, Bulgaria, pp. 567–575

ways to finance public tasks, only a few of them take into account the share, for example, of taxes, in central and local budgets. The structure of revenues is important as it reflects a local administration's financial authority and the revenue policy determined by the fiscal federalism approach.

At the local level, dependency on governmental transfers is a crucial fiscal distress risk factor. This dependence on the central budget is expressed by the share of taxes to revenues and the share of intra-governmental transfers to revenues. Local authorities that are highly dependent on governmental transfers and cannot rely on alternative sources are more likely to be vulnerable to financial problems. The same issue arises with debt financing. Local authorities strongly dependent on issuing debt are more prone to financial distress risk as they have to meet debt service requirements at all times, even with a deteriorating financial stance

(Trussel and Patrick 2009, 593). Generally, the size of the government in question matters when considering financial distress risk factors. One very common indicator currently in use that reflects this consideration is administrative expenditure.

Identifying the risk factors and their causes occurs at an early stage in the process of financial distress risk management. They are the fundamental considerations for decision making in the scope of dealing with financial distress and preventing it. A wide variety of instruments can be used in financial distress risk management during either the prevention phase or the restriction stage. The toolkit of preventative instruments is usually focused on prediction and financial planning. In this category, prediction models and plans matter.

Generally, short- and long-term instruments support financial distress risk management. In the short term, the instruments are dedicated to liquidity management. In the long term, multi-year financial plans are the core instrument. These plans are especially important as they support debt management, including debt limits, which are the crucial factor that need to be addressed from a short- and long-term perspective. The most important instruments for detecting financial distress risk in this category are early warning systems, stress tests, and financial control measures.

Once the risk of financial distress has been identified, possible ways of responding at the local level include reduced spending, increased taxes and fees, shifting the timing of payments, and borrowing money. The local authority may also be strengthened by the central government in terms of financial distress risk management if the central government increases state aid, allows additional tax collection, provides oversight, or assumes control (Fiscal Stress… 2010, 6–8).

Financial distress risk management is a new scope of interest and activity in the public sector. In many countries, public sector entities do not manage risk in a complex manner and are only focused on budget execution and financial control. Experiences from the financial crisis of 2008 brought to light the weaknesses of existent financial solutions and instruments. Financial control in the public sector turned into comprehensive risk management with special emphasis on financial risk management, which is supported by a performance approach to public task execution.

The financial distress phenomenon as an early stage on the road to insolvency is of special interest to this work. Because it is flexible and suitable to identifying financial distress risk characteristics, we used the Mullarkey Report to provide the following recommendations in the field of financial distress risk management (Risk Management… 2004, 5):

(a) The financial distress risk assessment and management process should be integrated into existing management systems and should be kept as simple and straightforward as possible.
(b) In introducing a financial distress risk management strategy, full use should be made of existing systems, processes, procedures, and reporting structures.
(c) Each department should be involved and have clearly defined risk management structures and responsibilities, taking into consideration its role in mitigating financial distress risk threat.
(d) The process of risk identification should be ongoing and repeated by departments at least once a year.
(e) Departments should evaluate and assess any identified financial distress risks factors according to the increasing threat of occurrence at least once a year.
(f) When risks factors have been identified and assessed, departments should determine an appropriate method for addressing them.
(g) A department's risk management system should provide for monitoring and reporting at various levels of management.

Measuring and predicting the risk of a financial distress occurring is a difficult and sophisticated research task. Based on the literature and data collected from experience, there are at least three factors responsible for the challenges that are faced. According to Trussel and Patrick (2009, 593), the main constraints in the process of financial distress prediction are as follows:

(a) the problem of defining the phenomenon
(b) the issue of identifying the risk factors responsible for fiscal distress
(c) the use of the risk factors as predictors of fiscal distress

With regard to the first problem, it is difficult to find one coherent definition because researchers use the terms 'fiscal distress' and 'financial distress' synonymously. One simple definition of fiscal distress is proposed by Trussel and Patrick (2009, 584), who have pointed out that fiscal distress is a kind of serious financial distortion that may lead to insolvency. Both public and private entities may become financially or fiscally distressed. The same is true for non-governmental organizations (NGOs). The results of financial/fiscal distress differ only based on the specific characteristics of a given organization (for profit or non-profit). Gilson and Lang (1990, 320) describe the results for profit-oriented entities as a decline on stock returns and earnings while the results for non-profit organizations are decreasing resources, assets, and revenues.

The second problem arises when attempting to identify a complete and comprehensive list of risk factors that can determine whether financial distress will occur, and that are crucial and important for the final results of the analysis. The risk factors impacting financial distress are generally financial in nature so the analysis of these determinants requires a comprehensive and comparable data set. The difficulty with finding such information has been raised by Cahill et al. (1994, 254), who pointed out the uncertainty of information used in the diagnosis of fiscally distressed municipalities. The financial data set problem is a common one in many countries; it questions the comprehensiveness of information and its reliability with regard to the financial situation of public sector entities. This data plays a significant role in building the prediction models, and the data's quality strongly impacts the scope of the analysis and its final results. Selecting the most appropriate prediction model is a crucial task since there are a variety of models to choose from, all while taking into account numerous qualitative and quantitative factors.

4 Methodology and Variables

4.1 Examination of Fiscal Distress at the General Government Level

This section provides an analysis of fiscal distress at the general government sector for 26 countries (Belgium, Bulgaria, the Czech Republic, Denmark, Germany, Ireland, Spain, France, Croatia, Italy, Cyprus, Latvia, Lithuania, Luxembourg, Hungary, Malta, the Netherlands, Austria, Poland, Portugal, Romania, Slovenia, Slovakia, Finland, Sweden, and the United Kingdom). Countries were selected based on the quality, completeness, and availability of data for the 2009–2014 period. All of the general government sectors were classified into two clusters. The following representative variables were adopted for each of the sectors.

DISTRESS: Takes a value equal to 0 (not fiscally distressed) or 1 (fiscally distressed). Values were computed based on two criteria: the first assumes the existence of a deficit for three consecutive years, while the second claims there existed about a 5 % cumulative deficit in relation to revenue over the same period (three years). The presence of these two criteria at the same time determines the existence of fiscal distress.

DEBT: Takes a value equal to the natural logarithm of a government's consolidated gross debt (the raw data before transformation was in €millions).

DEBT.REV: The ratio of a government's consolidated gross debt (in €millions) and its revenues (in €millions).

IGT.REV: The ratio of inter-governmental lending within EU28 in the context of the financial crisis (in €millions) and various government revenues (in €millions).

TAX.REV: The ratio of tax revenues (from taxes on production and imports; current taxes on income, wealth, etc.; and capital taxes in €millions) and total government revenues (in €millions).

EXP.GDP: The ratio of government expenditure (in €millions) and GDP (in €millions).

REV.CHANGE: The relative change of total government revenues in comparison to the previous year.

SIZE: Takes a value equal to the natural logarithm of total government revenues (the raw data before transformation was in €millions).

The first step of the examination is to detect the absence or presence of fiscal distress for each country in each year (Table 11.4) on the basis

Table 11.4 Countries and years with a fiscally distressed status (1) and a not fiscally distressed status (0) for the general government sector

Country	2009	2010	2011	2012	2013	2014	Sum
Austria	1	1	1	1	0	0	4
Belgium	0	1	1	1	1	1	5
Bulgaria	0	0	1	1	0	0	2
Croatia	1	1	1	1	1	1	6
Cyprus	0	0	1	1	1	1	4
Czech Republic	1	1	1	1	1	1	6
Denmark	0	0	0	1	0	0	1
Finland	0	0	0	0	0	0	0
France	1	1	1	1	1	1	6
Germany	0	1	1	0	0	0	2
Hungary	1	1	1	1	1	1	6
Ireland	0	1	1	1	1	1	5
Italy	1	1	1	1	1	1	6
Latvia	1	1	1	1	0	0	4
Lithuania	1	1	1	1	1	1	6
Luxembourg	0	0	0	0	0	0	0
Malta	1	1	1	1	1	1	6
Netherlands	0	0	1	1	1	1	4
Poland	1	1	1	1	1	1	6
Portugal	1	1	1	1	1	1	6
Romania	1	1	1	1	1	1	6
Slovakia	1	1	1	1	1	1	6
Slovenia	1	1	1	1	1	1	6
Spain	0	1	1	1	1	1	5
Sweden	0	0	0	0	0	0	0
United Kingdom	1	1	1	1	1	1	6
Sum	15	19	22	22	18	18	114

Source: Own calculations based on data from Eurostat, http://ec.europa.eu/eurostat/data/database (accessed 07/07/2015)

of the criteria discussed above. As shown in the table below, Croatia, the Czech Republic, France, Hungary, Italy, Lithuania, Malta, Poland, Portugal, Romania, Slovakia, Slovenia, and the United Kingdom met the criteria to qualify as fiscally distressed units for the period under examination, while Finland, Luxembourg, and Sweden would not be considered as fiscally distressed units at the same time. The highest number of fiscally distressed units was recorded for the years 2011 and 2012, while the lowest number was observed in 2009.

The second stage of the examination is to classify the cases (for the general government sector) into clusters with similar testing characteristics (features). The clustering of cases by *k*-means using 156 cases was performed, where each *i*-th country in the *j*-th year as a separate case was analysed. The results from this analysis are shown in Table 11.5.

According to the data (presented in Table 11.5), the first cluster consists of twelve countries: Bulgaria, the Czech Republic, Croatia, Cyprus, Latvia, Lithuania, Luxembourg, Hungary, Malta, Romania, Slovenia, and Slovakia. The second cluster includes fourteen countries: Belgium, Denmark, Germany, Ireland, Spain, France, Italy, the Netherlands, Austria, Poland, Portugal, Finland, Sweden, and the United Kingdom. Basic descriptive statistics were computed for each of the clusters (Table 11.6).

The biggest differences in both clusters were characterized by the following variables: REV.CHANGE (378.6 % for the first cluster and 329.3 % for the second cluster) and IGT.REV (180.6 % for the first cluster and 122.5 % for the second cluster). The least amount of fluctuation was seen for SIZE and DEBT. Generally, only three variables were characterized by low volatility: SIZE, DEBT, and EXP.GDP. For the first cluster, TAX.REV can also be added to the list, but it should be noted that this variable has a high variation coefficient for the second cluster. Half of the variation coefficients in both clusters were similar, with the exceptions being DISTRESS, IGT.REV, TAX.REV, and REV.CHANGE, which were significantly different between the two clusters. Figure 11.1 illustrates how the two clusters were differentiated. As can be seen, the variables DEBT, SIZE, and DEBT.REV were the main influencers for the distribution of the observations made involving the two clusters.

The next step of the examination is to evaluate the parameters using General Discriminant Analysis. First, the model was constructed using stepwise regression (backward). The results of the GDA are presented

Table 11.5 Elements of clusters for the general government sector

Cluster 1							
Obs	Country	Year	Distance	Obs	Country	Year	Distance
7	Bulgaria	2009	0.619372	**79**	Luxembourg	2009	0.598401
8	Bulgaria	2010	0.573499	**80**	Luxembourg	2010	0.503047
9	Bulgaria	2011	0.477339	**81**	Luxembourg	2011	0.495011
10	Bulgaria	2012	0.421747	**82**	Luxembourg	2012	0.452567
11	Bulgaria	2013	0.501805	**83**	Luxembourg	2013	0.426528
12	Bulgaria	2014	0.370180	**84**	Luxembourg	2014	0.428926
13	Czech Republic	2009	0.583326	**85**	Hungary	2009	0.638914
14	Czech Republic	2010	0.632994	**86**	Hungary	2010	0.653614
15	Czech Republic	2011	0.662034	**87**	Hungary	2011	0.618581
16	Czech Republic	2012	0.686511	**88**	Hungary	2012	0.644747
17	Czech Republic	2013	0.671859	**89**	Hungary	2013	0.653051
18	Czech Republic	2014	0.657850	**90**	Hungary	2014	0.656074
49	Croatia	2009	0.110280	**91**	Malta	2009	0.886212
50	Croatia	2010	0.148831	**92**	Malta	2010	0.859844
51	Croatia	2011	0.201060	**93**	Malta	2011	0.831313
52	Croatia	2012	0.243539	**94**	Malta	2012	0.806430
53	Croatia	2013	0.334192	**95**	Malta	2013	0.772501
54	Croatia	2014	0.372885	**96**	Malta	2014	0.730110
61	Cyprus	2009	0.482085	**121**	Romania	2009	0.391969
62	Cyprus	2010	0.460379	**122**	Romania	2010	0.438360
63	Cyprus	2011	0.379578	**123**	Romania	2011	0.488909
64	Cyprus	2012	0.462735	**124**	Romania	2012	0.508724
65	Cyprus	2013	0.645481	**125**	Romania	2013	0.543303
66	Cyprus	2014	0.593057	**126**	Romania	2014	0.576686
67	Latvia	2009	0.496004	**127**	Slovenia	2009	0.218001
68	Latvia	2010	0.435734	**128**	Slovenia	2010	0.178834
69	Latvia	2011	0.402315	**129**	Slovenia	2011	0.100035
70	Latvia	2012	0.368088	**130**	Slovenia	2012	0.079806
71	Latvia	2013	0.459348	**131**	Slovenia	2013	0.187604
72	Latvia	2014	0.434459	**132**	Slovenia	2014	0.276431
73	Lithuania	2009	0.398409	**133**	Slovakia	2009	0.181860
74	Lithuania	2010	0.295362	**134**	Slovakia	2010	0.203729
75	Lithuania	2011	0.242994	**135**	Slovakia	2011	0.252928
76	Lithuania	2012	0.198997	**136**	Slovakia	2012	0.320565
77	Lithuania	2013	0.184448	**137**	Slovakia	2013	0.353774
78	Lithuania	2014	0.149799	**138**	Slovakia	2014	0.357680

(*continued*)

Table 11.5 (continued)

Cluster 2

Obs	Country	Year	Distance	Obs	Country	Year	Distance
1	Belgium	2009	0.302821	**97**	Netherlands	2009	0.294884
2	Belgium	2010	0.202876	**98**	Netherlands	2010	0.282377
3	Belgium	2011	0.189646	**99**	Netherlands	2011	0.176647
4	Belgium	2012	0.176354	**100**	Netherlands	2012	0.158834
5	Belgium	2013	0.165565	**101**	Netherlands	2013	0.160729
6	Belgium	2014	0.176413	**102**	Netherlands	2014	0.159697
19	Denmark	2009	0.730594	**103**	Austria	2009	0.322062
20	Denmark	2010	0.689755	**104**	Austria	2010	0.300567
21	Denmark	2011	0.650330	**105**	Austria	2011	0.280325
22	Denmark	2012	0.620950	**106**	Austria	2012	0.268405
23	Denmark	2013	0.654984	**107**	Austria	2013	0.331548
24	Denmark	2014	0.649921	**108**	Austria	2014	0.314006
25	Germany	2009	0.773643	**109**	Poland	2009	0.461676
26	Germany	2010	0.787366	**110**	Poland	2010	0.387661
27	Germany	2011	0.804753	**111**	Poland	2011	0.392037
28	Germany	2012	0.846562	**112**	Poland	2012	0.340023
29	Germany	2013	0.851139	**113**	Poland	2013	0.326426
30	Germany	2014	0.860511	**114**	Poland	2014	0.369589
31	Ireland	2009	0.756424	**115**	Portugal	2009	0.598736
32	Ireland	2010	0.724997	**116**	Portugal	2010	0.584536
33	Ireland	2011	0.811017	**117**	Portugal	2011	0.592615
34	Ireland	2012	0.854555	**118**	Portugal	2012	0.656908
35	Ireland	2013	0.839074	**119**	Portugal	2013	0.622514
36	Ireland	2014	0.736067	**120**	Portugal	2014	0.631220
37	Spain	2009	0.316381	**139**	Finland	2009	0.809783
38	Spain	2010	0.259408	**140**	Finland	2010	0.748402
39	Spain	2011	0.290814	**141**	Finland	2011	0.715817
40	Spain	2012	0.381229	**142**	Finland	2012	0.675418
41	Spain	2013	0.434327	**143**	Finland	2013	0.649746
42	Spain	2014	0.479455	**144**	Finland	2014	0.621195
43	France	2009	0.679391	**145**	Sweden	2009	0.611138
44	France	2010	0.700781	**146**	Sweden	2010	0.582560
45	France	2011	0.730888	**147**	Sweden	2011	0.578971
46	France	2012	0.754967	**148**	Sweden	2012	0.563834
47	France	2013	0.773592	**149**	Sweden	2013	0.549648
48	France	2014	0.788672	**150**	Sweden	2014	0.506209
55	Italy	2009	0.690238	**151**	United Kingdom	2009	0.503099
56	Italy	2010	0.714310	**152**	United Kingdom	2010	0.581314
57	Italy	2011	0.729142	**153**	United Kingdom	2011	0.636057
58	Italy	2012	0.749647	**154**	United Kingdom	2012	0.680229
59	Italy	2013	0.774212	**155**	United Kingdom	2013	0.693602
60	Italy	2014	0.793759	**156**	United Kingdom	2014	0.758617

Source: Own calculations based on data from Eurostat, http://ec.europa.eu/eurostat/data/database (accessed 07/07/2015)

Table 11.6 Basic descriptive statistics of clusters for the general government sector

	Cluster 1				Cluster 2			
Variables	Mean	Standard deviation	Variance	Variation coefficient	Mean	Standard deviation	Variance	Variation coefficient
DISTRESS	0.805556	0.398550	0.158842	0.494751	0.66667	0.474236	0.224900	0.711354
DEBT	9.820190	0.896139	0.803065	0.091255	12.92593	1.094746	1.198469	0.084694
DEBT.REV	1.236069	0.512664	0.262824	0.414753	1.77898	0.703887	0.495456	0.395668
IGT.REV	0.013475	0.024335	0.000592	1.805902	0.01735	0.021261	0.000452	1.225238
TAX.REV	0.554557	0.071322	0.005087	0.128612	0.60779	0.102073	0.010419	0.167941
EXP.GDP	0.429694	0.048733	0.002375	0.113412	0.50315	0.051445	0.002647	0.102245
REV.CHANGE	0.016921	0.064070	0.004105	3.786305	0.01734	0.057109	0.003261	3.293203
SIZE	9.704836	0.865028	0.748273	0.089134	12.43464	0.953488	0.909139	0.07668

Source: Own calculations based on data from Eurostat, http://ec.europa.eu/eurostat/data/database (accessed 07/07/2015)

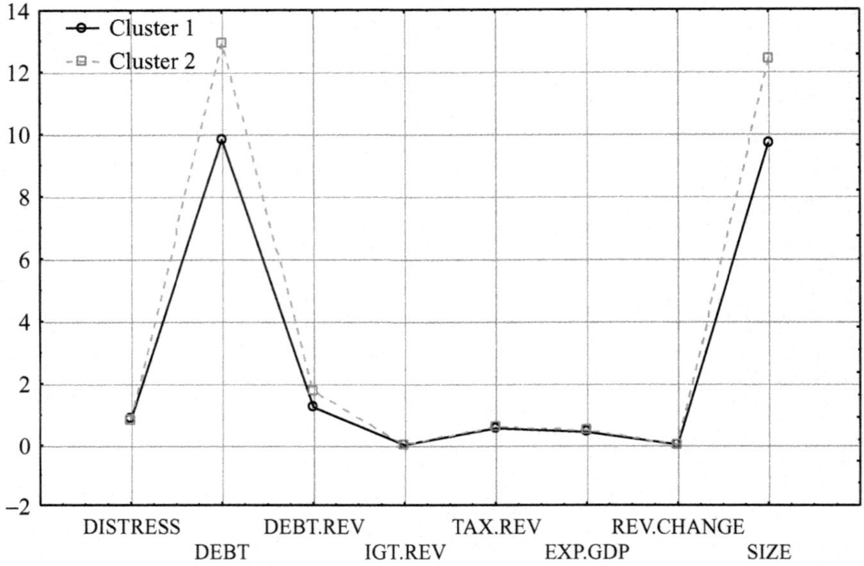

Fig. 11.1 Means of clusters of general government sector (*Source*: Own elaboration based on data from Eurostat http://ec.europa.eu/eurostat/data/database (access: 07/07/2015))

in Table 11.7. According to the evaluation of the parameters, only three variables were significant: DEBT, TAX.REV, and SIZE, as evidenced by the *p*-value that was lower than 0.05. The strongest influencer concerning the recognition of fiscally distressed units were first DEBT and then SIZE and TAX.REV, as evidenced by the standardized coefficient β (beta). The standardized coefficient β highlights the variables that are the most efficient in discriminating between fiscally distressed (1) and not fiscally distressed countries (0). DEBT (contribution above 123 %) was the most efficient in distinguishing between these two groups, followed by SIZE (with a contribution above 115 %) and TAX.REV (contribution equal to 37.5 %). Again, DEBT offered a positive contribution to the accurate recognition of a given unit as fiscally distressed while TAX.REV and SIZE had negative contributions. On the other hand, the correct recognition of a unit as not being fiscally distressed had the opposite contribution with the same level of influence. Table 11.8 presents the means of the predictors in the fiscally distressed group (1) and the not fiscally distressed group (0).

Table 11.7 Evaluation of parameters done with GDA for the general government sector (cluster 1)

Not fiscal distress											
Variables	Comment. – (O/Z/P)	0 – Param.	0 – Er.Std.	0 – t	0 – p	−95 % – CL	+95 % – CL	0 – Beta (ß)	0 – Er.Std.ß	−95 % – CL	+95 % – CL
Intercept		−0.719129	0.688182	−1.04497	0.299737	−2.09237	0.654116				
DEBT		−0.550451	0.073453	−7.49389	0.000000	−0.69703	−0.403877	−1.23769	0.165160	−1.56726	−0.908118
DEBT.REV	Connect.										
IGT.REV	Connect.										
TAX.REV		2.095851	0.566794	3.69773	0.000437	0.96483	3.226870	0.37506	0.101430	0.17266	0.577464
EXP.GDP	Connect.										
REV.CHANGE	Connect.										
SIZE		0.531368	0.080016	6.64079	0.000000	0.37170	0.691037	1.15330	0.173669	0.80675	1.499853
Fiscal distress											
Variables	Comment. – (O/Z/P)	1 – Param.	1 – Er. Std.	1 – t	1 – p	−95 % – CL	+95 % – CL	1 – Beta (ß)	1 – Er.Std.ß	−95 % – CL	+95 % – CL
Intercept		1.71913	0.688182	2.49807	0.014910	0.34588	3.092375				
DEBT		0.55045	0.073453	7.49389	0.000000	0.40388	0.697025	1.23769	0.165160	0.90812	1.567260
DEBT.REV	Connect.										
IGT.REV	Connect.										
TAX.REV		−2.09585	0.566794	−3.69773	0.000437	−3.22687	−0.964831	−0.37506	0.101430	−0.57746	−0.172661
EXP.GDP	Connect.										
REV.CHANGE	Connect.										
SIZE		−0.53137	0.080016	−6.64079	0.000000	−0.69104	−0.371699	−1.15330	0.173669	−1.49985	−0.806750

Source: Own calculations based on data from Eurostat http://ec.europa.eu/eurostat/data/database (access: 07/07/2015)

It should be noted that if the value for DEBT exceeds a mean equal to 9.82 (Table 11.8), then the given country should qualify as being fiscally distressed. If the value is below the mean, then the country would not be labelled as fiscally distressed. If the value for TAX.REV exceeds a mean of 0.55, then the country being analysed should be classified as not fiscally distressed; a value below that translates to a fiscally distressed country. If the value for SIZE exceeds a mean of 9.70, then the country in question should be considered to be fiscally distressed. It is worth mentioning that the values of DEBT and SIZE were transformed using a natural logarithm.

Table 11.9 shows the values of a Wilk test for the decomposition of effective hypotheses, presenting the importance of the variables tested in the identification of fiscal distress. The Wilk test value should be less than 1, and the lower the value, the better.

Table 11.8 The means of the predictors in the fiscally distressed group (1) and the not fiscally distressed group (0) for the general government sector (cluster 1)

Item	0 – p = 0.1944	1 – p = 0.8056	General – mean
DEBT	**9.006973**	**9.951354**	**9.82019**
DEBT.REV	0.663119	1.328481	1.236069
IGT.REV	0.010756	0.013914	0.013475
TAX.REV	**0.621223**	**0.543804**	**0.554557**
EXP.GDP	0.4256	0.430355	0.429694
REV.CHANGE	0.011636	0.017774	0.016921
SIZE	**9.558762**	**9.728396**	**9.704836**

Source: Own calculations based on data from Eurostat, http://ec.europa.eu/eurostat/data/database (accessed 07/07/2015)

Table 11.9 Multivariate tests of significance for the general government sector (cluster 1)

Item	Test	Value	F	Effect – df	Error – df	p
Intercept	Wilks	0.984196	1.09196	1	68	0.299737
DEBT	Wilks	0.547688	56.15838	1	68	0.000000
DEBT.REV	Wilks	1.000000		0		
IGT.REV	Wilks	1.000000		0		
TAX.REV	Wilks	0.832586	13.67321	1	68	0.000437
EXP.GDP	Wilks	1.000000		0		
REV.CHANGE	Wilks	1.000000		0		
SIZE	Wilks	0.606601	44.10007	1	68	0.000000

Source: Own calculations based on data from Eurostat, http://ec.europa.eu/eurostat/data/database (accessed 07/07/2015)

Table 11.10 Classification matrix to identify fiscal distress (1) or a lack of fiscal distress (0) for the general government sector (cluster 1)

Item	Percent – correct	0 – p = 0.1944	1 – p = 0.8056
0	64.28571	9.00000	5.00000
1	96.55172	2.00000	56.00000
Total	90.27778	11.00000	61.00000

Source: Own calculations based on data from Eurostat, http://ec.europa.eu/eurostat/data/database (accessed 07/07/2015)

Table 11.10 contains percentages for the units that have been correctly classified as fiscally distressed (1) or not fiscally distressed (0). The model enabled the accurate classification of 90.28 % of cases from both groups. It can be seen that the likelihood of correctly classifying units as being fiscally distressed is 96.55 %. This model also facilitates the correct prediction of units as not fiscally distressed 64.28 % of the time.

A similar analysis for the second cluster was carried out, where the construction of the model was also preceded by a stepwise regression (backward). Table 11.11 shows the evaluation of parameters done with GDA.

In Table 11.12 the means of the predictors for both the fiscally distressed group and the not fiscally distressed group are listed.

As seen in Table 11.12, the value for DEBT is higher than the overall mean, which is equal to 12.92593. This results in the classification of a given country as being fiscally distressed. When the DEBT value is lower than the overall mean, it identifies a unit as not being fiscally distressed. A similar outcome is observed with SIZE: a value higher than the mean of 12.43 translates to a fiscally distressed group, while a value lower than the mean signals a not fiscally distressed group. Based on the results of a Wilk test, Table 11.13 presents the significance of the variables tested for the identification of fiscal distress.

Table 11.14 contains percentages regarding the proper categorization of units as being fiscally distressed (1) or not fiscally distressed (0). The model enabled the correct classification of 83.33 % of cases from both groups. It can be seen that the likelihood of properly identifying a group as fiscally distressed was 94.64 %. The GDA model predicts that there is a 60.71 % likelihood of correctly classifying units as not being fiscally distressed. Thus, it is easier to determine the presence of fiscal distress than a lack of fiscal distress.

Table 11.11 Evaluation of parameters done with GDA for the general government sector (cluster 2)

Not fiscal distress											
Variables	Comment. (o/z/p)	–0 – Coeff.	0 – Er. Std.	0 – t	0 – p	–95 % – CL	+95 % – CL	0 – Beta (ß)	0 – Er.Std.ß	–95 % – CL	+95 % – CL
Intercept		1.077256	0.504799	2.13403	0.035865	0.072863	2.081649				
DEBT		–0.741812	0.090676	–8.18088	0.000000	–0.922229	–0.561394	–1.71243	0.209321	–2.12891	–1.29595
DEBT.REV	Connect.										
IGT.REV	Connect.										
TAX.REV	Connect.										
EXP.GDP	Connect.										
REV.CHANGE	Connect.										
SIZE		0.711294	0.104110	6.83215	0.000000	0.504148	0.918440	1.43011	0.209321	1.01363	1.84660
Fiscal distress											
Variables	Comment. (O/Z/P)	–1 – Coeff	1 – Er.	1 – t	1 – p	–95 % – CL	+95 % – CL	1 – Beta (ß)	1 – Er.Std.ß	–95 % – CL	+95 % – CL
Intercept		–0.077256	0.504799	–0.15304	0.878745	–1.08165	0.927137				
DEBT		0.741812	0.090676	8.18088	0.000000	0.56139	0.922229	1.71243	0.209321	1.29595	2.12891
DEBT.REV	Connect.										
IGT.REV	Connect.										
TAX.REV	Connect.										
EXP.GDP	Connect.										
REV.CHANGE	Connect.										
SIZE		–0.711294	0.104110	–6.83215	0.000000	–0.91844	–0.504148	–1.43011	0.209321	–1.84660	–1.01363

Source: Own calculations based on data from Eurostat http://ec.europa.eu/eurostat/data/database (access: 07/07/2015)

Table 11.12 The means of the predictors for the fiscally distressed group (1) and the not fiscally distressed group (0) for the general government sector (cluster 2)

Item	0 – p=0.3333	1 – p=0.667	General – mean
DEBT	**12.31859**	**13.22960**	**12.92593**
DEBT.REV	1.15964	2.08866	1.77898
IGT.REV	0.01392	0.01907	0.01735
TAX.REV	0.65069	0.58634	0.60779
EXP.GDP	0.52243	0.49352	0.50315
REV.CHANGE	0.01140	0.02031	0.01734
SIZE	**12.23650**	**12.53370**	**12.43464**

Source: Own calculations based on data from Eurostat, http://ec.europa.eu/eurostat/data/database (accessed 07/07/2015)

Table 11.13 Multivariate tests of significance for the general government sector (cluster 2)

Item	Test	Value	F	Effect – df	Error – df	p
Intercept	Wilks	0.946770	4.55407	1	81	0.035865
DEBT	Wilks	0.547568	66.92676	1	81	0.000000
DEBT.REV	Wilks	1.000000		0		
IGT.REV	Wilks	1.000000		0		
TAX.REV	Wilks	1.000000		0		
EXP.GDP	Wilks	1.000000		0		
REV. CHANGE	Wilks	1.000000		0		
SIZE	Wilks	0.634407	46.67824	1	81	0.000000

Source: Own calculations based on data from Eurostat, http://ec.europa.eu/eurostat/data/database (accessed 07/07/2015)

Table 11.14 Classification matrix to identify fiscal distress (1) or a lack of fiscal distress (0) for the general government sector (cluster 2)

Item	Percent – correct	0 – p = 0.3333	1 – p = 0.6667
0	60.71429	17.00000	11.00000
1	94.64286	3.00000	53.00000
Totality	83.33333	20.00000	64.00000

Source: Own calculations based on data from Eurostat, http://ec.europa.eu/eurostat/data/database (accessed 07/07/2015)

4.2 Examination of Fiscal Distress at the Local Government Level

The same analysis was conducted for the ten units representing local government sectors (for Belgium, Hungary, Italy, Luxembourg, the Netherlands, Portugal, Romania, Slovenia, Spain, and the United Kingdom). However, the examination did not include IGT.REV due to the lack of data available at the local level. First, the fiscal distress for each unit of the local government sector and year was determined (Table 11.15). As shown in Table 11.15, seven of the ten countries met the criteria to qualify as fiscally distressed units for the period under examination. None of the countries could be classified as not being fiscally distressed for 2009–2014. Moreover, all of the countries experienced fiscal distress for three years (2011–2013).

The next Table 11.16 presents the classification of cases for the local government sector into two clusters. The clustering of cases by *k*-means using 60 cases was performed (Table 11.15). As is shown, there are two resultant clusters. The first one consists of Belgium, Spain, Italy, the Netherlands, Portugal, and the United Kingdom while the second cluster includes Luxemburg, Hungary, Romania, and Slovenia.

Table 11.15 Units and years with a fiscally distressed status (1) or a not fiscally distressed status (0) for the local government sector

Country	2009	2010	2011	2012	2013	2014	Sum
Belgium	1	1	1	1	1	1	6
Hungary	1	1	1	1	1	1	6
Italy	1	1	1	1	1	1	6
Luxembourg	0	1	1	1	1	0	4
Netherlands	0	0	1	1	1	1	4
Portugal	1	1	1	1	1	1	6
Romania	1	1	1	1	1	1	6
Slovenia	1	1	1	1	1	1	6
Spain	0	1	1	1	1	1	5
United Kingdom	1	1	1	1	1	1	6
Sum	7	9	10	10	10	9	55

Source: Own calculations based on data from Eurostat, http://ec.europa.eu/eurostat/data/database (accessed 07/07/2015)

Table 11.16 Elements of clusters for the local government sector

Obs	Country	Year	Distance	Obs	Country	Year	Distance
Cluster 1							
1	Belgium	2009	0.390553	**31**	Netherlands	2009	0.656951
2	Belgium	2010	0.358577	**32**	Netherlands	2010	0.633147
3	Belgium	2011	0.324842	**33**	Netherlands	2011	0.477679
4	Belgium	2012	0.304309	**34**	Netherlands	2012	0.37912
5	Belgium	2013	0.29124	**35**	Netherlands	2013	0.36463
6	Belgium	2014	0.279195	**36**	Netherlands	2014	0.345813
7	Spain	2009	0.379075	**37**	Portugal	2009	0.76147
8	Spain	2010	0.102631	**38**	Portugal	2010	0.688002
9	Spain	2011	0.095267	**39**	Portugal	2011	0.659415
10	Spain	2012	0.31793	**40**	Portugal	2012	0.717312
11	Spain	2013	0.513839	**41**	Portugal	2013	0.662246
12	Spain	2014	0.588587	**42**	Portugal	2014	0.670534
13	Italy	2009	0.576124	**55**	United Kingdom	2009	0.745034
14	Italy	2010	0.631621	**56**	United Kingdom	2010	0.724866
15	Italy	2011	0.664386	**57**	United Kingdom	2011	0.709134
16	Italy	2012	0.690932	**58**	United Kingdom	2012	0.758377
17	Italy	2013	0.74768	**59**	United Kingdom	2013	0.745873
18	Italy	2014	0.79772	**60**	United Kingdom	2014	0.768477
Cluster 2							
Obs	Country	Year	Distance	Obs	Country	Year	Distance
19	Luxembourg	2009	0.860048	**43**	Romania	2009	0.291516
20	Luxembourg	2010	0.649656	**44**	Romania	2010	0.274049
21	Luxembourg	2011	0.631141	**45**	Romania	2011	0.283963
22	Luxembourg	2012	0.556572	**46**	Romania	2012	0.304888
23	Luxembourg	2013	0.50287	**47**	Romania	2013	0.342895
24	Luxembourg	2014	0.607998	**48**	Romania	2014	0.387257
25	Hungary	2009	0.5548	**49**	Slovenia	2009	0.407399
26	Hungary	2010	0.558745	**50**	Slovenia	2010	0.367997
27	Hungary	2011	0.508375	**51**	Slovenia	2011	0.304131
28	Hungary	2012	0.528779	**52**	Slovenia	2012	0.312653
29	Hungary	2013	0.540888	**53**	Slovenia	2013	0.416046
30	Hungary	2014	0.542605	**54**	Slovenia	2014	0.528496

Source: Own calculations based on data from Eurostat, http://ec.europa.eu/eurostat/data/database (accessed 07/07/2015)

Table 11.17 provides descriptive statistics for both clusters. Note that the coefficient of variation for REV.CHANGE from the first cluster was 483.6 % while it is 372.4 % for the second cluster. These coefficients reflect the greatest amount of fluctuation relative to the other variables. Other highly volatile variables include DISTRESS and DEBT.REV; it should be noted that EXP.GDP is only volatile for the first cluster. The other variables are characterized by low volatility.

Figure 11.2 illustrates the differentiation between the variables in each cluster, which is also influenced by the distribution of the observations. Cluster diversity was mainly influenced by DEBT, DEBT.REV, and SIZE.

As before, an important step in the analysis is to evaluate the parameters using stepwise regression (backward), as shown in Table 11.18. The significant variables in this analysis are DEBT, EXP.GDP, and REV.CHANGE. The most efficient variable in discriminating between the two groups (fiscally distressed and not fiscally distressed) is DEBT.REV, with a contribution of about 133.6 %; SIZE had a contribution of 130.3 %. Thus, these two variables balance each other. The other variables, EXP.GDP and REV.CHANGE, have less influence in discriminating between the two groups ('influence' refers to the likelihood that a variable will correctly categorize a unit). With regard to a valid diagnosis of fiscal distress, DEBT, EXP.GDP, and REV.CHANGE all had positive contributions, while SIZE had a negative contribution.

Table 11.19 presents the means of the predictors in the fiscally distressed group (1) and the not fiscally distressed group (0).

Table 11.19 contains values that define whether a unit is fiscally distressed or not fiscally distressed. If the value of DEBT is higher than 13.2994213, then the local government sector in question is fiscally distressed. If this value is lower than the overall mean, then the unit is not fiscally distressed. It should be noted that the DEBT value was transformed using a natural logarithm; therefore the original value should be read through the lens of function $e^{13.29942}$. A similar situation exists with the variable of SIZE, so it also should be read

Table 11.17 Basic descriptive statistics of clusters for the local government sector

	Cluster 1				Cluster 2			
Variables	Mean	Standard deviation	Variance	Variation coefficient	Mean	Standard deviation	Variance	Variation coefficient
Distress	0.91667	0.280306	0.078571	0.305787	0.91667	0.282330	0.079710	0.307996
DEBT	13.29942	0.851896	0.725726	0.064055	10.16509	0.900218	0.810392	0.08856
DEBT.REV	3.31965	0.911107	0.830117	0.274459	1.62366	0.758030	0.574610	0.466864
TAX.REV	0.79805	0.085279	0.007273	0.106859	0.76515	0.073144	0.005350	0.095594
EXP.GDP	0.31644	0.07133	0.005088	0.225414	0.31533	0.039403	0.001553	0.124956
REV.CHANGE	0.01459	0.070554	0.004978	4.835778	0.01890	0.070389	0.004955	3.723864
SIZE	12.13808	0.866738	0.751235	0.071407	9.81075	0.532333	0.283379	0.05426

Source: Own calculations based on data from Eurostat, http://ec.europa.eu/eurostat/data/database (accessed 07/07/2015)

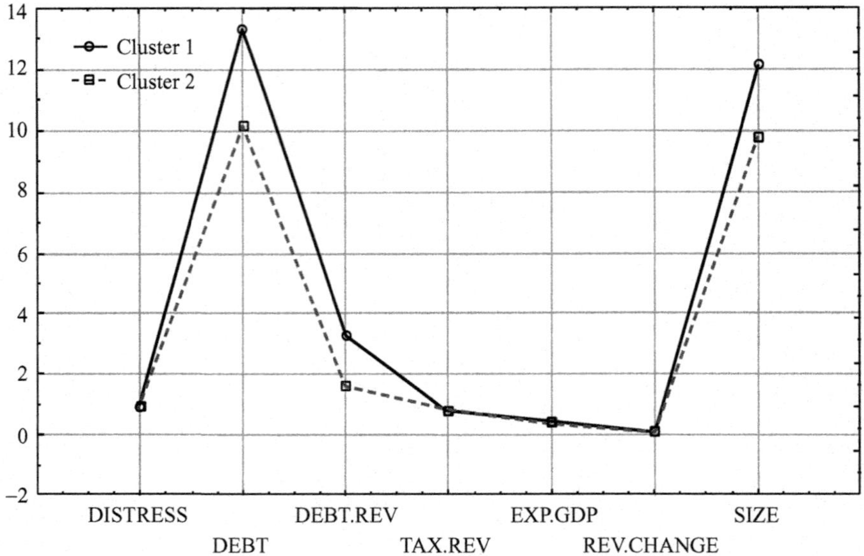

Fig. 11.2 Differentiation of clusters for the local government sector (*Source*: Own elaboration based on data from Eurostat, http://ec.europa.eu/eurostat/data/database (accessed 07/07/2015))

through the lens of function $e^{12.13808}$. Thus, if the SIZE value for the selected unit is higher than the overall mean, then this unit is categorized as being fiscally distressed. The analysis of EXP.GDP and REV.CHANGE reflects the same considerations as the other variables that were not transformed by a natural logarithm. Table 11.20 provides values of significance for the variables based on a Wilk test.

The last step of the examination for this cluster is to verify whether units were correctly classified as being fiscally distressed or not fiscally distressed. As Table 11.21 shows, the model correctly classifies a given unit into one of the groups 91.67 % of the time. The likelihood of correctly identifying a unit as being fiscally distressed is 93.94 %. On the other hand, 67.67 % of the time, a unit will be accurately categorized as not experiencing fiscal distress.

The second cluster should also be examined in addition to the first cluster. Thus, duplicating the steps of the GDA, the next table provides

Table 11.18 Evaluation of parameters done with GDA for the local government sector (cluster 1)

Not fiscal distress											
Variables	Comment. – (O/Z/P)	0 – Coeff.	0 – Er. std.	0 – t	0 – p	−95 % – CL	+95 % – CL	0 – Beta (ß)	0 – Er.Std.ß	−95 % – CL	+95 % – CL
Intercept		1.30285	0.680771	1.91379	0.064919	−0.08559	2.691295				
DEBT		−0.43963	0.161619	−2.72013	0.0106	−0.76925	−0.11	−1.33609	0.491187	−2.33788	−0.33431
DEBT.REV	Connect.										
TAX.REV	Connect.										
EXP.GDP		−1.48699	0.646533	−2.29995	0.028346	−2.8056	−0.16838	−0.3784	0.164524	−0.71394	−0.04285
REV.CHANGE		−1.25311	0.58984	−2.1245	0.041707	−2.4561	−0.05013	−0.31541	0.148465	−0.61821	−0.01262
SIZE		0.42149	0.162211	2.5984	0.014207	0.09066	0.752321	1.30329	0.501575	0.28033	2.326264
Fiscal distress											
Variables	Comment. – (O/Z/P)	1 – Coeff.	1 – Er.	1 – t	1 – p	−95 % – CL	+95 % – CL	1 – Beta (ß)	1 – Er.Std.ß	−95 % – CL	+95 % – CL
Intercept		−0.30285	0.680771	−0.44487	0.659505	−1.69129	1.085587				
DEBT		0.439625	0.161619	2.72013	0.0106	0.11	0.76925	1.33609	0.491187	0.33431	2.337876
DEBT.REV	Connect.										
TAX.REV	Connect.										
EXP.GDP		1.486992	0.646533	2.29995	0.028346	0.16838	2.805604	0.3784	0.164524	0.04285	0.713943
REV.CHANGE		1.253114	0.58984	2.1245	0.041707	0.05013	2.456101	0.31541	0.148465	0.01262	0.618211
SIZE		−0.42149	0.162211	−2.5984	0.014207	−0.75232	−0.09066	−1.30329	0.501575	−2.32626	−0.28033

Source: Own calculations based on data from Eurostat, http://ec.europa.eu/eurostat/data/database (accessed 07/07/2015)

Table 11.19 The means of the predictors for the fiscally distressed group (1) and the not fiscally distressed group (0) for the local government sector (cluster 1)

Item	0 – p = 0.0833	1 – p = 0.9167	General – mean
DEBT	**12.83005**	**13.34209**	**13.29942**
DEBT.REV	2.48187	3.39582	3.31965
TAX.REV	0.82126	0.79594	0.79805
EXP.GDP	**0.27**	**0.32067**	**0.31644**
REV.CHANGE	**–0.06653**	**0.02197**	**0.01459**
SIZE	**11.9526**	**12.15495**	**12.13808**

Source: Own calculations based on data from Eurostat, http://ec.europa.eu/eurostat/data/database (access: 07/07/2015)

Table 11.20 Multivariate tests of significance for the local government sector (cluster 1)

Item	Test	Value	F	Effect – df	Error – df	p
Intercept	Wilks	0.894336	3.662601	1	31	0.064919
DEBT	Wilks	0.80731	7.399118	1	31	0.0106
DEBT.REV	Wilks	1		0		
TAX.REV	Wilks	1		0		
EXP.GDP	Wilks	0.854235	5.28976	1	31	0.028346
REV. CHANGE	Wilks	0.872908	4.51349	1	31	0.041707
SIZE	Wilks	0.821155	6.751699	1	31	0.014207

Source: Own calculations based on data from Eurostat, http://ec.europa.eu/eurostat/data/database (accessed 07/07/2015)

Table 11.21 Classification matrix to identify fiscal distress (1) or a lack of fiscal distress (0) for the subnational government sector (cluster 1)

Item	Percent – correct	0 – p = 0.0833	1 – p = 0.9167
0	66.66667	2	1
1	93.93939	2	31
Total	91.66667	4	32

Source: Own calculations based on data from Eurostat, http://ec.europa.eu/eurostat/data/database (accessed 07/07/2015)

the evaluation parameters. As is shown in Table 11.22, DEBT, with a contribution of 43.9 %, is the most efficient variable in discriminating between a fiscally distressed group and a not fiscally distressed group.

Table 11.22 Evaluation of parameters done with GDA for local government sector (cluster 2)

Not fiscal distress											
Variables	**Comment. – (O/Z/P)**	**0 – Coeff.**	**0 – Er. std.**	**0 – t**	**0 – p**	**–95 % – CL**	**+95 % – CL**	**0 – Beta (ß)**	**0 – Er.Std.ß**	**–95 % – CL**	**+95 % – CL**
Intercept		1.48428	0.612834	2.42199	0.024126	0.21334	2.75522				
DEBT		–0.13782	0.060063	–2.29459	0.031669	–0.26238	–0.01326	–0.43944	0.191512	–0.83661	–0.04227
DEBT.REV	Connect.										
TAX.REV	Connect.										
EXP.GDP	Connect.										
REV.CHANGE	Connect.										
SIZE	Connect.										
Not fiscal distress											
Variables	**Comment. – (O/Z/P)**	**0 – Coeff.**	**0 – Er. std.**	**0 – t**	**0 – p**	**–95 % – CL**	**+95 % – CL**	**0 – Beta (ß)**	**0 – Er.Std.ß**	**–95 % – CL**	**+95 % – CL**
Intercept		–0.48428	0.612834	–0.79023	0.437829	–1.75522	0.78666				
DEBT		0.137819	0.060063	2.294589	0.031669	0.01326	0.262382	0.439441	0.191512	0.04227	0.836613
DEBT.REV	Connect.										
TAX.REV	Connect.										
EXP.GDP	Connect.										
REV.CHANGE	Connect.										
SIZE	Connect.										

Source: Own calculations based on data from Eurostat, http://ec.europa.eu/eurostat/data/database (access: 07/07/2015)

Table 11.23 presents the mean values of the predictors. If the value of DEBT is higher than 10.16509, then the unit in question should be classified as being fiscally distressed. If the DEBT value is lower than the overall mean, then the unit should be classified as not being fiscally distressed. Note, however, that the value of DEBT should be read through the lens of function $e^{10.16509}$.

In addition, Table 11.24 provides the values of significance for the variables as reflected from a Wilk test.

Table 11.25 shows the likelihood that each unit will be accurately categorized. As can be seen, the model is able to recognize 100 % of the units belonging to the fiscally distressed group and not a single case from the not fiscally distressed group. However, the model's ability to make sound predictions is good at 91.67 %.

Table 11.23 The means of the predictors for the fiscally distressed group (1) and the not fiscally distressed group (0) for the local government sector (cluster 2)

Items	0 – p = 0.0833	1 – p = 0.9167	General – mean
DEBT	**8.880686**	**10.28186**	**10.16509**
DEBT.REV	0.589681	1.71766	1.62366
TAX.REV	0.869948	0.75562	0.76515
EXP.GDP	0.32	0.31491	0.31533
REV.CHANGE	0.02507	0.01834	0.0189
SIZE	9.431343	9.84524	9.81074

Source: Own calculations based on data from Eurostat, http://ec.europa.eu/eurostat/data/database (access: 07/07/2015)

Table 11.24 Multivariate tests of significance for the local government sector (cluster 2)

Item	Test	Value	F	Effect – df	Error – df	p
Intercept	Wilks	0.789491	5.866056	1	22	0.024126
DEBT	Wilks	0.806891	5.265137	1	22	0.031669
DEBT.REV	Wilks	1		0		
TAX.REV	Wilks	1		0		
EXP.GDP	Wilks	1		0		
REV. CHANGE	Wilks	1		0		
SIZE	Wilks	1		0		

Source: Own calculations based on data from Eurostat, http://ec.europa.eu/eurostat/data/database (access: 07/07/2015)

Table 11.25 Classification matrix to identify fiscal distress (1) or a lack of fiscal distress (0) for the local government sector (cluster 2)

Item	Percent – correct	0 – p = 0.0833	1 – p = 0.9167
0	0	0	2
1	100	0	22
Totality	91.6667	0	24

Source: Own calculations based on data from Eurostat, http://ec.europa.eu/eurostat/data/database (access: 07/07/2015)

5 Conclusions

Detecting financial distress risk and identifying risk factors is crucial and fundamental to understand further the process of risk management. Financial distress risk management in the public sector has become a real challenge since the 2008 crisis, because almost every single European country has dealt with or is dealing with the threat of financial distress. Taking into account experience from the past and works related to financial distress risk and risk factors, the most important factor in predicting the process is financial variables. It is also worth mentioning that the significance of financial variables is different when detecting and managing financial distress risk. For this reason the selection of variables impacts the efficiency of financial distress risk management.

The study bases of financial variables that are used to determine financial distress risk are selected according to results of a variety of financial distress analyses and risk factors. We have compared differences and similarities between financial distress risk factors at the governmental and local or regional tier. The final result shows that a common risk factor for government tiers is their debt level. In this context debt management should be strictly integrated with financial distress risk management. It is especially important for monitoring the debt dynamic and structure, as usually the reasons for issuing debt and determining debt structure are different at government (financing current expenditure) and local or regional (financing of capital expenditure) tiers. The second risk factor is revenue dynamic. This risk factor is important at local or regional level. Local government entities usually have limited authority in creating their own revenue policy and rely strictly on taxes (central and local), which are very prone to conjectural cycle. In this case the capability of the national government to respond and slow down the crisis is stronger as it is powerful enough to create and influence tax policy at local, regional, and state level. The level of authority in tax policy in local government is determined by a fiscal federalism model. An important risk factor at the local level is size, as this determines the current expenditure for financing and maintaining local and regional authorities.

Size as a financial variable is also significant at the national governmental level as well. It is important to note that we have proposed different approaches to defining size as it is usually the total amount of revenue, and in this paper we assume the natural logarithm of total government revenues. However, the influence of the size variable does have a negative contribution, similar to the results of others studies (Trussel and Patric). Based on these result we can expect that general and sub-national government levels need to strengthen the collection of taxes and take actions that focus on eliminating tax evasion. These actions are the most significant and necessary scopes of financial distress management, as well as determining the possibility of stabilizing the general government budget and regional budgets. It is still a challenge in the crisis period as tax revenue decreases and it is difficult to keep budgets balanced. However, if in periods before the crisis the government had ensured efficient tax collection, this would secure budgets and prevent them from being impacted by external shocks and financial distress risk.

It is interesting that there is no significant proof that public expenditures related to GDP are crucial factors in determining financial distress at governmental level. We expect this variable will be important as it reflects the model of the state, and in the case of welfare states this usually impacts the financial distress risk. It may be explained in the post-crisis era by austerity programs which impact the level of public spending in most European countries.

We also expect that inter-governmental lending will make a positive contribution to detecting financial distress, especially at local government level. One of the future analyses we are going to do in depth will explain more details of the role variables have at different tiers of local government. We expect that it may have a higher influence over municipal levels of government and will be especially significant in unitary countries.

Future work should be covered by analysis of countries in three groups: unitary, federal, and regional. Recognizing that local government is organized differently and can vary is important when taking into account fiscal federalism. We will also select entities which may be 'too large for insolvency', and will propose stress tests and provide methodology that will detect stress at general governmental and local tiers. The number of variables and regional governments will be extended and we intend to provide more analysis regarding the pre-crisis period.

Bibliography

Adeyemi, B. (2011). Bank failure in Nigeria: A consequence of capital inadequacy, lack of transparency and non-performing loans. *Banks and Bank System, 6*(1), 99–109.

Altman, E. I. (1983). Exploring the road to bankruptcy. *Journal of Business Strategy, 4*(2), 36–41.

Asquith, P., Gertner., R., et al. (1994). Anatomy of financial distress: An examination of junk-bond issuers. *Quarterly Journal of Economics, 109*(3), 625–658.

Bahl, R., & Schroeder, L. (1984). The role of multi-year forecasting in the annual budgeting process of local governments. *Public Budgeting & Finance, 4*(1), 3–13.

Balakrishnan, R., Danninger, S., Elekdag, S., & Tytell, I. (2011). The transmission of financial stress from advanced and emerging economies. *Emerging Markets Finance and Trade, 47*, 40–68.

Borge L. E. & Hopland A. O. (2015). Investments and maintenance: Easy targets when governments cut budget http://lagv2015.idepfr.org/submission/index.php/LAGV2015/LAGV14/paper/viewFile/1388/291. Accessed 2 July 2015.

Bradbury, K. L. (1982, November/December). Fiscal distress in large U.S. *New England Economic Review*, 33–43.

Cahill, A. G., James J. A., Lavigne E., & Stacey A. (1994). State Government responses to Municipal Fiscal Distress: A brave new world for State-Local Intergovernmental. *Public Productivity & Management Review, 17*(3), Changing Government: Pressures, Reality, Responses: Proceedings of the Sixth National Public Sector Productivity Conference.

Capalbo, E., Grossi, G., Ianni, L., & Sargiacomo, M. (2010). Financial distress and Italian local governments. Debating the national special.

Carlson, M. A., King T., & Lewis K. (2008). Distress in the financial sector and economic activity. *The B.E. Journal of Economic Analysis & Policy Contributions, 11*(1), art 35.

Carlson, Mark A. and King, Thomas B. and Lewis, Kurt F., Distress in the Financial Sector and Economic Activity (November 3, 2010). FEDS Working Paper No. 2008–43. Available at SSRN: http://ssrn.com/abstract=1702316 or http://dx.doi.org/10.2139/ssrn.1702316

Cerami, A. (2008). New social risks in Central and Eastern Europe: The need for a new empowering politics of the Welfare State. *Sociologický časopis/Czech Sociological Re-view, 44*(6), 1089–1110.

Duca, J. V. (1999). What credit market indicators tell us. Economic and Financial Review of the Federal Reserve Bank of Dallas.

Financially Distressed Municipalities Program State Pennsylvania. (1997). Chapter 115 adopted July 7, 1989, effective July 8, 1989, 19 Pa.B. 2948; renumbered from 16 Pa. Code Chapter 36, May 16, 1997, effective May 17, 1997, 27 Pa.B. 2415. Immediately preceding text appears at serial pages (138237) to (138242) and (158559) to (158560).

Fiscal Stress Faced by Local Governments. (2010). Congressional Budget Office, December 31.

Gilchrist, S., Yankov, V., & Zakrajšek, E. (2009). Credit market shocks and economic fluctuations: Evidence from corporate bond and stock markets. *Journal of Monetary Economics, 56*, 471–493.

Gilson, S., John, K., & Lang, L. (1990). Troubled debt restructurings: An empirical study of private reorganization of firms in default. *Journal of Financial Economics, 27*, 315–353.

Gordon, M. J. (1971). Towards the theory of financial distress. *Journal of Finance, 26*(2), 347–356.

Groves, S., Godsey, W., & Shulman, M. (1981). Financial indicators for local government. *Public Budgeting and Finance, 1*(2), 5–19.

Illing, M., & Liu, Y. (2006). Measuring financial stress in a developed country: An application to Canada. *Journal of Financial Stability, 2*, 243–265.

King, T. B., A. T. Levin, and R. Perli (2007). Financial Market Perceptions of Recession Risk. Finance and Economics Discussion Series Paper No. 2007–57, Federal Reserve Board.

Kloha, P., Weissert, C., & Kleine, R. (2005). Developing and testing a composite model to predict local fiscal distress. *Public Administration Review, 65*(3), 313–323.

Lavigne, R. (2006). The institutional and political determinants of fiscal adjustment. Bank of Canada working paper.

McNamara, R., Duncan, K., & Kelly, S. (2011). Micro and macro determinants of financial distress, 15th International Business Research Conference. Sydney, Australia. Nov. 2011. http://epublications.bond.edu.au/business_pubs/542. Accessed 3 July 2015.

Measuring Fiscal Distress in South African Local Government. (2014). Chapter 10, Submission for the 2014/15 Division of Revenue. 118. PART 3. www.fcc.co.za. Accessed data 28 June 2015.

Park, C.-Y., & Mercado, R. V. (2013). Determinants of financial stress in emerging market economies ADB economics working paper series. Asian Development Bank No. 356|July 2013.

Pindado, J., & Rodriquez, L. (2005). Determinants of financial distress costs. Swiss Society for Financial Market Research.

Platt, H., & Platt, M. (1994). Business cycle effects on state corporate failure rates. *Journal of Economics and Business, 46*(2), 13–127.

Porada-Rochoń, M. (2013). *Modele decyzji finansowych MŚP w wybranych krajach Europy środkowo-wschodniej w warunkach zaburzeń finansowych*. Szczecin: Wydawnictwo PTE.

Post, G. V., & Moon, S. Y. (1998). A pooled cross-section time-series approach to business. Failures in 18 U.S. Cities. *Journal of Economics and Business, 40*, 45–57

Powell, A. W. (2013) Future planning in fiscal distress, economics of social issues ED.700.301.61, Sheldon F. Greenberg 1–11.

Raman, K. (1982). Alternative accounting measures as predictors of municipal financial distress. *Journal of Accounting, Auditing, and Finance, 6*(1), 44–50.

Rossi, F. M., Zito, M., & Costanzo, A. (2012). How to prevent distress in local government: A new model applied in Italy, Advanced Research in Scientific Areas.

Risk Management Guidance for Government Departments and Offices. (2004). Government Accounting Sector, Department of Finance, March.

Shyan-Rong Chou, Ender Su, Sheng-Jung Li, & Hsien-Chao Cheng (2010). An empirical study of the relationship between corporate information disclosure and financial distress. *International Research Journal of Finance and Economics Issue 4*, Inc.

Trussel, J. M., & Patrick, P. A. (2009). A predictive model of fiscal distress in local governments. *Journal of Public Budgeting Accounting & Financial Management, 21*(4), 578–616.

Trussel, J. M., & Patrick, P. A. (2012). A survival analysis of U.S. municipalities in fiscal distress. *International Journal of Public Administration, 35*(9), 620–633.

Trussel, J. M., & Patrick, P. A. (2013). Predicting fiscal distress in special district governments. *Journal of Public budgeting, Accounting & Financial management, 25*(4), 589–616.

Wadhwani, B. S. (1986). Inflation, bankruptcy, default premia and the stock market. *The Economic Journal, 96*, 120–138.

Ziolo, M. (2014). 'Predicting municipalities' Fiscal Distress. The empirical analysis of West Pomeranian Municipalities after the Crisis 2008, SGEM Conference on Political Sciences, Law, Finance, Economics & Tourism, Conference Proceedings, Volume II, International Multidisciplinary Scientific Conferences on Social Sciences & Arts, 3–9 September 2014, Bulgaria.

12

Impact of Insurance Companies' Investment Policy on Risk Management in the Public Sector

Teresa Czerwińska

1 Introduction

To a large extent, the operation of the public sector is determined by the appropriate fulfilment of the functions served by the insurance sector, both in the economic as well as the social sphere. The insurance sector has a special position in the financial system of the economic system because, in line with the principle of certainty of the insurance cover, it is a safety buffer for the continued operation of many enterprises of the real economy as well as individuals, especially in the context of retirement security. The significance of the insurance sector for the public one is examined in the context of the so-called critical functions: (1) fulfilment of the function of insurance coverage; and (2) the mechanisms of long-term allocation of capital. The importance of insurance institutions both for the stability of the public sector and the whole

T. Czerwińska (✉)
University of Warsaw, Warsaw, Poland

K. Raczkowski (ed.), *Risk Management in Public Administration*,
DOI 10.1007/978-3-319-30877-7_12

economic system arises from the fact that these institutions perform the critical—from the perspective of society as well as the economy—function of insurance coverage which allows the management of risk and ensures continuity of operation. The capability of ensuring infallible fulfillment of insurance coverage constitutes a synthetic indicator of the stability of the socio-economic system. Performance of the functions of critical importance for the stability of the public sector by the insurance sector is also concerned with the mechanism of long-term allocation of capital, especially in the case of life insurance companies, which is invested on the financial market and in the real economy e.g. in infrastructural projects.

The performance of the function of insurance coverage is of critical importance for risk management in the public sector and for stakeholders, broadly understood in a social sense, especially in terms of (see FSB 2014):

a) compulsory insurance (mainly general liability insurance)—materialization of the risk of default by an insurance company may lead to disruption to economic activity and diminish the stature and image of the profession which is required to ensure insurance coverage, e.g. in the healthcare or tourism sector,
b) meeting the obligations of acting as financial security measures for people, i.e. payments on account of health insurance, and pensions.

Performance of the functions of critical importance for the stability of the public sector by the insurance sector is also concerned with the mechanism of long-term allocation of capital, especially in the case of life insurance companies, which is invested on the financial market and in the real economy e.g. in infrastructural projects. It should also be highlighted that the functions of insurance companies in financial markets are evolving gradually. Insurers are now competing with other financial intermediaries, particularly in the areas of: asset management (e.g. policies linked to insurance capital funds); financing business ventures by acquiring financial instruments and providing loans and guarantees.

Their investment activities are essential for the economic situation in the capital market and the cost of capital.

The EU insurers' investment policies will be influenced strongly by the implementation of Solvency II regulations, on the one hand, and the dynamics of economic phenomena, on the other hand. A threat to the financial system stability may be generated by a loop of factors such: as general economic downturn; an anti-crisis policy of central banks resulting in a low interest rate environment; the debt crisis having major consequences for the default risk level in financial markets. There are also factors generated to some extent by the financial sector environment itself, through the so-called regulatory tsunami in the financial sector—simultaneous implementation of new regulations in the banking, insurance and other financial intermediaries sectors, tightening of prudential requirements, and development of new macro-prudential tools that are not as yet well understood as regards their effectiveness and impact on the system in holistic terms.

Thus, a need arises to identify the insurance sector's potential to generate systemic risks in a changing regulatory and economic environment in order to strengthen supervision of financial sector and guarantee capacities to absorb potential losses and market shocks. The aim of this chapter is to identify the areas where insurance companies' investment policies influence the stability of the public sector in the EU countries and to analyse the model of their investment portfolio allocation. The research period is 2005–2013. In the study, statistical analysis tools, i.e. cluster analysis and time-series data and indices analysis, are used. The first part describes the position of investment activities in insurers' financial management based on their cash flows, reflecting the real dynamics of cash flows and investment policy goals. On this basis, potential areas where insurers' investment activities impact the financial system's stability are subsequently examined. The investment portfolio allocation model in life and non-life sectors is examined. For the purposes of the analysis, insurers' investment portfolios have been decomposed into two essential elements: a portfolio of shares and other variable-yield instruments and a portfolio of debt instruments.

2 Investment Policy Objectives and Creation of Value for the Stability of the Public Sector

2.1 The Model of an Insurance Company's Financial Flows

Insurance companies as highly specialised financial intermediaries implement—to put it in a somewhat simplified manner—a financial management model comprising two cash flows (generated by the insurer ($CF_{ICPF,t}$)) (Cummins and Weiss 1993, 463–481; Santomero and Babbel 1997, 231–270; Brockett et al. 2005, 393–412, Nissim 2010; Mishkin 2012), where the basic cash flow is determined by the core business, that is insurance activities (incomes from ($CIF_{INSA,t}$) and expenditure on ($COF_{INSA,t}$) conclusion and performance of insurance contracts) whereas an additional cash flow is generated mainly by investment activities in financial markets (income from ($CIF_{INVA,t}$) and expenditure on ($COF_{INVA,t}$) investment activities):

$$CF_{ICPF,t} = \sum_{i=1}^{n} CIF_{INSA,t}, CIF_{INVA,t}, COF_{INSA,t}, COF_{INVA,t} \qquad \text{(Eq. 12.1)}$$

An insurance company's core business involves transferring certain loss probability distribution from the policyholder for a defined corresponding price (premium), hence insurance premiums, on the one hand, and claims, on the other hand, form basic cash flows triggered by insurance activities. Financial flows are modelled based on both deterministic models (Cummins et al. 1999, 417–458; Hodes et al. 2003, 41–69; Hilli et al. 2011, 329–343) and stochastic models (Wilkie 1986; Daykin and Hey 1990, 173–259; Artikis and Voudouri 2000, 87–90; Halliwell 2003; Stenberg et al. 2006). In classical terms, the basic cash inflow ($CIF_{ICPF,t}$) of each insurance company comprises a contractual premium ($CIF_{CONT,t}$), income from investment activities ($CIF_{INVA,t}$), reinsurance ($CIF_{RE,t}$) and others ($CIF_{Others,t}$), i.e. recourses, recoveries, income from the issue of securities:

$$CIF_{ICPF,t} = \underbrace{\sum_{i=1}^{n} CIF_{CONT,_t}}_{Insurance\ module}, \underbrace{CIF_{RE,_t}, CIF_{INVA,_t}, CIF_{Others,_t}}_{Non\text{-}insurance\ module} \qquad \text{(Eq. 12.2)}$$

Looking at the expenditure of an insurance company from the model perspective also, two modules can be distinguished: (1) the basic module consisting of expenditure on: claims incurred ($COF_{CLAIM,_t}$), solicitation and administration ($COF_{SAL,_t}, COF_{ADM,_t}$), reinsurance ($COF_{RE,_t}$) and (2) a non-insurance module consisting of investment expenditure ($COF_{INVA,_t}$) and others ($COF_{Others,_t}$), i.e. payment of dividends, repayment of loans:

$$COF_{ICPF,t} = \underbrace{\sum_{i=1}^{n} COF_{CLAIM,_t}, COF_{SAL,_t}, COF_{RE,_t}, COF_{ADM,_t}}_{Insurance\ module}, \underbrace{COF_{INVA,_t} COF_{Others,_t}}_{Non\text{-}insurance\ module} \qquad \text{(Eq. 12.3)}$$

The inverse insurance services provision cycle allows for using leverage to bridge the gap between the current value of collected premiums and the value of future liabilities resulting from concluded policies (Hancock et al. 2001, 1–9). The size of an insurance company's investment portfolio is determined by the size of its business proxied by written premiums, on the one hand, and by the achieved weighted average rate of return on assets (i) held in the portfolio, on the other hand, with that rate being a result of an insurer's investment policy:

$$CIF_{INVA,_t} = \bar{i} \times INV_{PORT} \qquad \text{(Eq. 12.4)}$$

Insurance companies also invest their own funds (S_{CAP}) and may manage investment portfolios for the account and at the risk of policyholders (F_{POL}) (e.g. life insurance policies linked to insurance capital funds). Insurance companies' investment portfolios are determined by portfolios of their liabilities since an investment portfolio is primarily designed to secure current and future contract-related payments for which provisions are made ($T_{PROV,t}$). The type and structure of an insurance company's contractual liabilities determine: the investment time horizon, the expected rate of return, and the acceptable level of risk and liquidity needs (Wilkie

1986; Davis 2001b; Charupat and Milevsky 2002, 199–209;Hipp and Plum 2000, 215–228; Yang and Zhang 2005, 615–634;Schmidli 2005, 25–35). An insurance company's investment portfolio should be designed taking into account the maturity structure of contractual liabilities and restrictions set forth in legal regulations on liquidity and solvency (art. 132, Directive 2009/138/EC (Solvency II)). Because of the priority attached to the liquidity and solvency of insurance companies, a degree of attention is given to asset liability management (ALM) within their financial management (Chaim 2010; Josa-Fombellida and Rincon-Zapatero 2006, 81–98; Waring 2004, 8–20;Blake 1999, 327–357;Ziemba and Mulvey 1998; Elton and Gruber 1992, 869–890). One of the fundamental principles governing financial management of insurance companies, highlighted commonly both in the relevant literature and in legal regulations, is balancing the value of provisions to cover current and future contractual liabilities against the investment portfolio:

$$NV_{PORT,t} \geq T_{PROV,t} \qquad \text{(Eq. 12.5)}$$

The income from investment activities results from the size and risk-yield profile of an insurance company's investment portfolio (INV_{PORT}) and is determined by the income from realisation of securities ($CIF_{CAP,t}$), i.e. sale of shares, participating interests ($CIF_{SHAR,t}$), redemption of debt securities by their issuer ($CIF_{DEBT,t}$), withdrawal of bank deposits ($CIF_{DEP,t}$) and others, e.g. sale of property ($CIF_{CAP\_OTHERS,t}$) and capital inflows, i.e. interest ($CIF_{INTEREST,t}$), dividends on securities held in the portfolio ($CIF_{DIV,t}$), others, e.g. rents for property ($CIF_{INT\_OTHERS,t}$):

$$INV_{PORT,t} = f\left(T_{PROV,t}, S_{CAP,t}, F_{POL,t}\right) \qquad (12.6)$$

$$CIF_{INVA,t} = f\left(INV_{PORT}\right) \qquad (12.7)$$

On the other hand, expenditure on implementation of an insurance company's investment policy usually includes: expenditure on purchase of financial instruments and tangible fixed assets, fees for and commissions on transactions concluded in the financial market.

To sum up, by issuing non-monetary financial instruments, insurance companies as financial intermediaries raise capital in the form of premiums that is leveraged in the financial market, making prices of insurance services sensitive to changes in interest rates (Doherty and Kang 1988; Allen and Santomero 1998, 1461–1485). The efficiency of insurance companies' investment policies is largely determined by the amount of insurance premiums, which is part of their pricing policies and often defines their competitive position in the market (Dickinson 2000; Shiu 2004, 1079–1110; Chen and Wong 2004, 469–499).

2.2 Investment Policy Objectives and Creation of Value for the Stability of the Public Sector

Investment activities are identified as the so-called critical functions of insurance companies because such activities could be "(...) *performed for third parties where failure would lead to the disruption of services that are vital for financial stability and the real economy due to the insurer's size or market share, external and internal interconnectedness, complexity or cross-border activities*" (Recovery and Resolution Planning for Systemically Important Insurers 2014). Insurance companies as financial intermediaries influence the financial system stability through implemented investment policies. This may destabilise the situation in the capital market, e.g. create speculative bubbles through excessive demand, and influence the real economy through over-rating some sectors at the expense of others, thus determining the cost of capital. Allocation of funds for instruments issued by the government and transformation of capital into investment in the real economy sector are of particular systemic importance. Assuming a relatively widely accepted view that the financial system stability is manifested as its ability to operate smoothly and to fulfil appropriately functions that are of key importance for the economy and individual actors (Crockett 1997; Schinasi 2004; Mishkin 1999, 3–20;Davis 2001a, 92–110; Houben et al. 2004, 38–42; Allen and Wood 2006, 152–172), the value created for the financial system stability by insurers' investment activities can be considered in the following areas:

(a) micro—referring to the view that the financial system can be stable only when each individual component thereof is stable (Crockett 2000)—creating value for shareholders and policyholders, the impact of investment decisions made by an insurer on its financial situation, which is associated with liquidity and solvency risks; the level and intensity of which are a function of the company size and sector concentration (too-big-to-fail institutions);
(b) macro—the impact of investment policies implemented by insurance companies through: (1) accumulation of government debt securities; (2) influencing the situation in financial markets where they belong to the group of significant long-term investors; (3) determining the cost of capital for the real economy enterprises, and paying pension benefits.

The investment activity pursued—based on consensus-seeking—is aimed at securing funds for claims incurred, on the one hand, and maximizing the rate of return on capital invested by the company owners, on the other hand (see e.g.: Heyman and Rowland 2006). Having in mind that liquidity and solvency are overarching principles of financial management, a particularly important aspect is the generation of financial surplus, understood as a difference between the investment portfolio and the liabilities portfolio (Brockett et al. 2005, 393–412), by ensuring an efficient investment policy whereby provisions made of premiums and equity are invested. Such surplus is a safety buffer when the value of claims incurred exceeds net premiums collected. Ultimately, however, claim payments are guaranteed with all assets of an insurer. This model highlights the role of efficient investment activity as a source for generating financial surplus that is strategically important for an insurance company, as such surplus, on the one hand, allows for achieving a competitive position in the financial services market by offering policies at attractive prices and, on the other hand, ensures that owners receive competitive return on their capital—as remuneration for their being residual bearers of risk transferred under insurance contracts (Brockett et al. 2005, 393–412).

As shown by recent experience, a conflict of policyholders' and shareholders' interests is becoming more and more meaningful for investment policies developed by insurance companies. The sources of this conflict are not obvious because, in the long term, both policyholders and shareholders are interested in the financial stability of a given company and the entire sector. Nevertheless, two principal sources of the growing conflict over the goals of such policies can be defined:

(a) high insurance market saturation, in particular in highly developed countries, and high capital barriers to entry are drivers for seeking opportunities to provide a stronger leverage to the capital raised as insurance premiums, which allows for achieving satisfactory rates of return for shareholders, on the one hand, and, on the other hand, for competing by offering lower prices which—as shown by studies—have recently become more important as customers' sensitivity to prices, and willingness to compare different products has definitely increased (Insurance in 2015); price competition, combined with the agency conflict, may contribute to excessive investment risk-taking that could pose a threat to an insurer's liquidity and solvency and thereby undermine the certainty of the insurance cover, which is a priority for policyholders;
(b) short-termism of financial management in financial institutions that increases moral hazard since—as demonstrated by many authors and practitioners—managers essentially make their assessments for not more than a year ahead, which encourages excessive investment risk taking.

Reducing vulnerability provides a specific value for the financial system stability. By implementing their investment policies, insurers may contribute to reducing vulnerability of financial markets since their investment is long-term by nature and they stimulate and transform household savings. In the classical view, insurers' investment activities, being auxiliary to their core insurance business, provide protection against depreciation and reduce the cost of insurance through low leverage of collected premiums, and are not a catalyst for systemic risk (Systemic Risk in Insurance 2010; Insurance and Financial Stability, IAIS 2011; Fitzpatrick 2013; Thimann 2014; Eling and Pankoke 2014). The vast majority of systemic risk is generated by insurance companies pursuing quasi-banking activities involving: the use of high financial leverage resulting in big exposure to market and liquidity risks, requiring the use of sophisticated financial instruments and risk management strategies, i.e.: hedging, derivatives, requiring changes of payment dates, SDC issuance, default risk transfer, e.g. through repos—exceeding what is justified by the scale and needs of insurance activities (Systemic Risk in Insurance 2010; Weiss 2010; Global Systemically Important Insurers: Policy Measures 2013; Fitzpatrick 2013). It is here where strong links with other financial institutions and exposure to non-insurance risks inherent in financial markets occur. Studies show that an increased value of non-insurance liabilities and bigger income from investment activities are accompanied by a greater potential for systemic risk generation (Weiss and Muhlnickel 2014).

Insurance companies provide an important value for financial system stability through capital participation in the government debt market. Given the public finance crisis in many countries, attention should be paid to the greater significance of insurance companies as actors accumulating government debt instruments. The role of the government as an additional stakeholder of insurers' investment policies is growing. In this respect, there are two issues that are key to the financial system stability: (1) ensuring stable demand for government debt securities, which is extremely important in the context of the debt crisis in many countries; (2) the risk of excessive concentration of debt of low investment quality in insurers' portfolios.

Insurance companies can contribute to reducing vulnerability of the government debt market through long-term participation and stable demand. This is crucial for public finance sustainability. The Solvency II regulations provide for preferential default risk assessment of bonds issued and guaranteed by the member states and central banks, European Economic Area (EEA) countries and supranational institutions, i.e. the International Monetary Fund (IMF), and the European Bank for Reconstruction and Development (EBRD). When calculating the capital requirement, they were considered to be risk-free instruments of the highest investment quality, hence are not subject to capital requirements to hedge the insurer's exposure to risk (art. 44, Commission Delegated Regulation (EU) 2015/35). Simultaneously, preferential default risk assessment of government securities, without differentiating their actual investment quality, may consequently deteriorate the financial situation of insurance companies. This is due to the fact that they will accumulate much bigger volumes of instruments of actually low investment quality than now, given that the capital requirement is calculated under obvious preferences. The realities of the debt crisis in many countries have clearly shown that treating government securities as risk-free rapidly deteriorated the financial situation of many European banks (the case of Greek bonds).

Investment activities of insurance companies may contribute to a reduction in price volatility in financial markets and the property market. The run risk is relatively low for insurance companies and arises basically only in the case of the life insurance sector and pension funds (Eling and Pankoke 2014; Thimann 2014), hence the relatively low risk of fire sale of assets. Stable demand for corporate instruments among insurance companies contributes to rational development of the cost of capital for enterprises. However, there arises the risk of insurance companies being overstimulated to allocate their portfolios for government debt instruments, which may contribute to reducing demand for private-sector instruments issued by the private sector that have lower investment quality rating (Al-Darwish et al. 2011), thus limiting the insurance sector participation in generating economic growth.

3 The Analysis of Investment Activities of Insurance Companies in the EU Countries

The impact of insurers' investment policies on the stability of the public sector can be considered with reference to two fundamental aspects: (1) the size of investment activities, associated with insurance companies pursuing excessive investment activities not justified by their core business, with increased moral hazard and with a drive for higher leverage of their investment portfolios (the problem of insurance companies being transformed into quasi-banking institutions), and (2) investment portfolio allocation models in the insurance sector and the problem of investing in entities affiliated by capital and subsidiaries, i.e. insufficient portfolio diversification.

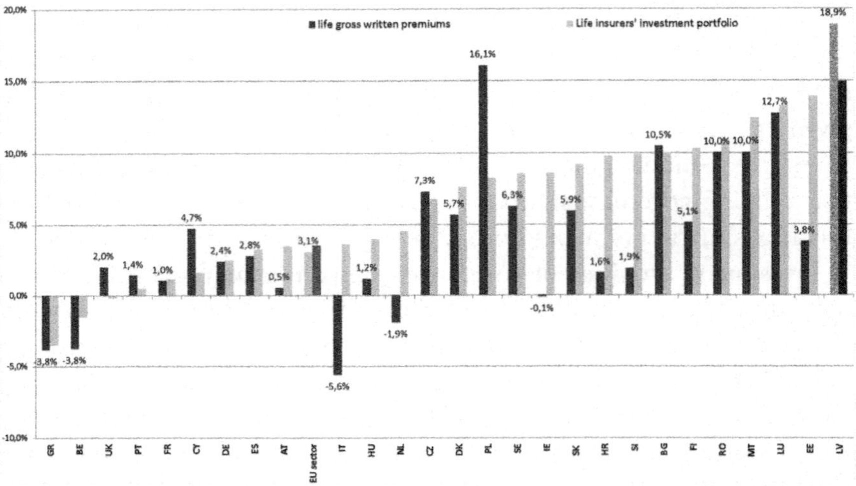

Fig. 12.1 Average annual rates of change in the value of life insurers' investment portfolios and life gross written premiums in EU countries in 2005–2013 (%) (*Source*: Own calculation based on Insurance Europe data)

Considering the size of insurers' investment activities as compared with the pace of changes in gross written premiums, it may be concluded that in many EU countries, the average annual change in the value of investment portfolio was disproportionally large relative to the average annual change in the value of gross written premiums (Figs. 12.1 and 12.2). The most meaningful changes in both investment portfolio and gross written premiums took place in countries with emerging insurance markets, i.e. Bulgaria, Poland, Romania, Malta, Latvia. In the vast majority of countries, the average annual growth rate of the investment portfolio value was significantly higher than the growth rate of gross written premiums despite the downturn in financial markets. Changes in both the investment portfolio and gross written premiums in highly developed markets were more proportional and less dynamic (except Luxemburg's life sector). The situation in Ireland (life sector), the Netherlands (life sector), Italy (life and non-life sector), Cyprus (non-life sector), Czech Republic (non-life sector), Sweden, Portugal and Croatia (non-life sector), where a decrease in gross written premiums was accompanied by a major increase in the investment portfolio value, is particularly notable. This provides evidence that the situation in the insurance market deteriorated disproportionately in relation

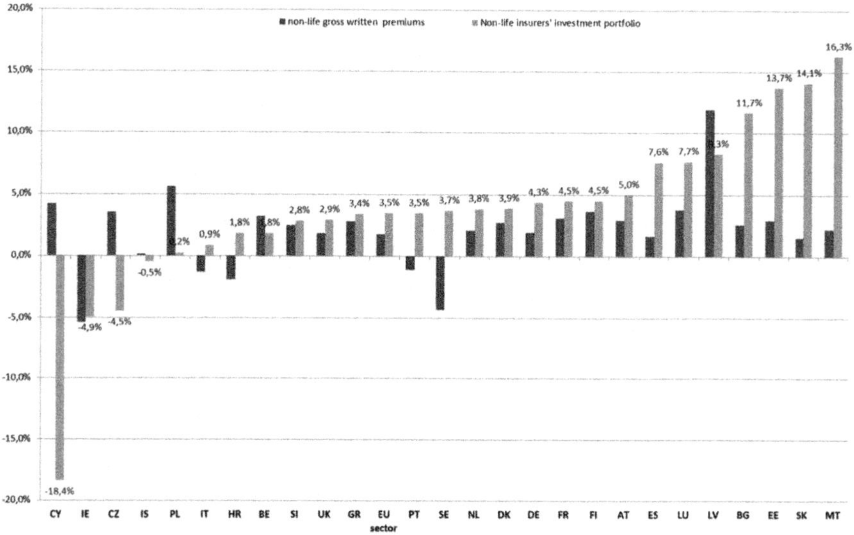

Fig. 12.2 Average annual rates of change in the value of non-life insurers' investment portfolios and non-life gross written premiums in EU countries in 2005–2013 (%) (*Source*: Own calculation based on Insurance Europe data)

to the situation in the capital market. The situation in the insurance sector proved to be more sensitive to the economic crisis than the situation in the capital market. Nevertheless, taking into account that—to put it in a somewhat simplified manner —the size of the investment portfolio is determined by gross written premiums, there may be concerns about excessive leverage of the investment portfolio, and excessive investment activity where the growth rate of the investment portfolio value significantly exceeds the growth rate of gross written premiums, e.g. Ireland, Slovenia, Estonia, Croatia, Finland (in the life sector) and Malta, Slovakia, Estonia, Bulgaria, Czech Republic, Sweden (in the non-life sector). This requires even further and more thorough research.

The starting point for the analysis of risk transmission channels between the insurance sector and the financial sector in its broad meaning is identifying the investment portfolio allocation model in the insurance sector in EU countries. Taking into account J. Tobin's separation theorem (1958), the investment portfolio allocation model in the insurance sector may be considered from the perspective of a portfolio comprising two elements, notably: shares and other variable-yield securities (e.g.

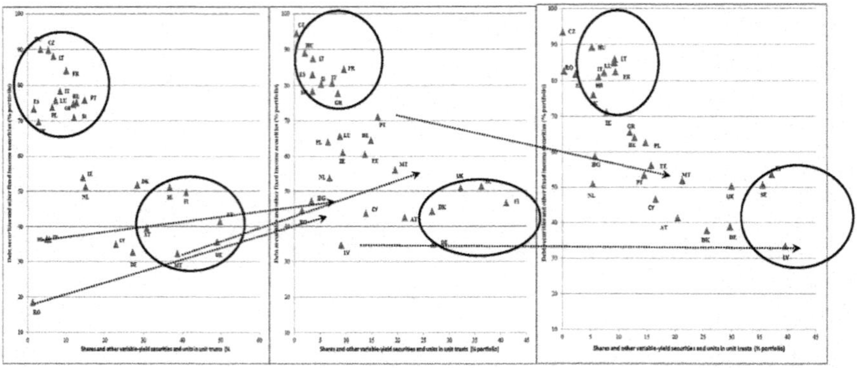

Fig. 12.3 Evolution of life insurers' investment portfolios in EU countries in 2007 (*left*), 2010 (*middle*), 2013 (*right*) (*Source*: Own calculation based on The European Insurance and Occupational Pensions Authority (EIOPA) data)

units in unit trusts) and debt securities and other fixed-income securities (Figs. 12.3 and 12.4). Based on the conducted research, a simplification can be made to distinguish two investment portfolio allocation models in both life and non-life sectors: (1) the classical model—where debt securities and other fixed-income securities account for a dominant proportion (more than 60 % of the portfolio), the remainder being mainly shares and other variable-yield securities (e.g. units in unit trusts), complemented chiefly by bank deposits, (2) the diversified model, bearing remarkable resemblance to the allocation of investment funds, where the proportion of debt securities and other fixed-income securities and that of shares and other variable-yield securities in the portfolio are comparable, the remainder being loans or bank deposits. Differences in the structure of the investment portfolio allocation in the insurance sector among the various countries result from the specificity of life and non-life sectors and may be partly related to normative constraints governing portfolio allocation, e.g. in some new EU member states such as Poland, Slovakia, Hungary. In the classical sense, non-life insurers invest mainly in shorter-term, higher credit quality and more liquid debt securities as compared to life insurers (Davis 2001a; Liu and Yang 2004, 11–31; Nissim 2010). Nevertheless, a clearly classical portfolio allocation model with a dominant proportion of debt securities in the portfolio (median of over 80 % in the period concerned) can be identified

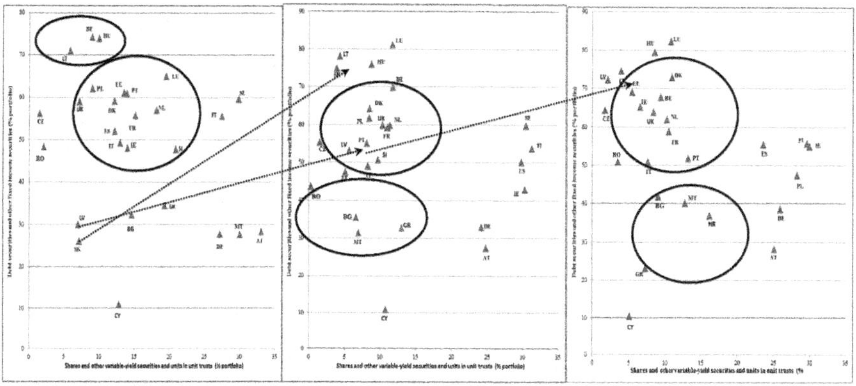

Fig. 12.4 Evolution of non-life insurers' investment portfolio in EU countries in 2007 (*left*), 2010 (*middle*) and 2013 (*right*) (*Source*: Own calculation based on EIOPA data)

in the life sector in: the Czech Republic, Hungary, Lithuania, Croatia, Estonia, Slovakia, Slovenia, France, Italy, and in the non-life sector in: Belgium, Hungary, Lithuania, Luxembourg (median of over 70 % in the period concerned) (Figs. 12.3 and 12.4). Within the diversified model, basically two allocation submodels can be indicated: (1) a portfolio with a greater investment risk where shares and other variable-yield securities, corporate bonds and loans account form its significant part; (2) a portfolio with a relatively low investment risk where debt securities and other fixed-income securities as well as bank deposits and property constitute its considerable proportion. A substantial similarity is noticeable in investment portfolio allocation models in: Lithuania, Bulgaria, Romania, Malta, where debt securities and other fixed-income securities and bank deposits clearly dominate (Figs. 12.3 and 12.4). Such an allocation model generates a relatively low rate of return in a low interest rate environment. Furthermore, the research found that:

a) life insurers' investment portfolios changed more dynamically than those of non-life insurers;
b) investment portfolio allocation was more stable in highly developed markets, i.e. Germany, France, the UK, Austria, Sweden, Denmark, the Netherlands, and changed very dynamically in emerging markets,

particularly in: Romania, Bulgaria, Slovakia, Latvia—the structure of portfolio allocation changed considerably (there were much more bonds in portfolios) which may be interpreted as a kind of strategy to seek allocation carrying relatively lower risk in such rapidly changing market conditions;

c) non-life insurers were significantly exposed to the market risk as a consequence of a greater proportion of shares and other variable-yield securities in their investment portfolios in 2005 and 2007–2010 than the proportion of shares held by life insurers (Figs. 12.3 and 12.4).

Certain evolution of changes in both life and non-life insurers' investment portfolios can be observed in the period in question—generally, the proportion of shares and other variable-yield securities in the portfolio decreased, in particular in 2007–2009, and the proportion of debt securities and other fixed-income securities rose, especially in 2008–2012.

In addition, an attempt may be made to distinguish groups of countries with similar investment portfolio allocation models in the insurance sector, that partly being a consequence of the fact that insurers adopt a business model reflecting the socio-economic profile of the geographic region. In countries without highly developed capital markets, shares and other variable-yield securities constitute a much smaller part of investment portfolios, e.g. Romania, Bulgaria, Cyprus, Greece, Latvia. A meaningful similarity is found in allocation models in: (1) Germany, Austria, the UK (life and non-life sectors)—portfolios including more shares and other variable-yield securities, corporate bonds and loans than in other EU countries; (2) Finland, Sweden, Denmark (life and non-life sectors)—portfolios including more shares and other variable-yield securities than in other EU countries; (3) Cyprus, Greece, Malta, Bulgaria (non-life sector), where investment portfolios include a significant proportion of bank deposits and property, whereas shares and other variable-yield securities constitute a very small part (Figs. 12.3 and 12.4).

The analysis of the structure of investment portfolio allocation in the EU insurance and reinsurance sector in 2005–2013 as an indirect systemic risk transmission channel showed that:

a) in both life and non-life sectors, debt instruments (mainly bonds) were a basic component of the investment portfolio: for the life sector, the median proportion of the portfolio ranged from 53.8 % in 2007 to 68.3 % in 2012, while for the non-life sector, it ranged from 53.7 in 2010 to 58.4 in 2011 (Tables 12.1 and 12.2);
b) the proportion of bonds in insurers' investment portfolios tended to increase in terms of both value and portfolio structure, notably for insurers operating in: Romania, Bulgaria, Ireland, Malta (life insurers) and in: Denmark, Ireland, Latvia, Luxembourg (non-life insurers) (Fig. 12.5);
c) the highest proportion of bonds in the investment portfolio was noticed for life insurers in: Italy, France, Lithuania, Hungary (on average, over 80 % of the portfolio in the period under analysis) and non-life insurers in: Belgium, Luxembourg, Lithuania, Hungary (median of over 70 % of the portfolio in that period) (Figs. 12.3 and 12.4);

Table 12.1 The structure of investment portfolio allocation in the life sector in EU countries in 2005–2013

Insurance companies in EU countries (percentile)	2005	2006	2007	2008	2009	2010	2011	2012	2013
Proportion of shares and other variable-yield securities and units in unit trusts in the investment portfolio (%)									
0.1	1.9	2.9	3.2	1.1	1.3	2.8	2.9	3.0	4.1
0.25	6.6	7.0	6.0	2.9	3.3	4.4	5.3	6.8	6.1
0.5	**10.4**	**14.3**	**12.1**	**8.0**	**7.8**	**9.1**	**10.6**	**10.6**	**12.0**
0.75	25.4	26.5	27.8	18.7	15.7	17.8	19.9	19.4	20.9
0.9	34.3	37.2	39.6	25.2	27.3	29.0	30.8	30.0	32.3
Proportion of debt securities and other fixed-income securities in the investment portfolio (%)									
0.1	41.3	35.2	33.9	39.6	40.0	43.2	42.0	40.2	40.2
0.3	51.0	46.9	37.9	45.7	50.1	46.9	51.2	51.6	50.6
0.5	**57.9**	**54.4**	**53.8**	**60.7**	**64.5**	**60.8**	**65.1**	**68.3**	**62.5**
0.75	78.3	79.3	75.4	77.4	79.3	79.3	82.4	82.4	82.0
0.9	88.0	86.5	85.7	86.8	86.0	85.6	87.9	83.5	85.3

Source: Own calculation based on EIOPA data

Table 12.2 The structure of investment portfolio allocation in the non-life sector in EU countries in 2005–2013

Insurance companies in EU countries (percentile)	2005	2006	2007	2008	2009	2010	2011	2012	2013
Proportion of shares and other variable-yield securities and units in unit trusts in the investment portfolio (%)									
0.1	4.0	4.27	6.6	1.6	3.0	4.1	2.3	2.5	3.8
0.25	7.7	8.09	9.0	6.2	7.0	6.8	5.9	4.9	6.8
0.5	**10.7**	**11.20**	**13.5**	**10.1**	**9.7**	**9.7**	**8.3**	**7.9**	**9.9**
0.75	17.2	18.74	19.4	14.9	14.6	12.4	10.1	12.0	15.5
0.9	25.9	27.05	28.4	22.9	25.6	30.0	23.6	23.0	27.1
The share of debt securities and other fixed income securities in the investment portfolio (%)									
0.1	31.4	26.8	27.6	28.4	28.8	32.2	35.4	36.0	32.4
0.3	47.6	43.3	33.3	43.7	46.8	43.2	47.1	47.9	43.1
0.5	**55.3**	**54.5**	**55.4**	**56.6**	**56.9**	**53.7**	**58.4**	**57.2**	**55.5**
0.75	62.7	60.3	60.2	62.0	64.0	60.8	65.6	64.5	67.0
0.9	70.5	70.5	67.3	71.3	69.6	75.3	80.6	81.0	73.6

Source: Own calculation based on EIOPA data

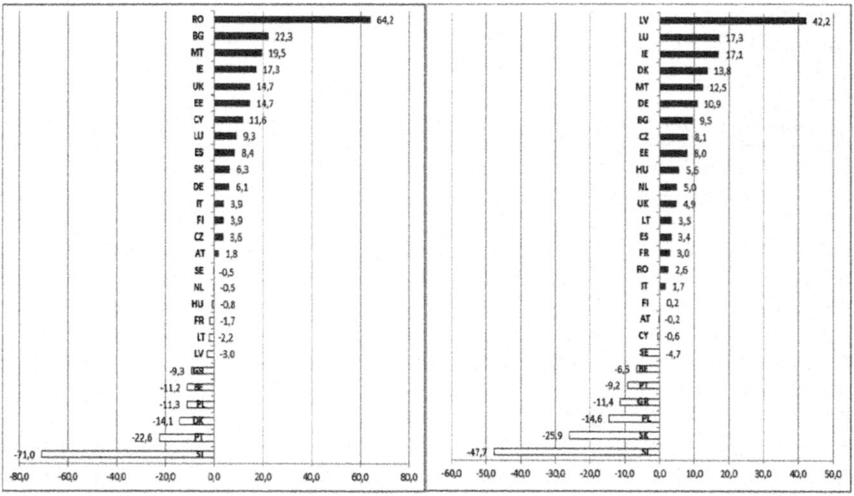

Fig. 12.5 Change in proportion of bonds (in %) in life insurers' (*left*) and non-life insurers' (*right*) investment portfolios in selected EU countries in 2013 in comparison to 2007 (*Source*: Own calculation based on EIOPA data)

d) the proportion of shares and other variable-yield securities in insurers' investment portfolios is clearly linked with the situation in stock exchange markets, being much higher in 2007 (before the economic downturn) in all analysed countries and much lower in 2009 (Tables 12.1 and 12.2),
e) the proportion of shares and other variable-yield securities gradually increased primarily in the life sector and changed slightly in the non-life sector in 2009–2013 (Tables 12.1 and 12.2);
f) the most dynamic growth in the period analysed was observed for the proportion of shares and other variable-yield securities in investment portfolios of insurance companies in: Latvia (life sector), Poland (life and non-life sectors), Spain (non-life sector) (Fig. 12.6);
g) the analysis based on statistical measures revealed that (Tables 12.1 and 12.2),
   a) the proportion of bonds in both life and non-life insurers' investment portfolios was less volatile—in one fourth of the analysed countries, bonds accounted for 77–82 % of life insurers' investment portfolios and 60–67 % in the non-life sector throughout the period concerned (except 2007);

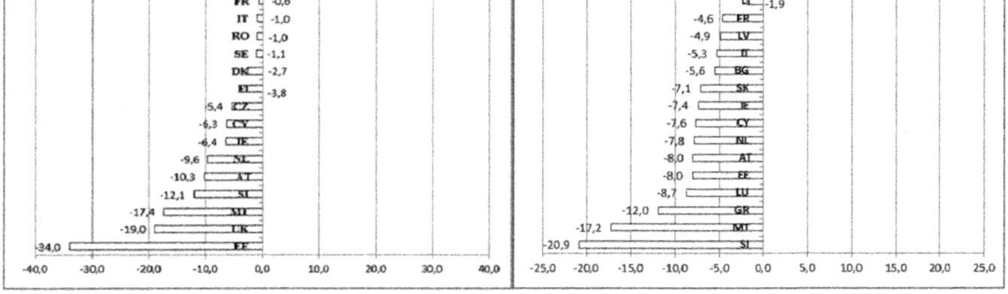

Fig. 12.6 Change in proportion of shares (in %) in life insurers' (*left*) and non-life insurers' (*right*) investment portfolios in selected EU countries in 2013 in comparison to 2007 (*Source*: Own calculation based on EIOPA data)

b) in some countries (10th percentile), especially those without highly developed capital markets, e.g. Romania, Bulgaria, Cyprus, Croatia, Latvia, Greece, Malta, the proportion of shares in the investment portfolio was negligible throughout that period.

In line with the so-called freedom of investment and *Prudent Person Role*, Solvency II abolishes the principle of territoriality, i.e. insurance risks located within the territory of the EU do not require that the assets covering technical provisions for those risks be located in the EU (or in certain member states). Territorial allocation of the assets portfolio should ensure their availability (art. 133, Directive 2009/138/EC). Restrictions on investment concentration in a single entity or a group of affiliates and in investment assets with low liquidity (i.e. property, instruments traded on non-regulated markets) do not apply to investments in government debt securities. The most significant risks in the insurance sector primarily include exogenous risks, i.e. low interest rate risk, default risk of government securities, macro-environment risk, and market risk in financial markets arising out of share price fluctuations. Exposure of insurance companies to default risk and interest rate risk is meaningful. The research shows that insurers invested primarily in bonds issued by public issuers, mainly government bonds. Where an investment portfolio is dominated by government debt securities, there is more exposure to political risk, and greater sensitivity to the public finance quality. At the same time, despite much turbulence, government guarantees are still often regarded as the most reliable instruments in the financial market. The debt crisis and deteriorating financial situation of many EU countries did not contribute to any major fall in the proportion of bonds in insurers' portfolios in view of the increased default risk. In the case of government securities, the perception of default risk is much more complex and very different from other instruments as factors that play a role are not only strictly economic. A high proportion of private bonds in investment portfolios is found in: Austria, the UK, Portugal, Spain, and Ireland (Fig. 12.7). A high share of bonds issued by the private sector in investment portfolios involves greater default risk and have been a source of vulnerability (increasing the probability of corporate defaults, widening of corporate spreads) (OECD 2011).

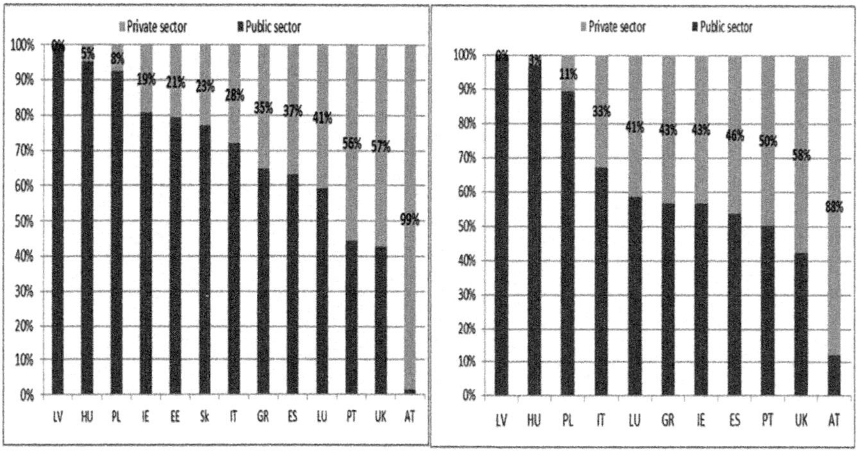

Fig. 12.7 The structure of bonds in life insurers' (*left*) and non-life insurers' (*right*) investment portfolios in 2013 (%) (*Source*: Own calculation based on OECD.StatiLibrary)

In most EU countries, portfolios of government bonds held by insurance companies include more than 60 % of national bonds (Long-Term Guarantees Assessment). This is important for financing public debt, especially in the current economic reality. At the same time, this essentially increases insurers' exposure to the default risk because the debt crisis and the difficult situation of public finances in a large number of member states make the risk of the issuer's insolvency most realistic (Russell 2011). In some countries, especially those with low levels of debt and countries that basically do not issue any government debt securities, insurers' portfolios of government bonds are dominated by bonds of foreign issuers, e.g. in: Luxembourg, Finland, Estonia, Lithuania, and Latvia (Fig. 12.8). Among foreign government debt securities held in insurers' investment portfolios, instruments with the highest investment rating account for the largest part (Czerwińska 2014, 41–56). Those are mostly government securities issued by: Germany (AAA rating), France (AA rating), Austria (AA+ rating), the Netherlands (AA+ rating), Belgium (AA rating), the UK (AAA rating). Italian government debt instruments with BBB rating are an exception. Bonds issued by the German government constitute 43 % and

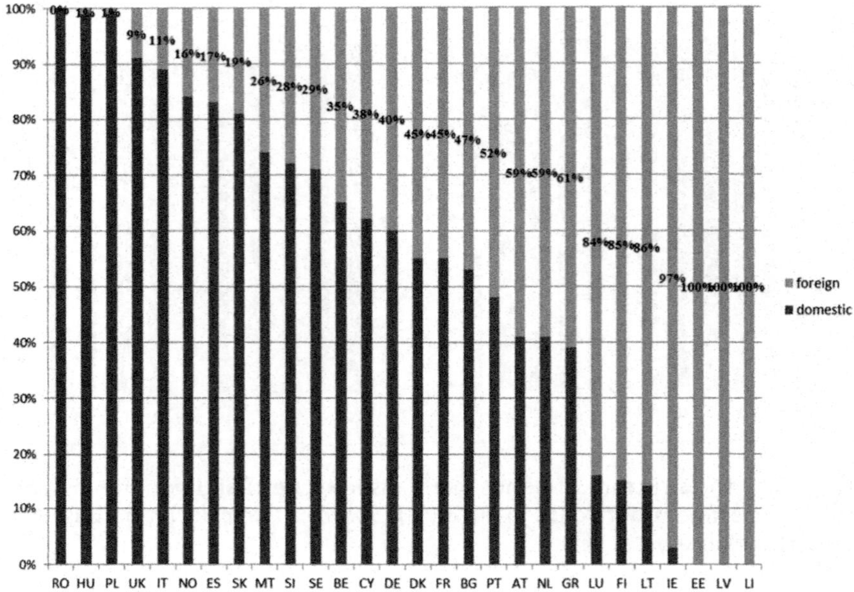

Fig. 12.8 The structure of insurers' portfolios of government bonds in the EU by country of allocation in 2011 (in %) (*Source*: Own calculation based on Long-Term Guarantees Assessment, Appendix 1: Methodology for the calibration of the adaptation (CCP) (as tested in the assessment), 14 June 2013 (EIOPA/13/297))

44 % of the portfolio of government debt securities in Finland and Liechtenstein, respectively, and over 30 % of such portfolios in Ireland, the Netherlands and Lithuania (Fig. 12.9).

4 Conclusions

The investment activity of insurance institutions that act on the market of treasury debt securities through long-term allocation of capital is of immense importance for the stability of the public sector. Insurance companies as investors accumulating long-term capital are vital for the financial system stability and, to a large extent, influence the situation in the capital market. In view of current increasing customers' price sensitivity,

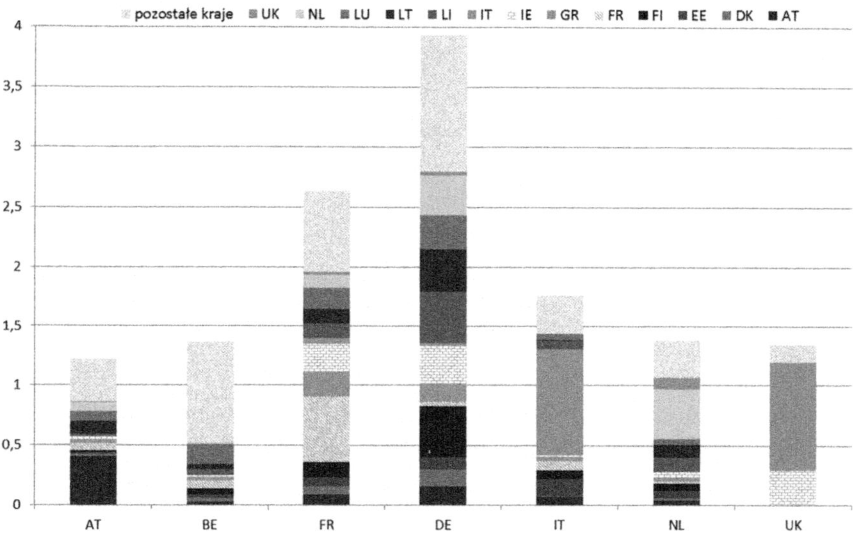

Fig. 12.9 Aggregated proportions of government debt securities issued by selected European Union countries in insurers' investment portfolios (by country of issuer) in 2011 (*Source*: Own calculation based on Long-Term Guarantees Assessment, Appendix 1: Methodology for the calibration of the adaptation (CCP) (as tested in the assessment), 14 June 2013 (EIOPA/13/297))

and willingness to compare different products, investment policy is essential for the competitive position of an insurance company. Under the new regulations of the Financial Stability Board (Recovery and Resolution Planning for Systemically Important Insurers..., FSB 2014), investment activities of insurance companies are identified as the so-called critical functions since they have an impact on the financial system stability, in particular: (1) by investing funds in instruments issued by the government, which is of particular systemic importance in the context of debt crisis in many EU member states; (2) by influencing the situation on the stock and bond markets, e.g. creating speculative bubbles, assets fire sale; (3) by transforming capital into investment in the real economy sector—an effect on the real economy through overrating some sectors at the expense of others, thus determining the cost of capital. Taking into account socio-economic reality, the significance of the insurance sector for the stability of the public sector is growing. Ensuring incessant demand for treasury debt securities in times of the public debt crisis in many (not only European) countries is particularly important for maintaining stability. Simultaneously, there is a worrying possibility of accumulation of debt of low investment quality and default on obligations towards the beneficiaries, especially under the circumstances of continuing low (or negative) interest rates and deflation.

The analysis of the investment portfolio allocation model in the insurance sector indicates particular sensitivity of this sector to low interest rate risk and default risk of government securities. The conducted research found that:

a) a simplification can be made to distinguish two investment portfolio allocation models among both life and non-life insurers: (1) the classical model—where debt securities and other fixed-income securities account for a dominant proportion, the remainder being mainly shares and other variable-yield securities (e.g. units in unit trusts), complemented chiefly by bank deposits, (2) the diversified model—where the proportion of debt securities and that of shares and other variable-yield securities in the portfolio are comparable, the remainder being loans or bank deposits;
b) investment portfolio allocation was more stable in highly developed markets, i.e. Germany, France, the UK, Austria, Sweden, Denmark, the Netherlands, and changed very dynamically in emerging markets, particularly in: Romania, Bulgaria, Slovakia, Latvia;
c) the proportion of bonds in both life and non-life insurers' investment portfolios was less volatile than that of shares;
d) exposure of insurance companies to default risk and interest rate risk is systemically important; the research shows that insurers invested primarily in debt securities and other fixed-income securities issued by public issuers, mainly government bonds.
e) The research carried out allows for identifying potential areas where insurers' investment activities influence the EU financial sector stability, which—in the context of planned macro-prudential regulations in the insurance sector—can guide works on prudential instruments and solutions for non-insurance, i.e. investment, activities.

Bibliography

Al-Darwish, A., Hafeman, M., Impavido, G., Kemp, M., & O'Malley, P. (2011). Possible unintended consequences of Basel III and Solvency II. IMF working paper (WP/11/187), IMF Working Paper. http://www.truesaleinternational.de/fileadmin/tsi_downloads/ABS_Research/Finanzmarktstabilisierung/imf_wp201108_Monetary_and_Capital_Markets_Department.pdf

Allen, F., & Santomero, A. M. (1998). The theory of financial intermediation, "Journal of Banking & Finance" nr 21 1461-1485.

Allen, W., & Wood, G. (2006). Defining and achieving financial stability. *Journal of Financial Stability, 2*, 152–172.

Artikis, T., & Voudouri, A. (2000). A stochastic integral arising in discounting continuous cash flows and certain transformed characteristic functions. *Applied Mathematical Letters, 13*, 87–90.

Blake, D. (1999). Portfolio choice models of pension funds and life assurance companies, similarities and differences. *Geneva Papers on Risk and Insurance, 24*, 327–357.

Brockett, P. L., Cooper, W. W., Golden, L. L., Rousseau, J. J., & Wang, Y. (2005). Financial intermediary versus production approach to efficiency of marketing distribution systems and organizational structure of insurance companies. *The Journal of Risk and Insurance, 72*(3), 393–412.

Chaim, R. M. (2010). Dynamic asset and liability management. In M. Micocci, G. N. Gregoriou, & G. B. Masala (Eds.), *Pension fund risk management: Financial and actuarial modeling*. New York: CRC Press/Chapman& Hall Book.

Charupat, N., & Milevsky, M. A. (2002). Optimal asset allocation in life annuities: A note. *Insurance: Mathematics and Economics, 30*, 199–209.

Chen, R., & Wong, K. A. (2004). The determinants of financial health of Asian insurance companies. *The Journal of Risk and Insurance, 71*(3), 469–499.

Commission Delegated Regulation (EU) 2015/35 of 10 October 2014 supplementing Directive 2009/138/EC of the European Parliament and of the Council on the taking-up and pursuit of the business of Insurance and Reinsurance (Solvency II). (2015). Official Journal of the European Union L 12, Vol. 58.

Crockett, A. (1997). *Theory and practice of financial stability*. Essays in International Finance, No. 203, 60 p.

Crockett, A. (2000). Marrying the micro- and macro-prudential dimensions of financial stability. Speech in Basel before the 11th International Conference

of Banking Supervisors. http://www.bis.org/speeches/sp000921.htm. Accessed 26 June 2015.
Cummins, J. D., & Weiss, M. (1993). Measuring cost efficiency in the property – Liability insurance industry. *Journal of Banking and Finance, 17*, 483–496.
Cummins, J. D., Grace, M. F., & Philips, R. D. (1999). Regulatory solvency prediction in property-liability insurance: Risk-based capital, audit ratios, and cash flow simulation. *Journal of Risk and Insurance, 66*, 417–458.
Czerwińska, T. (2014). Credit risk of insurance companies investment portfolio in the light of Solvency II requirements. *Journal of Management and Finance, 12*(1), 12–35.
Davis, E. (2001a). A typology of financial instability, OesterreichischeNationalbank. *Financial Stability Report, 2*, 92–110.
Davis, E. P. (2001b). Portfolio regulation of life insurance companies and pension funds. London: The Pensions Institute, Discussion paper PI-0101.
Daykin, C. D., & Hey, G. B. (1990). Managing uncertainty in a general insurance company. *Journal of the Institute of Actuaries, 117*, 173–277.
Dickinson, G. (2000). The implications of lower interest rates for insurers: A comment. *Geneva Papers on Risk and Insurance – Issues & Practice, 25*(1), 59–63.
Directive 2009/138/EC of the European Parliament and of the Council of 25 November 2009 on the taking-up and pursuit of the business of Insurance and Reinsurance (Solvency II). (2009).
Doherty, N. A., & Kang, H. B. (1988). Interest rates and insurance price cycles. *Journal of Banking and Finance, 62*, 199–214.
Eling, M., & Pankoke, D. (2014). Systemic risk in the insurance sector – What do we know? Working papers on risk management and insurance, No. 124, Ed. H. Schmeiser, University of St. Gallen.
Elton, E. J., & Gruber, M. J. (1992). Optimal investment strategies with investor liabilities. *Journal of Banking and Finance, 16*, 869–890.
Fitzpatrick, J. H. (2013). Cross industry analysis 28 G-SIBs vs. 28 Insurers – Comparison of systemic risk indicators. The Geneva Association.
Global Shadow Banking Monitoring Report. (2013). Financial Stability Board, Basel. http://www.financialstabilityboard.org/publications/r_121118c.htm
Halliwell, L. J. (2003). The valuation of stochastic cash flows. CAS Forum, pp. 1–68. www.casact.org/pubs/forum/03spforum/03spf001.pdf
Hancock, J., Huber, P., & Koch, P. (2001). Value creation in the insurance industry. *Risk Management and Insurance Review, 4*(2), 1–9.

Heyman, W. H., & Rowland, D. D. (2006). An investment management methodology for publicly held property/casualty insurers. *Journal of Applied Corporate Finance, 18*(1), 36–53.

Hilli, P., Koivu, M., & Pennanen, T. (2011). Cash-flow based valuation of pension liabilities. *European Actuarial Journal, 1*, 329–343. doi:10.1007/s13385-011-0023-3.

Hipp, C., & Plum, M. (2000). Optimal investment for insurers. *Insurance: Mathematics and Economics, 27*, 215–228.

Hodes, D. M., Neghaiwi, T., Cummins, J. D., Phillips, R., Sh. Feldblum, & The Financial Modeling of Property/Casualty Insurance Companies. 2003. https://www.casact.org/pubs/forum/96spforum/96spf003.pdf

Houben, A., Kakes, J., Schinasi, G. (2004). Toward a framework for safeguarding financial stability. IMF working papers (WP/04/101). International Capital Markets Department IMF.

Insurance and Financial Stability. (2011). IAIS.

Insurance companies: bridging low interest rates and higher capital requirements, w: Financial Stability Review. (2013). Deutsche Bundesbank, Frankfurt am Main. http://www.bundesbank.de

Insurance in 2015 – Determining the Position. 2015. New coordinates in the German-speaking insurance market. Institute of Insurance Economics, University of St. Gallen.

Josa-Fombellida, R., & Rincon-Zapatero, J. P. (2006). Optimal investment decisions with a liability: The case of defined benefit pension plans. *Insurance Mathematics and Economics, 39*, 81–98.

Liu Ch, S., & Yang, H. (2004). Optimal investment for an insurer to minimize its probability of ruin. *North American Actuarial Journal, 8*(2), 11–31.

Mishkin, F. S. (1999). Global financial instability: framework, events, issues. *Journal of Economic Perspectives, 13*(4), 3–20.

Mishkin, F.S. (2012). The economics of money, banking and financial markets, Global Edition. PEARSON.

Nielsen, J., & Sandmann, K. (1995). Equity-linked life insurance: A model with stochastic interest rates. *Insurance: Mathematics and Economics, 16*, 225–253.

Nissim, D. (2010). Analysis and valuation of insurance companies, Columbia Business School Center for excellence in accounting & security analysis.

Pennanen, T. (2011). Superhedging in illiquid markets. *Math Finance, 21*(3), 519–540.

Recovery and Resolution Planning for Systemically Important Insurers. (2014). Guidance on identification of critical functions and critical shared services, FSB, 16.

Risk Centre. (2014). The London School of Economics and Political Science, SRC special paper nr 3.

Russell, D. (2011). European insurance: Government crisis potentially leading to further dilution of Solvency II principles. J.P. Morgan Europe Equity Research.

Santomero, A. M., & Babbel, D. F. (1997). Financial risk management by insurers: An analysis of the process. *Journal of Risk and Insurance, 62*, 253–270.

Schinasi, G. (2004). Defining financial stability. IMF working paper no. WP/04/187. https://www.imf.org/external/pubs/ft/wp/2004/wp04187.pdf

Schmidli, H. (2005). On optimal investment and subexponential claims. *Insurance: Mathematics and Economics, 36*, 399–420.

Shin, H. S., & Shin, K. (2011). *Macroprudential policy and monetary aggregates.* NBER Working Paper No. 16836. Paper prepared for the 2010 Bank of Korea Research Conference.

Shiu, Y. (2004). Determinants of United Kingdom General insurance company performance. *British Actuarial Journal, 10*(5), 1079–1110.

Stenberg, F., Manca, R., & Silvestrov, D. (2006). Semi-Markov reward models for insurance. *Theory of Stochastic Processes, 12*, 239–254.

Systemic Risk in Insurance. (2010). *An analysis of insurance and financial stability.* Geneva: The Geneva Association.

The Impact of the Financial Crisis On The Insurance Sector And Policy Responses, OECD. (2011).

Thimann, Ch. (2014). How insurers differ from banks: A primer on systemic regulation. Systemic Risk Centre, The London School of Economics and Political Science. SRC special paper no. 3. http://www.systemicrisk.ac.uk/sites/default/files/downloads/publications/sp-3_1.pdf

Tobin, J. (1958). Liquidity preference as behavior toward risk. *Review of Economic Studies, 25*(2), 65–86.

Waring, M. B. (2004). Liability – Relative investing. Be dual duration – Matched and on the surplus efficient frontier. *The Journal of Portfolio Management, Summer.*

Weiss, M. A. (2010). Systemic risk and the U.S. insurance sector. Working paper, National Association of Insurance Commissioners, Washington, DC.

Weiss, G. N. F., & Muhlnickel, J. (2014). Why do some insurers become systemically relevant? *Journal of Financial Stability, 13*, 95–117.

Wilkie, A. D. (1986). A stochastic investment model for actuarial use. *Transactions of the Faculty of Actuaries, 39*, 391–403.

Yang, H., & Zhang, L. (2005). Optimal investment for insurer with jump-diffusion risk process. *Insurance: Mathematics and Economics, 37*, 1066–1096.

Ziemba, W. T., & Mulvey, J. M. (1998). *Worldwide asset and liability modeling.* Cambridge: Cambridge University Press.

13

Personal Income Tax and the Risk of Revenue Fluctuations in the European Union

Bogdan Mróz and Mariusz Sokołek

1 Introduction

Tax collection has been the subject of heated disputes for as long as taxes have been around, and the questions asked have always been about the same things: how to define the tax base, whom to tax, with or without concessions, at what rate, under a progressive, regressive or perhaps flat-tax regime? There doesn't seem to be a single fix for all those points of dispute, even though opinions can be heard—among academics and taxpayers alike—claiming this to be a simple matter. Some argue that government interference should be strictly limited and that neither high tax rates nor rate-cutting reforms have any major impact on the economy, especially as measured by GDP (Gross Domestic Product) growth.

B. Mróz (✉)
Warsaw School of Economics, Warszawa, Poland

M. Sokołek
University of Social Sciences, Warszawa, Poland

K. Raczkowski (ed.), *Risk Management in Public Administration*,
DOI 10.1007/978-3-319-30877-7_13

Others see in taxes a powerful instrument for the state which, they reason, should impose high progressive rates in order to facilitate income redistribution between various social groups and taxpayer categories.

Despite years and decades of trying, financial and economic theories have yet to find a golden mean for tax rates, i.e. such level of rational fiscal burdens which would please the taxpayer and the finance minister alike. In 1945 C. Clark[1] defined the limit of a country's taxable capacity as 25 % of GDP (Weralski 1990, 211), even if actual figures in many economies were higher. Many factors contribute to influence this value, including the economic system, structure of the economy, the current stage of a business cycle, or how the tax revenue is spent (Gomułowicz 1995, 1). The taxable capacity can surely be regarded as exceeded when an increase in tax rates, far from producing a corresponding increase in tax receipts, in fact brings about their fall. In taxpayers' reactions, 'certain symptoms tend to emerge in accordance with the law of increasing resistance: activity is shifted from the official economy to the informal sector, employment in the latter is on the rise, propensity to invest is down, while passive and active tax resistance grows more intense' (Gomułowicz 1995, 1).

Both parties to the dispute give strong arguments either for state intervention (especially through tax regulations) and against it, and nothing seems to indicate that this debate, which has continued throughout the history of taxes, can be satisfactorily settled. All the more so as taxes, whose burden is perceptibly shouldered by citizens, have become an important element of electoral games played by politicians—and hardly any general election passes without a fierce debate on tax reforms. Meanwhile matter-of-fact discussion, devoid of orthodox ossification and ideological obstinacy, might produce new insights and solutions, bringing us closer to an optimal design of the tax system.

---

[1] Colin Grant Clark (1905–1989), the British economist and statistician, who worked in the UK and in Australia, a pioneer of using the gross national product as the basis for studying national economies. Together with A.G.B. Fisher he developed one of the earliest models of economic development, the Fisher-Clark model, where a tertiary sector of the economy (services) is separated from the sectors of manufacturing and agriculture (previously, services and manufacturing were believed to be interdependent).

Attempts to develop a close-to-ideal tax model are frequently undertaken in the context of personal income taxation. By burdening citizens in a direct way, this tax is highly sensitive to changes, especially changes which broaden the taxpayer population, increase the tax base or raise the tax rates. Meanwhile, taxpayers would like to see new concessions introduced and the rates cut down. Income tax is applied to as large a group of taxpayers as possible—all those who receive any income, from whatever source. Most frequently this is income from work (under various types of employment contract); other sources include social transfers, lease, dividends, sale of, or rent from, personal property, etc. The addition of a source of income to, or its exemption from, the roster of taxable items serves to pursue certain goals but it also gives rise to certain consequences—it either adds to or takes away from fiscal revenues.

In the present article, after taking a historical look at taxes and their evolution, the authors attempt to identify the impact of ongoing changes in the tax structure and the level of fiscal revenues in EU countries. The discussion is confined to the taxation of the populace, where there are great numbers of taxable persons. Emotions tend to run high with this kind of tax, and therefore decisions about it should be taken only after a thorough analysis of statistical data from available sources (in this publication, OECD and Eurostat numbers are quoted).

Ongoing discussions about the tax system designs and globalisation of European economies offer encouragement to pursue comparative studies of different economies and systems. Such comparisons have a not inconsiderable value for integration processes.

2 A Brief Historical Overview of Taxation, with Emphasis on Taxes Levied on the Population in EU Countries

A part and parcel of state organization at any stage, taxes today form the bulk (80–90 %) of fiscal revenues. According to common definitions, tax is a compulsory and non-refundable financial charge collected by the state in order to obtain budget revenue to cover public expenditures. The tax system, being compulsory, is based on legal norms from which arise the rights and duties of the parties, i.e. the state authority and the taxpayers. These norms place the latter under an obligation to pay, and a failure to pay triggers enforcement action by the former.

The earliest indications of public levies having been collected (clay tablets at burial sites) were found in the south of Egypt, dating back to an estimated 3200–3000 BCE. These were in-kind taxes, provided in the form of agricultural produce such as linen or oil. In ancient Mesopotamia, such taxes emerged around 2500 BCE (cf. Lymer 2002, 39).

References to taxes, serving to support priesthood and collected for redistribution purposes, can be found in the Bible, too. The Gospel of Mathew tells us about Pharisees asking Jesus if it was lawful to pay taxes to Caesar, and about Jesus' unambiguous reply, 'Render unto Caesar the things that are Caesar's.'

In Athens at the time of the Solonian reforms, ca. 596 BCE, the first property taxes emerged, assessed initially in relation to land, and then cattle, houses, furniture and, finally, money holdings. In ancient Egypt ca. 700 BCE, and much later under the Emperor Augustus (6 BCE), the testator was required to bequeath to the state 5 % of the value of his property. As of the end of the twelfth century, property taxes were common in Italy and the Netherlands. These taxes basically formed the backbone of tax systems in European states.

The late eighteenth century saw the first moves towards taxing income, directed at the bourgeoisie. In Great Britain, under the Triple Assessment Act of 1798, an income tax was imposed to finance the war against Napoleon. That tax was rescinded in 1802 but just a year later it was introduced again, only to be suspended in 1816, with the end of the Napoleonic wars. The tax was collected from all citizens with annual income in excess of 60 pounds; and to annual income of above 200 pounds a top rate of 10 % applied. With the average income staying below 20 pounds a year, most Britons were not liable for the tax, whose initial basic rate stayed at 3 %. With the passage of time, tax revenues were used to finance not only wars but—increasingly—social expenditure as well. Towards the end of the nineteenth century the income tax rate was raised to 10 %, and by 1918 it had reached 30 %. Further increase in tax burdens was brought by World War II—initially to 40 %, and later to 50 %. Simultaneously, the tax-free allowance was being lowered, thus effectively increasing the taxpayer population.

The income tax *sensu stricto* has been a fixed element of European states' fiscal policy since the latter half of the nineteenth century (in the UK it was resumed in 1840), with most countries imposing relatively high tax rates (of which more later). In the USA, income tax was born in 1862, its purpose being to finance the civil war. The initial tax rates were 3 % and 5 %, for incomes exceeding $600 and $10,000, respectively. In 1913 the rate ran at 7 %, and Congress was vested with the right of laying down the tax rules. In addition to that, in 1909, a 1 % corporate tax was introduced. Canada saw the launch of income taxation in 1917.[2]

As previously mentioned, two diametrically different views of taxes have been espoused by economists. According to one school of thought, the state should have a strong presence in the economy, especially through tax regulations. Within this current, a system which held sway in the formative time of capitalism, between the sixteenth and the eighteenth centuries, was mercantilism—with a classical example of a mercantilist state being provided by England. The chief theoreticians included Thomas Mun, sir Josiah Child, and (in France) Jean Bidon, an ardent advocate of state intervention and high tariffs to stave off imports (Spychalski 1999, 73–74). But the state's robust interference, as propounded by the mercantilists, failed to stand the test of time and lost to the principle of economic liberalism, which underlies classical economics. Opponents of an authoritarian role for the state argue that if more money is left with the citizenry, they will manage it in a much better way than the government would—thus contributing to an increase in investments and consumption, which in turn will broaden the tax base and, consequently, produce higher tax revenues. Among prominent economic liberals was the founder of classical economics, Adam Smith, who laid down his views in a two-volume magnum opus, *An Inquiry into the Nature and Causes of the Wealth of Nations*, published in 1776. Smith called for the state not to interfere with the economy, and for the market mechanism to regulate economic relations between individual and public interests. He believed that the state should confine its role to that

[2] This historical overview of income tax is based on: Lymer 2002.

of a night watchman, focusing on key public works (road construction, education, and elementary health care), defence, justice and indispensable public administration.

Discussions of the state's presence in the economy resumed with the economic crises of the early twentieth century, when the 'invisible hand' of the market proved incapable of preventing deterioration in economic trends. The Cambridge economist, J. M. Keynes, spearheaded a new approach to the state's role, which stood in opposition to the liberal view. His work, *The General Theory of Employment, Interest and Money*, published in 1936, ushered in what is sometimes termed the 'Keynesian revolution' in economics. Regarding the tax system, Keynes argued that it should be used by the state as one of the instruments influencing the propensity to consume, and he advocated progressive taxation (Keynes 1985, 410).

Strong interventionism was espoused outside Europe, too. In the USA, the Franklin D. Roosevelt administration pursued a policy known as the New Deal, with a progressive tax system employed to achieve social goals via budgetary redistribution (Sommers 2012).

A barrage of criticism of state interventionism and Keynes's theory came from the US economist and 1976 Nobel Prize winner, Milton Friedman, who presented his views on limiting the role of fiscal policy in a 1968 publication in *The American Economic Review* (Friedman 1968, 1–2). Friedman threw new light on the market mechanism's impact on the economy, and he blazed the trail for monetarist theory. He was the first to demand that the progressive income tax—then reigning supreme—be abandoned in favour of proportional tax, and in the early 1960s he proposed the introduction of a flat tax rate (Friedman 1968, 174–176). In his view, a low flat tax rate on taxable income, for example 20 %, would produce more revenue than a complex tax scale with a plethora of deductions, exemptions, etc. Taxpayers' benefits would include savings on the costs of hiding income from tax authorities. In other words, such policy would curtail the extent of the informal sector of the economy. Overall, the entire economy would stand to gain, tax considerations playing a perceptibly smaller role in resource allocation. The only ones to lose would be members of certain professions—lawyers, accountants, public officials, and legislators—who could then turn to activities that are more productive than filling out tax returns, or searching for and closing legislative loopholes (Friedman and Friedman 1994, 296).

A host of other neoliberal ideas followed. One of them, a theory developed by R.E. Luckas, posited the helplessness of government intervention in the economy: human behaviours are always a step ahead of government reaction, and all government moves are delayed (Luckas 1972, 103–124). In this context, however, the focus today is on an active fiscal policy, where the condition of the economy is analysed on a continuous basis and government reacts speedily. In the tax field, this policy boils down to actively influencing the economy through tax rate changes, revisions of tax rules, imposition or removal of tax concessions, and changes in subsidy rules. But the government's reaction to changes in the business environment will also be late, due to factors which include the time-consuming nature of legislative procedures: changes in law must be preceded by proper diagnosis, detailed statistical analysis and selection of adequate tools, all of which requires time. And finally, a certain *vacatio legis* is needed, as is the verification of whether the assumed outcomes have indeed been achieved (Bain and Howells 1987, 93–94).

An important contribution to discussions about income tax was made by A.B. Laffer, who proposed to stimulate the economy by lowering taxes and introducing tax concessions. The 'Laffer curve' theory posits a direct linkage between tax rates and budget revenue. As the former increases, so does the latter —but only up to a critical point at which rate increases begin to be accompanied by decreases in revenue (Begg et al. 2003, 480). The Laffer curve has been often cited by opponents of higher taxes, and it underlay the Reagan administration's tax reform in 1981, when marginal tax rates were lowered from 14 to 11 % for bottom rates and from 70 to 50 % for top rates (but with as many as 14 tax brackets retained). Such reforms provided a major impulse to ideas about reducing the burden of taxes levied on the population. Initiated by Margaret Thatcher and Ronald Reagan, the radical tax reforms led to a situation where 'governments across the globe have been racing to lower tax rates on productive behaviour. Personal and corporate income tax rates have been dramatically reduced, and the tax burden on saving and investment has been lowered (Mitchell, 2008, 1).' Another consequence was that flat tax rates began to be applied to the taxation of income.

The idea of a flat tax was originally put forward by R. Hall and A. Rabushka from Stanford University's Hoover Institution, in a 1981 article in Wall Street Journal and in the book *The Flat Tax*, first published in 1983 and reprinted later on (Hall and Rabushka 1995). Averring that their plan was not just an 'academic abstraction', the two questioned in particular the notion of vertical equity, or tax progression, where the tax rate goes up as the taxpayer's income increases (Ostaszewski et al. 2008, 117–118).

D.J. Mitchell, in his *The Global Flat Tax Revolution*, professes that this revolution has the effect of changing the world (Mitchell 2008, 8), and he points out that the flat tax has been introduced in countries pursing an aggressive course in the economy, such as Estonia or Hong Kong. Their performance, he argues, validates the Laffer curve claim: the economic growth and high budget revenues come as a result of reasonable tax rates. Finding it paradoxical that this fiscal arrangement, although masterminded in the USA, is most frequently found in Central and Eastern Europe, among post-communist countries, Mitchell proposes that Western Europe countries should consider introducing the flat tax themselves (Mitchell 2008, 8–9).

3 Income Tax Evolution in EU Countries

A common feature of personal income tax (PIT) systems in UE-15[3] is tax progression, even though there are differences in the numbers and values

[3] **EU symbols** –member states of the European Union.

EA symbols—eurozone members.

EU-27 European Union—(BE, BG, CZ, DK, DE, EE, IE, EL, ES, FR, IT, CY, LV, LT, LU, HU, MT, NL, AT, PL, PT, RO, SI,

SK, FI, SE, UK).

EU-28 European Union (BE, BG, CZ, DK, DE, EE, IE, EL, ES, FR, HR, IT, CY, LV, LT, LU, HU, MT, NL, AT, PL, PT, RO,

SI, SK, FI, SE, UK).

EU-15 European Union (BE, DK, DE, IE, EL, ES, FR, IT, LU, NL, AT, PT, FI, SE, UK).

EA-17 Euro area (BE, DE, IE, EE, EL, ES, FR, IT, CY, LU, MT, NL, AT, PT, SI, SK, FI).

EA-18 Euro area (BE, DE, IE, EE, EL, ES, FR, IT, CY, LV, LU, MT, NL, AT, PT, SI, SK, FI).

of tax brackets and in tax rates. Another similarity is the tax-free allowance, reflecting concern for taxpayers' ability-to-pay and complying with the welfare state idea. The tax-free allowance corresponds to the poverty threshold, or the minimum level of income needed to meet the basic needs (Krajewska 2012, 91).

Despite differences in territorial size and historical experiences, the countries in the EU have similar tax systems, influenced as they are by social, civilizational and political determinants and sets of values. PIT codes are not harmonized at the EU level—each member state being free to apply its own PIT scope, rates, deductions and allowances—but the general rules on the scope and subject of taxation show many similarities. As far as indirect taxes are concerned, the EU's principle of free movement of goods and services has effectively enforced harmonization, especially in the case of VAT (value-added tax), as required by European treaties under Article 116 TFEU (ex Article 96 TEC).[4]

As a result of integration processes in Europe, a shared classification of taxes was developed, in line with OECD requirements (Table 13.1).

Table 13.2 shows what proportion of the total tax burden in EU member states is accounted for by the main types of taxes combined, i.e. direct and indirect taxes (but excluding compulsory social contributions, or CSC).

As demonstrated by Table 13.2 figures, the combined share of direct and indirect taxes as a proportion of total tax burden dropped in 2012 (compared to 1995) in 13 member states, most pronouncedly in Lithuania. In Greece this proportion was stable over the whole period, although changes could be noticed in individual years. On the other hand, in 14 member states, the direct and indirect taxes (combined) increased their share of total tax burden, with Sweden leading the pack (up 9.4 percentage points).

As found in a 2005 study by Mendoz and Tesar, a high share of indirect taxes in total taxation in individual countries is conducive to eco-

[4] The Treaty on European Union (TUE) is an international agreement binding on—currently—27 European member states and providing, along with the Treaty on the Functioning of the European Union (TFUE), the legal foundation for the establishment and operation of the European Union.

Table 13.1 The OECD classification of taxes

OECD classification of taxes						
Taxes on income, profit and capital gains	Social security contributions	Taxes on payroll and workforce	Taxes on property	Taxes on goods and services	Other	
1.Tax on personal income, profit and capital 2. Corporate income tax 3. Other income taxes	1. Payable by employees 2. Payable by employers 3. Payable by sole traders and persons not in employment	1. Payable by employers	1. Recurrent taxes on immovable property 2. Recurrent taxes on net wealth 3. Estate, inheritance and gift taxes 4. Taxes on financial and capital transactions 5. Other	1. On value added 2. On sales 3. Excises 4. Profits from fiscal monopolies 5. Import duty 6. Export taxes 7. Other	Other taxes on economic activity	Other tax burdens

Source: Authors' compilation based on Revenue…, 1981, 35–36

Table 13.2 Total taxes as % of total taxation, 1995–2012

Member state	1995–2012						Change	Ranking in 2012
	1995	2000	2003	2006	2009	2012		
Belgium	67.3	69.2	68.1	69.5	66.6	67.8	0.5	16
Bulgaria	68.9	65.6	66.8	73.0	73.4	74.2	5.3	6
Czech Republic	58.7	55.6	55.9	55.8	55.5	55.5	−3.2	28
Denmark	97.8	96.4	97.5	97.6	97.9	98.1	0.3	1
Germany	57.6	58.7	56.5	58.7	59.7	60.2	2.6	23
Estonia	66.1	64.7	65.6	67.1	63.1	64.7	−1.4	19
Ireland	85.0	86.1	84.7	85.1	79.5	84.7	−0.3	2
Greece	67.9	69.7	63.5	66.2	65.8	67.9	0.0	15
Spain	63.3	64.7	64.0	67.1	59.5	63.2	−0.1	20
France	56.5	63.5	61.9	62.6	60.1	62.1	5.6	22
Croatia	–	68.2	68.1	68.6	66.6	67.9	−0.3	14
Italy	68.5	71.2	70.4	70.4	68.1	69.2	0.7	12
Cyprus	75.7	77.9	78.1	78.1	75.4	74.1	−1.6	7
Latvia	63.9	66.5	68.9	71.2	68.0	69.8	5.9	11
Lithuania	74.0	66.9	67.9	69.6	58.0	59.7	−14.3	24
Luxembourg	73.5	74.3	71.8	72.4	70.2	70.7	−2.8	9
Hungary	63.9	66.6	66.8	66.4	67.1	66.2	2.3	17
Malta	77.2	77.0	79.4	81.7	82.3	82.0	4.8	4
Netherlands	60.5	61.4	63.1	64.1	63.8	59.0	−1.5	26
Austria	64.0	65.8	66.3	65.4	65.0	65.4	1.4	18
Poland	69.5	60.3	60.3	63.9	64.3	62.3	−7.2	21
Portugal	73.7	74.3	72.8	73.8	70.9	72.0	−1.7	8
Romania	72.2	63.3	65.9	66.0	65.1	68.8	−3.4	13
Slovenia	57.0	61.9	62.8	63.4	59.9	59.5	2.5	25
Slovakia	62.7	58.5	58.0	59.9	56.4	55.8	6.9	27
Finland	69.2	74.8	73.3	72.1	70.1	70.2	1.0	10
Sweden	74.4	75.8	77.2	80.7	82.6	83.8	9.4	3
United Kingdom	82.5	83.2	81.9	81.6	80.6	81.2	−1.3	5
EU-28 averages								
Weighted			67.3	68.7	66.5	67.6	0.3	
arithmetic			69.2	70.4	68.4	69.1	−0.1	
EU-27 averages								
weighted	65.5	68.5	67.3	68.7	66.5	67.6	2.1	
arithmetic	69.3	69.4	69.2	70.5	68.5	69.2	−0.1	

(continued)

Table 13.2 (continued)

Member state	1995–2012						Change	Ranking in 2012
	1995	2000	2003	2006	2009	2012		
EA-18 averages								
Weighted	61.1	64.5	63.4	64.8	62.9	63.9	2.8	
arithmetic	67.4	68.9	68.3	69.4	66.9	67.7	0.3	
EA-17 averages								
weighted	65	64.5	63.4	64.8	62.9	63.9	−1.1	
arithmetic	69.2	69.0	68.3	69.3	66.9	67.6	−1.6	

Source: Authors' compilation based on, Taxation..., 2013, 174–176

nomic growth. And high revenues from income taxes are indicative of a high level of a country's economic development. On average, the revenue from indirect and direct taxes accounts for close to 70 % of all budget revenues and nearly 90 % of tax revenue. Exceptions include countries such as Denmark, Sweden and the UK, where these taxes represent as much as 80 % or even 90 % of total budget revenues.

A more detailed breakdown of taxation is presented in Table 13.3, which shows the percentage contributions of direct taxes and indirect taxes, with the biggest subsets of respectively VAT and PIT being singled out. The data cover the period of 1995–2012.[5]

It can be seen from Table 13.3 that the contribution of VAT, an indirect tax, to total taxation rose in most EU member states (22), while it dropped in just four of them. The highest increases, of over 10 percentage points, were seen in Romania and Bulgaria. The picture is different when it comes to PIT, whose share of total tax burden increased in only 12 member states, while decreasing in 16. But the overall average for EU-28 did not show any major fluctuations.

The structure of taxation can also be analysed in terms of the proportions of individual taxes (in this case, VAT and PIT) as percentages of gross domestic product (GDP) (Table 13.4).

An analysis of Table 13.4 yields conclusions which are similar to those from Table 13.3. VAT's share of GDP grew in most EU member states—especially in Cyprus, but also in countries such as Bulgaria, Romania,

[5] These data are published in Eurostat's 2013 report. The 2014 report contains newer figures, but they go back only to 2000, rather than 1995 (as in the 2013 publication).

Table 13.3 Major types of taxes (indirect, direct, VAT, PIT) as a percentage of total taxation

	Indirect taxes as % of total taxation					VAT as % of total taxation					Direct taxes as % of total taxation					PIT as % of total taxation				
Member state	1995	2000	2006	2012	Change 1995/ 2012	1995	2000	2006	2012	Change 1995/ 2012	1995	2000	2006	2012	Change 1995/ 2012	1995	2000	2006	2012	Change 1995/ 2012
Belgium	29.3	30.2	30.6	29.4	0.1	15.1	15.9	15.9	15.8	0.7	38.0	38.9	38.9	38.3	0.3	30.8	29.4	27.9	28.2	–2.6
Bulgaria	37.7	43.8	56.1	55.3	17.6	22.5	26.4	34.9	33.8	11.3	29.1	21.9	16.9	18.8	–10.3	13.5	12.7	8.4	10.6	–2.9
Czech Republic	32.9	32.1	30.7	35.0	2.1	16.8	18.4	18.0	20.6	3.8	25.8	23.5	25.1	20.5	–5.3	12.9	13.0	11.8	10.8	–2.1
Denmark	34.9	34.9	36.4	35.0	0.1	19.4	19.4	20.8	20.7	1.3	63.5	61.8	61.8	63.6	0.1	53.9	51.9	50.1	50.9	–3.0
Germany	27.2	27.3	28.0	29.2	2.0	16.3	16.6	16.5	18.6	2.3	30.4	31.4	30.7	31.0	0.6	23.5	22.9	21.3	22.5	–1.0
Estonia	36.2	39.7	44.1	43.7	7.5	26.5	27.2	29.6	26.6	0.1	30.0	25.0	23.0	20.9	–9.1	23.3	22.1	18.2	16.5	–6.8
Ireland	43.9	42.9	44.1	39.1	–4.8	21.2	23.0	24.1	21.7	0.5	41.2	43.2	41.0	45.6	4.4	31.3	29.8	27.3	33.8	2.5
Greece	44.1	40.9	40.1	37.6	–6.5	21.1	20.9	22.5	21.0	–0.1	23.8	28.8	36.2	30.3	6.5	12.5	14.4	14.6	20.6	8.1
Spain	33.2	35.1	34.9	32.9	–0.3	16.3	18.1	17.8	17.0	0.7	32.1	31.2	33.4	32.6	0.5	24.1	19.5	19.5	23.8	–0.3
France	37.5	35.8	35.3	34.9	–2.6	17.5	16.9	16.6	15.6	–1.9	19.7	28.3	27.7	27.7	8.0	22.3	19.0	17.9	18.8	–3.5
Croatia	–	–	50.1	50.8	0.7	–	–	32.7	34.4	1.7	–	–	18.5	17.1	–1.4	–	–	9.8	10.3	0.5
Italy	31.1	36.4	36.0	34.5	3.4	13.9	15.6	14.9	13.9	0.0	37.6	34.8	34.4	34.7	–2.9	26.2	27.5	26.2	27.8	1.6
Cyprus	42.6	40.6	48.0	42.7	0.1	17.2	18.2	27.1	25.2	8.0	33.1	37.2	30.2	31.4	–1.7	14.8	12.2	12.8	11.3	–3.5
Latvia	42.4	41.8	43.3	42.2	–0.2	27.8	23.9	28.1	25.5	–2.3	21.5	24.7	27.9	27.6	6.1	16	18.8	19.8	20.4	4.4
Lithuania	43.5	40.6	38.0	41.9	–1.6	26.9	24.4	25.3	28.1	1.2	30.4	27.2	31.8	18.0	–12.4	22.7	24.8	22.5	12.9	–9.8
Luxembourg	31.9	35.8	35.7	33.0	1.1	14.0	14.3	16.1	18.2	4.2	41.6	38.4	36.7	37.7	–3.9	21.7	18.3	20.9	22.0	0.3
Hungary	42.8	41.8	41.0	47.1	4.3	18.4	22.3	20.4	23.9	5.5	21.1	24.9	25.3	19.2	–1.9	16	18.5	18.1	13.8	–2.2
Malta	45.9	44.1	45.4	40.7	–5.2	23.1	21.0	23.8	23.3	0.2	31.3	32.9	36.3	41.3	10.0	18.9	17.5	20.9	20.1	1.2
Netherlands	29.3	31.4	33.6	30.4	1.1	16.2	17.3	18.9	17.8	1.6	31.2	30.0	30.5	28.6	–2.6	19.2	15.0	17.8	19.6	0.4
Austria	35.8	35.3	34.5	34.4	–1.4	18.6	18.8	18.4	18.6	0.0	28.3	30.6	31.0	31.1	2.8	22.4	23.3	23.2	23.5	1.1
Poland	38.3	38.8	42.8	40.4	2.1	16.8	21.3	24.1	22.5	5.7	31.6	22.1	22.2	22.3	–9.3	22.6	13.5	13.6	14.1	–8.5
Portugal	45.6	43.5	47.0	42.9	–2.7	23.4	24.6	26.6	26.2	2.8	28.1	30.8	268.0	29.1	1.0	18.1	17.1	16.3	18.3	0.2
Romania	33.7	40.2	44.9	47.2	13.5	18.0	21.4	27.8	30.1	12.1	38.5	23.1	21.1	21.6	–16.9	25.1	11.4	10.0	12.3	–12.8

(*continued*)

Table 13.3 (continued)

Member state	Indirect taxes as % of total taxation					VAT as % of total taxation					Direct taxes as % of total taxation					PIT as % of total taxation				
	1995	2000	2006	2012	Change 1995/ 2012	1995	2000	2006	2012	Change 1995/ 2012	1995	2000	2006	2012	Change 1995/ 2012	1995	2000	2006	2012	Change 1995/ 2012
Slovenia	39.5	42.2	39.8	38.8	–0.7	–	23.1	22.3	21.8	–1.3	17.7	19.8	23.8	20.8	3.1	15	15.0	15.0	15.6	0.6
Slovakia	35.9	36.7	39.2	36.1	0.2	20.8	20.4	25.5	21.5	0.7	26.8	21.9	20.7	19.7	–7.1	8.9	9.9	8.6	9.2	0.3
Finland	31	29.5	31.8	33.3	2.3	17.4	17.4	19.9	20.8	3.4	38.2	45.3	40.3	37.0	–1.2	31.1	30.6	30.3	29.4	–1.7
Sweden	33.2	31.9	34.7	42.3	9.1	18.9	16.7	18.5	21.0	2.1	41.2	43.9	46.0	41.4	0.2	34.8	35.2	37.5	34.4	–0.4
United Kingdom	38.8	37.8	35.2	38.5	–0.3	18.4	17.9	18.0	20.5	2.1	43.7	45.4	46.5	42.7	–1.0	29.5	29.4	28.6	27.1	–2.4
EU-28 averages																				
weighted	–	–	34.3	34.5	0.2	–	–	17.8	18.1	0.3			34.6	33.4	–1.2			23.3	23.9	0.6
arithmetic	–	–	39.3	38.9	–0.4	–	–	22.3	22.3	0.0			31.2	30.4	–0.8			20.3	20.7	0.4
EU-27 averages																				
weighted	32.9	33.9	34.3	34.5	1.6	16.8	17.3	17.7	18.1	1.3	32.4	34.8	34.6	33.5	1.1	23.4	24.3	23.3	24.0	0.6
arithmetic	37.0	37.5	38.9	38.5	1.5	17.6	20.0	21.9	21.9	4.3	32.4	32.1	31.7	30.9	–1.5	22.3	21.2	20.7	21.0	–1.3
EA-18 averages																				
weighted	–	32.9	33.6	32.8	–0.1		17.0	17.1	17.0	0.0		31.8	31.5	31.4	–0.4		22.3	21.3	22.9	0.6
arithmetic	–	37.2	38.4	36.5	–0.7		19.6	21.4	20.5	0.9		31.8	31.1	31.4	–0.4		20.1	19.9	21.2	1.1
EA-17 averages																				
weighted	31.8	32.9	33.6	32.8	1.0	16.4	17.0	17.1	17.0	0.6	29.6	31.9	31.5	31.4	1.8	21.3	22.3	21.3	22.9	1.6
arithmetic	36.5	36.9	38.1	36.1	–0.4	18.6	19.4	21.0	20.2	1.6	31.1	32.3	31.3	31.6	0.5	20.8	20.2	19.9	21.2	0.4

Source: Authors' compilation based on Taxation..., 2013, 172–188, Taxation..., 2014, 174–189

Table 13.4 VAT and PIT as percentage of GDP, 1995–2012

Member state	VAT as % of GDP					PIT as % of GDP				
	1995	2000	2006	2012	Change 1995/2012	1995	2000	2006	2012	Change 1995/2012
Belgium	6.6	7.2	7.1	7.2	0.6	13.5	13.2	12.4	12.7	–0.8
Bulgaria	7	8.3	10.7	9.4	2.4	4.2	4.0	2.6	3.0	–1.2
Czech Republic	6	6.2	6.4	7.2	1.2	4.6	4.4	4.2	3.8	–0.8
Denmark	9.4	9.6	10.3	10.0	0.6	26.3	25.6	24.9	24.5	–1.8
Germany	6.5	6.8	6.4	7.3	0.8	9.4	9.5	8.2	8.8	–0.6
Estonia	9.6	8.4	9.1	8.7	–0.9	8.4	6.8	5.6	5.3	–3.1
Ireland	6.9	7.2	7.7	6.2	–0.7	1.2	9.4	8.8	9.7	8.5
Greece	6.1	7.2	7.1	7.1	1.0	3.6	5.0	4.6	6.9	3.3
Spain	5.2	6.2	6.5	5.5	0.3	7.7	6.7	7.2	7.7	0.0
France	7.5	7.4	7.3	7.0	–0.5	5.3	8.4	7.9	8.5	3.2
Croatia	–	–	12.2	12.3	0.1	–	–	3.6	3.7	0.1
Italy	5.5	6.5	6.2	6.1	0.6	10.4	11.4	10.9	12.2	1.8
Cyprus	4.6	5.5	9.7	8.9	4.3	4.0	3.7	4.6	4.0	0.0
Latvia	9.2	7.1	8.6	7.1	–2.1	5.3	5.6	6.1	5.7	0.4
Lithuania	7.4	7.5	7.6	7.7	0.3	6.2	7.7	6.8	3.5	–2.7
Luxembourg	5.2	5.6	5.8	7.1	1.9	8.0	7.2	7.5	8.6	0.6
Hungary	7.5	8.9	7.6	9.4	1.9	6.6	7.3	6.8	5.4	–1.2
Malta	6.1	5.7	7.9	7.8	1.7	5.0	4.8	6.9	6.7	1.7
Netherlands	6.5	6.9	7.4	7.0	0.5	7.7	6.0	6.9	7.7	0.0
Austria	7.7	8.1	7.6	8.0	0.3	9.3	10.0	9.6	10.1	0.8
Poland	6.2	6.9	8.1	7.3	1.1	8.4	4.4	4.6	4.6	–3.8
Portugal	6.9	7.6	8.6	8.5	1.6	5.4	5.3	5.3	5.9	0.5
Romania	4.9	6.5	7.9	8.5	3.6	6.9	3.5	2.8	3.5	–3.4
Slovenia	4.7	8.6	8.5	8.2	3.5	5.8	5.6	5.7	5.8	0.0
Slovakia	8.4	7.0	7.5	6.1	–2.3	3.6	3.4	2.5	2.6	–1.0
Finland	7.9	8.2	8.7	9.2	1.3	14.2	14.5	13.3	13.0	–1.2
Sweden	9.1	8.6	8.9	9.3	0.2	16.7	18.1	18.1	15.2	–1.5
United Kingdom	6.4	6.5	6.5	7.3	0.9	10.1	10.7	10.3	9.6	–0.5
EU-28 averages										
weighted			7.0	7.1	0.1			9.2	9.4	0.2
arithmetic			8.0	7.9	–0.1			7.8	7.8	0.0
EU-27 averages										
weighted	6.6	7.0	7.0	7.1	0.5	9.2	9.8	9.2	9.4	0.2
arithmetic	6.7	7.3	7.8	7.7	1.0	8.4	8.2	8.0	8.0	–0.4

(*continued*)

Table 13.4 (continued)

Member state	VAT as % of GDP 1995	2000	2006	2012	Change 1995/2012	PIT as % of GDP 1995	2000	2006	2012	Change 1995/2012
EA-18 averages										
weighted		7.0	6.8	6.9	−0.1			8.5	9.2	0.7
arithmetic		7.1	7.6	7.4	0.3			7.4	7.9	0.5
EA-17 averages										
weighted	6.5	7.0	6.8	6.9	0.4	8.5	9.1	8.5	9.2	0.7
arithmetic	6.3	7.1	7.6	7.4	1.1	7.7	7.7	7.5	8.0	0.3

Source: as in Table 13.2

Slovenia and Hungary. Actually it is the emerging economies, admitted to the block only recently, which form the bulk of this group. As for PIT's proportion of GDP, it fell in 14 countries, most noticeably in Poland, and also in Romania, Lithuania, Estonia and Hungary—again, the new entrants with expanding economies. Decreases in PIT's share of GDP were also seen in Denmark, Sweden, Finland and the UK.

Another factor influencing changes in the structure of budget revenues in individual member states is the changing numbers of tax brackets. These numbers have been declining across the EU, reflecting moves to simplify income tax codes and lower the tax burdens on the higher earners. Some have actually argued, citing the theory of tax equity, that smaller diversification—as reflected in fewer tax brackets and, especially, in a flat tax rate for all taxpayers, no matter their income level—signifies an equitable distribution of tax burdens and represents a more just tax system. In Italy, for example, the number of tax brackets has been reduced by as many as 27 over the past 30 years. In Spain, 23 tax brackets were shorn off, with Belgium, Sweden and Greece coming next on the list (Table 13.5).

In step with the curtailment of tax-bracket numbers in the period under review, i.e. from 1995 to 2014, the top marginal tax rates on personal incomes were being gradually brought down. Only a few member states—among them Ireland, Malta, Austria and Slovenia—did not change their top rates, and in only one country, the UK, was the top PIT rate actually increased (by 5 percentage points). Elsewhere in

Table 13.5 Numbers of tax brackets in selected EU member states, 1981–2014

Member state	1981	1990	2000	2010	2014	Change
Belgium	24	7	7	5	5	**−19**
Czech Republic	–	–	4	1	1	**−3**
Denmark	3	3	3	2	2	**−1**
Germany	–	3	3	4	4	**1**
Estonia	–	–	1	1	1	**0**
Ireland	5	3	2	2	2	**−3**
Greece	15	9	5	8	3	**−12**
Spain	30	16	6	4	7	**−23**
France	12	12	6	4	4	**−8**
Italy	32	7	5	5	5	**−27**
Luxembourg	21	24	16	16	19	**−2**
Hungary	–	4	3	2	1	**−3**
Netherlands	10	3	4	4	4	**−6**
Austria	11	5	4	3	3	**−8**
Poland	–	–	3	2	2	**−1**
Portugal	12	5	5	8	5	**−7**
Slovenia	–	–	5	3	4	**−1**
Slovakia	–	–	7	1	2	**−5**
Finland	–	5	6	4	5	**0**
Sweden	18	4	2	2	2	**−16**
United Kingdom	6	2	3	3	3	**−3**

Source: Trends..., 2012, 30, Taxing..., 2015, 159–523

the EU the top rates of personal income tax went down—including a decrease by 40 percentage points in Bulgaria (over 1995–2014). And once again, one can see that countries with robust economies, such as Bulgaria, the Czech Republic, Poland, Hungary, Lithuania, Romania and Slovakia, lowered their top income tax rates to a perceptible degree (Table 13.6).

The tax-free allowance (income tax threshold) is an important element of the income tax system, common for progressive tax arrangements. It is not present in arrangements involving the flat tax rate, which is applied to all incomes with no deductions. The tax-free allowances in EU member states have been changing, too, as can be seen in Table 13.7.

Over 2006–2014, the personal income tax threshold rose across the EU, although its absolute levels differ from one member state to the other. The highest tax-free allowance is provided in Sweden (which also boasts the highest absolute increase), followed by Spain and Cyprus.

Table 13.6 Top tax rates in EU member states, 1995–2014

Member state	1995	2000	2006	2012	2014	Change
Belgium	60.6	60.6	53.7	53.7	53.7	–6.9
Bulgaria	50.0	40.0	24.0	10.0	10.0	–40.0
Czech Republic	43.0	32.0	32.0	15.0	22.0	–21.0
Denmark	65.7	62.9	62.3	55.4	56.6	–9.1
Germany	57.0	53.8	44.3	47.5	47.5	–9.5
Estonia	26.0	26.0	23.0	21.0	21.0	–5.0
Ireland	48.0	44.0	42.0	48.0	48.0	0.0
Greece	45.0	45.0	40.0	49.0	46.0	1.0
Spain	56.0	48.0	45.0	52.0	52.0	–4.0
France	59.1	59.0	45.8	50.6	53.3	–5.8
Croatia	42.9	41.3	53.1	47.2	47.2	4.3
Italy	51.0	45.9	44.1	47.3	47.9	–3.1
Cyprus	40.0	40.0	30.0	35.0	35.0	–5.0
Latvia	25.0	25.0	25.0	25.0	24.0	–1.0
Lithuania	33.0	33.0	27.0	15.0	15.0	–18.0
Luxembourg	51.3	47.2	39.0	41.3	43.6	–7.7
Hungary	44.0	44.0	36.0	20.3	16.0	–28.0
Malta	35.0	35.0	35.0	35.0	35.0	0.0
Netherlands	60.0	60.0	52.0	52.0	52.0	–8.0
Austria	50.0	50.0	50.0	50.0	50.0	0.0
Poland	45.0	40.0	40.0	32.0	32.0	–13.0
Portugal	40.0	40.0	42.0	49.0	56.5	16.5
Romania	40.0	40.0	16.0	16.0	16.0	–24.0
Slovenia	50.0	50.0	50.0	41.0	50.0	0.0
Slovakia	42.0	42.0	19.0	19.0	25.0	–17.0
Finland	62.2	54.0	50.9	49.0	51.5	–10.7
Sweden	61.3	51.5	56.6	56.6	56.9	–4.4
United Kingdom	40.0	40.0	40.0	50.0	45.0	5.0
EU-28 averages	**47.2**	**44.6**	**39.9**	38.7	39.4	–7.8
EU-27 averages	**47.4**	**44.8**	**39.4**	38.4	39.2	–8.2
EA-18 averages	**47.7**	**45.9**	**40.6**	42.5	43.8	–3.9
EA-17 averages	**49.0**	**47.1**	**41.5**	43.6	45.0	–4.0

Source: Taxation…, 2013, 172–188, Taxation… 2014, 32–33

At the other end of the spectrum—with the lowest level of tax-free allowance, and also its lowest absolute increase—comes Poland. In 2015, an attempt was made to raise the Polish threshold to some €2,000, but it was defeated in Parliament. Even if that proposal had been granted, the tax-free allowance in Poland would have still remained the lowest in Europe.

Table 13.7 Tax-free allowance (income tax threshold) in selected EU member states in 2006 and 2014 (in euro terms at the exchange rate for the calendar year)

Member state	2006	2014	Change
Belgium	6,800.0	8,590.0	1,790.0
Czech Republic	1,265.0	3,822.0	2,557.0
Germany	7,664.0	8,354.0	690.0
Greece	10,000.0	12,000.0	2,000.0
Spain	3,400.0	12,450.0	9,050.0
Italy	7,500.0	8,000.0	500.0
Cyprus	10,000.0	19,500.0	9,500.0
Luxembourg	9,750.0	11,265.0	1,515.0
Malta	7,130.0	8,500.0	1,370.0
Austria	10,000.0	12,000.0	2,000.0
Poland	698.0	725.0	27.0
Finland	12,000.0	16,300.0	4,300.0
Sweden	32,850.0	45,700.0	12,850.0
United Kingdom	6,880.0	12,800.0	5,920.0

Source: Wach 2006,41–44 (data for 2006); Praca 2015, 9–107 (data for 2014)

4 Conclusion

The longstanding argument about the state's role in the economy is thrown into particularly sharp relief when tax burdens on the populace enter the picture. Taxes are an indispensable feature of any state, enabling it to carry out its functions but also directly affecting citizens' finances. Where should the limit be set for state intervention in economic processes, and especially in the sphere of taxation? This recurring question has been heatedly debated by scholars and researchers representing different currents of contemporary economics. The so-called Washington Consensus, promoted by the World Bank, the IMF and other influential institutions, put emphasis on tight fiscal policy and tax reforms towards a broader tax base and lower rates of taxation (Williamson 1993, 1332). In the past three decades tax codes were frequently modified along these lines, although these tax reforms can hardly be described as thorough going. Rather, the focus was on broadening the tax base and trimming tax concessions, credits and deductions. It was only with a broader tax base that the income tax rates, particularly for top earners, could be reduced. Initially rates tended to run in the 14–70 % range, to be brought down later to 15–40 % (Belka 1991, 102). While as recently as the early 1990s many countries in Europe had a dozen-plus tax rates and brackets (and even 25, as in Luxembourg), today's standard is between two and six. Luxembourg still stands out, this time with over ten tax rates (The Essential Guide… 2012, 1). The tax-free allowances have been revised, too. Looking at how systems to tax the population evolved between 1995 and 2012, a number of conclusions can be drawn:

(a) Personal income tax reforms seek to reduce the tax rates.
(b) With a view to simplifying tax assessment and collection, the numbers of tax brackets have been drastically reduced.
(c) Cuts in tax rates and fewer tax brackets do not lead to a simultaneous reduction of tax-free allowances, which in some cases have actually increased perceptibly.
(d) The reductions of tax rates and increases in tax-free allowances are usually accompanied by moves to eliminate tax breaks and broaden the tax base.
(e) Revenue losses from lower direct taxes are offset by increased proportions of indirect taxes (especially VAT).
(f) While these reforms were carried out, in most EU member states no drastic budget revenue decreases were registered, which means that the risk of budget revenues fluctuating in response to the reforms was insignificant.

It looks like the objectives for the tax reforms espoused by the OECD in the late 1980s, and put into practice from the early 1990s, have been gradually achieved. They were underpinned by the premise that too high tax burdens restrict economic activity and bring output down. It has also been proposed that the tax system should be streamlined towards cutting down on tax administration and collection costs. According to the theory of equity in taxation, people with a similar ability to pay taxes should be taxed in the same way and the tax system should help level off inequalities in after-tax income (Hagemann and Montador 1988, 187; Kay 1990, 89).

Reforms seeking to liberalize tax codes are thus the right way to follow. Where personal income is taxed according to taxpayer-friendly rules, the costs of labour shrink, with employment rising and unemployment going down. Private capital is consequently put to effective uses, stimulating the economy via job creation and higher personal income tax revenues. All this warrants the conclusion that the risk of budget revenue fluctuations in response to taxpayer-friendly changes in income tax codes is relatively small—and worth taking, with economic growth in mind.

Bibliography

Bain, K., & Howells, P. (1987). *Government and the economy*. London: Longman.

Begg, D., Fischer, S., & Dornbusch, R. (2003). *Mikroekonomia*. Warszawa: PWE.

Belka, M. (1991). Reaganomika, Sukces czy porażka, Ossolineum, Wrocław–Warszawa–Kraków.

Friedman, M. (1962). *Capitalism and freedom*. Chicago: University of Chicago Press.

Friedman, M. (1968). *The role of monetary policy* (p. 3). Princeton: American Economic Review.

Friedman, M., & Friedman, R. (1994). *Wolny wybór*. Sosnowiec: Panta.

Gomułowicz, A. (1995). Granice fiskalizmu. Glosa, 1.

Hagemann, R., & Montador, B. (1988). Tax reform in OECD countries, motives, constraints and practices. *OECD Economic Studies, 10*, 185–226.

Hall, R., & Rabushka, A. (1995). *The flat tax*. Stanford: Hoover Institution Press.

Kay, J. A. (1990). Tax policy: A survey. In A. Krajewska (Ed.), The Economic Journal, *100*, 18–75. Warszawa: Podatki w Unii Europejskiej, Polskie Wydawnictwo Ekonomiczne.

Keynes, J. M. (1985). *Ogólna teoria zatrudnienia, procentu i pieniądza*. Warszawa: PWN.

Krajewska, A. (2012). *Podatki w Unii Europejskiej, długookresowe tendencje w reakcje na kryzys* (2nd ed. vol. 91). Warszawa: Polskie Wydawnictwo Ekonomiczne.

Luckas, R. E. (1972). Expectations and naturality of money. *Journal of Economic Theory, 4*, 103–124.

Lymer, A. (2002). History of taxation. In A. Lymer, et al. (Ed.), *The international taxation system*. Boston: Kluwer Academic Publishers.

Mitchell, D. J. (2008). The global flat tax revolution. *Prosperitas, VIII*(I), 1–12.

OECD. (1981). *Revenue statistics of OECD member countries 1965–1980*. Paris: OECD.

Ostaszewski, J., et al. (2008). *Finanse*. Warszawa: Difin.

Praca w UE – podatki i składki. (2015, March). *PWC*.

Sommers, A. T. (2012). Ends and means: Market vs. government, economic impact 2. In A. Krajewska (Ed.), *Podatki w Unii Europejskiej, długookresowe tendencje w reakcje na kryzys* (2nd ed.). Warszawa: Polskie Wydawnictwo Ekonomiczne.

Spychalski, G. B. (1999). *Zarys historii myśli ekonomicznej*. Warszawa: PWN.

Taxation Trends in the European Union. (2013). Taxation and customs.

Taxation Trends in the European Union. (2014). Taxation and customs.

Taxing Wages 2013–2014. (2015). Special feature: Modelling the tax burden on labour income in Brazil, China, India, Indonesia and South Africa. Paris: OECD.

The Essential Guide for Individuals in Luxembourg. Tax, Social Security. (2012). *Labor environment, immigration*. Deloitte, 1.

Trends in Personal Income Tax and Employee Social Security Contribution Schedules. (2012). *Taxing wages*. Paris: OECD.

Wach, K. (2006). *Systemy podatkowe krajów Unii Europejskiej*. Kraków: Oficyna Wydawnicza.

Weralski, M. (1990). Współczesna teoria społecznych granic opodatkowania. Państwo i Prawo.

Williamson, J. (1993). Democracy and the "Washington consensus". *World Development, 21*(8), 1329–1336.

14

VAT Fraud in Selected European Union Countries and Its Possible Macroeconomic Implications

Czesław Jędrzejek

1 Introduction

This work is devoted to analysis of VAT compliance and the efficiency of measuring and analysing 'compliance gaps', which is a powerful first step to addressing non-compliance. VAT collection efficiencies, mostly in the three neighbouring countries of Poland, the Czech Republic, and Slovakia, are presented. Table 14.1 shows summarized characteristics of these countries.

Based on OECD statistics, Poland experienced the fastest GDP growth in the last among these three countries particularly since 2008. In 2009 the Polish government came with the nickname of Poland as a 'Green Island' government in 2009 (as the only country in the EU without negative GDP growth) in the post-crisis period (Fig. 14.1).

It is to be taken into consideration that since 2014 the EU switched European System of National and Regional Accounts measures from

C. Jędrzejek (✉)
Poznan University of Technology, Poznan, Poland

K. Raczkowski (ed.), *Risk Management in Public Administration*,
DOI 10.1007/978-3-319-30877-7_14

Table 14.1 Population and development statistics for the Czech Republic, Poland, and Slovakia

Country	Population [mln]	Standard VAT rate	GDP purchasing power parity	GDP purchasing power parity per capita [$bln]	Export [$bln]	Trade balance [$bln]	Human Development Index	Gini coefficient	Average annual wages [$]
Czech Rep.	10.5	21 %	319.6	30,366	174.6	21.2	0.87	24.9	15266.3
Poland	38.5	23 %	943.3	24510	220.0	3.3	0.83	32.7	13689.5
Slovakia	5.4	20 %	149.4	27584	86.8	4.7	0.83	25.7	15239.1

Source: OECD https://data.oecd.org, Wikipedia: Human Development Index, Gini coefficient represent 2013 data, the other entries represent year 2014

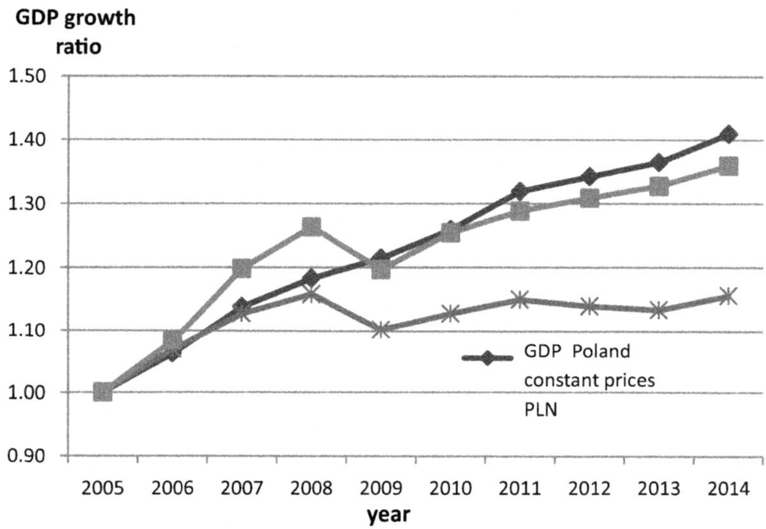

Fig. 14.1 GDP growth ratio for the Czech Republic, Poland, and Slovakia in the 10 years since 2005 (*Source*: OECD https://data.oecd.org)

the ESA 95 to ESA 2010. Accordingly, GDP values have been recalculated. The Polish GDP values increased by between 1.2 and 1.7 % in the period of 2010–2013 (GUS 2014b, 9), these corrections being among the highest in the UE. The yearly GDP growth ratio in Fig. 14.1 changed little.

While the Czech Republic and Slovakia have recovered to pre-crisis collection levels in GDP terms, the weak performance of Poland continues. The goal is to assess reasons for this situation from several angles:

(a) political
(b) economic
(c) revenue, statistics and judicial system management
(d) technical (analytic IT support)

First, there is a comparison between the economic situations in the three countries in question, in order to exclude economic reasons for the fiscal performance difference. Next, the fiscal statistics of Poland, the Czech Republic, and Slovakia are presented; then this study concentrates on the analytic capability of the administrations in the three countries. The final section analyses the effects of VAT fraud on macro-economic accounts.

2 Fiscal Background

2.1 General Characteristics

The Czech Republic, and Slovakia are trying to move up in the ranking within the class of the advanced EU countries. The Czech Republic (the most advanced of the three) and Slovakia are classified as advanced countries (Poland is still emerging) and have higher ratings than Poland, and so are considered fiscally more stable. On 10 December 2013, the European Council issued a new recommendation for Poland and an excessive deficit procedure (EDP).

On 19 June 2015, the Council closed excessive deficit procedures for Poland, which happens when a country reduces its deficit below the EU's 3 % of GDP reference value (Poland's general government deficit amounted to 3.2 % of GDP in 2014). However, the Council found Poland to be eligible for specific provisions under the excessive deficit procedure dealing with systemic pension reforms, because its deficit is close to the reference value and its debt-to-GDP ratio is below the 60 % reference value for government debt (but only because people's private retirement funds in pension-plan portfolios are being transferred to the government ZUS fund). Typically, toward the end of a year the Ministry of Finance blocks planned expenses. E.g. in 2014, out of the budget plans for science of 7bn PLN (Polish złoty), only 5bn PLN was spent.

The Czech Republic and Slovakia also went through the excessive deficit procedures. These procedures were closed (with the conclusion that the countries do not have the excessive deficit) in June 2014 because:

(a) the general government deficit in the Czech Republic was brought down and reached 1.5 % of GDP in 2013 and the debt-to-GDP ratio did not exceed 46 %, and in 2014 it fell;
(b) the general government deficit in Slovakia was brought down to 2,8 % of GDP in 2013 and the debt-to-GDP ratio reached 55.4 % of GDP in 2014.

These fiscal data are much more favourable compared to those of Poland.

2.1.1 Tax Structure for Selected EU Countries Poland, Czech Republic, and Slovakia

Table 14.2 presents a comparison of tax structures for selected older EU countries with those of Poland, the Czech Republic, and Slovakia. Indirect tax and VAT structures of Poland, Czech Republic, and Slovakia are very similar to each other and the OECD average.

Table 14.2 Comparison of tax structure for selected EU countries (values are expressed in national currencies in bn) in 2013; also ratios with regard to total tax values are given

	Poland	Czech Rep.	Slovakia	UK	Belgium	Greece	Italy	Portugal	OECD[a]
Taxes on goods and services (indirect tax, IT)	187.4	463.5	7.2	180.1	42.5	24.8	177.6	21.0	
VAT	114.4	286.1	4.3	113.9	26.9	13.9	96.1	14.0	
IT/TOTAL [%]	36	34	35	33	25	38	26	40	33
VAT/TOTAL [%]	22	21	21	21	15	21	14	26	20

Source: OECD, Consumption Tax Trends (10 Dec 2014) http://stats.oecd.org
[a]Unweighted average

2.2 Vat Collection Measures

There is an effort throughout the world towards being able to estimate and understand the difference between tax due and tax collected but even in advanced economies this proves difficult (IMF May 2015, 1).

The extent of compliance with legal obligations should be the predominant concern in any country. It affects the revenue yield, efficiency and fairness of any tax system. Non-compliance undermines revenue, distorts competition (putting the non-compliant at an advantage), and compromises equity. In a weak revenue management regime (Poland being a prime example) governments anxious for revenue may concentrate their efforts on more compliant taxpayers, amplifying the distortions and leading to strengthening of organized financial crime. Perception of unequal treatment can become a media theme and at the same time encourages resistance to measures that could enforce conditions for wider willingness to comply (IMF April 2015, Ex. Summary page).

2.2.1 Recent VAT Collection Data for Poland

Poland experiences several problems with VAT collection. After 2011 the standard VAT rate increased from 22 to 23 %. In spite of this and the fact that final consumption expenditure growth for 2011–2013 was positive, the decrease in VAT revenues in 2013 was dramatic. In Fig. 14.2 VAT collection details are presented.

The Polish Ministry of Finance claimed that the decrease in VAT revenue was due to the economy slow-down after the worldwide crisis of 2008, increased exports, and a growing informal economy and VAT fraud.

In reality, most of the effect came from a sharp rise in VAT refunds over the period 2010–2013.

It can be argued that the ratio of VAT tax refund values to gross VAT revenues is the best measure of VAT fraud because it is independent of GDP, total consumption expenditure and the values of consumer price changes. One can claim that weak VAT collection data are partly due to, say, deflation, but the ratio is insensitive to this. It is characteristic of the Polish Ministry of Finance that, having next to zero analytical ability, and

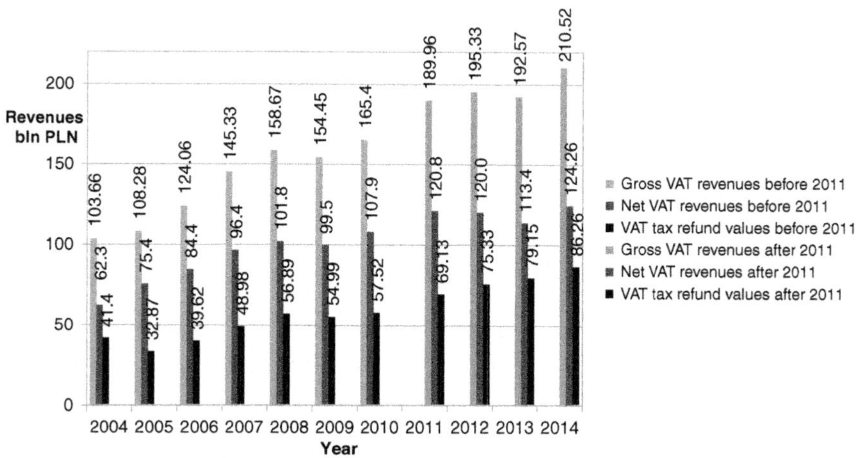

Fig. 14.2 Gross VAT revenues, net VAT revenues and VAT refund values between 2004 and 2013 (*Source*: The Polish Ministry of Finance)

having hidden the raw tax financial data for years, it only disclosed the scale of VAT refunds in February 2014.

The rise in VAT revenues in 2014 is illusory. It happened because of a large rise in the number of VAT refunds that the Polish tax authority had delayed to pay (a similar 44 % rise happened in the UK in the fiscal year 2012–2013) (FT 2013). The ratio of C values to gross VAT revenues stayed as high as in 2013 (41 %) (Fig. 14.3).

$$\text{Ratio} = \text{VAT refunds} / \text{VAT revenues}$$

Unfortunately, there is little work and data on what determines the level of refunds. The (IMF 2005) work presented data from the 1999 to 2001 period and a model was used that had not account for fraud, explicitly.

2.2.2 Recent VAT Collection Data for Czech Republic and Slovakia

The latest complete data for the Czech Republic and Slovakia are not available as they were for Poland. Slovakia had a large decrease in net VAT revenues in 2012.

Overall, VAT tax collection in the two countries increased over 2009–2014 (Fig. 14.4).

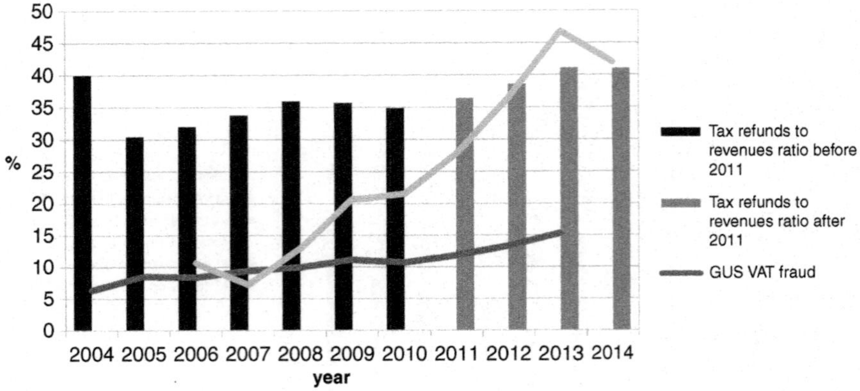

Fig. 14.3 The ratio of VAT tax refund values to gross VAT revenues, between 2004 and 2014 (*left axis*) (*Source*: The Polish Ministry of Finance data. The data described on the *right axis* represents VAT fraud (GUS, private information) and (PWC 2014) calculated tax gap)

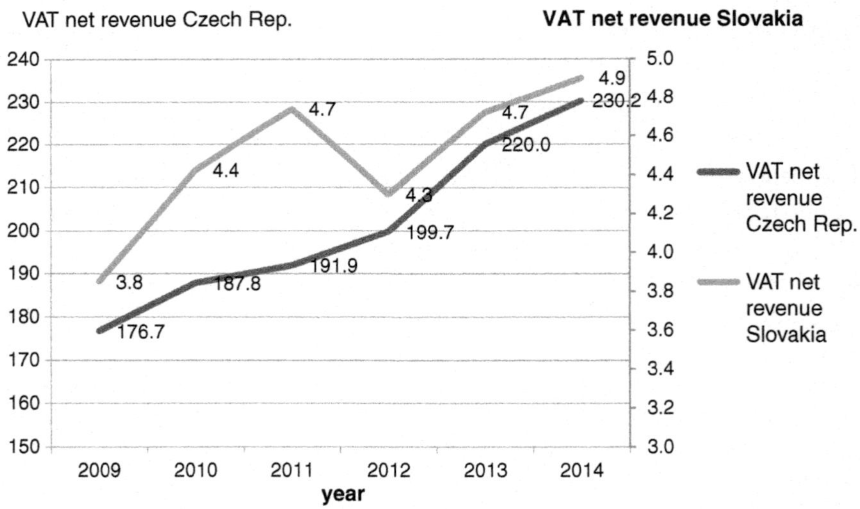

Fig. 14.4 Net VAT tax revenues in national currencies 2009–2014 for: Czech Republic in KCZ (*left axis*) and Slovakia tin EUR (*right axis*) (*Source*: The Polish Ministry of Finance data. Sources: MFSR (2015); (Kurzy 2016))

In the Czech Republic in 2013 GDP growth was negative in constant prices but VAT collection increased by 10 % compared with 2012. As for the first half of 2015 the Czech VAT collection amounted to 106.2bn

CZK (Czech koruna) compared to 111.5bn CZK, which is a 4.79 % drop (Kurzy 2016). In the same period Poland collected 88.21bn PLN in indirect taxes (MF 2015), over three billion PLN less than in the same period in 2014: 92.39bn PLN. Since in current prices the result is worse than in 2011, Poland, at best, by the end of 2015 will achieve the level of collection of 2011, after more than a 10 % increase in GDP. It is telling that the Finance Ministry of the Czech Republic openly wrote about a delay in VAT refunds in November and December 2014, which explains that drop in VAT revenues in the first half of 2015. The Polish Finance Ministry instead inaccurately suggested that a real improvement in VAT collection occurred, and has appeared to make decisions based on an incorrect judgment of the financial situation.

Finally, we should look at VAT in the three analysed countries as percentages of GDP. It has been judged that it would be more appropriate to use GNP or related concept gross national income (GNI), (preferred by the World Bank and Eurostat). GNI represents total primary income receivable by resident institutional units: compensation of employees, taxes on production and imports less subsidies, property income (receivable less payable), gross operating surplus and gross mixed income.

In Table 14.3 VAT values in relations to GDP and GNI (in millions of national currencies for 2013) are presented. VAT to GDP/GNI ratios are in percentages.

Poland has the lowest GNI/GDP ratio, which indicates that the ratio of average wages to GDP is also very low (and falling). This is characteristic of the economy of low innovation capacity, and a consequently low-paid workforce. If the Polish GNI to GDP ratio were equal to that of

Table 14.3 VAT to GDP/GNI ratios

Country	GNI	GDP	GNI/ GDP ratio	VAT/ GDP	VAT/ (GDP*VAT(rate))	VAT/GNI
Czech Rep.	3661746	4,086,260	0.896	5.40	0.26	6.02
Poland	1367426	1,662,678	0.822	6.82	0.30	8.29
Slovakia	64388	73,593	0.875	6.42	0.32	7.34

Source: *Eurostat* (2015a, 2015b)

the Czech Republic then the VAT revenues (taking the average VAT rate) would be larger by 20.2 bl PLN.

Nevertheless, the results seem to indicate that VAT/GDP ratio is highest for Poland.

However, if this ratio is divided by the standard VAT rate, that ratio is largest for Slovakia. For the Czech Republic, the OECD data for the VAT/GDP ratio: 7.1 % in 2012 shown in Table 14.1. A1.6 (OECD 2014, 39), is not compatible with the results in Table 14.3.

2.3 Analysis of the VAT Gap

So far this chapter has been devoted to the last direct measures of VAT collection efficiency. Now we will consider several measures that relate to VAT liability. The first one is the VAT gap—the difference between the theoretical tax liability according to the tax law and the actual revenue collected (Barbone et al. 2013, p. 29) on a timely basis.

There have been many studies on measuring the top-down tax gap. Several of them considered EU countries (Reckon 2009, 41; Barbone et al. 2013, 37–38; Barbone et al. 2015). The latest data come from 2012 (Barbone et al. 2015).

Many countries estimate tax gaps, either value-added tax (VAT) gap or the goods and services tax (GST) gaps, e.g. the UK since 1992. Since 2009, the UK has estimated the direct tax gap. Gemmell and Hasseldine (2013) and Fedeli and Fortel (2011, 2012) mention that the studies are highly politicized and subject to disagreement, because many economist believe that there are no reliable estimates of the overall tax gap. However, the tax gap as a whole can be examined, as indicated by Raczkowski (2015).

The UK's HMRC (Her Majesty's Revenue & Customs) data for the VAT gap up to 2012 agree with the ones obtained by Barbone et al. (2013), although there are claims the amounts are several times larger (HMRC 2015).

For France Barbone et al. (2013) estimated the VAT gap as €32bn. French authorities have claimed it is several times smaller (Euroactiv 2013). This might be explained by the use of different data sources—however, data discrepancies should not be so huge.

The IMF has prepared a new method of measuring VAT gaps for roll-out to Uganda. In particular, it assessed the UK HMRC's tax gap analysis program and provided advice and guidance on further improving it (IMF 2013b).

The tax gap measure does not give direct indication of the tax fraud.

Top-down tax gap methodologies consist of the following steps:

(a) calculation of total consumption portion of the taxable income (tax base), broken down by products and services;
(b) calculation of theoretical VAT revenue through 'taxation' theoretical tax base VAT rates relevant for particular goods and services;
(c) comparison of theoretical income calculated over the actual budget from VAT proceeds for each year.

The tax base is calculated separately for the following consumption categories (sales/purchases) of goods and services:

(a) final consumption of households
(b) final consumption of public entities and public benefit organizations
(c) intermediate consumption
(d) investment

In the UK report (HMRC 2015, 27) in Fig. 9 it was revealed that the following sources of HMRC's were used for VAT gap estimates:

(a) 'top-down' estimates of tax due from macroeconomic data
(b) 'bottom-up' random enquiries into tax returns,
(c) HMRC's own intelligence on tax risk
(d) cross-checking with other sources of data

In May 2013 PWC Poland published a report (PWC 2013, p. 14–15) in which an estimate of the minimal and maximal tax gap was given. As for the EU-related cases, a final figure for consumption by households was obtained with COICOP classification (Classification of individual consumption by purpose) for the period 2006–2011. This particular work used EUROSTAT macro-economic data. Use Tables for flows between 47 sectors related to consumption goods and services were employed. According to PwC, the VAT gap in the period 2011–2013 increased dramatically and might have ranged in 2012 from 36.5 to 58.5bn PLN ($12.1–19.4bn). In Fig. 14.2 it is shown that the gap decreased in 2014.

The second group of measures is C-efficiency methods. It has been observed that the changes in VAT revenues have been driven much less by changes in the standard rate than by changes in C-efficiency (Keen 2013). C-efficiency is an indicator of the departure of VAT from a perfectly enforced tax levied at a uniform rate on all consumption. The final consumption expenditure is a better tax base indicator than the GDP, particularly if an export value to GDP ratio changes. This ratio is steadily growing for Poland and in 2014 it amounted 47.45 %.

$$\text{C-efficiency} = R(\text{VAT}) / B * r \tag{14.1}$$

where R(VAT)/are VAT revenues, r – standard VAT rate, and B the tax base.

Usually, a variant of the final consumption (FC) expenditure is taken as a tax base, sometimes called tax base indicator—although there is some difference between final consumption and the VAT base. National accounts contain data on final consumption expenditure but may not contain some other data.

There are several variations of the C-efficiency methods. In the simplest version

$$\text{C-efficiency } 2 = R\left(\text{VAT}\right) / \text{FC} * r \tag{14.2}$$

This number would be 1, if VAT revenue collected was applied at the standard rate to all final consumption.

More justifiable is to remove VAT revenues from FC—the theoretical basis for taxation should not include the tax itself. Then the Eq. 14.2 is transformed to the form:

$$\text{C-efficiency } 1 = R\left(\text{VAT}\right) / \left(\text{FC} - R\left(\text{VAT av}\right)\right) * r \quad \text{(Eq. 14.3)}$$

where R(VAT av) is theoretical VAT to be raised.

Finally, a VAT Revenue Ratio (VRR) is used that reads:

$$VRR = R\left(VAT\right)/\left(FC - R\left(VAT\right)\right) * r \qquad \text{(Eq. 14.4)}$$

which is defined as the ratio between the actual VAT revenue collected and the revenue that would be collected if VAT was applied at the standard rate to all final consumption.

The Central Statistical Office of Poland, GUS does not calculate R(VAT av). This is done by the Polish Ministry of Finance, that calculated the average VAT rate in the period 2004–2011. In 2011 this value was 16.5 %, and the same numbers have been used for 2012–214.

Figure 14.5 shows a decrease of C-efficiency factor for Poland in recent years. The rise of this factor in 2014 was in part caused by delaying VAT refund payments. It is expected that 2015 results will be close to the 2013 results.

In Table 14.4 VRR, VAT gaps for selected EU countries are presented. A change of these over years for a country indicates VAT collection trends. A comparison of these quantities for different countries is not straightforward.

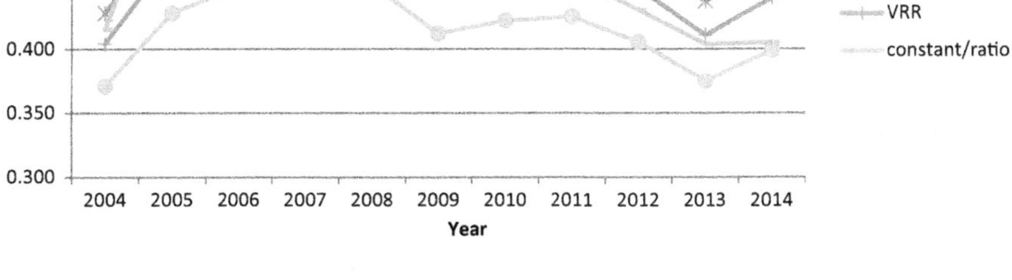

Fig. 14.5 C-efficiency 1, C-efficiency 2, VRR measures together with const/ ratio (proportional to the inverse ratio of VAT refund values to gross VAT revenues)

Table 14.4 VRR, VAT Gaps for selected EU countries

VRR										
Year	Poland	Czech OECD	Czech Eurostat	Slovakia	UK	Belgium	Greece	Italy	Portugal	OECD*
2008	0.50	0.58	0.34	0.54	0.46	0.48	0.46	0.41	0.51	0.58
2011	0.47	0.56	0.35	0.49	0.44	0.48	0.37	0.41	0.47	0.56
2012	0.45	0.57	0.37	0.43	0.44	0.48	0.37	0.38	0.47	0.55
2013	0.41		0.40	0.47						
2014	0.44		0.41	0.475						

VAT GAP [%]									
Year	Poland	Czech	Slovakia	UK	Belgium	Greece	Italy	Portugal	EU (26)**
2011	19	17	33	10	12	38	32	11	16
2012	25	22	39	10	10	33	33	10	16

Source: VRR: OECD (for 2008–2012), This work: Eurostat and national Statistical Offices for the Czech Republic, Poland, and Slovakia data. VAT Gap: (Barbonne et al. 2015) Table 3.1 VAT gap estimates, 2011–2012

Note: There is a tremendous difference for VRR for the Czech Republic, that cannot come from methodology difference. In crude comparison, one would expect strong a correlation between VRR and the VAT gap (the larger the first quantity, the smaller the second quantity). UK, Belgium, and Portugal VAT gaps are too small for their VRR and reverse situation happens for Slovakia

OECD*Unweighted average

EU (26)**Weighted average

2.4 Vat Fraud: The Effect on Balance of Trade and National Accounts

2.4.1 Transnational Transactions

VAT mechanisms contain inherent risks that facilitate fraud. VAT is applied to sales both to private consumers and to other businesses (in contrast to the retail sales taxes, which generally tax sales to final consumers only). In the direct VAT scheme, business sellers, within the country where a transaction takes place, pay the output VAT to the tax office.

Business purchasers are able to offset the VAT they have paid on their purchases ('input VAT') against their 'output VAT' liability on their sales. The most fraud-prone feature of the current system is that exported goods are VAT zero-rated. This means that a zero tax rate is applied to their sale but also that the seller is entitled to reclaim the VAT paid on taxed production inputs in his own country.

At the beginning, the EU relied on various means to decrease fraud risk. The first was the VAT Information Exchange System (VIES)—an electronic means of communicating information related to the validity of VAT numbers obtained by legal business entities upon registration in the EU. EU law requires that, where goods or services are procured within the EU, VAT must be paid only in the member state where the purchaser resides. For this reason, suppliers need an easy way to validate the VAT numbers presented by purchasers. This validation is performed through VIES.

Intrastat is the system for collecting information and producing statistics on the trade in goods between countries of the EU. It replaced customs declarations as the source of trade statistics within the EU on 1 January 1993. The requirements of Intrastat are similar in all member states of the EU, although there are important differences (threshold values below which a business is not required to file Intrastat forms).

Trade statistics are an essential part of a country's balance of payments account and are regarded as an important economic indicator of the performance of any country. Intrastat is also used as a tool against VAT fraud, permitting the comparison between Intrastat and VAT declarations.

The commercial world uses the statistics to assess markets within the country (e.g. to gauge how imports are penetrating the market) and externally (e.g. to establish new markets for their goods).

In addition, the statistics are passed on to European and International bodies such as Eurostat (the Statistical Office of the European Communities), the United Nations and the IMF.

Intrastat data forms an integral part of these statistics and therefore it is important that the data submitted be of a high quality. In order to envision which macro-economic account is affected by VAT fraud one has to consider detailed mechanisms of a particular type of fraud scheme.

Several fraudulent schemes use the right to deduct input VAT for fictitious transactions. We distinguish between three schemes (with some variations), Table 14.5.

Acquisition fraud is where the goods are imported from the EU into the UK by a trader who then goes missing without completing a VAT return or Intrastat declaration. He sells the goods to a buyer in the UK and they are eventually bought by a final consumer (VAT with complicity). Because a missing trader pays with real money such transactions cause increased import.

Carousel fraud is similar to acquisition fraud in the early stage. After moving through a series of bogus transactions through intermediaries, the goods are then re-exported to another member state, completing a 'carousel'.

Table 14.5 VAT fraud schemes. Scheme no 1 (mostly UK). Schemes 2 and 3 (mostly Poland)

Scheme no	No of border crossings	border crossing	Time ordering of VAT refund and VAT return	Isolation of exporter	Carousel	Nature of fraud (first stage)
1	1 or 2	Paper real	VAT refund later	Large	Yes	Import
2	2	Fictitious	VAT refund earlier	Exporter known	Yes	Export
3	1	Fictitious	VAT refund earlier	Exporter known	No	Export

Source: VAT fraud schemes according to the author's classification

Since the Missing trader intra-community (MTIC) fraud problem originated in the UK I will address definitions used in analysis regarding the UK typology (Ruffles et al. 2003).

Carousel fraud is currently regarded as the dominant type in terms of loss of government revenue in the UK (and in many other EU countries).

The fraud impacts on intra-EU trade statistics as these are collected via the VAT system. Carousel transactions are captured in export data (otherwise exporters could not apply for a VAT refund). However, the acquisition of the goods in MTIC frauds is not included in import data. Imports are, therefore, under-recorded. This fraud is also a factor contributing to asymmetry between the UK's and other EU member states' trade data, and thus can be used to estimate (although not directly) the scale of VAT fraud.

Moreover, such trade asymmetries can impact GDP estimates and the balance of payments, thus potentially causing severe distortion of macro-economic data. Macro-economic statistics are essential for the functioning of any country. They are used by government departments to help set overall trade, development, and fiscal policies.

According to the European system of accounts (ESA 2010), GDP at market prices is the final result of the production activity of resident producer units. It can be defined in three ways:

(a) The production approach: GDP is the sum of gross value added of the various institutional sectors or the various industries plus taxes and less subsidies on products (which are not allocated to sectors and industries). It is also the balancing item in the total economy production account.
(b) The expenditure approach: GDP is the sum of final uses of goods and services by resident institutional units (final consumption and gross capital formation), plus exports and minus imports of goods and services.
(c) The income approach: GDP is the sum of uses in the total economy (generation of income, account compensation of employees, taxes on production and imports less subsidies, gross operating surplus and mixed income of the total economy).

The Central Statistical Office of Poland derives GDP using information from production and expenditure/distribution. The expenditure approach is often considered more reliable than the income production. Advanced countries are able to reconcile data coming from different areas of economy as well as expenditure. GDP revisions will be much smaller than those to imports or exports.

The Effect of VAT Fraud on Exports and GDP

For the UK typology it was found that the effects of VAT fraud were strong on UK imports but rather small on GDP (Ruffles et al., 2003). This work mentioned that most fraud was of the carousel type not acquisition. It is not easy to understand why there was an asymmetry.

Most Polish cases are of the export type and it should show large asymmetry. The value of fictitious invoices in a given year is not exactly known. It has been reported (Pogroszewska 18.03.2015) that the value of fictitious invoices in 2014 amounted to 34bn PLN. However, this pertained to cases occurring between 2010 and 2014. Assuming that transnational VAT fraud constitutes around 90 % of VAT fraud—the number comes only from UKS (Control Offices), and only 20 % of taxpayers are controlled, because the Polish tax offices do not have advanced risk assessment tools—then fictitious exports recorded by the GUS Polish National Office of Statistics will be 120bn PLN compared to the official exports figure of 811.1bn PLN. This is over-reporting of exports by more than 17 %. Since GUS uses only two methods for GDP estimation, and results of both methods have to agree, there is a significant possibility of the GDP being over-reported, even in the 0.5–1 % range.

3 Conclusions

VAT mechanisms contains inherent risks that facilitate fraud. Preventing VAT fraud is difficult even for advanced EU countries. Poland copes with the task much worse than neighbouring countries: Czech Republic and Slovakia. This can be attributed to severe shortcomings of the Polish administration, particularly in the area of IT analytic support.

Very limited analytic capability contributes to opacity surrounding tax revenues (Moure 2013). It is not an exaggeration to say that most decisions of the Polish Ministry of Finance concerning VAT fraud combatting were not correct. The effects of VAT fraud are so large in Poland that they definitely affect balance of payments statistics, and possibly also the national accounts. A more detailed analysis will be the subject of the work to follow.

Acknowledgement This work was supported by the 04/45/DSPB/0122 PUT grant.

Bibliography

Barbone, L., Belkindas, M. V., Bettendorff, L., Bird, R., Bonch-Osmoloskiy, M., & Smart, M. (2013, July). Study to quantify and analyze the VAT gap in the EU-27 member states. Center for Social and Economic Research Project Report. http://ec.europa.eu/taxation_customs/resources/documents/common/publications/studies/vat-gap.pdf. Accessed 4 Nov 2014.

Barbone, L., Bonch-Osmolovskiy, M., & Poniatowski, G. (2015). Study to quantify and analyse the VAT GAP in the EU member states; CASE Network Reports 124; CASE – Centrum Analiz Społeczno-Ekonomicznych.

Financial Times [FT]. (2013, April 8). Sharp rise in delays of VAT refunds. http://www.ft.com/cms/s/0/9e58c368-9f8b-11e2-968b-00144feabdc0.html

Gemmell, N., & Hasseldine, J. (2013). Taxpayers' behavioural responses and measures of tax compliance 'Gaps': A critique, UK Tax Administration Research Centre, Discussion Paper: 002-13.

Euroactiv. (2013). http://www.euractiv.com/section/euro-finance/news/france-s-30-billion-vat-gap-revealed. Accessed 8 Sept 2016.

European Commission. (2014a). Excessive deficit procedure Czech Republic. http://ec.europa.eu/economy_finance/economic_governance/sgp/deficit/countries/czech_republic_en.htm

European Commission. (2014b). Excessive deficit procedure Slovakia. http://ec.europa.eu/economy_finance/economic_governance/sgp/deficit/countries/slovakia_en.htm

European Commission [EC]. (2015). Excessive deficit procedure Poland. http://ec.europa.eu/economy_finance/economic_governance/sgp/deficit/countries/poland_en.htm

Estimates of VAT tax realization. (n.d.). Daňové příjmy – DPH. http://www.kurzy.cz/cnb/ekonomika/danove-prijmy-dph/

Eurostat. EUROINDICATORS 72/2015 (2015a, April 21). Provision of deficit and debt data for 2014 – first notification. http://ec.europa.eu/eurostat/

documents/2995521/6796757/2-21042015-AP-EN.pdf/2a3922ae-2976-4aef-b6ce-af19bde6a236

Eurostat. (2015b). GNI data collection 2013 and 2014. http://ec.europa.eu/eurostat/statistics-explained/index.php/Monitoring_GNI_for_own_resource_purposes

EC. (2013, November). Manual on the changes between ESA 95 and ESA 2010. http://ec.europa.eu/eurostat/documents/3859598/5936825/ KS-GQ-14-002-EN.PDF/b247b032-6910-4db8-8f29-cb71d575752f.

Fedeli, S., & Fortel, F. (2011). International VAT fraud: The carousel game. Journal of *Modern Accounting and Auditing, 7*(3), 211–226.

Fedeli, S., & Fortel, F. (2012). Border tax adjustment without borders: The EU carousel of VAT fraud. *Review of Economics & Finance, 2*, 55–70.

GUS. (2014a). CZĘŚĆ III Roczne wskaźniki makroekonomiczne. http://stat.gov.pl/cps/rde/xbcr/gus/roczne_wskazniki_makroekonomiczne_cz_III_.xls

GUS. (2014b). Central Statistical Office of Poland [GUS], Wdrożenie Europejskiego Systemu Rachunków Narodowych i Regionalnych w Unii Europejskiej (ESA2010)1 do polskich rachunków narodowych. Zmiany metodologiczne oraz ich wpływ na główne agregaty makroekonomiczne. (Eng. Implementation of the European System of National and Regional Accounts in the European Union (ESA2010) Rachunków Narodowych i Regionalnych w Unii Europejskiej (ESA2010)1 do polskich rachunków narodowych. http://stat.gov.pl/download/gfx/portalinformacyjny/pl/defaultaktualnosci/5526/8/1/1/notatka_informacyjna_esa_2010-29_09_2014_28_09_2014_ostat_1.pdf

H.M. Revenue & Customs. (2013). Preliminary estimates of the VAT gap for 2012–13. London: HMRC. Available at. https://www.gov.uk/government/uploads/system/ uploads/ attachment_data/ file/263638/est-vat-gap-2013.pdf

HM Revenue & Customs. (2015, July 16). Annual report and accounts 2014–15. Report by the Comptroller and Auditor General. https://www.gov.uk/government/uploads/system/uploads/attachment_data/file/449343/HMRC_Annual_Report_and_Accounts_2014-15__Web_accessible_version_.pdf

International Monetary Fund. (2013a). IMF Country Report No. 13/220, Republic of Poland: Selected Issues.

International Monetary Fund. (2013b, October). United Kingdom: Technical assistance report – Assessment of HMRC's Tax Gap Analysis, IMF Country Report No. 13/314.

International Monetary Fund. (2014). Estonia: Report of the findings from the Revenue Administration Gap Analysis Program – the Value-Added Tax Gap in Estonia. http://www.imf.org/external/pubs/ft/scr/2014/cr14133.pdf

International Monetary Fund. (2015, April). Current challenges in revenue mobilization: Improving tax compliance.

IMF Country Report. (2013b). United Kingdom: Technical assistance report – Assessment of HMRC's Tax.

IMF Country Report No. 14/133. (2014). Republic of Estonia technical assistance report – Revenue Administration Gap Analysis Program – The Value-Added Tax Gap.

IMF [International Monetary Fund]. (2015, May). Republic of Poland technical assistance report – Tax administration – Modernization challenges and strategic priorities, IMF Country Report No. 15/112.

IMF Working Paper WP/05/218. (2005, November). Graham Harrison and Russell Krelove, VAT Refunds: A Review of Country Experience.

Keen, M. (2013). The anatomy of the VAT. *National Tax Journal, 66*, 423–446.

kurzy. (2016). http://www.kurzy.cz/makroekonomika/hdp/ . Accessed 8 Sept 2016.

MF, Ministerstwo Finansów. (2015, lipiec). Szacunkowe dane o wykonaniu budżetu państwa w 2015 r., Polish Ministry of Finance, Estimates of budget implementation.

MFCR. (2015). Finance Ministry of Czech Republic, The state budget deficit for 2014 is about 34 billion, less than planned. http://www.mfcr.cz/cs/aktualne/tiskove-zpravy/2015/pokladni-plneni-statniho-rozpoctu-cr-20131

MFSR. (2015). Finance Ministry of Slovak Republic, Continuous implementation of the state budget, Notifikace deficitu a dluhu vládních institucí – 2014. http://www.mfsr.sk/Default.aspx?CatID=10171

Mourre, G. (2013). Policy paper tax policy challenges in Eu countries: A few lessons from the 2012 commission tax reform report and the European semester. *The Economic and Social Review, 44*(4), 489–510.

OECD. (2014, December 10). Consumption Tax Trends 2014 VAT/GST and excise rates, trends and policy issues. http://www.oecd.org/tax/consumption-tax-trends-19990979.htm

Pisani, S. (2014). An approach to assess how the activity of the Italian Revenue Agency affects compliance. www.agenziaentrate.gov.it/wps/file/Nsilib/Nsi/Documentazione/ Rivista/Argomenti+di+discussione/Pubblicazioni/2014-01/2014_01.pdf. Accessed 15 July 2015.

Pogroszewska, M. (2015, March 18). Rzeczpospolita, Mimo kontroli rośnie wartość wyłudzeń VAT, prawo.rp.pl/artykul/1186885.html

PricewaterhouseCoopers [PwC]. (2013). *Raport Straty Skarbu Państwa w VAT – luka podatkowa, oszustwa, wyłudzenia oraz problematyka podatku od towarów i usług w Polsce*. Warszawa: Fundacja Naukowa – Instytut Badań Strukturalnych.

PWC. (2014). http://www.pwc.pl/pl/biuro-prasowe/2014/2014-11-27-luka-vatowska-spada-po-raz-pierwszy-od-7-lat.jhtml

Raczkowski, K. (2015). Measuring the tax gap in the European economy. *Journal of Economics and Management*, *21*(3).

Reckon LLP. (2009). *Study to quantify and analyze the VAT gap in the EU-25 Member States*. London. https://ec.europa.eu/taxation_customs/sites/taxation/files/docs/body/reckon_report_sep2009.pdf

Ruffles, D., Tily, G., Caplan, D., & Tudor, S. (2003). VAT missing trader intracommunity fraud: The effect on balance of payments statistics and U.K. national accounts. *Economic Trends*, *597*, 58–70.

Summary and Conclusions

Risk management in public administration certainly requires further examination, which would allow new theoretical concepts to be created as well as practical implementations in the operations of the public sector. If the activity of the public sector is based exclusively on the existing classic approach to public governance which promotes transparency, responsibility, and readiness to provide public services, it is by far insufficient to meet new challenges. Public administration of any country should have a risk management system applicable to all forms of state operations, which means that it is necessary, and not only advisable, to engage in networking based on all types of inter-institutional and/or inter-organizational interactions within the economy. This type of cooperation requires formal coordination by state authorities at one central point, however, it is also essential to create other more or less formalized channels and coordinating centres within the whole system, whose work will be co-contributing to the success of the entire system. In the democratic system nowadays, it would not be possible or would be absolutely ineffective to have such a system of central control that would be deferring or distorting the decision-making process and performance of tasks,

K. Raczkowski (ed.), *Risk Management in Public Administration*,
DOI 10.1007/978-3-319-30877-7

and disregarding the involved risks which can multiply on many levels at the same time and, to make matters worse, as part of systematic limiting and incapacitating of the decision-making process in the public sphere. Equally ineffective and simultaneously intrinsically threatening would be such democratic acceptance of social participation that distorts the original ideals through blurred lobbying and always to some extent accords a given social group or groups with privilege as part of apparent equality before the law or apparent sustenance of competitiveness of individuals and economic entities.

Based on conclusions aggregated from all the chapters of this monograph, it may be summed up that risk management in public administration requires the following facts to be taken into consideration (which also serve as recommendations for future research):

- risk should be examined through the prism of economic categories but simultaneously paying regard to other humanist and social functions of the global system,
- risk should be explicitly taken into consideration in public governance with respect to all groups of stakeholders,
- adherence to trade agreements, as seen especially on the example of the Transatlantic Trade and Investment Partnership (TTIP), shows that liberalization of free trade is burdened with grave risk which, if not dispersed before the agreement is approved, will create competition asymmetry between involved parties (e.g. the USA – the European Union).
- rating agencies exert considerable influence over investment decisions and determine the cost of capital, which should drive a given public sector to support economic growth to such an extent that could dislodge speculative operations and support investment instead,
- the process of financial risk management must take into account all the stakeholders and not merely the state budget, or the budget of local authorities, banks, and other financial institutions,
- in principle, the risk in public safety management is perceived as a negative phenomenon, while it should also be seen through the prism of chances and from a positive perspective,

- IT tools are an inextricable element of risk management, however, they need to be adjusted to a specific type of enterprise or organisational environment in cooperation with external and internal experts,
- public authorities must safeguard the services offered by the social security system as well as social services, which would enhance the operations of social enterprises and facilitate the general welfare,
- intellectual capital is the main asset of any organisation but, at the same time, the quality of this capital determines the level of risks generated by knowledge, employee skills, communication within a company, mutual trust and cooperation, or reputation on the market,
- qualitative assessment of regulatory risk should be a useful tool aiding the process of designing many provisions of the law, especially the ones regarding the financial system,
- identification of risk factors and detection of risk itself are of cardinal importance for the sound management of risk,
- financial institutions that have a large capacity for accumulating capital serve as an important stabiliser of the financial system, for they influence the capital market,
- tax avoidance and tax evasion (especially with regard to VAT) are constant elements of operation of economic entities, which creates risk that widens the tax gap and strengthens unfair competition.

The conclusions presented above prove that risk management in public administration requires the capability for real deciphering of the emerging information whose value is often inversely proportional to the activity that is actually undertaken by all types of organizational entities, both on the micro-organizational and macro-organizational level. This also means that, already in the very planning phase, the process of creation of law just as its implementation into the existing legal order must take into consideration the capacity for extreme modelling of the consequences and effects in order to disperse or eliminate possible risk beforehand. Thus it is necessary to adopt especially such perspectives that would be relevant for households, companies, national states, and the international (global) sphere, where one approach would take into account legal activity, the second approach – semi-legal operations, and the third one – completely illegal actions undertaken by domestic and foreign entities within the system. Finally, it should be accepted that creation of risk and protection of national interests should be part of the vital interest of any country and any public administration that understands what common good is, in particular within the framework of sustainable development and securing the strategic areas of state activity in the socio-economic sphere.

About the Authors

Patrycja Chodnicka Lecturer at the Faculty of Management at Warsaw University in the Department of Banking and Money Markets, author and co-author of many scientific publications. Participant of numerous conferences and seminars, both scientific and commercial, of domestic and international range. Member of a team carrying out the study within the project Regulatory determinants of pro-cyclicality in bank lending, which was awarded by the Director of the National Science Centre. Research manager for, among others: credit rating on the international financial market, the efficiency of the banking sector and money laundering. Member of Scientific Committees for several journals (*The Advances in Business Related Scientific Research Journal* and *The International Journal of IT–based Management for Smart Business*) and for international conferences (Advances in Business Related Scientific Research Conference in Venice, Rome, Milan and Olbia, and Workshop on Business in Korea). Co-editor of the scientific journal *Faculty of Management Working Paper Series*. Awards laureate, including the Scholarship of the Ministry of Science and Higher Education for the best PhD students (2012/2013). Winner of the Congress of the Capital Market and XVI Scientific Conference of Young Economists.

K. Raczkowski (ed.), *Risk Management in Public Administration*,
DOI 10.1007/978-3-319-30877-7

Zbigniew Ciekanowski Specialist in social sciences and telecommunications engineer. Academic at Cardinal Stefan Wyszyński University in Warsaw and Bronisław Markiewicz State Higher School of Technology and Economics in Jarosław, where he heads the Faculty of Management and Internal Security and is advisor to the Scientific Club for Internal Security. His scientific interests revolve around issues concerned with human resources management as well as internal security with regard to state security, economics, telecommunication, anti-terrorism and crisis management.

Teresa Czerwińska Professor at the Faculty of Management at the University of Warsaw. Her research is focused on systemic risk in the insurance sector and investment policy of insurance companies and pension funds. As a researcher and consultant, she is also interested in questions regarding socially responsible investing (SRI) on the capital market and the relationship between portfolio risk management and socially responsible strategies, such as investment funds and pension funds, applied by financial institutions.

Katarzyna Dohn Based at the Institute of Management and Administration, Faculty of Organization and Management, Technical University of Silesia. Currently, her research interests are concentrated on the following areas: logistics, supply chain management, production management, organization of production process, and knowledge management. She has been involved in many research projects. She is the author or co-author of over 80 publications, mostly in Polish periodicals.

Aldona Frączkiewicz-Wronka Professor and Head of the Department of Public Management and Social Sciences at the University of Economics in Katowice. Her research interests focus on issues related to the management of public sector organizations, and she is head of research team in many projects funded by the Ministry of Science and Higher Education as well as by the EU. She is the author of numerous publications on the functioning of the public sector in Poland, has experience with a proven track record for successfully training managers in the health care sector and public administration, and is an expert for the National Foresight

Programme 'Poland 2000', and the Technology Foresight for development of public services in the Upper Silesian Industrial Region (GOP). She has designed and facilitated courses for a broad range of clients i.e. public entities, such as the Ministry of Science and Higher Education, the Ministry of Regional Development, the Ministry of Health, and the Marshal's Office in Katowice among others.

Adam Gumiński Based at the Institute of Management and Administration, Faculty of Organization and Management, Technical University of Silesia. Currently, his research interests are concentrated on the following areas: investment management, project management, knowledge management, human resource management. He participated in numerous research projects. He is the author or co-author of over 70 publications, mostly in Polish periodicals.

Prof. Czesław Jędrzejek Professor, currently heading the Division of Computer Systems and Technologies at Poznan University of Technology (PUT) in Poland (since 2003). His previous positions were at Jagiellonian University, Cracow, four American universities (among others University of Chicago, and Texas A&M University – where he was a vice-director of Nanofab Laboratory) over the course of ten years, and École Franco-Polonaise des Nouvelles Technologies d'Information et Telecommunication in Poznan. He has over 200 scientific publications to his credit in the areas of physics, telecommunications, information engineering and economy. He has been a (co)principal investigator in 4 American, 6 European Union, and 5 Polish research grants. He has managed around ten implementations of commercial IT systems. At present, his main interests lie in analytic rule-based systems for public administration in the area of law enforcement. Within the Polish Platform for Homeland Security, he managed development of Analyzer of Facts and Relations with 2 modules: Billlings—a phone records analysis tool currently being deployed countrywide, and Money Transfers. He is a cofounder of two technology startups: Mobilfuture (analytic tools) and Kognitek (recommendation techniques for large-scale datasets), which aim at commercializing academic research.

Jolanta Jurczak Head of the Organization and Management Department at the Chodkowska University (UTH); teacher at the University of Social Sciences in Warsaw; scientific interest area concerns the knowledge and intellectual capital management as well as methods and techniques used in increasing human capital value; practical experience as a director and manager of Polish companies.

Stanisław Kasiewicz Professor at the Warsaw School of Economics. Employee of WSE since 1971. Presently, employee of the Institute of Corporate Finance and Investments at the Collegium of Business Administration of the Warsaw School of Economics. He was a member of supervisory boards of the open pension funds Orzeł, Warta, PKO Bank Polski S.A. and the Bank Guarantee Fund. He took part in research on competitiveness, globalization, business value management, insolvency, risk and regulations. He has conducted lectures on Regulatory Impact Assessment (RIA) and was a long-term member of the team headed by Professor Leszek Balcerowicz, which prepared the reform of the Polish economy. Author of more than 250 scientific publications, member of the Program Council of four financial quarterlies, and present Research Director of ALTERUM Centre for Research and Analysis of Financial System.

Lech Kurkliński Specialist in banking, risk management, cross-cultural management, Assistant Professor in the Institute of Corporate Finance and Investments at the Warsaw School of Economics (previously Warsaw University, Department of Banking and Finance). Studied at the University of Virginia, University of Oklahoma City. In banking since 1991: Director of Craftsmanship Bank in Warsaw, CEO of PBI Bank SA, management board member of BIG Bank Gdański SA, responsible for the retail and SME department (of the bank), head of greenfield retail banking project Millennium— BIG Bank SA executive vice president, managing director of Household International in Poland, head of consumer finance division and deputy CEO of HSBC in Poland, member of supervisory boards e.g. the Warsaw Stock Exchange. Author of several publications on banking, regulations, foreign direct investments, risk management, and cross-cultural management. At present

Managing Director of ALTERUM Centre for Research and Analysis of Financial System.

Barbara Kożuch Professor of Economics, Doctor of Economic Science, specializing in organization and management with scientific achievements in economic sciences and humanities. Based at the Institute of Public Affairs of Jagiellonian University. Her research and works are focused on organizational theory, systems, and methods of management, public management and human resource management. In particular, she examines the theoretical basis of management science, conditions of effective and efficient functioning of the public sector, public management in public and civic organizations, as well as organizational cooperation and change management in health care, education and culture, and public order.

Konrad Laska Member of the ACCA. MSc, graduate of the University of Rzeszów, and the University of Huddersfield in the UK. Co-author of management and leadership related papers in national publications. Current research interests focused on social and public management.

Bogdan Mróz Full Professor at Warsaw School of Economics. He completed his post-graduate studies in Milan (Scuola Superiore Enrico Mattei) and Ottawa (School of Business, Carleton University). Responsible for many research projects conducted in Poland, he has also been involved in international research cooperation programmes, e.g., joint Polish-German and Polish-Japanese research projects. His research interests include, *inter alia*, the shadow economy, tax evasion and informal labour markets.

Małgorzata Porada-Rochoń Associate Professor of Finance. She is coordinator of several research projects. Her research is focused on corporate finance, financial analysis, financial distress and corporate turnaround. She has 7 years' experience in finance as an expert in EU funds. Currently she is working on insolvency in the private sector, and insolvency risk management.

Marta Postuła Professor of Economics. Head of the Department of Corporate Finances at the Faculty of Management, University of Warsaw, professor at Kozminski University, member of the TIGER research team. She has specialized in 'organization and management'. Since 1999 she has been involved in the public administration sector, holding high-ranking posts. The core scope of her professional experiences include: operations of the public finance system in Poland and worldwide, budget processes and the effectiveness of public expenditures

Author and co-editor of books devoted to public finances and over 70 other scientific publications. She has participated in numerous national and international conferences and scientific seminars. Represented Poland in the group devoted to public finance quality operating at the European Commission. She also takes part in the working group Senior Budget Officials in OECD.

Konrad Raczkowski Professor of Economics and Management. Specializes in management in economic system, public finances and informal economy. Since 2012 Head of the Economic Institute at the University of Social Sciences in Warsaw and Chair of the Department of Economic Security Management. Since 2010 has served as an expert for the Parliamentary Research Bureau of the Chancellery of Parliament, and for economic organizations, enterprises and international institutions. From 2015, Undersecretary of State in the Ministry of Finance and member of the National Development Council of the President of the Republic of Poland. Author of about 100 scientific papers.

Katarzyna Sienkiewicz-Małyjurek Assistant Professor in the Institute of Management and Administration of the Silesian University of Technology. She specializes in management sciences. Her research and works are focused on management in the public sector, especially regarding public safety and emergency management, coordination theory, complexity theory, complex adaptive systems, inter-organizational collaboration, collaborative networks, collaborative leadership and performance management.

Mariusz Sokołek Faculty member of the Accounting Institute of SAN University of Social Sciences in Warsaw. His research interests focus on the tax system and accounting at business entities. He works as chief accountant and runs an accounting office.

Elżbieta Szaruga Has specialized in managerial economics, and is currently an assistant at the Faculty of Economics and Management Services, where she is also a PhD student. Her scientific interests revolve around issues such as spatial econometrics, rationalization of transport energy intensity, sustainable transport, the valuation of external costs of road accidents, decarbonization policy, programming in R and creating applications in VBA.

Piotr Tworek Assistant Professor in Risk Management and Finance at the University of Economics in Katowice. His research revolves around risk management issues in such fields as corporate finance, investments, project management, construction economics and public management. A member of the Polish Economic Society (PTE), the International Project Management Association (IPMA), and the Public Risk Management Association (PRMA). Author of over 100 papers and 2 scientific monographs, and co-author of 2 monographs and editor of 1 monograph devoted to risk issues in economics, finance and management. Holder of a scholarship granted by the Dekaban-Liddle Foundation (2014/2015) for an internship at the Adam Smith Business School, University of Glasgow (Scotland, UK).

Sylwia Wojciechowska-Filipek Based in the Economic Institute of the University of Social Sciences in Warsaw, where she is the Assistant Professor (adjunct) in the Faculty of Banking and Insurance. She specializes in information management, management information systems, information technologies application in products and services as well as in trading and virtualization of business operations.

Martyna Wronka-Pośpiech Assistant Professor in Management at the University of Economics in Katowice. Her research is focused on entrepreneurship, innovation, and strategic management in social and public sector. With a proven track record of engagement in social projects, she has over 7 years' experience of successfully empowering trainees working in the non-profit sector through counselling, consulting, coaching and development strategy.

Magdalena Zioło Associate Professor of Finance, Head of Department of Banking and Comparative Finance. She has published several articles in national and international journals. Her research is focused on finance and banking, in particular public finance, banking union and fiscal union, financial analysis, fiscal distress, financial planning, financial policy, and financial risk management. She has as 5 years' experience in the banking sector. She is a former Dekaban Liddle Fellow. Recently she has been working on fiscal policy, insolvency risk management, banking union, and the economics of the public sector.

Wojciech Zoleński Based at the Institute of Management and Administration, Faculty of Organization and Management, at the Technical University of Silesia. His current research concentrates on the following areas: production management, organization of production processes, knowledge management, and artificial intelligence tools in management. He has participated in many research projects, and is the author or co-author of over 30 publications, mostly in Polish periodicals.

Katarzyna Żukrowska Professor of Economics and International Relations. Director of International Studies Institute, Socio-Economic Collegium, Warsaw School of Economics.

Index

K. Raczkowski (ed.), *Risk Management in Public Administration*,
DOI 10.1007/978-3-319-30877-7

Printed by Printforce, the Netherlands